TAKING SIDES

Clashing Views in

World Politics

THIRTEENTH EDITION

TAKING SIDES

Clashing Views in

World Politics

THIRTEENTH EDITION

Selected, Edited, and with Introductions by

John T. Rourke
University of Connecticut

Contemporary Learning Series

A Division of The McGraw-Hill Companies

For my son and friend—John Michael

Cover image: Cartesia/Getty Images

Cover Acknowledgment:
Maggie Lytle

Compositor: ICC Macmillan Inc.

Library of Congress Cataloging-in-Publication Data Main entry under title:
Taking sides: clashing views on controversial issues in world politics/selected, edited, and with
introductions by John T. Rourke.—13th ed.
Includes bibliographical references and index.
1. World Politics—1989–. I. Rourke, John T., *comp.*
909.82

MHID: 0-07-339720-2
ISBN: 978-0-07-339720-7
ISSN: 1094-754X

Printed on Recycled Paper

Preface

In the first edition of *Taking Sides: Clashing Views in World Politics,* I wrote of my belief in informed argument: [A] book that debates vital issues is valuable and necessary. . . . [It is important] to recognize that world politics is usually not a subject of absolute rights and absolute wrongs and of easy policy choices. We all have a responsibility to study the issues thoughtfully, and we should be careful to understand all sides of the debates.

It is gratifying to discover, as indicated by the success of *Taking Sides* over 12 editions, that so many of my colleagues share this belief in the value of a debate-format text.

The format of this edition follows a formula that has proved successful in acquainting students with the global issues that we face and in generating discussion of those issues and the policy choices that address them. This book addresses 19 issues on a wide range of topics in international relations. Each issue has two readings, one pro and one con. Each is also accompanied by an issue *introduction,* which sets the stage for the debate, provides some background information on each author, and generally puts the issue into its political context. Each issue concludes with a *postscript* that summarizes the debate, gives the reader paths for further investigation, and suggests additional readings that might be helpful. I have also provided relevant Internet site addresses (URLs) in each postscript and on the *Internet References* page that accompanies each part opener. At the back of the book is a listing of all the *contributors to this volume,* which will give you information on the political scientists and other commentators whose views are debated here.

I have continued to emphasize issues that are currently being debated in the policy sphere. The authors of the selections are a mix of practitioners, scholars, and noted political commentators.

Changes to this edition The dynamic, constantly changing nature of the world political system and the many helpful comments from reviewers have brought about significant changes to this edition. Of the 38 readings in this edition 27 are new, with 11 readings being carried over from the previous edition.

The kaleidoscopic dynamism of the international system is also evident in the high turnover in issues from one edition to the next of this reader. More than half of the issues have changed entirely or in part. Only 3 (16 percent) of the 19 issues and their readings are carried over directly from the previous edition. In contrast, 8 issues (42 percent) and their readings are completely new. They are: Will China Soon Become a Threatening Superpower? (Issue 5); Should All Foreign Troops Soon Leave Iraq? (Issue 7); Is World Trade Organization Membership Beneficial? (Issue 9); Should the United States Take a Hard-line with China About Its International Economic Policies? (Issue 10); Is Immigration an Economic Benefit to the Host Country? (Issue 11); Is Patient Diplomacy the

Best Approach to Iran's Nuclear Program? (Issue 14); Does the United Nations Deserve Support? (Issue 16); and Should Accused Terrorists Have Legal Rights Similar to Prisoners of War? (Issue 18). Another 8 issues (42 percent) that were included in the last edition have one or more new readings to reflect changes in their ongoing and dynamic nature. These debates are: Is Economic Globalization a Positive Trend? (Issue 1); Is U.S. Global Dominance Destructive? (Issue 3); Has Russia Become Undemocratic and Antagonistic? (Issue 4); Would It Be an Error to Establish a Palestinian State? (Issue 6); Does the United States Have a Sound Strategy for the War on Terrorism? (Issue 13); Is North Korea an Aggressive Rogue State? (Issue 15); Is U.S. Refusal to Join the International Criminal Court Wise? (Issue 17); and Can Destructive Impacts from Global Warming Be Confidently Predicted? (Issue 19).

It is important to note that the changes to this edition from the last should not disguise the fact that most of the issues address enduring human concerns, such as global political organization, arms and arms control, justice, development, and the environment. Also important is the fact that many of the issues have both a specific and a larger topic. For instance, Issue 16 is about the specific topic of the performance of the United Nations, but it is also about more general topics. These include the proper role of international organizations in the global system and the degree to which countries should subordinate their sovereignty to them.

A word to the instructor   An *Instructor's Manual with Test Questions* (multiple-choice and essay) is available through the publisher for instructors using *Taking Sides* in the classroom. A general guidebook, *Using Taking Sides in the Classroom,* which discusses methods and techniques for integrating the pro-con approach into any classroom setting, is also available. An online version of *Using Taking Sides in the Classroom* and a correspondence service for *Taking Sides* adopters can be found at http://www.mhcls.com/usingts/. *Taking Sides: Clashing Views in World Politics* is only one title in the *Taking Sides* series. If you are interested in seeing the table of contents for any of the other titles, please visit the *Taking Sides* Web site at http://www.mhcls.com/takingsides/.

A note especially for the student reader   You will find that the debates in this book are not one-sided. Each author strongly believes in his or her position. And if you read the debates without prejudging them, you will see that each author makes cogent points. An author may not be "right," but the arguments made in an essay should not be dismissed out of hand, and you should work to remain tolerant of those who hold beliefs that are different from your own. There is an additional consideration to keep in mind as you pursue this debate approach to world politics. To consider divergent views objectively does not mean that you have to remain forever neutral. In fact, once you are informed, you ought to form convictions. More important, you should try to influence international policy to conform better with your beliefs. Write letters to policymakers; donate to causes you support; work for candidates who agree with your views; join an activist organization. *Do* something, whichever side of an issue you are on!

Acknowledgments   I received many helpful comments and suggestions from colleagues and readers across the United States and Canada. Their suggestions have markedly enhanced the quality of this edition of *Taking Sides*. If as you read this book you are reminded of a selection or an issue that could be included in a future edition, please write to me in care of McGraw-Hill/Contemporary Learning Series with your recommendations or e-mail them to me at john.rourke@uconn.edu.

My thanks go to those who responded with suggestions for the 13th edition. I would also like to thank Jill Peter, my editor for this volume, for her help in refining this edition.

John T. Rourke
University of Connecticut

Contents In Brief

Contents

Anne O. Krueger, special adviser to the managing director of the International Monetary Fund, asserts that the growth of economic globalization is the best approach to improving the economies of Africa and, by extension, other countries as well. Hugo Chavez, the president of Venezuela, tells a summit meeting of the Group of 15 (G-15), a coalition of now 17 economically less developed countries (LDCs) in Latin America, Africa, and Asia that cooperate to press the International Monetary Fund and other international financial organizations to·adopt policies more favorable to the LDCs, that globalization is a process controlled by the wealthy and powerful, economically developed countries for their benefit and has harmed the LDCs.

Julia Galeota of McLean, Virginia, who was seventeen years old when she wrote her essay that won first place for her age category in the 2004 *Humanist* Essay Contest for Young Women and Men of North America, contends that many cultures around the world are gradually disappearing due to the overwhelming influence of corporate and cultural America. Philippe Legrain, chief economist of Britain in Europe, an organization supporting the adoption by Great Britain of the euro as its currency, counters that it is a myth that globalization involves the imposition of Americanized uniformity, rather than an explosion of cultural exchange.

Louis Janowski, a former U.S. diplomat with service in Vietnam, France, Ethiopia, Saudi Arabia, and Kenya, maintains that the view that the 9/11 attacks ushered in a new geo-strategic reality requiring new foreign policy approaches is based on a false and dangerous premise and is leading to an age of American neo-imperialism. Michael Mandelbaum, Christian A. Herter Professor of American Foreign Policy and director of the American Foreign Policy Program at The Johns Hopkins University Paul H. Nitze School of Advanced International Studies, contends that U.S. power and leadership help maintain global security and prosperity and that most other countries want American leadership, even if they sometimes disagree with U.S. policy.

Tucker Herbert and Diane Raub, both of whom are on the staff of the *Stanford Review,* an independent, student-run newspaper at Stanford University, argue that under President Vladimir Putin, Russia has fallen from the ranks of democracies and is engaged in a foreign policy that pits U.S. interests against those of Russia. Eugene B. Rumer, a senior research fellow at the National Defense University's Institute for National Strategic Studies in Washington, D.C., recognizes that Russian democracy falls short of full scale and that Russian policy sometimes clashes with the United States, but argues that compared to the history of Russian democracy, which was zero before the 1990s, the country is not doing poorly and that Russia's pursuit of its own interests should not be construed as necessarily antagonistic.

Robert T. McLean, a research associate at the Center for Security Policy in Washington, D.C., contends that the U.S. Defense Department is correct in its view that China is an expanding danger based on its expansive aspirations in the economic and political arenas coupled with an equally bold foreign policy. Alice Lyman Miller, editor of the Hoover Institution journal, *China Leadership Monitor,* projects that it will be a long time before China acquires the global political, strategic, and economic reach of a superpower.

Peter F. Allgeier, Deputy U.S. Trade Representative, Office of the U.S. Trade Representative, describes the World Trade Organization as beneficial to U.S. strategic and economic interests and argues that there is overwhelming value to be gained through continued U.S. participation in the organization. Lori Wallach, director of Public Citizen's Global Trade Watch, part of Public Citizen, a Washington, D.C.–based advocacy group, maintains that Congress should demand a transformation of WTO trade rules because they have failed to achieve the promised economic gains and have also undercut an array of nontrade, noneconomic policies and goals advantageous to the public interest in the United States and abroad.

Robert Baugh, executive director, Industrial Union Council, AFL-CIO, asserts that the litany of China's failures to meet its trade obligations is extensive and that the failure of the U.S. government to respond strongly has put the country on a dangerous path. John Frisbie, president of the U.S.–China Business Council in Washington, D.C., concedes that there are some difficult issues to resolve with China but argues that jeopardizing the U.S. economy with tariffs or other protectionist measures is not an acceptable way to inform China that it must change some of its policies.

strategy needs to change from waging a global war on terrorism that overemphasizes military action to a broader global counterinsurgency approach that adds equally critical political, economic, diplomatic, and developmental efforts to the military campaign.

Frank G. Wisner, vice chairman for External Affairs of the American International Group, in New York City, says it is not clear that Iran is determined to build nuclear weapons and urges a policy signaling that the United States not only seeks agreement that will contain the nuclear crisis but is prepared to consider normalizing relations with and giving security guarantees to Iran. James Phillips, research fellow for Middle Eastern Affairs in the Douglas and Sarah Allison Center for Foreign Policy Studies at the Heritage Foundation in Washington, D.C., tells Congress that the United States should mobilize an international coalition to pressure Iran to cease its nuclear weapons development program and, if that fails, should consider military options to set back Iran's nuclear weapons program.

Nicholas Eberstadt, Henry Wendt Scholar in Political Economy at the American Enterprise Institute, Washington, D.C., asserts that North Korea's acquisition of nuclear weapons is designed to facilitate the reunification of the now-divided Korean peninsula under the rule of the Pyongyang regime. Leon V. Sigal, director of the Northeast Cooperative Security Project at the Social Science Research Council, New York City, contends that since 1988, North Korea has been trying to end its historic enmity against the United States but has been frustrated by U.S. policy.

Betty McColllum, member of the United States House of Representatives (D-MN), admits that the United Nations has flaws and needs reforms, but argues that the world is far better off than it would be if the UN did not exist. Clifford D. May, president of the Foundation for the Defense of Democracy, argues that the UN has largely been a failure, that the prospects to reform it are dim, and that the United States and other democracies should create a new international organization to promote global peace, prosperity, and democracy.

Issue 17.   Is U.S. Refusal to Join the International Criminal Court Wise?   306

John R. Bolton, at the time U.S. Under Secretary State for Arms Control and International Security and beginning in 2005, U.S. Ambassador to the United Nations, explains why President George W. Bush had decided to reject membership in the International Criminal Court. Briony MacPhee, a professional volunteer associate with the American Non-Governmental Organizations Coalition for the International Criminal Court, a program of the United Nations Association of the United States of America, argues that conservatives should join many liberals in supporting the United States to become a party to the International Criminal Court.

Issue 18.   Should Accused Terrorists Have Legal Rights Similar to Prisoners of War?   325

Katherine Newell Bierman, Counterterrorism Counsel, U.S. Program of Human Rights Watch, urges Congress to ensure that terrorist suspects captured on the battlefield are prosecuted according to the standards of the Uniform Code of Military Justice. Steven G. Bradbury, Acting Assistant Attorney General, U.S. Department of Justice, contends that it is neither necessary nor wise to require that military commissions follow all of the procedures of a court-martial when dealing with terrorists for their war crimes.

Ralph J. Cicerone, president, National Academy of Sciences, tells Congress that while future climate change and its impacts cannot be precisely forecast, a broad-brush picture of how global warming may affect the Earth is emerging and it contains a range of worrisome impact. John R. Christy, professor of atmospheric science and director of the Earth System Science Center at the University of Alabama in Huntsville, argues that projections of drastic climate changes in the future from global warming have not been adequately proved, and it is important not to make radical changes in energy policy based on such projections.

Introduction

World Politics and the Voice of Justice

John T. Rourke

Some years ago, the Rolling Stones recorded "Sympathy With the Devil." If you have never heard it, go find a copy. It is worth listening to. The theme of the song is echoed in a wonderful essay by Marshall Berman, "Have Sympathy for the Devil" (*New American Review*, 1973). The common theme of the Stones' and Berman's works is based on Johann Goethe's *Faust*. In that classic drama, the protagonist, Dr. Faust, trades his soul to gain great power. He attempts to do good, but in the end he commits evil by, in contemporary paraphrase, "doing the wrong things for the right reasons." Does that make Faust evil, the personification of the devil Mephistopheles among us? Or is the good doctor merely misguided in his effort to make the world better as he saw it and imagined it might be? The point that the Stones and Berman make is that it is important to avoid falling prey to the trap of many zealots who are so convinced of the truth of their own views that they feel righteously at liberty to condemn those who disagree with them as stupid or even diabolical.

It is to the principle of rational discourse, of tolerant debate, that this reader is dedicated. There are many issues in this volume that appropriately excite passion—for example, Issue 6 on whether or not Israel should agree to an independent Palestinian state, or Issue 18 which examines whether or not those accused of terrorism should have legal protections similar to those given prisoners of war. If not, then the question is what are the boundaries? Can such prisoners be held without trial? Can interrogators use torture?

As you will see, each of the authors in all the debates strongly believes in his or her position. If you read these debates objectively, you will find that each side makes cogent points. They may or may not be right, but they should not be dismissed out of hand. It is important to repeat that the debate format does not imply that you should remain forever neutral. In fact, once you are informed, you *ought* to form convictions, and you should try to act on those convictions and try to influence international policy to conform better with your beliefs. Ponder the similarities in the views of two very different leaders, a very young president in a relatively young democracy and a very old emperor in a very old country: In 1963 President John F. Kennedy, in recalling the words of the author of the epic poem *The Divine Comedy* (1321), told a West German audience, "Dante once said that the hottest places in hell are reserved for those who in a period of moral crisis maintain their neutrality." That very same year, while speaking to the United Nations, Ethiopia's emperor Haile Selassie (1892–1975) said, "Throughout history it has been the inaction of those who could have acted, the indifference of those who should have known better, the silence of the voice of justice when it mattered most that made it possible for evil to triumph."

The point is: Become Informed. Then *do* something! Write letters to policy-makers, donate money to causes you support, work for candidates with whom you agree, join an activist organization, or any of the many other things that you can do to make a difference. What you do is less important than that you do it.

Approaches to Studying International Politics

As will become evident as you read this volume, there are many approaches to the study of international politics. Some political scientists and most practitioners specialize in *substantive topics,* and this reader is organized along topical lines. Unit 1 (Issues 1 through 3) features debates on the evolution of the international system in the direction of greater globalization. In Issue 1, Anne O. Krueger and Venezuelan President Hugo Chavez debate the general topic of economic globalization. Krueger is optimistic, maintaining that economic globalization is a positive trend; Chavez sees it as a trend that benefits the wealthy and harms the poor. Issue 2 addresses the accompanying phenomenon of cultural globalization. American student Julia Galeota fears that American culture is wiping away cultural diversity in the world, while British analyst Phillippe Legrain rejects these charges and points to the positive aspects of cultural diversity. The current power arrangement of the international system has left the United States as the dominant power, and in Issue 3 diplomat Louis Janowski and scholar Michael Mandelbaum have very different views on the impact of U.S. hegemony.

Unit 2 (Issues 4 through 8) focuses on regional and country-specific issues, including trends in Russian domestic and foreign policy, whether China should be considered a growing threat, the possibility of a Palestinian state, whether U.S. and other foreign troops should withdraw quickly from Iraq or stay for an extended time to try to stabilize and democratize the country, and the ongoing U.S. sanctions against Cuba.

Unit 3 (Issues 9 through 11) deals with specific concerns of the international economy, a topic introduced more generally in Issue 1. Issue 9 takes up the general topic of free trade and the more specific topic of whether membership in the World Trade Organization is beneficial or not. Monetary relations are another aspect of economic globalization, and Issue 10 turns to whether the United States should take strong measures against China in response to its refusal to let its currency, the yuan, fluctuate freely against the U.S. dollar. Robert Baugh from the AFL-CIO charges that China is not playing according to the international rules, that the U.S. economy is being harmed, and that the United States should retaliate against China. John Frisbie or the U.S.-China Business Council argues that China is improving its adherence to international standards and counsels patience will yield better results than sanctions. In Issue 11, the debate turns to the impact of immigration on host countries. The flow of both legal and illegal immigration is a contentious topic in many countries, and here the debate focuses on the United States as an example the controversy.

Unit 4 (Issues 12 through 15) examines violence and the attempts to limit it in the international system. The past few decades have witnessed a rising concern about terrorism and the spread of nuclear, chemical, biological, and radiological weapons of mass destruction, not only among countries, but also to terrorist groups. Partly in response to these changes, President George W. Bush proclaimed that the United States had the right to take preemptive military action against threats before any direct or even immediately impending attack against Americans. In the first reading under Issue 12, the report of a committee appointed by the UN secretary general rejects preemptive action, while a report authored at the U.S. Army War College supports it. Issue 13 turns to what has become a high-profile threat: terrorism. President George W. Bush argues that the war on terrorism, which his administration is waging, is being won. Bruce Hoffman of the RAND research organization disagrees. The next two issues focus on nuclear nonproliferation in general, with Issue 14 taking up the specific case of Iran and Issue 15 addressing the particular case of North Korea. One clear difference between the two is that Iran has an alleged nuclear weapons program that is, at soonest, some years away from producing a weapons, while North Korea has nuclear weapons.

Unit 5 (Issues 16 through 18) addresses controversies related to international law and organizations. The ability of the United Nations to deploy effective peacekeeping forces is severely constrained by a number of factors. Similarly, the UN has not been able to resolve the world's many social and economic inequities. Moreover, the UN has suffered some mismanagement. Is the organization a failure that should be abandoned, as columnist Mark Steyn argues? Congresswoman Betty McCollum does not think so. Issue 17 evaluates the wisdom of establishing a permanent international criminal court to punish those who violate the law of war. It is easy to advocate such a court as long as it is trying and sometimes punishing alleged war criminals from other countries. But one has to understand that one day a citizen of one's own country could be put on trial. The third debate in Unit 5 takes up the treatment of terrorist combatants, such as the al-Qaeda fighters captured by U.S. forces in Afghanistan. Katherine Newell Bierman of the organization Human Right Watch testifies before Congress that such prisoners should be considered prisoners of war subject to all the protections of the Geneva Conventions. U.S. Assistant Attorney General Steven G. Bradbury counters that the Geneva Conventions were not designed to cover terrorists and that it is neither wise nor feasible to treat them as prisoners of war.

Unit 6, which consists of Issue 19, addresses the environment. Over the past few decades there has been a growing concern about global warming. Many people believe that it is mostly being caused by human activities, especially the burning of petroleum and other fossil fuels that discharge carbon dioxide into the atmosphere. There is also widespread belief that global warming will bring increasingly catastrophic results and that strong measures should be quickly taken to greatly reduce the emission of carbon dioxide and similar gases. Scientist Ralph J. Cicerone represents this view in the first reading. In the second reading, however, another scientist, John R. Christy, says that neither the causes nor the potential impacts of global warming are anywhere near as certain as some contend.

Political scientists also approach their subject from differing *methodological perspectives*. You will see, for example, that world politics can be studied from different *levels of analysis*. The question is, What is the basic source of the forces that shape the conduct of politics? Possible answers are world forces, the individual political processes of the specific countries, or the personal attributes of a country's leaders and decision makers. Various readings will illustrate all three levels.

Another way for students and practitioners of world politics to approach their subject is to focus on what is called the realist versus the idealist (or liberal) debate. Realists tend to assume that the world is permanently flawed and therefore advocate following policies in their country's narrow self-interests. Idealists take the approach that the world condition can be improved substantially by following policies that, at least in the short term, call for some risk or self-sacrifice. This divergence is an element of many of the debates in this book. Issue 13 is a particular example. In the first reading, President Bush advocates a very realpolitik approach of unilateral, preemptive military action when it is deemed necessary to preserve U.S. interests. John Steinbruner argues that coercive preemption is dangerous. He favors a more liberal approach involving multilateral diplomacy and action through the UN and other international organizations.

Dynamics of World Politics

The action on the global stage today is vastly different from what it was a few decades ago, or even a few years ago. *Technology* is one of the causes of this change. Technology has changed communications, manufacturing, health care, and many other aspects of the human condition. Technology has given humans the ability to create biological, chemical, and nuclear compounds and other material that in relatively small amounts have the ability to kill and injure huge numbers of people. Another negative by-product of technology may be the vastly increased consumption of petroleum and other natural resources and the global environmental degradation that has been caused by discharges of waste products, deforestation, and a host of other technology-enhanced human activities.

Another dynamic aspect of world politics involves the *changing axes* of the world system. For about 40 years after World War II ended in 1945, a bipolar system existed, the primary axis of which was the *East-West* conflict, which pitted the United States and its allies against the Soviet Union and its allies. Now that the Cold War is over, one broad debate is over what role the United States should play. In Issue 3, former U.S. diplomat Louis Janowski argues that the United States should reduce its global presence; Michael Mandelbaum believes doing so will harm global stability. Issue 4 looks at Russia, the last rival to the U.S. super power status before the Soviet Union's collapse in 1991, and assesses whether Moscow is once again becoming undemocratic and hostile. Then Issue 5 deals with China. Some people believe that China is the next superpower and that it will pose a threat to U.S. security and interests. Others do not see China as a threat, but believe that treating it as one could become a self-fulfilling prophecy.

Technological changes and the shifting axes of international politics also highlight the *increased role of economics* in world politics. Economics have always played a role, but traditionally the main focus has been on strategic-political questions—especially military power. This concern still strongly exists, but now it shares the international spotlight with economic issues. One important change in recent decades has been the rapid growth of regional and global markets and the promotion of free trade and other forms of international economic interchange. As Issue 1 on economic interdependence indicates, many people support these efforts and see them as the wave of the future. But there are others who believe that free economic globalization and interdependence undermine sovereignty and the ability of governments to control their destinies. One related topic, which is taken up in Issue 9 is free trade and its oversight body, the World Trade Organization, are making a positive contribution to the world as a whole.

Another change in the world system has to do with the main *international* actors. At one time states (countries) were practically the only international actors on the world stage. Now, and increasingly so, there are other actors. Some actors are regional. Others, such as the United Nations, are global actors. Turning to the most notable international organization, Issue 16 examines the UN and, by extension, the role of that world organization and the proper approach of member countries to it and to global cooperation. Issue 17 focuses on whether or not a supranational criminal court should be established to take over the prosecution and punishment of war criminals from the domestic courts and ad hoc tribunals that have sometimes dealt with such cases in the past.

Perceptions Versus Reality

In addition to addressing the general changes in the world system outlined above, the debates in this reader explore the controversies that exist over many of the fundamental issues that face the world.

One key to these debates is the differing *perceptions* that protagonists bring to them. There may be a reality in world politics, but very often that reality is obscured. Many observers, for example, are alarmed by the seeming rise in radical actions by Islamic fundamentalists. However, the image of Islamic radicalism is not a fact but a perception; perhaps correct, perhaps not. In cases such as this, though, it is often the perception, not the reality, that *is* more important because policy is formulated on what decision makers *think,* not necessarily on what *is.* Thus, perception becomes the operating guide, or *operational reality,* whether it is true or not. Perceptions result from many actors. One factor is the information that decision makers receive. For a variety of reasons, the facts and analyses that are given to leaders are often inaccurate or represent only part of the picture. The conflicting perceptions of Israelis and Palestinians, for example, make the achievement of peace in Israel very difficult. Many Israelis and Palestinians fervently believe that the conflict that has occurred in the region over the past 50 years is the responsibility of the other. Both sides also believe in the righteousness of their own policies. Even if both sides are well-meaning, the perceptions of hostility that each holds means that the operational reality often has to be violence. These differing perceptions are a key element in the debate in Issue 6.

A related aspect of perception is the tendency to see oneself differently than some others do. Specifically, the tendency is to see oneself as benevolent and to perceive rivals as sinister. This reverse image is partly at issue in the debate on preemptive war (Issue 12). Many Americans see themselves as threatened by terrorists and rogue nations and support preemptive war as a legitimate defensive strategy. Other countries worry that the Bush Doctrine is an excuse for the United States to try to dominate others and attack those who offer serious opposition to U.S. imperialism. For example, one aspect of Issue 15 on how to deal with North Korea's nuclear weapons program centers on whether the North Koreans are trying to increase their power for aggressive purposes or are trying to deter any chance of a U.S. attack on them. Perceptions, then, are crucial to understanding international politics. It is important to understand objective reality, but it is also necessary to comprehend subjective reality in order to be able to predict and analyze another country's actions.

Levels of Analysis

Political scientists approach the study of international politics from different levels of analysis. The most macroscopic view is *system-level analysis*. This is a top-down approach that maintains that world factors virtually compel countries to follow certain foreign policies. Governing factors include the number of powerful actors, geographic relationships, economic needs, and technology. System analysts hold that a country's internal political system and its leaders do not have a major impact on policy. As such, political scientists who work from this perspective are interested in exploring the governing factors, how they cause policy, and how and why systems change.

After the end of World War II, the world was structured as a *bipolar* system, dominated by the United States and the Soviet Union. Furthermore, each superpower was supported by a tightly organized and dependent group of allies. For a variety of reasons, including changing economics and the nuclear standoff, the bipolar system has faded. Some political scientists argue that the bipolar system is being replaced by a *multipolar* system. In such a configuration, those who favor *balance-of-power* politics maintain that it is unwise to ignore power considerations. Or it may be that something like a one-power (unipolar) system exists, with the United States as that power, as taken up in Issue 3.

State-level analysis is the middle and most common level of analysis. Social scientists who study world politics from this perspective focus on how countries, singly or comparatively, make foreign policy. In other words, this perspective is concerned with internal political dynamics, such as the roles of and interactions between the executive and legislative branches of government, the impact of bureaucracy, the role of interest groups, and the effect of public opinion. This level of analysis is very much in evidence in Issue 11 and the debate over immigration to the United States, a topic that has cultural, as well as economic, ramifications. The dangers to the global environment, which are debated in Issue 19 extend beyond rarified scientific controversy to important issues of public policy. For example, should the United States and other industrialized countries adopt policies that are costly in terms of economics and lifestyle to significantly reduce the emission of carbon dioxide and other harmful gases? This debate pits interest groups against one another as they try to get the governments of their respective countries to support or reject the steps necessary to reduce the consumption of resources and the emission of waste products.

A third level of analysis, which is the most microscopic, is *human-level analysis.* This approach focuses, in part, on the role of individual decision makers. This technique is applied under the assumption that individuals make decisions and that the nature of those decisions is determined by the decision makers' perceptions, predilections, and strengths and weaknesses. Part of Issue 8 on U.S. sanctions on Cuba is based on conjectures about whether Cuba will experience a basic change in its political system once long-time President Fidel Castro is no longer in power.

The Political and Ecological Future

Future *world alternatives* are discussed in many of the issues in this volume. Abraham Lincoln once said, "A house divided against itself cannot stand." One suspects that the sixteenth president might say something similar about the world today if he were with us. Issue 1, for example, debates whether growing globalization is a positive or negative trend. The world has responded to globalization by creating and strengthening the UN, the IMF, the World Bank, the World Trade Organization, and many other international organizations to try to regulate the increasing number of international interactions. There can be little doubt that the role of global governance is growing, and this reality is the spark behind specific debates about the future that are taken up in many of the selections. Far-reaching alternatives to a state-centric system based on sovereign countries include international organizations' (Issue 16) taking over some (or all) of the sovereign responsibilities of national governments, such as the prosecution of international war criminals (Issue 17). The global future also involves the ability of the world to prosper economically while not denuding itself of its natural resources or destroying the environment. This is the focus of Issue 19 on the environment.

The Axes of World Division

The world is politically dynamic, and the nature of the political system is undergoing profound change. As noted, the once-primary axis of world politics, the East-West confrontation, has broken down. Yet a few vestiges of the conflict on that axis remain. These can be seen in Issue 5 about future relations with still-communist and increasingly powerful China and Issue 4 about relations with the former heart of the so-called communist bloc, Russia/ the Soviet Union.

In contrast to the moribund East-West axis, the *North-South axis* has increased in importance and tension. The wealthy, industrialized countries

(North) are at one end, and the poor, less developed countries (LDCs, South) are at the other extreme. Economic differences and disputes are the primary dimension of this axis, in contrast to the military nature of the East-West axis. Issue 1 explores these differences with regard to globalization.

Something of military relations between the North and the South are present in the war with Iraq and the crisises with North Korea and Iran, which are taken up in Issues 7 and 14 and 15, respectively. There are some, especially in the South, who believe that the negative U.S. reactions to Iraqi, Iranian, and North Korean power, especially their possible possession of weapons of mass destruction, constitute evidence that the powerful countries are determined to maintain their power by keeping weak countries from obtaining the same types of weapons that the United States and other big powers have.

Increased Role of Economics

As the growing importance of the North-South axis indicates, economics are playing an increased role in world politics. The economic reasons behind the decline of the East-West axis is further evidence. Economics have always played a part in international relations, but the traditional focus has been on strategic political affairs, especially questions of military power.

Political scientists, however, are increasingly focusing on the international political economy, or the economic dimensions of world politics. International trade, for instance, has increased dramatically, expanding from an annual world export total of $20 billion in 1933 to $7.9 trillion in 2002. The impact has been profound. The domestic economic health of most countries is heavily affected by trade and other aspects of international economics. Since World War II there has been an emphasis on expanding free trade by decreasing tariffs and other barriers to international commerce. In recent years, however, a downturn in the economies of many of the industrialized countries has increased calls for more protectionism. Yet restrictions on trade and other economic activity can also be used as diplomatic weapons. The intertwining of economies and the creation of organizations to regulate them, such as the World Trade Organization, is raising issues of sovereignty and other concerns. This is a central matter in the debate in Issue 1 over whether or not the trend toward global economic integration is desirable and in Issue 9 on the benefits of free trade.

Conclusion

Having discussed many of the various dimensions and approaches to the study of world politics, it is incumbent on this editor to advise against your becoming too structured by them. Issues of focus and methodology are important both to studying international relations and to understanding how others are analyzing global conduct. However, they are also partially pedagogical. In the final analysis, world politics is a highly interrelated, perhaps seamless, subject. No one level of analysis, for instance, can fully explain the events on the world stage. Instead, using each of the levels to analyze events and trends will bring the greatest understanding.

Similarly, the realist-idealist division is less precise in practice than it may appear. As some of the debates indicate, each side often stresses its own standards of morality. Which is more moral: defeating a dictatorship or sparing the sword and saving lives that would almost inevitably be lost in the dictator's overthrow? Furthermore, realists usually do not reject moral considerations. Rather, they contend that morality is but one of the factors that a country's decision makers must consider. Realists are also apt to argue that standards of morality differ when dealing with a country as opposed to an individual. By the same token, most idealists do not completely ignore the often dangerous nature of the world. Nor do they argue that a country must totally sacrifice its short-term interests to promote the betterment of the current and future world. Thus, realism and idealism can be seen most accurately as the ends of a continuum—with most political scientists and practitioners falling somewhere between, rather than at, the extremes. The best advice, then, is this: think broadly about international politics. The subject is very complex, and the more creative and expansive you are in selecting your foci and methodologies, the more insight you will gain. To end where we began, with Dr. Faust, I offer his last words in Goethe's drama, "*Mehr licht,*" . . . More light! That is the goal of this book.

Internet References . . .

The Ultimate Political Science Links Page

Under the editorship of Professor P. S. Ruckman, Jr., at Rock Valley College in Rockford, Illinois, this site provides a gateway to the academic study of not just world politics but all of political science. It includes links to journals, news, publishers, and other relevant resources.

http://www.rvc.cc.il.us/faclink/pruckman/PSLinks.htm

Poly-Cy: Internet Resources for Political Science

This is a worthwhile gateway to a broad range of political science resources, including some on international relations. It is maintained by Robert D. Duval, director of graduate studies at West Virginia University.

http://www.polsci.wvu.edu/polycy/

The WWW Virtual Library: International Affairs Resources

Maintained by Wayne A. Selcher, professor of international studies at Elizabethtown College in Elizabethtown, Pennsylvania, this site contains approximately 2,000 annotated links relating to a broad spectrum of international affairs. The sites listed are those that the Webmaster believes have long-term value and that are cost-free, and many have further links to help in extended research.

http://www.etown.edu/vl/

The Globalization Website

The goals of this site are to shed light on the process of globalization and contribute to discussions of its consequences, to clarify the meaning of globalization and the debates that surround it, and to serve as a guide to available sources on globalization.

http://www.sociology.emory.EDU/globalization/

Globalization and the International System

*T*he most significant change that the international system is experiencing is the trend toward globalization. Countries are becoming interdependent, the number of international organizations and their power are increasing, and global communications have become widespread and almost instantaneous. As reflected in the issues that make up this part, these changes and others have led to considerable debate about the value of globalization and what it will mean with regard to human governance.

- Is Economic Globalization a Positive Trend?

- Does Globalization Threaten Cultural Diversity?

- Is U.S. Global Dominance Destructive?

ISSUE 1

Is Economic Globalization a Positive Trend?

YES: Anne O. Krueger, from "An Enduring Need: The Importance of Multilateralism in the 21st Century," Lecture Presented at the 2006 Annual Meetings, Boards of Governors of the International Monetary Fund and World Bank Group (September 19, 2006)

NO: Hugo Chavez, from Address to the Opening of XII G-15 Summit (March 1, 2004)

ISSUE SUMMARY

YES: Anne O. Krueger, special adviser to the managing director of the International Monetary Fund, asserts that the growth of economic globalization is the best approach to improving the economies of Africa and, by extension, other countries as well.

NO: Hugo Chavez, the president of Venezuela tells a summit meeting of the Group of 15 (G-15), a coalition of now 17 economically less developed countries (LDCs) in Latin America, Africa, and Asia that cooperate to press the International Monetary Fund and other international financial organizations to adopt policies more favorable to the LDCs, that globalization is a process controlled by the wealthy and powerful, economically developed countries for their benefit and has harmed the LDCs.

Globalization is a process that is diminishing many of the factors that divide the world. Advances in travel and communication have made geographical distances less important, people around the world increasingly resemble one another culturally, and the United Nations and other international organizations have increased the level of global governance. Another aspect, economic integration, is the most advanced of any of the strands of globalization. Tariffs and other barriers to trade have decreased significantly since the end of World War II. As a result, all aspects of international economic exchange have grown rapidly. For example, global trade, measured in the value of exported goods and services, has grown about 2,000 percent since the mid-twentieth century and now comes to about 12 trillion annually. International investment in real estate and stocks and bonds in other countries, and in total, now exceeds 25 trillion. The flow of currencies is so massive that there is no accurate measure, but it certainly is more than $1.5 trillion a day.

In this liberalized atmosphere, huge multinational corporations (MNCs) have come to dominate global commerce. Just the top 500 MNCs have combined annual sales of over 15 trillion. The impact of all these changes is that the economic prosperity of almost all countries and the individuals within them is heavily dependent on what they import and export, the flow of investment in and out of each country, and the exchange rates of the currency of each country against the currencies of other countries.

The issue here is whether this economic globalization and integration is a positive or negative trend. For about 60 years, the United States has been at the center of the drive to open international commerce. The push to reduce trade barriers that occurred during and after World War II was designed to prevent a recurrence of the global economic collapse of the 1930s and the war of the 1940s. Policymakers believed that protectionism had caused the Great Depression, that the ensuing human desperation provided fertile ground for the rise of dictators who blamed scapegoats for what had occurred and who promised national salvation, and that these fascist dictators had set off World War II. In sum, policymakers thought that protectionism caused economic depression, which caused dictators, which caused war. They believed that free trade, by contrast, would promote prosperity, democracy, and peace.

Based on these political and economic theories, American policymakers took the lead in establishing a new international economic system, including helping to found such leading global economic organizations as the International Monetary Fund (IMF), the World Bank, and the World Trade Organization (WTO). During the entire latter half of the twentieth century, the movement toward economic globalization has been strong, and there have been few influential voices opposing it.

In the following selection, Anne O. Krueger focuses on the benefits of economic globalization for Africa as part of her general view and that of the IMF that globalization not only benefits economically developed countries but is also a key to the economic development of poorer countries. Not everyone agrees, though, and in recent years the idea that globalization is necessarily beneficial has come under increasing scrutiny and has met increasing resistance. Within countries, globalization has benefited some, while others have lost jobs to imports and suffered other negative consequences. Similarly, some countries, notably those in sub-Saharan Africa, have not prospered. Reflecting this uneven impact, one line of criticism of globalization comes from those who believe that the way global politics work is a function of how the world is organized economically. These critics contend that people within countries are divided into "haves" and "have-nots" and that the world is similarly divided into have and have-not countries. Moreover, these critics believe that, both domestically and internationally, the wealthy haves are using globalization to keep the have-nots weak and poor in order to exploit them. Representing this view, Venezuela's President Hugo Chavez argues in the second selection that economic globalization benefits the few at the expense of the many.

YES

Anne O. Krueger

An Enduring Need: The Importance of Multilateralism in the 21st Century

Multilateralism has been the key to the huge economic successes of the past half century. My theme . . . is that the achievements of the multilateral economic system are increasingly underappreciated as it is ever more taken for granted, while the need for a well-functioning multilateral international economic system is greater than ever as globalization proceeds. I shall argue that the multilateral financial institutions have performed remarkably well in underpinning economic success of unimagined proportions over the past sixty years. However, just as we take the air we breathe for granted, so, too, do many now take those successes and the multilateral economic system underpinning them for granted. They ignore the "public good" benefits that the multilateral system provides and focus instead on a narrow view of the short-term costs and benefits to them.

On the face of it, there is wide support for the multilateral institutions and for the principle of multilateralism. But too often these days, that support is little more than lip service. On almost all issues, the cumulative impact of decisions that affect the strength and health of the institutions is usually underestimated, if it is recognized at all, and the "common good" is generally under-represented in global fora.

I shall start by considering some of the many reasons why multilateralism is so important. Then I want to remind us of some of the successes of the system over the past sixty years. After that I shall turn to some of the reasons why support for the system is not as strong as one would expect in light of its great accomplishments. Finally I'll examine some of the practical issues on which the common good seems to be underestimated relative to the particular concerns of individual countries or groups of countries.

The Role of Multilateralism

To their enormous credit, the founders of the post-war international economic system knew, and understood, the importance of multilateralism. They knew it in theory, but they also knew it because they had all experienced the

From lecture presented at the 2006 Annual Meetings, Boards of Governors of the International Monetary Fund and World Bank Group, Singapore, by Anne O. Krueger (September 19, 2006).

enormous cost of individual actions taken outside a multilateral framework in the 1930s. Then, governments, struggling to offset the impact of the Great Depression, undertook measures that, in effect, were designed to export their problems and that could only succeed if other countries did not take similar measures.

Competitive devaluations were designed to boost exports, but could have succeeded only if other countries did not respond in kind. But, of course, there were irresistible pressures on countries against which devaluation had been undertaken to follow suit and retaliate, and competitive devaluations worsened the situation.

Countries also raised their own tariff barriers, hoping to stimulate their own economic activity by reducing imports (again exporting both unemployment and reduced output to other countries). But, again, the fact that other countries were undertaking similar measures negated any beneficial effect. The volume of world trade shrank and high tariff barriers increased distortions and inefficiencies in the global economy. The American Smoot-Hawley tariff of 1930 was followed by such calamitous events that after the Second World War protectionism in much of the world was held at bay, if not defeated, for years by the mere mention of the name.

Interestingly, most European countries had learned the difficulties of negotiating tariff levels bilaterally (and therefore discriminating among countries) back in the 19th century. They had therefore adopted most favored nation (MFN) clauses in their trade treaties, insuring that imports of each commodity would be treated similarly regardless of country of origin. It was not, however, until the 1920s that the United States government recognized the drawbacks of bilateral trade treaties (at least as seen from an American perspective): the trading partner with which the United States was negotiating would have to lower its tariff for all its MFN partners, while the American tariffs were not extended to others. Most countries chose to offer more favorable tariffs to countries where they would receive larger reciprocal reductions (across other partners) in exchange. Thus, MFN countries could reduce tariffs with each other, leaving the US (and other countries that did not have MFN clauses) confronting the higher tariff rates. The United States was therefore in a position of bargaining with all MFN countries while being excluded from tariff reductions already undertaken among MFN members. It was largely because of this manifestly unfavorable experience that, in the 1930s, Cordell Hull, the American Secretary of State, so enthusiastically supported "reciprocal tariff agreements" in an MFN context.

But the experience of competitive devaluations was equally compelling: an action taken by one country could be in its self-interest unless others followed, in which case all would be worse off. A multilateral framework to avoid this possible outcome seemed clearly warranted.

Correctly, the founders of the postwar international economic system recognized that multilateralism was desirable, not only to reduce and, they hoped, to eliminate the possibility of any recurrence of the 1930s, but also to promote nondiscrimination in international transactions. For my purposes today, I shall focus on the three key organizations: the International Monetary

Fund, charged with maintaining international financial stability; the World Bank, responsible for the provision of development capital; and the World Trade Organization (earlier the General Agreement on Tariffs and Trade) supervising the world's multilateral trading system.

The founders of the postwar system recognized the benefits to be had from a resumption of international capital flows, but believed that the experience of the 1930s had destroyed prospects for a resumption of most private capital flows. They therefore were concerned with enabling official capital flows through the International Bank for Reconstruction and Development—now the World Bank—and did not focus on difficulties that might arise either from discriminatory treatment by source of private capital flows **or** from the lack of an agreed international framework governing treatment of foreign capital. Hence, the postwar international economic system and organization was assumed to be complete when, in addition to the GATT for multilateral trade relations and the World Bank for official capital flows, the IMF was charged with international financial and macroeconomic stability and rules governing current account transactions. The absence of a regime for private capital flows resulted from the assumption that these flows would be relatively unimportant.

What was enshrined in the Fund's Articles of Agreement was provision for convertibility of domestic currencies for current account transactions. By definition, if a currency is convertible without restrictions, it is multilateral and there can be no discrimination for current account transactions. Issues relating to discrimination on the capital account were not addressed, on the assumption that there were relatively few such transactions. Obviously, trade credits and perhaps some other short-term credits might enter international trade, but it was not thought that issues of discrimination would arise. Interestingly, this oversight led to problems even when private capital flows had resumed at very low levels: difficulties arose because of governments' terms for granting official export credit, aid tying, and related issues.

One of the most striking ways in which the world has changed has been the emergence of private capital flows as a major force in the world economy. I shall return to this issue later and argue that the absence of a multilateral, nondiscriminatory framework governing international capital flows (and exchange control mechanisms) is an important and potentially costly gap in the multilateral economic system.

The arguments for a level playing field in which all transactions with foreigners are subject to the same regime are straightforward, glaringly obvious, and hence very dull. Each country's citizens will be better off sourcing imports and finance from the cheapest available source; and selling goods and services and undertaking capital transactions where they can obtain the best terms. And, as I shall note later, efforts to discriminate by country of origin or destination also confront enormous practical problems that normally can be addressed, if at all, only with a highly complex, distortionary, and costly set of regulations.

While the arguments for multilateral regimes for trade, current account transactions, exchange regimes, and capital flows are profoundly correct, they do not provide a dramatic demonstration of the virtues of multilateralism. Experience with efforts to depart from multilateralism has provided more dramatic illustrations of the need for multilateral solutions to international economic policy issues.

Let me mention just [two]: efforts to impose trade sanctions bilaterally . . . and anti-dumping and countervailing duty administration.

Efforts to impose trade sanctions against a country or group of countries are of course an extreme form of trade discrimination. Yet experience shows that they are seldom very effective unless all countries participate or those imposing sanctions can prevent trade through a blockade or other means. Even in cases where "most countries" are supportive, even one open border (whether the authorities are openly permissive, simply turn a blind eye, or cannot enforce) has generally been sufficient to mitigate most of the potential impact of trade sanctions. . . .

Anti-dumping and countervailing duty measures are, by design, discriminatory against countries (and firms) that are found to be using "unfair" means to lower their selling price in the market to which they export. In many instances, firms have been able to shift production from a plant in the country against which the AD or CVD measures is applied to one elsewhere. But when that has not been the case, third country producers are often the big beneficiaries. A famous case was Polish golf carts; the full story is too long to recount, but the main effect of the American effort to impose a CVD on Polish imports was to induce entry of Spanish carts into the American market.

I hope I have said enough to indicate the crucial importance of multilateralism in a well-functioning international economic system. And, since there are occasions when individual countries can perceive it to be in their self interest to pursue discriminatory policies if it is believed that others will not do the same, an international economic regime underpinning and enforcing multilateralism in international transactions is vital. Third country effects; the temptation to retaliate; the fact that an open international economic system has many aspects of a "public good": all of these are arguments that underpinned the postwar international economic system.

But the experience of the postwar years [since World War II], and the unquestionable success of the system, speak even more strongly as to its importance. In most discussions of globalization today, it seems to be forgotten exactly how far the world has come in the sixty years of the postwar international economic system.

Recall that the war-torn European and Asian economies were devastated and, in the aftermath of the war, had output levels significantly below those of the prewar years. Most had severe exchange controls, often with bilateral clearing arrangements, high tariffs and often quantitative restrictions on imports. The average European tariff on manufactured goods imports stood at over 40 percent, but that number understates the extent of trade restrictiveness as quantitative restrictions often kept imports below even the quantities demanded at those high tariff levels. Only 4 countries in the world had full currency convertibility. And, of course, many countries were still very poor, or underdeveloped, as they were then called, with very low per capita incomes and correspondingly poor indicators of health, nutrition, literacy, and other measures of well being.

But starting in the late 1940s, the global economy embarked upon a quarter-century-long period of rapid economic growth, greatly outperforming any prior period of comparable length in world economic history. European recovery accelerated rapidly, and most countries had re-attained their prewar output levels by the early 1950s. But they sustained their growth rates well into the 1960s and early 1970s. At the same time, Japan's economy began growing and by the 1960s was achieving rates of economic growth of 7–9 percent—well above anything that had earlier been thought possible.

Expanding world trade was the "engine of growth" in the postwar years. While real [controlled for inflation] GDP [gross domestic product] was growing at rates far in excess of those realized in earlier eras, world trade was growing at almost twice the rate of real GDP growth. In part, the recovery from wartime conditions and growth of GDP spurred trade growth. But in addition, successive rounds of tariff reductions under GATT and other trade liberalizing measures spurred growth in trade and GDP. At the same time, bilateral trading agreements were gradually abandoned and then multilateral clearing of balances, and, finally, full current-account convertibility followed. It was a virtuous circle: reduction of trade barriers spurred economic growth; and economic growth enabled the further reduction of trade barriers. To leap ahead of my story, by the end of the 20th century, tariffs on manufactured goods among developed countries had fallen from over 40 percent in the late 1940s to an average of less than 5 percent, and quantitative restrictions on trade in manufactures were largely a thing of the past.

Several points about this phenomenal success deserve noting in connection with the role of multilateralism. Perhaps most important, the developing countries, with a few exceptions, failed to participate in trade liberalization in the quarter century after 1950. They mostly erected high trade barriers against imports of manufactures as it was believed that protectionism for "infant industries" was the appropriate policy to achieve more rapid economic growth.

Despite their failure to participate, however, developing countries grew at rates well above those that had been achieved in earlier eras. The fact that the world economy was growing rapidly enabled relatively favorable terms of trade and growth of export earnings (although their share of world trade declined as the industrial countries' trade liberalization led to even more rapid growth there). While the East Asian "tigers," whose policies included increasing integration with the international economy, were growing at spectacular rates, other developing countries benefited substantially from the rapid growth of the world economy, despite their failure to liberalize. In an important sense, those "inner-oriented" developing countries were "free riders" of the multilateral system: the rapid growth of trade benefited them even though they had not themselves liberalized their trade at that time. It enabled them to enter markets more readily than they otherwise would have done, and to increase their exports when domestic incentives were appropriate. That same growth enabled even greater benefits to accrue to them when they liberalized their own trade regimes in the 1980s and 1990s, encouraged by the examples of East Asian success. Trade barriers, both tariffs and quantitative restrictions, have been lowered dramatically in most of the economies now referred to as "emerging markets," thereby contributing to their further growth.

A second, and related, point, is that "globalization" was certainly occurring during the golden quarter century. Trade as a share of global GDP was rising, not only because of falling trade barriers but also because transport and communications costs were dropping sharply. It bears repeating that in 1931 a 3 minute phone call between London and New York had cost $293 in constant 1998 prices. By 2001, that same call cost $1; and today it costs at most just a few cents. Ocean shipping added about 30 percent to the f.o.b. value of exports in the late 1940s; that figure had fallen to 3 percent by the late 1990s. Air freight, a rarity in the immediate postwar years, now accounts for 40 percent of world trade in value terms. Those cost reductions meant that more and more goods were tradable; that many services were increasingly tradable; and hence that globalization was proceeding during the period.

In that connection, the tremendous advances in living standards around the world that accompanied rapid global growth should also be recognized. For example, life expectancy in India has risen from about 39 years in the early 1950s to over 60 years today. Similar dramatic increases have taken place in most developing countries. Since 1960, life expectancy in the developing countries has risen at roughly double the rate in the richest, with the result that the gap in life expectancy between rich and poor countries has shrunk from 30 years in the 1950s to around ten years today. Literacy rates have risen sharply, and other indicators of well being have improved dramatically in most countries.

But the main point is that the trade liberalization and globalization that took place during the first quarter century after 1945 was undertaken in a multilateral context. Bilateral trading agreements fell dramatically in importance; more and more countries adopted Article VIII convertibility [of currencies]; tariff and non-tariff barriers fell sharply.

Almost all of this took place in a multilateral system underpinned by the IMF, the World Bank and the then—GATT. . . .

Let us turn to the next thirty years after the Golden quarter century [1945–1970, during which Europe recovered amid a generally prosperous global economy]. The 1970s represented a major turning point. Perhaps most importantly, the "Bretton Woods system" of fixed exchange rates had to be abandoned, as major countries were unwilling or unable to follow the domestic economic policies that would have been necessary had it been decided to maintain fixed exchange rate regimes. It was probably fortunate for the international economy that that abandonment took place before the quadrupling of the oil price in 1973, as flexible exchange rates between the major currencies enabled the absorption of a significant portion of the shock with less economic dislocation than might have occurred had countries been trying to sustain their earlier, fixed exchange rates.

But several other, related, phenomena occurred. Worldwide inflation accelerated. Many oil-importing countries accessed private capital markets to borrow to finance their oil imports in the years immediately after the oil price increase, with the private capital markets in effect "recycling" the windfall gains from oil producers to the oil-importing developing countries. When, in the 1980s, industrial countries adopted anti-inflationary policies, the higher debt-servicing costs faced by developing countries, and other factors, led to the "debt crisis" of the 1980s.

The official international community—both the IMF and the World Bank—reacted, supporting adjustment efforts in many of the afflicted countries. By the late 1980s, growth in emerging markets was accelerating, and debt "overhangs" were addressed through the [U.S. Secretary of the Treasury Nicholas] Brady plan and other measures. The Paris Club [19 high income countries]—another multilateral effort—found its role in the restructuring of official debt to official creditors greatly enhanced. I should note in passing that these efforts were necessarily in a multilateral context, as the debt which had to be restructured under the Brady Plan was held by a large number of industrial countries, and any country that had alone tried to enable a restructuring of developing country debt held by its nationals would have confronted the awkward fact that nationals from other creditor countries would benefit by its actions. Multilateralism was essential for the resolution of these difficulties.

Over this period, the International Monetary Fund had adapted significantly to its new role. The Fund shifted toward greater emphasis on support and surveillance of economic policies in developing countries, and greater focus on the consistency of exchange rates with monetary and fiscal policies, largely in the context of current account issues.

But in the 1990s there was another sea change in the international economic system. The world economy was growing rapidly, fuelled by growth in world trade, in turn the result at least in part of further trade liberalization under the Uruguay Round. At the same time, the collapse of the Soviet Union led to major challenges in transforming those economies into functioning market economies. Again, bilateral efforts to support the transition would, by themselves, have been far clumsier. The existence of the GATT, subsequently the WTO, as a means of bringing trade regimes into the multilateral system, was essential. So, too, was the admission of economies in transition to the Fund and the Bank, enabling them to adopt the rules of the game for their exchange rate regimes and current account transactions.

Simultaneously, many of the developing countries whose economic performance in the 1980s had contrasted poorly with that of the successful East Asian economies began undertaking policy reforms, including shifting to a more open economy, in the hope and expectation that their economic performance could be improved. By the mid-1990s, China's rapid economic growth was recognized by all, and India's economic reforms were beginning to bring results.

Earlier, some of the East Asian economies had profitably utilized large private capital inflows—in the case of Korea averaging almost 10 percent of GDP during the high growth years—and had shown their creditworthiness. This, combined with the improved prospects of many emerging markets, had led private creditors to pay much more attention to emerging markets. As a consequence, private capital flows to emerging markets mushroomed: whereas in the early 1980s, less than half of capital flows to developing countries had originated from private sources, by the mid 1990s, private capital flows predominated. And whereas a small number of developing countries had been significant borrowers from private markets even in the 1980s, a much larger number of countries, including economies in transition, were able to access them by the mid 1990s. . . .

While private capital flows were increasing in absolute and relative importance, and countries continued to liberalize, a series of events diverted attention from these trends. These were the crises in Mexico in 1994, Thailand, Indonesia, Korea and Malaysia in 1997–98, Russia in 1998, and Brazil in 1999. These crises, especially in the Asian countries, came as a major shock, in part because the rapid and sustained growth of those countries over such a long period had led most observers to believe they were invulnerable, and in part because of the rapidity and severity with which the crises erupted. These were different from earlier current account crises, in part because the capital account was more open and thus permitted more sizeable outflows relative to trade flows. It is not my intention here to analyze these episodes: for present purposes, the only point is to note that there was a great deal of learning to be done by all about the factors contributing to the crises and about the appropriate policy responses when crises did occur. Focus on those issues significantly distracted the international community from attention to the larger questions that arose in response to the emergence of such very large private capital flows and the drift away from multilateral international economic relations.

Lessons have been learned, and many countries' economic policies have changed in ways that make them less vulnerable to financial crises: there have been shifts to more flexible exchange rate regimes, attention has been paid to issues of debt sustainability, reserve levels are higher, and there is greater focus on the consistency of monetary and fiscal policy with exchange rate regimes. And, of course, the IFIs [international financial institutions, such as the IMF and World Bank] played an important role both in facilitating economic reform and disseminating the lessons learned: yet again something multilateralism was best equipped to do.

Where We are Today

The international economy has prospered over the past few years. World real GDP has grown well in excess of 4 per cent annually for four years running and is projected to sustain this pace into 2007. And all regions of the world are sharing in this growth. The world is a far more affluent place than it was a half century ago. Living standards, measured by indicators such as life expectancy, infant mortality, nutritional status, and literacy, have all improved. To be sure, some parts of the world have been more successful than others, and some have failed to share in the gains, and these problems need to be addressed.

Nonetheless, the broad brush picture is one of phenomenal economic success encompassing virtually the entire world, unparalleled by any period in economic history. And the multilateral system has underpinned much of that success. Countries undertaking reforms have realized gains far greater than they would have had the world economy been significantly less vibrant. And experience with reforms has been applied elsewhere, in part because the IFIs have enabled rapid transmission of lessons learned. The fact that trade and capital flows take place on a level multilateral playing field enhances efficiency, and increases competition in ways that are further growth-enhancing. On the surface, therefore, the outlook appears extremely promising. . . .

The very success of the multilateral system over the past six decades is both a cause for celebration and a strong argument for doing all we can to preserve both the system and the benefits it has brought. The international economy has been hugely successful over the past sixty years. Real rates of economic growth and, with them, poverty reduction, have surpassed what anyone thought possible at the end of the Second World War. There is still a great deal to be learned and done—not least to extend the benefits of economic growth to all citizens—but progress has already exceeded expectations by a wide margin.

The dramatic progress we have seen was made possible by the multilateral economic system and the liberalization that has come about through unilateral actions, through compliance with the conditions of membership of the multilateral institutions, and through multilateral negotiations. The fact that globalization has greatly intensified economic linkages and interdependence among countries increases the importance of open multilateralism. In addressing the challenges we face, therefore, we must be careful to appreciate the continuing—even growing—importance of the multilateral system, and to strengthen it.

Of course, international institutions need to adapt to changes in the international economy. They have and they are. But as calls are made for them to achieve those objectives, the message should be clear that changing roles are in the context of a multilateral system: and that multilateralism has been a success that must be fought for and preserved.

 **NO**

Speech at the Opening of XII G-15 Summit

Welcome to Venezuela, the land where a patriotic people has taken over again the banners of Simon Bolivar, its Libertador, whose name is well known beyond these frontiers!

Yes, ladies and gentlemen: Bolivar, . . . who on this very same land of South America tried to unite the Rising Republics in a single, strong and free Republic.

In his letter to Jamaica in 1815, Bolivar said talking about the Panama isthmus and his idea of convening there a Amphictyonic Congress:

> I wish one day we would have the opportunity to install there an august congress with the representatives of the Republics, Kingdoms and Empires to debate and discuss the highest interests of Peace and War with the countries of the other three parts of the world.

[Note: The Great Amphictyonic League was established by several Greek city-states about 1100 B.C. to protect and administer the major Greek temples. As such, it was one of the earliest international organizations.]

Bolivar reveals himself as an anti-imperialist leader, in the same historic perspective that 140 years after that insightful letter at Kingston materialized in the Bandung [Indonesia] Conference in April 1955. Inspired by [India's Prime Minister Jawaharlal] Nerhu, Yugoslavia's Prime Minister Josip Broz] Tito and [Egypt's President Gamal Abdel] Nasser, a group of important leaders gathered at this conference to face great challenges and expressed their wish of not being involved in the East-West conflict and rather work together toward national development. This was the first key milestone: the first Afro-Asian conference, the immediate precedent of the Non-Aligned Countries that gathered 29 heads of state and from which the "Conscience of the South" was born.

Two events of great political significance occurred in the 1960's: the creation of the Non-Aligned Movement in Belgrade [Yugoslavia] in 1961 and the Group of the 77 in 1964. Two milestones and a clear historic trend: the need of the self-awareness of the South and of acting together in a world reality characterized by imbalance and unequal exchange.

In the 1970's a proposal, arising from the IV Summit of Heads of State of the Non-Aligned Countries in Algiers [Algeria] in 1973, became important: the

From Venezuelanalysis.com, March 1, 2004. Copyright © 2004 by Venezuelanalysis.com. Reprinted by permission.

need to create a new international economic order. In 1974 the UN Assembly ratified this proposal, which maintains full effectiveness, but ended up becoming a mere historical reference.

Two events that were very important for the struggles in the South occurred during the 1980's: the creation of the Commission of the South in Kuala Lumpur [Malaysia] in 1987 under the leadership of [President] Julius Nyerere, the unforgettable fighter of Tanzania and the world.

Two years later, in September 1989, the Group of the 15 was born within the framework of the meeting of the Non-Aligned Countries, with the purpose of strengthening the South-South cooperation. [Note: The G-15 now has 17 member countries: Algeria, Argentina, Brazil, Chile, Egypt, India, Indonesia, Jamaica, Kenya, Malaysia, Mexico, Nigeria, Peru, Senegal, Sri Lanka, Venezuela, and Zimbabwe.]

In 1990, the South-Commission submitted its strategic proposal: "A Challenge for the South." And later on . . . later on came the Flood [the dominance of the U.S. and its allies] with the fall of the Berlin Wall and the implosion of the Soviet Union; unipolarity [one global superpower, the United States] appears and the "happy 1990's" arrived, as [economist] Joseph Stiglitz said.

All those struggles, ideas and proposals sunk in the Neoliberal Flood and the world began to witness the so-called "end of History" and the triumphant chant of the Neoliberal Globalization, which today, besides an objective reality, is a weapon of manipulation intended to force us to passiveness faced to an Economic World Order that excludes our South countries and condemns them to the never-ending role of producers of wealth and recipients of leftovers. [Note: Neoliberalism, as the term is used here, applies to the theory that holds that the best path to global prosperity is for all countries to eliminate external barriers to the free flow of trade and investment and to institute a free enterprise (capitalist) system internally.]

Never before had the world such a tremendous scientific-technical potential, such a capacity to generate wealth and well-being. Authentic technological wonders that have made any place in the world to be always close with regard to distances and communications and have not been capable of bringing well-being for everybody, but only for a meager 15% [of the world population that is] living in the countries of the North [the United States, Japan, Western Europe, and other economically developed countries].

Globalization has not brought the so-called interdependence, but an increase in dependency. Instead of wealth globalization, there is poverty wide spreading. Development has not become general, or been shared. To the contrary, the abyss between North and South is now so huge, that the unsustainability of the current economic order and the blindness of the people who try to justify continuing to enjoy opulence and waste, are evident.

The face of this world economic order of globalization with a neoliberal sign is not only Internet, virtual reality or the exploration of the space.

This face can also be seen, and with a greater dramatic character in the countries of the South, in the 790 millions of people who are starving, 800 millions of illiterate adults, 654 millions of human beings who live today in the south and who will not grow older than 40 years of age. This is the harsh and

NO / Hugo Chavez

hard face of the work economic order dominated by the neoliberalism and seen every year in the South [the less economically developed countries, those not of the North], the death of over 11 millions of boys and girls below 5 years of age caused by illnesses that are practically always preventable and curable and who die at the appalling rate of over 30 thousand every day, 21 every minute, 10 each 30 seconds. In the South, the proportion of children suffering of malnutrition reaches up to 50% in quite a few countries, while according to the FAO [the UN's Food and Agriculture Organization], a child who lives in the First World [the North] will consume throughout his or her life, the equivalent to what 50 children consume in an underdeveloped country.

The great possibilities that a globalization of solidarity and true coopera- tion could bring to all people in the world through the scientific-technical wonders, has been reduced by the neoliberal model to this grotesque carica- ture full of exploitation and social injustice.

Our countries of the South were repeated a thousand times that the sole and true "science" capable of ensuring development and well-being for every- body, without exception, was synthesized in leaving the markets operate without regulation, privatizing everything and creating the conditions for transnational capital investment, and banning the State from intervening the economy.

Almost the magic and wonderful philosopher's stone!!

Neoliberal thought and politics were created in the North to serve their interests, but it should be highlighted that they have never been truly applied there, but they have been spread throughout the South in the past two decades and reached the disastrous category of a single thought.

Through the application of the sole thought, the world economy as a whole grew less than in the three decades between 1945 and 1975, when the Keynesian theories promoting market regulation through State intervention were applied. The gap separating the North and the South continued to grow, not only with regard to economic indicators, but also in the strategic sector of access to knowledge, from which the fundamental possibility of integral development in our times arises. [Note: "Keynesian theories" refers to those of British economist John Maynard Keynes (1883–1946), who argued that governments should use fiscal measures, such as raising or lowering interest rates and budget spending to avoid or ease the "boom and bust" cycle of economies.]

The countries of the North with 15% of the world population count with over 85% of Internet users and control 97% of the patents. These countries have an average of over 10 years of schooling, while in the countries of the South schooling hardly reaches 3.7 years and in many countries is even lower.

The tragedy of underdevelopment and poverty in Africa, which historic roots lay in colonialism and the slavery of millions of its children, is now reinforced by the neoliberalism from the North. In this region, the rate of infant mortality in children under 1 year of age is 107 per each thousand children born alive, while in the developed countries this rate is 6 per each thousand children born alive; also, life expectancy is 48 years, thirty years less than in countries of the North.

In Asia, economic growth in some countries has been remarkable, but the region, as a whole, still presents a delay with regard to the North in basic economic and social development aspects.

We are, dear friends, in Latin America, the favorite scenario of the neoliberal model in the past decades. Here, neoliberalism reached the status of a dogma and was applied with greatest severity.

Its catastrophic results can be easily seen and are the explanation for the growing and uncontrollable social protest that the poor people and the excluded people of Latin America have been expressing, every day more vigorously, for some years now, claiming their right to life, to education, to health, to culture, to a decent living as human beings.

I saw with my own eyes, a day like today but exactly 15 years ago, the 27 of February 1989, when an intense day of protest broke out on the streets of Caracas against the neoliberal package of the International Monetary Fund and ended in a real massacre known as "The Caracazo" [as in Caracas].

The neoliberal model promised Latin Americans greater economic growth, but during the neoliberal years growth has not even reached half the growth achieved in the 1945–1975 period with different politics.

The model recommended the most strict financial liberalization and exchange freedom to achieve a greater influx of foreign capitals and greater stability. But in neoliberal years the financial crises have been more intense and frequent than ever before, the external regional debts non-existent at the end of the Second World War amounts today to 750 billion dollars, the per capita highest debt in the world and in several countries is equal to more than half the GDP. Only between 1990 and the year 2002, Latin America made external debt payments amounting to 1 trillion 528 billions of dollars, which duplicates the amount of the current debt and represented an annual average payment of 118 billion. That is, we pay the debt every 6.3 years, but this evil burden continues to be there, unchanging and inextinguishable.

It is a never-ending debt!

Obviously, this debt has exceeded the normal and reasonable payment commitments by any debtor and has turned into an instrument to undercapitalize our countries additionally to the imposition of socially adverse measures that subsequently generate powerful politically destabilizing factors for the governments that insist in their implementation.

We were asked to be ultraliberal in trade and to lift any barrier, which may obstruct the imports coming from the North, but the oral champions of free trade actually are the champions in the praxis of protectionism. The North spends 1 billion dollars a day in practicing what has been banned from doing, that is, subsidizing inefficient products.

I want to tell you—and this is a true and verifiable data—that each cow grazing in the European Union receives in its four stomachs 2.20 dollars a day in subsidies, thus having a better situation than 2.5 billion poor people in the South who hardly survive with an income less than 2 dollars a day.

With the FTAA [the proposed Free Trade Area of the Americas], the government of the United States wants us to reach a zero tariff situation in their benefit and wants us to give away our markets, our oil, our water resources and biodiversity, in addition to our sovereignty, whereas walls of subsidies for agriculture keep access closed to the market of that country. It is a peculiar way of relieving the huge commercial deficit of the United States, to do exactly the contrary to what they present as a sacred principle in economic policy.

Neoliberalism promised Latin American people that if they accepted the demands of the multinational capital, investments would overflow the region. Indeed, the incoming capital increased. A portion to buy state-owned companies sometimes at bargain prices, another portion was speculative capital to seize the opportunities involved in the financial liberalization environment.

The neoliberal model promised that after a painful adjustment period necessary to deprive the State of its regulatory power over economy and liberalize trade and finance, wealth would spread over Latin America and the long-lasting history of poverty and underdevelopment would be left behind. But the painful and temporary adjustment became permanent and appears to become everlasting. The results cannot be concealed.

Taking 1980 as the conventional year of the commencement of the neoliberal cycle, by that time around 35 percent of the Latin American population were poor. Two decades thereafter, 44 percent of Latin American men and women are poor. Poverty is particularly cruel to children. It is a sad reality that in Latin America most of the poor people are children and most children are poor. In the late 1990's, the Economic Commission for Latin America reported that 58 percent of children under 5 were poor, as well as 57% of children with ages ranging from 6 to 12.

Poverty among children and teenagers tends to reinforce and perpetuate inequalities of access to education, as shown by a survey conducted by the Inter-American Development Bank on 15 countries where householders in 10 percent of the population with the highest income had an average schooling of 11 years, whereas among householders in 30 percent of the lowest income population such average was 4 years.

Neoliberalism promised wealth. And poverty has spread, thus making of Latin America the most unequal region over the world in terms of income distribution. In the region, the wealthiest 10 percent of the population—those who are satisfied with neoliberalism and feel enthusiastic about the FTAA— receive nearly 50 percent of the total income, where the poorest 10 percent— those who never appear in high class society chronicles of the oligarchic mass media—barely receive 1.5 percent of such total income.

This exploitation model has turned Latin America and the Caribbean into a social bomb ready to explode, should anti-development, unemployment and poverty keep increasing.

Even though the social struggles are growing sharp and even some governments have been overthrown by uprisings, we are told by the North that the neoliberal reform has not yielded good results because it has not been implemented in full.

So, they now intend to recommend the formula of suicide. But we know, brothers and sisters, that countries do not commit suicide. The people of our countries awake, stand up and fight!

As a conclusion, because of its injustice and inequality, the economic and social order of neoliberal globalization appears to be a dead-end street for the South.

Therefore, the passive acceptance of the excluding rules imposed by this economic and social order cannot be the behavior to be exercised by the Heads of State and Government who have the highest responsibility before our peoples.

The history of our countries does not admit any doubt—passivity and grieving are useless, instead, the joined and firm action is the sole conduct enabling the South to rise from its sad role of exploited and humiliated rearguard.

Thanks to the heroic struggle against colonialism, the developing countries broke the economic and social order condemning them to the condition of exploited colonies. Colonialism was not defeated by the accumulations of tears of sorrow or by the repentance of colonialists, but for centuries of heroic fights for independence and sovereignty in which the resistance, tenacity and sacrifice of our peoples worked wonders.

Here, in South America, this year we are precisely commemorating 180 years of the heroic deeds of Ayacucho battle, where people joined and became a liberating army after almost 20 years of revolutionary wars under the bright leadership of José de San Martin, Bernardo O'Higgins, José Inacio Abreu e Lima, Simon Bolivar and Antonio José de Sucre, sending away the Spanish empire hitherto extended from the warm Caribbean beaches to the cold lands of Patagonia, thus ending 300 years of colonialism. [Note: In the Battle of Ayacucho (Peru) in 1824, revolutionary forces made up of troops from several current South American countries defeated Spanish forces in the pivotal battle of the independence campaign.]

Today, vis-á-vis the obvious failure of neoliberalism and the great threat that the International Economic Order represents for our countries, it is necessary to retake the Spirit of the South.

POSTSCRIPT

Is Economic Globalization a Positive Trend?

Globalization is both old and new. It is old in that the efforts of humans to overcome distance and other barriers to increased interchange have long existed. The first canoes and signal fires are part of the history of globalization. The first event in true globalization occurred between 1519 and 1522, when Ferdinand Magellan circumnavigated the globe. MNCs have existed at least since 1600 when a group of British merchants formed the East India Company. In the main, though, globalization is mostly a modern phenomenon. The progress of globalization until the latter half of the 1800s might be termed "creeping globalization." There were changes, but they occurred very slowly. Since then, the pace of globalization has increased exponentially. A brief introduction to globalization is available in Jurgen Osterhammel, Niels P. Petersson, and Dona Geyer, *Globalization: A Short History* (Princeton University Press, 2005).

The recent rapid pace of globalization has sparked an increasing chorus of criticism against many of its aspects including economic interdependence. Now it is not uncommon for massive protests to occur when the leaders of the world countries meet to discuss global or regional economics or when the WTO, IMF, or World Bank hold important conferences.

One of the oddities about globalization, economic or otherwise, is that it often creates a common cause between those of marked conservative and marked liberal views. More than anything, conservatives worry that their respective countries are losing control of their economies and, thus, a degree of their independence. Echoing this view, archconservative political commentator Patrick Buchanan has warned that unchecked globalization threatens to turn the United States into a "North American province of what some call The New World Order."

Some liberals share the conservatives' negative views of globalization but for different reasons. This perspective is less concerned with sovereignty and security; it is more concerned with workers and countries being exploited and the environment being damaged by MNCs that shift their operations to other countries to find cheap labor and to escape environmental regulations. Referring to violent anti-WTO protests that had recently occurred, U.S. labor leader John J. Sweeney told reporters that they were "just the beginning" and that "If globalization brings more inequality, then it will generate a violent reaction that [these protests] will look tame." One widely read critique of economic globalization is Joseph E. Stiglitz, *Making Globalization Work* (W. W. Norton, 2006).

Despite the upsurge of criticism, globalization continues to have many supporters. Most national leaders, especially among the industrialized countries, continue to support free economic interchange. In the United States, both President Bill Clinton and George W. Bush took that stand, although they sometimes also applied protectionist practices to shield U.S. business and workers. The support for globalization is also strong among economists, including Jagdish Bhagwati, *In Defense of Globalization* (Oxford University Press, 2004).

What many analysts argue is that globalization is not good or bad, as such. Rather, it is how it is applied that makes the difference. A study that takes a balanced view is Danial Cohen, *Globalization and its Enemies* (MIT Press, 2006). A book that looks toward reform and discuss new ways of thinking is Frederic Mishkin, *The Next Great Globalization* (Princeton University Press, 2006) and Kemal Dervis, *A Better Globalization* (Center for Global Development, 2005). The Internet provides further resources that examine globalization. A good site is The Globalization Web site, http://www.sociology.emory.edu/globalization, hosted by Emory University. It is even-handed and is particularly meant to support undergraduates.

ISSUE 2

Does Globalization Threaten Cultural Diversity?

YES: Julia Galeota, from "Cultural Imperialism: An American Tradition," *The Humanist* (May/June 2004)

NO: Philippe Legrain, from "In Defense of Globalization," *The International Economy* (Summer 2003)

ISSUE SUMMARY

YES: Julia Galeota of McLean, Virginia, who was seventeen years old when she wrote her essay that won first place for her age category in the 2004 *Humanist* Essay Contest for Young Women and Men of North America, contends that many cultures around the world are gradually disappearing due to the overwhelming influence of corporate and cultural America.

NO: Philippe Legrain, chief economist of Britain in Europe, an organization supporting the adoption by Great Britain of the euro as its currency, counters that it is a myth that globalization involves the imposition of Americanized uniformity, rather than an explosion of cultural exchange.

Globalization is often thought of in terms of economic integration, but it is a much broader phenomenon. Another important aspect of globalization is the spread of national cultures to other countries, regions, and, indeed, the world. One impetus for cultural globalization is economic globalization, as products spread around the world and as huge multinational corporations establish global operations. Additionally, cultural globalization is a product of advances in transportation that allow an increasing number of people to travel to other countries and of radio, television, the Internet, and other advances in communications that permit people to interact passively or actively with others around the world.

To a degree, the culture of many nations is spreading, with Japanese shushi bars now a common site in the United States, Europe, and elsewhere. Cultural globalization also involves a certain amount of cultural amalgamation, with influences merging to create new cultural realities. A third possibility, and the one that is at the heart of this debate, is when the spread of one culture is far greater than the spread of others. Arguably, that is what is currently occurring, with American "cultural exports" much greater than those of any other country.

There is significant evidence of the spread of Western, particularly American, cultural. Casual dress around the world is more apt to include jeans, T-shirts, and sneakers than traditional dress. Young people everywhere listen to music by Beyonce, Jay-Z, and others artists, and fast-food hamburgers, fries, and milk shakes are consumed around the world. Adding to the spread of American culture, U.S. movies are everywhere, earning the majority of all film revenues in Japan, Europe, and Latin America, and U.S. television programming is increasingly omnipresent, with, for instance, about two-thirds of the market in Latin America.

Another indication of the spread of American culture is that English is increasingly the common language of business, diplomacy, communications, and even culture. Among Europeans, for instance, nearly all school children receive English instruction, and two-thirds of younger Europeans speak at least some English compared to less than 20 percent of retirement-age Europeans.

It is important to not trivialize cultural globalization even though it involves, in part, fast food, sneakers, rock music, and other elements of pop culture. Some scholars argue the elimination of culture differences will help reduce conflicts as people become more familiar with one another and, indeed, more similar to each other.

Others, however, believe the cultural globalization has negative aspects. One argument is that it is causing a backlash as people face the loss of their own cultures. Some analysts contend that the growth of religious fundamentalism and even terrorism is a reaction to cultural threats. Other analysts believe that defense of cultural traditionalism could even lead to culture wars in the future, with the world dividing itself into antagonist cultural groups. A third worry is represented by Julia Galeota in the first reading, who worries that the spread of American culture amounts for cultural imperialism that is destroying the rich cultural variety that has heretofore marked human society. Galeota suggests that the spread of American culture is a product of American economic and other forms of power, rather than the result of the superiority of American culture and its attractiveness to others. As such, she depicts the Americanization of global culture as cultural imperialism. Philippe Legrain is much more at ease with cultural globalization. He contends that it reflects new realities and is making many contributions, such as giving people the freedom to adopt whatever language, style of dress, or other cultural aspect that they find most compatible with their tastes and needs.

YES

Julia Galeota

Cultural Imperialism: An American Tradition

Travel almost anywhere in the world today and, whether you suffer from habitual Big Mac cravings or cringe at the thought of missing the newest episode of MTV's *The Real World*, your American tastes can be satisfied practically everywhere. This proliferation of American products across the globe is more than mere accident. As a byproduct of globalization, it is part of a larger trend in the conscious dissemination of American attitudes and values that is often referred to as *cultural imperialism*. In his 1976 work *Communication and Cultural Domination*, Herbert Schiller defines cultural imperialism as:

> The sum of the processes by which a society is brought into the modern world system, and how its dominating stratum is attracted, pressured, forced, and sometimes bribed into shaping social institutions to correspond to, or even to promote, the values and structures of the dominant center of the system.

Thus, cultural imperialism involves much more than simple consumer goods; it involves the dissemination of ostensibly American principles, such as freedom and democracy. Though this process might sound appealing on the surface, it masks a frightening truth: many cultures around the world are gradually disappearing due to the overwhelming influence of corporate and cultural America.

The motivations behind American cultural imperialism parallel the justifications for U.S. imperialism throughout history: the desire for access to foreign markets and the belief in the superiority of American culture. Though the United States does boast the world's largest, most powerful economy, no business is completely satisfied with controlling only the American market; American corporations want to control the other 95 percent of the world's consumers as well. Many industries are incredibly successful in that venture. According to the *Guardian*, American films accounted for approximately 80 percent of global box office revenue in January 2003. And who can forget good old Micky D's? With over 30,000 restaurants in over one hundred countries, the ubiquitous golden arches of McDonald's are now, according to Eric Schlosser's *Fast Food* Nation, "more widely recognized than the Christian cross." Such American domination inevitably hurts local markets, as the

From *The Humanist* by Julia Galeota, vol. 64, no. 3, May/June 2004, pp. 22–24, 46. Copyright © 2004 by American Humanist Association. Reprinted by permission.

majority of foreign industries are unable to compete with the economic strength of U.S. industry. Because it serves American economic interests, corporations conveniently ignore the detrimental impact of American control of foreign markets.

Corporations don't harbor qualms about the detrimental effects of "Americanization" of foreign cultures, as most corporations have ostensibly convinced themselves that American culture is superior and therefore its influence is beneficial to other, "lesser" cultures. Unfortunately, this American belief in the superiority of U.S. culture is anything but new; it is as old as the culture itself. This attitude was manifest in the actions of settlers when they first arrived on this continent and massacred or assimilated essentially the entire "savage" Native American population. This attitude also reflects that of the late nineteenth-century age of imperialism, during which the jingoists attempted to fulfill what they believed to be the divinely ordained "manifest destiny" of American expansion. Jingoists strongly believe in the concept of social Darwinism: the stronger, "superior" cultures will overtake the weaker, "inferior" cultures in a "survival of the fittest." It is this arrogant belief in the incomparability of American culture that characterizes many of our economic and political strategies today.

It is easy enough to convince Americans of the superiority of their culture, but how does one convince the rest of the world of the superiority of American culture? The answer is simple: marketing. Whether attempting to sell an item, a brand, or an entire culture, marketers have always been able to successfully associate American products with modernity in the minds of consumers worldwide. While corporations seem to simply sell Nike shoes or Gap jeans (both, ironically, manufactured *outside* of the United States), they are also selling the image of America as the land of "cool." This indissoluble association causes consumers all over the globe to clamor ceaselessly for the same American products.

Twenty years ago, in his essay "The Globalization of Markets," Harvard business professor Theodore Levitt declared, "The world's needs and desires have been irrevocably homogenized." Levitt held that corporations that were willing to bend to local tastes and habits were inevitably doomed to failure. He drew a distinction between weak multinational corporations that operate differently in each country and strong global corporations that handle an entire world of business with the same agenda.

In recent years, American corporations have developed an even more successful global strategy: instead of advertising American conformity with blonde-haired, blue-eyed, stereotypical Americans, they pitch diversity. These campaigns—such as McDonald's new international "I'm lovin' it" campaign—work by drawing on the United State's history as an ethnically integrated nation composed of essentially every culture in the world. An early example of this global marketing tactic was found in a Coca Cola commercial from 1971 featuring children from many different countries innocently singing, "I'd like to teach the world to sing in perfect harmony/I'd like to buy the world a Coke to keep it company." This commercial illustrates an attempt to portray a U.S. goods as a product capable of transcending political, ethnic, religious, social, and economic differences to unite the world (according to the Coca-Cola Company, we can achieve world peace through consumerism).

More recently, Viacon's MTV has successfully adapted this strategy by integrating many different Americanized cultures into one unbelievably influential American network (with over 280 million subscribers worldwide). According to a 1996 "New World Teen Study" conducted by DMB&B's BrainWaves division, of the 26,700 middle-class teens in forty-five countries surveyed, 85 percent watch MTV every day. These teens absorb what MTV intends to show as a diverse mix of cultural influences but is really nothing more than manufactured stars singing in English to appeal to American popular taste.

If the strength of these diverse "American" images is not powerful enough to move products, American corporations also appropriate local cultures into their advertising abroad. Unlike Levitt's weak multinationals, these corporations don't bend to local tastes; they merely insert indigenous celebrities or trends to present the facade of a customized advertisement. MTV has spawned over twenty networks specific to certain geographical areas such as Brazil and Japan. These specialized networks further spread the association between American and modernity under the pretense of catering to local taste. Similarly, commercials in India in 2000 featured Bollywood stars Hrithik Roshan promoting Coke and Shahrukh Khan promoting Pepsi (Sanjeev Srivastava, "Cola Row in India." BBC News Online). By using popular local icons in their advertisements, U.S. corporations successfully associate what is fashionable in local cultures with what is fashionable in America. America essentially samples the world's cultures, repackages them with the American trademark of materialism, and resells them to the world.

Critics of the theory of American cultural imperialism argue that foreign consumers don't passively absorb the images America bombards upon them. In fact, foreign consumers do play an active role in the reciprocal relationship between buyer and seller. For example, according to Naomi Klein's *No Logo,* American cultural imperialism has inspired a "slow food movement" in Italy and a demonstration involving the burning of chickens outside of the first Kentucky Fried Chicken outlet in India. Though there have been countless other conspicuous and inconspicuous acts of resistance, the intense, unrelenting barrage of American cultural influence continues ceaselessly.

Compounding the influence of commercial images are the media and information industries, which present both explicit and implicit messages about the very real military and economic hegemony of the United States. Ironically, the industry that claims to be the source for "fair and balanced" information plays a large role in the propagation of American influence around the world. The concentration of media ownership during the 1990s enabled both American and British media organizations to gain control of the majority of the world's news services. Satellites allow over 150 million households in approximately 212 countries and territories worldwide to subscribe to CNN, a member of Time Warner, the world's largest media conglomerate. In the words of British sociologist Jeremy Tunstall, "When a government allows news importation, it is in effect importing a piece of another country's politics—which is true of no other import." In addition to politics and commercials, networks like CNN also present foreign countries with unabashed accounts of the military and economic superiority of the United States.

The Internet acts as another vehicle for the worldwide propagation of American influence. Interestingly, some commentators cite the new "information economy" as proof that American cultural imperialism is in decline. They argue that the global accessibility of this decentralized medium has decreased the relevance of the "core and periphery" theory of global influence. This theory describes an inherent imbalance in the primarily outward flow of information and influence from the stronger, more powerful "core" nations such as the United States. Additionally, such critics argue, unlike consumers of other types of media, Internet users must actively seek out information; users can consciously choose to avoid all messages of American culture. While these arguments are valid, they ignore their converse: if one so desires, anyone can access a wealth of information about American culture possibly unavailable through previous channels. Thus, the Internet can dramatically increase exposure to American culture for those who desire it.

Fear of the cultural upheaval that could result from this exposure to new information has driven governments in communist China and Cuba to strictly monitor and regulate their citizens' access to websites (these protectionist policies aren't totally effective, however, because they are difficult to implement and maintain). Paradoxically, limiting access to the Internet nearly ensures that countries will remain largely the recipients, rather than the contributors, of information on the Internet.

Not all social critics see the Americanization of the world as a negative phenomenon. Proponents of cultural imperialism, such as David Rothkopf, a former senior official in Clinton's Department of Commerce, argue that American cultural imperialism is in the interest not only of the United States but also of the world at large. Rothkopf cites Samuel Huntington's theory from *The Clash* of Civilizations and the Beginning of the World Order that, the greater the cultural disparities in the world, the more likely it is that conflict will occur. Rothkopf argues that the removal of cultural barriers through U.S. cultural imperialism will promote a more stable world, one in which American culture reigns supreme as "the most just, the most tolerant, the most willing to constantly reassess and improve itself, and the best model for the future." Rothkopf is correct in one sense: Americans are on the way to establishing a global society with minimal cultural barriers. However, one must question whether this projected society is truly beneficial for all involved. Is it worth sacrificing countless indigenous cultures for the unlikely promise of a world without conflict?

Around the world, the answer is an overwhelming "No!" Disregarding the fact that a world of homogenized culture would not necessarily guarantee a world without conflict, the complex fabric of diverse cultures around the world is a fundamental and indispensable basis of humanity. Throughout the course of human existence, millions have died to preserve their indigenous culture. It is a fundamental right of humanity to be allowed to preserve the mental, physical, intellectual, and creative aspects of one's society. A single "global culture" would be nothing more than a shallow, artificial "culture" of materialism reliant on technology. Thankfully, it would be nearly impossible to create one bland culture in a world of over six billion people. And nor should we want to. Contrary to Rothkopf's (and George W. Bush's) belief that, "Good and evil, better and worse coexist in this world," there are no such absolutes in this world. The United States should not be able to relentlessly force other nations to accept its definition of what is "good" and "just" or even "modern."

Fortunately, many victims of American cultural imperialism aren't blind to the subversion of their cultures. Unfortunately, these nations are often too weak to fight the strength of the United States and subsequently to preserve their native cultures. Some countries—such as France, China, Cuba, Canada, and Iran—have attempted to quell America's cultural influence by limiting or prohibiting access to American cultural programming through satellites and the Internet. However, according to the UN Universal Declaration of Human Rights, it is a basic right of all people to "seek, receive, and impart information and ideas through any media and regardless of frontiers," Governments shouldn't have to restrict their citizens' access to information in order to preserve their native cultures. We as a world must find ways to defend local cultures in a manner that does not compromise the rights of indigenous people.

The prevalent proposed solutions to the problem of American cultural imperialism are a mix of defense and compromise measures on behalf of the endangered cultures. In *The Lexus and the Olive Tree,* Thomas Friedman advocates the use of protective legislation such as zoning laws and protected area laws, as well as the appointment of politicians with cultural integrity, such as those in agricultural, culturally pure Southern France. However, many other nations have no voice in the nomination of their leadership, so those countries need a middle-class and elite committed to social activism. If it is utterly impossible to maintain the cultural purity of a country through legislation, Friedman suggests the country attempt to "glocalize," that is:

> To absorb influences that naturally fit into and can enrich [a] culture, to resist those things that are truly alien and to compartmentalize those things that, while different, can nevertheless be enjoyed and celebrated as different.

These types of protective filters should help to maintain the integrity of a culture in the face of cultural imperialism. In *Jihad vs. McWorld,* Benjamin Barber calls for the resuscitation of nongovernmental, noncapitalist spaces—to the "civic spaces"—such as village greens, places of religious worship, or community schools. It is also equally important to focus on the education of youth in their native values and traditions. Teens especially need a counterbalance images of American consumerism they absorb from the media. Even if individuals or countries consciously choose to become "Americanized" or "modernized," their choice should be made freely and independently of the coercion and influence of American cultural imperialism.

The responsibility for preserving cultures shouldn't fall entirely on those at risk. The United States must also recognize that what is good for its economy isn't necessarily good for the world at large. We must learn to put people before profits. The corporate and political leaders of the United States would be well advised to heed these words of Gandhi:

> I do not want my house to be walled in on all sides and my windows to be stuffed. I want the culture of all lands to be blown about my house as freely as possible. But I refuse to be blown off my feet by any.

The United States must acknowledge that no one culture can or should reign supreme, for the death of diverse cultures can only further harm future generations.

Philippe Legrain  **NO**

In Defense of Globalization

Fears that globalization is imposing a deadening cultural uniformity are as ubiquitous as Coca-Cola, McDonald's, and Mickey Mouse. Many people dread that local cultures and national identities are dissolving into a crass all-American consumerism. That cultural imperialism is said to impose American values as well as products, promote the commercial at the expense of the authentic, and substitute shallow gratification for deeper satisfaction.

Thomas Friedman, columnist for the *New York Times* and author of *The Lexus and the Olive Tree,* believes that globalization is "globalizing American culture and American cultural icons." Naomi Klein, a Canadian journalist and author of *No Logo,* argues that "Despite the embrace of polyethnic imagery, market-driven globalization doesn't want diversity; quite the opposite. Its enemies are national habits, local brands, and distinctive regional tastes."

But it is a myth that globalization involves the imposition of American-ized uniformity, rather than an explosion of cultural exchange. And although— as with any change—it can have downsides, this cross-fertilization is over-whelmingly a force for good.

The beauty of globalization is that it can free people from the tyranny of geography. Just because someone was born in France does not mean they can only aspire to speak French, eat French food, read French books, and so on. That we are increasingly free to choose our cultural experiences enriches our lives immeasurably. We could not always enjoy the best the world has to offer.

Globalization not only increases individual freedom, but also revitalizes cultures and cultural artifacts through foreign influences, technologies, and markets. Many of the best things come from cultures mixing: Paul Gauguin painting in Polynesia, the African rhythms in rock 'n' roll, the great British curry. Admire the many-colored faces of France's World Cup-winning soccer team, the ferment of ideas that came from Eastern Europe's Jewish diaspora, and the cosmopolitan cities of London and New York.

Fears about an Americanized uniformity are overblown. For a start, many "American" products are not as all-American as they seem; MTV in Asia promotes Thai pop stars and plays rock music sung in Mandarin. Nor are American products all-conquering. Coke accounts for less than two of the 64 fluid ounces that the typical person drinks a day. France imported a mere $620 million in food from the United States in 2000, while exporting to

From *The International Economy* by Philippe Legrain, vol. 17, no. 3, Summer 2003, pp. 62–65.

America three times that. Worldwide, pizzas are more popular than burgers and Chinese restaurants sprout up everywhere.

In fashion, the ne plus ultra is Italian or French. Nike shoes are given a run for their money by Germany's Adidas, Britain's Reebok, and Italy's Fila. American pop stars do not have the stage to themselves. According to the IFPI, the record-industry bible, local acts accounted for 68 percent of music sales in 2000, up from 58 percent in 1991. And although nearly three-quarters of television drama exported worldwide comes from the United States, most countries' favorite shows are homegrown.

Nor are Americans the only players in the global media industry. Of the seven market leaders, one is German, one French, and one Japanese. What they distribute comes from all quarters: Germany's Bertelsmann publishes books by American writers; America's News Corporation broadcasts Asian news; Japan's Sony sells Brazilian music.

In some ways, America is an outlier, not a global leader. Baseball and American football have not traveled well; most prefer soccer. Most of the world has adopted the (French) metric system; America persists with antiquated British Imperial measurements. Most developed countries have become intensely secular, but many Americans burn with fundamentalist fervor—like Muslims in the Middle East.

Admittedly, Hollywood dominates the global movie market and swamps local products in most countries. American fare accounts for more than half the market in Japan and nearly two-thirds in Europe. Yet Hollywood is less American than it seems. Top actors and directors are often from outside America. Some studios are foreign-owned. To some extent, Hollywood is a global industry that just happens to be in America. Rather than exporting Americana, it serves up pap to appeal to a global audience.

Hollywood's dominance is in part due to economics: Movies cost a lot to make and so need a big audience to be profitable; Hollywood has used America's huge and relatively uniform domestic market as a platform to expand overseas. So there could be a case for stuffing subsidies into a rival European film industry, just as Airbus was created to challenge Boeing's near-monopoly. But France's subsidies have created a vicious circle whereby European film producers fail in global markets because they serve domestic demand and the wishes of politicians and cinematic bureaucrats.

Another American export is also conquering the globe: English. By 2050, it is reckoned, half the world will be more or less proficient in it. A common global language would certainly be a big plus—for businessmen, scientists, and tourists—but a single one seems far less desirable. Language is often at the heart of national culture, yet English may usurp other languages not because it is what people prefer to speak, but because, like Microsoft software, there are compelling advantages to using it if everyone else does.

But although many languages are becoming extinct, English is rarely to blame. People are learning English as well as—not instead of—their native tongue, and often many more languages besides. Where local languages are dying, it is typically national rivals that are stamping them out. So although, within the United States, English is displacing American Indian tongues, it is not doing away with Swahili or Norwegian.

Even though American consumer culture is widespread, its significance is often exaggerated. You can choose to drink Coke and eat at McDonald's without becoming American in any meaningful sense. One newspaper photo of Taliban fighters in Afghanistan showed them toting Kalashnikovs—as well as a sports bag with Nike's trademark swoosh. People's culture—in the sense of their shared ideas, beliefs, knowledge, inherited traditions, and art—may scarcely be eroded by mere commercial artifacts that, despite all the furious branding, embody at best flimsy values.

The really profound cultural changes have little to do with Coca-Cola. Western ideas about liberalism and science are taking root almost everywhere, while Europe and North America are becoming multicultural societies through immigration, mainly from developing countries. Technology is reshaping culture: Just think of the Internet. Individual choice is fragmenting the imposed uniformity of national cultures. New hybrid cultures are emerging, and regional ones re-emerging. National identity is not disappearing, but the bonds of nationality are loosening.

Cross-border cultural exchange increases diversity within societies—but at the expense of making them more alike. People everywhere have more choice, but they often choose similar things. That worries cultural pessimists, even though the right to choose to be the same is an essential part of freedom.

Cross-cultural exchange can spread greater diversity as well as greater similarity: more gourmet restaurants as well as more McDonald's outlets. And just as a big city can support a wider spread of restaurants than a small town, so a global market for cultural products allows a wider range of artists to thrive. If all the new customers are ignorant, a wider market may drive down the quality of cultural products: Think of tourist souvenirs. But as long as some customers are well informed (or have "good taste"), a general "dumbing down" is unlikely. Hobbyists, fans, artistic pride, and professional critics also help maintain (and raise) standards.

A bigger worry is that greater individual freedom may undermine national identity. The French fret that by individually choosing to watch Hollywood films they might unwittingly lose their collective Frenchness. Yet such fears are overdone. Natural cultures are much stronger than people seem to think. They can embrace some foreign influences and resist others. Foreign influences can rapidly become domesticated, changing national culture, but not destroying it. Clearly, though, there is a limit to how many foreign influences a culture can absorb before being swamped. Traditional cultures in the developing world that have until now evolved (or failed to evolve) in isolation may be particularly vulnerable.

In *The Silent Takeover*, Noreena Hertz describes the supposed spiritual Eden that was the isolated kingdom of Bhutan in the Himalayas as being defiled by such awful imports as basketball and Spice Girls T-shirts. But is that such a bad thing? It is odd, to put it mildly, that many on the left support multiculturalism in the West but advocate cultural purity in the developing world—an attitude they would tar as fascist if proposed for the United States.

Hertz appears to want people outside the industrialized West preserved in unchanging but supposedly pure poverty. Yet the Westerners who want this supposed paradise preserved in aspic rarely feel like settling there. Nor do most people in developing countries want to lead an "authentic" unspoiled life of isolated poverty.

In truth, cultural pessimists are typically not attached to diversity per se but to designated manifestations of diversity, determined by their preferences. Cultural pessimists want to freeze things as they were. But if diversity at any point in time is desirable, why isn't diversity across time? Certainly, it is often a shame if ancient cultural traditions are lost. We should do our best to preserve them and keep them alive where possible. Foreigners can often help, by providing the new customers and technologies that have enabled reggae music, Haitian art, and Persian carpet making, for instance, to thrive and reach new markets. But people cannot be made to live in a museum. We in the West are forever casting off old customs when we feel they are no longer relevant. Nobody argues that Americans should ban nightclubs to force people back to line dancing. People in poor countries have a right to change, too.

Moreover, some losses of diversity are a good thing. Who laments that the world is now almost universally rid of slavery? More generally, Western ideas are reshaping the way people everywhere view themselves and the world. Like nationalism and socialism before it, liberalism is a European philosophy that has swept the world. Even people who resist liberal ideas, in the name of religion (Islamic and Christian fundamentalists), group identity (communitarians), authoritarianism (advocates of "Asian values") or tradition (cultural conservatives), now define themselves partly by their opposition to them.

Faith in science and technology is even more widespread. Even those who hate the West make use of its technologies. Osama bin Laden plots terrorism on a cellphone and crashes planes into skyscrapers. Antiglobalization protesters organize by e-mail and over the Internet. China no longer turns its nose up at Western technology: It tries to beat the West at its own game.

Yet globalization is not a one-way street. Although Europe's former colonial powers have left their stamp on much of the world, the recent flow of migration has been in the opposite direction. There are Algerian suburbs in Paris, but not French ones in Algiers. Whereas Muslims are a growing minority in Europe, Christians are a disappearing one in the Middle East.

Foreigners are changing America even as they adopt its ways. A million or so immigrants arrive each year, most of them Latino or Asian. Since 1990, the number of foreign-born American residents has risen by 6 million to just over 25 million, the biggest immigration wave since the turn of the 20th century. English may be all-conquering outside America, but in some parts of the United States, it is now second to Spanish.

The upshot is that national cultures are fragmenting into a kaleidoscope of different ones. New hybrid cultures are emerging. In "Amexica" people speak Spanglish. Regional cultures are reviving. The Scots and Welsh break with British monoculture. Estonia is reborn from the Soviet Union. Voices that were silent dare to speak again.

Individuals are forming new communities, linked by shared interests and passions, that cut across national borders. Friendships with foreigners met on holiday. Scientists sharing ideas over the Internet. Environmentalists campaigning together using e-mail. Greater individualism does not spell the end of community. The new communities are simply chosen rather than coerced, unlike the older ones that communitarians hark back to.

So is national identity dead? Hardly. People who speak the same language, were born and live near each other, face similar problems, have a common experience, and vote in the same elections still have plenty in common. For all our awareness of the world as a single place, we are not citizens of the world but citizens of a state. But if people now wear the bonds of nationality more loosely, is that such a bad thing? People may lament the passing of old ways. Indeed, many of the worries about globalization echo age-old fears about decline, a lost golden age, and so on. But by and large, people choose the new ways because they are more relevant to their current needs and offer new opportunities.

The truth is that we increasingly define ourselves rather than let others define us. Being British or American does not define who you are: It is part of who you are. You can like foreign things and still have strong bonds to your fellow citizens. As Mario Vargas Llosa, the Peruvian author, has written: "Seeking to impose a cultural identity on a people is equivalent to locking them in a prison and denying them the most precious of liberties—that of choosing what, how, and who they want to be."

POSTSCRIPT

Does Globalization Threaten Cultural Diversity?

Cultural globalization, dominated by the spread of Western, primarily American, culture is likely to continue into the foreseeable future. For example, English may not be a common global language, but the possibility of that occurring is given some credence by a survey of people in 42 countries that recorded the vast majority in every region agreed with the statement, "Children need to learn English to succeed in the world today."

Attitudes toward cultural globalization are less clear-cut and are even contradictory. A global survey found that, on average, three-quarters of all people thought culture imports were good. Regionally, that favorable response ranged from 61 percent in the Middle East to 86 percent in western Europe. At the same time, though, an approximately equal percentage of people thought cultural imports were eroding their traditional way of life, with Africans, at 86 percent, the most likely to think so. Not surprisingly, this sense of cultural threat also leads to a desire to protect traditional cultures. The survey found that about 70 percent of its respondents felt that their way of life needed protection from foreign influence. At 79 percent each, people in Africa and the Middle East were most likely to feel their traditional cultures needed protection; western Europeans (56 percent) were the least insecure. Whether this sense of cultural loss is all due to globalization is unclear. It may well be that the changes that are unsettling most people worldwide are also part of the even broader phenomenon of rapid technological modernization that is spurring globalization.

An oddity of the cultural globalization phenomenon is that American attitudes are not much different from those of other people, despite the worry that American culture is becoming dominant. The poll showed that the overwhelming majority of Americans were favorable to the increased availability of goods, music, films, and other cultural imports. Yet two-thrids of all Americans replied to the survey that their traditional way of life was being lost, and a similar percentage responded that they believed that their way of life needed to be protected against foreign influences.

For more on the progress of globalization, visit the British Broadcasting Corporation's Web site at http://www.bbc.co.uk/worldservice/programmes/globalisation/ and Randolph Kluver and Wayne Fu, "The Cultural Globalization Index," posted on the Web site of *Foreign Policy* at http://www.foreignpolicy. An overview of cultural globalization is John Boli, *World Culture Origins and Consequences* (Blackwell Publishing, 2005). For a mostly negative view of F. Jan Nederveen Pieterse, *Globalization and Culture* (Rowman & Littlefield, 2003) views the process as a cultural hybridization rather than Americanization. Of all countries, the less-developed ones are the most strongly impacted by cultural globalization, as discussed by Jeff Haynesin *Religion, Globalization, and Political Culture in the Third World* (St. Martin's Press, 1999). A discussion of maintaining cultural distinctiveness can be found in Harry Redner, *Conserving Cultures: Technology, Globalization, and the Future of Local Cultures* (Rowman & Littlefield, 2003).

ISSUE 3

Is U.S. Global Dominance Destructive?

YES: Louis Janowski, from "Neo-Imperialism and U.S. Foreign Policy," *Foreign Service Journal* (May 2004)

NO: Michael Mandelbaum, from "David's Friend Goliath," *Foreign Policy* (January/February 2006)

ISSUE SUMMARY

YES: Louis Janowski, a former U.S. diplomat with service in Vietnam, France, Ethiopia, Saudi Arabia, and Kenya, maintains that the view that the 9/11 attacks ushered in a new geo-strategic reality requiring new foreign policy approaches is based on a false and dangerous premise and is leading to an age of American neo-imperialism.

NO: Michael Mandelbaum, Christian A. Herter Professor of American Foreign Policy and director of the American Foreign Policy Program at The Johns Hopkins University Paul H. Nitze School of Advanced International Studies, contends that U.S. power and leadership help maintain global security and prosperity and that most other countries want American leadership, even if they sometimes disagree with U.S. policy.

There can be little doubt that the United States is the most powerful country in the world—no other country can rival the U.S. military or launch a successful conventional attack on the United States. Few could withstand a U.S. conventional attack. It is true that Americans are subject to terrorist attack, and the possibility of nuclear attack remains. Still, the U.S. nuclear arsenal overshadows that of any other country, with the aging Russian arsenal the closest rival, and terrorists find themselves under constant U.S. pressure. The United States is also in an unparalleled economic position, accounting for over 25 percent of the world's measured economic production. Scholars debate whether the world is structured as a unipolar system with just one dominant power (the United States in this case), whether there is a limited unipolar system, or whether a multipolar system with numerous power centers is emerging. Whatever the precise answer may be, there can be little doubt that the United States is currently the world dominant power, even if it has not achieved complete hegemony, or power dominance.

The issue is what the United States should do with its immense power. What role should the United States play in the world? The answers, at least in the view of the current U.S. administration, were given in 2002 when President George W. Bush issued a document entitled "The National Security Strategy of the United States of America." The report characterized the United States as possessing "unprecedented—and unequaled—strength and influence in the world" and went on to argue that "this position comes with unparalleled responsibilities, obligations, and opportunity. The great strength of this nation must be used to promote a balance of power that favors freedom." A number of the report's sections pledged that the United States would use its strength globally to promote human dignity, democracy, and free economic interchange, and the document also declared that the United States intends to develop cooperation with "other main centers of global power." These sections drew relatively little notice, although some analysts objected that, if taken literally, the pledges would lead the country into an unending series of draining efforts around the world. Much more controversial were the sections on threats to the United States and its allies, especially by terrorism and weapons of mass destruction (biological, chemical, nuclear, and radiological weapons). President Bush not only promised that attacks on the United States and its allies would bring devastating consequences to perpetrators, he also indicated that the United States would not wait to be attacked but might act preemptively to destroy perceived enemies and their capabilities before an attack could occur. The president's far-reaching position reflected the strength of neoconservative (neocon) views in his administration. This perspective argues that the United States has the right to act aggressively and unilaterally if necessary to protect its interests. Moreover, neocons believe that democracy, free enterprise (capitalism), and other aspects of the "American way" are superior to other approaches to governance and that the United States has the right and responsibility to promote and defend these approaches worldwide.

The U.S. invasion of Iraq in 2003 without UN support and in opposition to the views of most U.S. allies and other countries was the clearest expression of the Bush doctrine. That effort was not only designed to end what the neocons saw as the threat from Iraq, it also importantly included the determination to bring democracy to Iraq and, by extension, the rest of the Middle East.

The result of the Bush doctrine and its application, according to Louis Janowski in the first reading, has been a disastrous foreign policy that amounts to quasi-imperialism and that unduly taxes U.S. resources. Janowski concludes that the United States should greatly reduce its worldwide commitments. In the second reading, Michael Mandelbaum does not defend the Bush doctrine or the president's foreign policy as such. Instead, Mandelbaum argues that U.S. leadership is mostly positive and that the world will be worse off if Americans retreat from their global leadership rule.

YES

Louis Janowski

Neo-Imperialism and U.S. Foreign Policy

American foreign policy at its best combines a clear understanding of our national interests, the limits of our power, and the real and psychological needs of the American people. Effective foreign policy in our democracy has always been a combination of realpolitik and moral idealism. Pearl Harbor remains the classic example: a Japanese attack created the catalyst that allowed President Franklin Roosevelt to unite the American people behind moral and idealistic policies which successfully structured U.S. policies and advanced U.S. interests for the remainder of the 20th century.

Yet the U.S. foreign policy record over the past half-century has been mixed. All too often, our political leadership appears to suffer from attention deficit disorder and the dangerous, self-destructive behaviors that too often accompany ADD.

The Vietnam War failed the test of meeting a clearly defined and limited national interest. In addition, the realities of conducting guerrilla warfare meant that the average American perceived a nightmare rather than an idealistic and moral crusade for a better world. Both the Korean and Persian Gulf Wars had clear causes, limited objectives (recall President Harry Truman's dismissal of Gen. Douglas MacArthur over widening the scope of the Korean War) and wide global support. The Persian Gulf War was a good example of clear causes, limited objectives, morality, and broad international support. By contrast, Somalia was an example of unrealistic moral idealism combined with a lack of concrete national interest.

The 2003 invasion of Iraq failed to meet these criteria. It lacked virtually every element of this formula for success: a clearly defined *casus belli* [cause of war], an overriding national interest, limited goals, and international legitimacy. Indeed, the Bush administration was able to win popular support for the war only by pandering to the worst fears of the American public, conjuring up a link of terror between the secular nationalist Baathist rulers of Iraq and the diametrically opposed pan-Islamic religious fundamentalists of al-Qaida. The two represent essentially opposing ends of the political spectrum in the Middle East with little in common other than shared anti-Americanism.

Equally unbelievable was the portrait of an "axis of evil" linking Iran and Iraq (and North Korea). Saddam Hussein's invasion of Iran and the

From *Foreign Policy Journal*, May 2004, pp. 55–60. Copyright © 2004 by American Foreign Service Association. Reprinted by permission.

ensuing 1980–88 Iran-Iraq War render such a linkage a grotesque distortion of historical reality, as does the participation of several senior officials from the current Bush administration in the Reagan administration's efforts to cultivate Saddam during that period.

More generally, the Bush administration has attempted to argue that the terrorist attacks on the World Trade Center ushered in a new geo-strategic reality requiring new domestic and foreign policy approaches. This is a false premise. All that changed with 9/11 was a naive assumption that somehow the U.S.—unlike any other nation—could involve itself in ever-expanding external acts without potential negative or retaliatory responses on its territory.

In this regard, it is useful to recall that terrorism is specifically designed to cause overreaction. Perhaps terrorism's greatest success in the past century was Austria-Hungary's overreaction to the assassination of Archduke Ferdinand by a Serbian Pan-Slav "terrorist" which, in turn, led to World War I and the destruction of the Austro-Hungarian Empire.

Empire Building

The 9/11 attacks have been used to redefine U.S. foreign policy along neoconservative lines. The new policies emphasize unilateralism, unlimited objectives, and the use of military force as a primary adjunct to policy. This set of characteristics has little in common with historic U.S. policy, which until the 1940s emphasized isolationism, limited foreign policy objectives and an aversion to the use of military force outside the Western Hemisphere.

In one respect, the neoconservatives do harken back to the past in their approach to foreign policy. Unfortunately, they do so by invoking the now-obsolete political-military premises of the Cold War, such as a perceived need for overwhelming military superiority. The administrations proposed military budget of $401 billion for FY 2004–2005 is as great as those of the next six powers combined. Where is the threat to justify this expenditure? Ongoing efforts to expand the forward deployment of U.S. forces to areas such as Central Europe and South Asia can hardly be justified on the basis of a military threat to the territorial integrity or national existence of the United States or of our principal allies. There was a sound rationale for a forward projection of U.S. forces during the Cold War. But there is no basis for transforming forward defense into a strategy of unilateral global political-military imperialism, as we are in the process of doing.

President Dwight Eisenhower's farewell address, in which he warned of the dangers posed by the "military-industrial complex," was perhaps the last example of a leadership vision coupling an emphasis on adequate power with an understanding of the dangers that excessive power creates. Since Eisenhower, American political leadership has actively sought an ever-expanding role on the world stage and an expansion of military presence into far-flung regions of the world where U.S. interests are marginal at best.

For the sake of argument, however, let us assume that the only way for the United States to remain secure in the post-9/11 environment is to forge an empire. The basic ingredients for success at such an enterprise are: skillful diplomacy to forge strong alliances; the ability to formulate and implement rational decisions based on realistic threat assessments; sound decisions about when to use military force; and the wherewithal to support the demands of running and defending a global presence (e.g., a sound economic base, military hardware and human resources).

Keeping Bad Company

The long-term viability of any American empire will be based on the ability to make alliances with nations and leaders who support the long-term goals and values of American democracy while, to the extent possible, avoiding alliances of convenience with known bad actors. Yet in the case of Iraq, we reversed that formula.

Nearly all our major allies were strongly opposed to the war, and the few who stood with us did so despite strong domestic opposition. Thus, major by-products of the war have been a fundamental weakening of the NATO [North Atlantic Treaty Organization] alliance, rifts in the longstanding unity of the West, and the under-mining of pro-American governments in the Arab and Muslim worlds.

The war on terror demonstrates a similar inconsistency on the other side of the equation. In our zeal to acquire new allies against al-Qaida, the Bush administration seems willing to over-look the very same human rights violations and brutal suppression of democracy that the State Department details in its latest set of worldwide country reports. Countries like Uzbekistan, Turkmenistan and Pakistan were quick to learn that lesson, and others seem poised to follow in their footsteps.

This phenomenon is nothing new, regrettably. In Afghanistan, U.S. covert operations in support of Islamic fundamentalists fighting the Soviets two decades ago paved the way for the Taliban to fill the vacuum created when Moscow withdrew. When we eventually turned to tribal surrogates to help us oust the Taliban, we conveniently overlooked the fact that some of them were major players in the international drug trade. The result? Afghanistan today is the world's largest source of opium and heroin prices have fallen around the globe. It is, therefore, hard to make a convincing case that Afghanistan is any less a global danger to U.S. interests now.

Getting the Threat Right

Whether or not one believes that the Bush administration politicized the findings of the intelligence community concerning Saddam Hussein's alleged weapons of mass destruction programs, that debate underscores the need for sound analysis of often-ambiguous and incomplete indications regarding what our foes are doing and planning.

Understandably, the various components of the U.S. intelligence community frequently disagree among themselves when it comes to assessing the data, but in general, the most unrealistic threat assessments tend to come from the Defense Intelligence Agency and the other military intelligence services. This is so for several reasons. First, military commanders understandably want to ensure that they do not inadvertently endanger their troops by underestimating the forces they face. Second, DOD [Department of Defense] budgets are directly related to threat projections, while State [Department], CIA [Central Intelligence Agency] and NSA [National Security Agency] budgets lack this seminal link. Third, DIA [Defense Intelligence Agency] assessments frequently ignore political, economic and cultural factors, and therefore misread both enemy intentions and capabilities. For example, the military threat the Soviet Union posed during the Cold War was never as serious as estimated. And in the post-Cold War period, our experiences in the Balkans, Iraq and elsewhere have clearly demonstrated the gaps between the military threat projected by DOD and actual conditions on the ground.

In the case of Iraq, Gen. Eric Shinseki [Armu chief of staff] and other combat-seasoned military officers were fully aware that our lack of cultural and language capability would seriously limit the utility of modern arms, particularly in non-traditional warfare. They therefore requested force levels higher than they otherwise would have. Yet the White House rejected the requests, citing the ability of our troops to destroy all conventional military resistance in Iraq. But the administration neglected to take into account the importance of destroying or forcing the surrender and disbanding of Iraqi units in place and securing weapons and ammunition dumps to ensure that most Iraqis perceived the likelihood of successful unconventional warfare as poor. It also ignored the reality that terrorism and unconventional warfare are the logical by-products of overwhelming military inferiority.

The other side of the threat assessment coin is formulating an appropriate response. Just as even the best analysts sometimes either overestimate or underestimate potential threats, policy-makers tend to favor the use of force to keep other countries from assessing U.S. decision-makers as weak or uncertain.

American military dominance has resulted in both the overuse of military force and errors in how we have applied it. Overuse is a natural result of being able to use military force in almost any scenario; as the saying goes, when you have a hammer, every problem looks like a nail. But it also reflects the desire for quick solutions to complex problems, and the political reality that the use of military force builds short- to midterm political support at the polls.

The potential for error exists in large part because there are major disconnects in our system between global political, economic, social and political-military knowledge and national decision-making power. America's foreign and strategic policy decision-making structures are so complex and multi-layered, and actual "on-the-ground" knowledge is so far removed from those with decision-making authority, that serious mistakes are inevitable. The collapse of the Soviet Union and its empire from within is an excellent example of this type of structural problem. The Soviet centralized economic planning system worked reasonably well when the system it ran was a relatively simple one. But as the Soviet Union became economically mature and far more complex, centralized planning became incapable of meeting the varied tasks it faced. A similar reality is faced by American foreign policy today, with a potentially parallel outcome.

Then there is the problem of developing the human resources necessary for maintaining a global empire. After all, "smart" weapons systems are only as "smart" as those who operate them. It is exceptionally difficult to identify, track and destroy irregular forces and terrorists when you don't speak the local language or understand the local norms and mores—much less the broader culture and its complicated subcultures. What was true in Vietnam 35 years ago is just as true today in Iraq and Afghanistan. Yet no administration has been willing to commit the funds to ensure that U.S. diplomats, intelligence operatives and military forces have adequate linguistic, cultural and area-specific skills.

Despite our relative under-investment in these areas, our military, intelligence and diplomatic services have amassed an immense amount of knowledge (especially compared to what the political leadership of the day possesses). But power rivalries at both the political and bureaucratic levels and complex hierarchical structures work to keep knowledge and power apart. The longtime rivalry between the FBI and the CIA was one of the main factors that prevented solid intelligence about terrorist training in U.S. flight schools from cutting through multiple levels of bureaucracy and preventing the 9/11 terrorist attacks.

Following 9/11, top Defense Department officials chose to confine decision-making and intelligence assessment with respect to Iraq to a small group of like-thinking individuals (the "Office of Special Plans"). The result was that policy was made in secret by individuals with only a limited knowledge of the region, who never allowed their recommendations to face the open and ongoing scrutiny of the entire intelligence community (much less the political system). The outcome demonstrated manifold errors. There were no weapons of mass destruction. The assumption that Iraqi Arabs would warmly welcome the U.S., particularly given our longstanding support for Israel, failed to stand up in the light of day. Exiled Iraqis were not warmly welcomed upon their return. The assumption that Iraq's clan structure—where nepotism is a virtue, not a vice—is amenable to democracy appears to be either a misguided assumption or a cynical ploy.

Finally, the administration's insistence on requesting military force levels well below what the Joint Chiefs wanted, and its refusal to draw up clear-cut plans for occupation and exit, clearly created conditions more favorable to insurgency, costing hundreds of American lives.

Again, the lesson is that decision-makers need to have access to, and be willing to consult, those diplomats, analysts, troops and agents with first-hand knowledge of conditions on the ground. For this to occur, of course, a certain amount of humility is required by the political leadership as well as a fair amount of structural change to reduce the rigidity of our foreign affairs bureaucracies.

When he first arrived at State, Secretary [Colin] Powell stunned the bureaucracy by occasionally leaving the 7th floor and personally going to desk officers to seek out knowledge. Coming from a military background and drawing on his experiences in Vietnam, Powell was undoubtedly aware that bad news is repeatedly filtered by multiple levels of bureaucracy before it reaches senior decision-makers. And, as any problem works its way through the system, more and more filtering is done by officials who, no matter how competent or capable, are less likely to have adequate knowledge of the realities on the ground. Furthermore, they have bureaucratic reasons not to disturb the status quo and existing chains of power and control. Few are prepared to appear disloyal by failing to cheerlead administration priorities and policies of the moment. Bureaucratic advancement is as much the result of the absence of perceived error as it is of actual accomplishment.

Paying the Tab

Finally, in an era of half-trillion dollar budget deficits, can we afford an empire?

One of the major consequences of seeking a global political-military—empire is the relegation of critical domestic and global economic, financial and other policy questions to secondary status rather than addressing them as key issues.

Except for the United States, almost every developed nation (and many aspiring to that status) has placed economic and financial policies, not political-military objectives, at the top of their respective agendas since the end of the Cold War. And, in large part, they did so precisely because they knew U.S. leadership—for its own reasons—was prepared to carry the burden for them. This was a rational decision both because of the lack of a pressing threat and in view of the lesson learned by other developed states from 1939 to 1989: namely, empires are expensive. The average citizen of a former colonial power may today regret the loss of his or her perceived superiority by association with an empire, but he or she certainly does not regret no longer having to pay the extravagant costs of maintaining an imperial system.

United States policy-makers desperately need to pay more attention to America's pressing financial and economic needs. Cordell Hull is almost completely forgotten today, but he deserves to be remembered not only for being the longest-serving Secretary of State in history (1933–1944) but for being the last one to concentrate on promoting U.S. economic interests. Admittedly, the collapse of the global economic and financial order left him and FOB with no alternative, but it is still disheartening to see how far we have gone in the opposite direction.

Today, U.S. policies seem to be assisting a collapse of the very international financial order we created in the aftermath of World War II. The disconnect between the United States and Western Europe on trade matters is growing. American restrictions on steel imports have caused greater harm to U.S. steel fabricators and consumers than the benefits they provided to domestic steel producers, and provoked threats of retaliatory measures from Europe, China and Japan. Coincidentally or not, Washington sharply increased subsidies to American agribusiness on the eve of global discussions on finding a way to increase and rationalize global agricultural trade, with predictable results.

If the United States were a minor player on the world stage instead of the major funding source for the International Monetary Fund [IMF] and the

World Bank, those organizations would be demanding that the U.S. administration make major fiscal and economic policy changes. The United States' staggering trade deficit (5 percent of GDP) would have to be addressed, as would its addiction to foreign investment capital to finance that trade deficit. The IMF and the World Bank would also demand progress toward a balanced U.S. budget. The rapid fall of the U.S. dollar relative to other major currencies over the past two years is a clear indication that investors worldwide are today far less comfortable with investing in the United States. Whatever else one may think of the policies of the Clinton administration, its fixation on a strong dollar and balanced budgets was, in part, based on a clear understanding of the need to assure foreign investors of the long-term strength of the U.S. economy.

A Return to Core Competencies

The impact of American unilateralism and its concentration on political-military matters is obvious. There is a vacuum of leadership in other international policy areas, be they political, economic, legal, or environmental. The vacuum exists by definition. If you have a unilateral policy, you can't lead, because you have been unwilling to make the compromises necessary for others to follow.

As with domestic issues, success in foreign policy means meeting the often-conflicting needs of concerned parties. For example, if we had shown some regard for the views of the United Nations and our traditional allies as we prepared for war (or even afterward), we might not be bearing the costs almost entirely alone—and the situation in Iraq, not to mention its prospects, would likely be considerably brighter. Compare the current mess with the handling of the Persian Gulf War. There, patient diplomacy ensured that the financial, political and human costs to the U.S. were minimal—as opposed to the open-ended costs of the present "Coalition of the Willing" in Iraq.

The unilateralist neoconservative policies of today are a badly mutated descendant of our isolationist heritage. Isolationism at least had the clear advantage of limited objectives, keeping the United States from entering two world wars until a national consensus existed for intervention. Our late entry into both conflicts spared the United States from most of the human, social and financial consequences of those two great conflicts.

Of course, isolationism is dead, buried by technology that makes it outmoded except in backwaters such as North Korea and Burma. But the concept of limiting commitments on the basis of national interest and real needs makes as much sense today as it always has. American foreign policy today needs to reexamine its commitments worldwide and redefine them. Our 60-year relationship with Europe is crumbling, and better solutions exist than moving U.S. military bases from Western to Central Europe.

U.S. foreign policy toward the Middle East has been a disaster since 1967. An even-handed policy with respect to the Israeli-Palestinian conflict would do more to reduce the threat of anti-American terrorism than any other step we could take. We also need to question why, in view of the end of the Cold

War and a vastly changed energy situation world-wide over the past three decades, we need a military presence in the Persian Gulf.

In sum, the primary need of the United States today is to greatly reduce U.S. commitments world-wide. The existing U.S. decision-making and intelligence structures are no more capable of running a global empire (at least one in accord with the moral and democratic views of the American public) than the centralized Soviet system was of controlling a far less complicated global equation. In the language of the business community, the United States needs to get back to its core competencies. In the 21st century, there is no reason for Americans to play the "Great Game" in the mode of 19th century European elites—particularly when no vital U.S. interests are at stake. To follow such a course is, in the words of Talleyrand, "Worse than wrong, monsieur. It is stupid."

Michael Mandelbaum

 **NO**

David's Friend Goliath

Everybody talks about the weather, Mark Twain once observed, but nobody does anything about it. The same is true of America's role in the world. The United States is the subject of endless commentary, most of it negative, some of it poisonously hostile. Statements by foreign leaders, street demonstrations in national capitals, and much-publicized opinion polls all seem to bespeak a worldwide conviction that the United States misuses its enormous power in ways that threaten the stability of the international system. That is hardly surprising. No one loves Goliath. What is surprising is the world's failure to respond to the United States as it did to the Goliaths of the past.

Sovereign states as powerful as the United States, and as dangerous as its critics declare it to be, were historically subject to a check on their power. Other countries banded together to block them.

Revolutionary and Napoleonic France in the late 18th and early 19th century, Germany during the two world wars, and the Soviet Union during the Cold War all inspired countervailing coalitions that ultimately defeated them. Yet no such anti-American alignment has formed or shows any sign of forming today. Widespread complaints about the United States' international role are met with an absence of concrete, effective measures to challenge, change, or restrict it.

The gap between what the world says about American power and what it fails to do about it is the single most striking feature of 21st-century international relations. The explanation for this gap is twofold. First, the charges most frequently leveled at America are false. The United States does not endanger other countries, nor does it invariably act without regard to the interests and wishes of others. Second, far from menacing the rest of the world, the United States plays a uniquely positive global role. The governments of most other countries understand that, although they have powerful reasons not to say so explicitly.

Benign Hegemon

The charge that the United States threatens others is frequently linked to the use of the term "empire" to describe America's international presence. In contrast with empires of the past, however, the United States does not control, or aspire to control, directly or indirectly, the politics and economics of other societies. True, in the post-Cold War period, America has intervened militarily in a few places outside its borders, including Somalia, Haiti, Bosnia, Kosovo, Afghanistan, and Iraq. But these cases are exceptions that prove the rule.

These foreign ventures are few in number and, with the exception of Iraq, none has any economic value or strategic importance. In each case, American control of the country came as the byproduct of a military intervention undertaken for quite different reasons: to rescue distressed people in Somalia, to stop ethnic cleansing in Bosnia, to depose a dangerous tyrant in Iraq. Unlike the great empires of the past, the U.S. goal was to build stable, effective governments and then to leave as quickly as possible. Moreover, unlike past imperial practice, the U.S. government has sought to share control of its occupied countries with allies, not to monopolize them.

One policy innovation of the current Bush administration that gives other countries pause is the doctrine of preventive war. According to this doctrine, the United States reserves the right to attack a country not in response to an actual act of aggression, or because it is unmistakably on the verge of aggression, but rather in anticipation of an assault at some point in the future. The United States implemented the doctrine in 2003 with the invasion of Iraq.

Were it to become central to American foreign policy, the preventive war doctrine would provide a broad charter for military intervention. But that is not its destiny. The Bush administration presented the campaign in Iraq not as a way to ensure that Saddam Hussein did not have the opportunity to acquire nuclear weapons at some point in the future, but rather as a way of depriving him of the far less dangerous chemical weapons that he was believed already to possess.

More important, the countries that are now plausible targets for a preventive war—North Korea and Iran—differ from Iraq in ways that make such a campaign extremely unattractive. North Korea is more heavily armed than Iraq, and in a war could do serious damage to America's chief ally in the region, South Korea, even if North Korea lost. Iran has a larger population than Iraq, and it is less isolated internationally. The United States would have hesitated before attacking either one of these countries even if the Iraq operation had gone smoothly. Now, with the occupation of Iraq proving to be both costly (some $251 billion and counting) and frustrating, support for repeating the exercise elsewhere is hard to find.

America the Accessible

The war in Iraq is the most-often cited piece of evidence that America conducts itself in a recklessly unilateral fashion. Because of its enormous power, critics say, the policies that the United States applies beyond its borders are bound to affect others, yet when it comes to deciding these policies, non-Americans have no influence. However valid the charge of unilateralism in the case of Iraq may be (and other governments did in fact support the war), it does not hold true for U.S. foreign policy as a whole.

The reason is that the American political system is fragmented, which means there are multiple points of access to it. Other countries can exert influence on one of the House or Senate committees with jurisdiction over foreign policy. Or countries can deal with one or more of the federal departments that conduct the nation's relations with other countries. For that matter, American think tanks generate such a wide variety of proposals for U.S. policies toward every country that almost any approach is bound to have a champion somewhere.

Even Sudan, which the U.S. government has accused of genocide, recently signed a $530,000 contract with a Washington lobbyist to help improve its image. Non-Americans may not enjoy formal representation in the U.S. political system, but because of the openness of that system, they can and do achieve what representation brings—a voice in the making of American policy.

Because the opportunities to be heard and heeded are so plentiful, countries with opposing aims often simultaneously attempt to persuade the American government to favor their respective causes. That has sometimes led the United States to become a mediator for international conflict, between Arabs and Israelis, Indians and Pakistanis, and other sets of antagonists. That's a role that other countries value.

The World's Government

The United States makes other positive contributions, albeit often unseen and even unknown, to the well-being of people around the world. In fact, America performs for the community of sovereign states many, though not all, of the tasks that national governments carry out within them. For instance, U.S. military power helps to keep order in the world. The American military presence in Europe and East Asia, which now includes approximately 185,000 personnel, reassures the governments of these regions that their neighbors cannot threaten them, helping to allay suspicions, forestall arms races, and make the chances of armed conflict remote. U.S. forces in Europe, for instance, reassure Western Europeans that they do not have to increase their own troop strength to protect themselves against the possibility of a resurgent Russia, while at the same time reassuring Russia that its great adversary of the last century, Germany, will not adopt aggressive policies. Similarly, the U.S.-Japan Security Treaty, which protects Japan, simultaneously reassures Japan's neighbors that it will remain peaceful. This reassurance is vital yet invisible, and it is all but taken for granted.

The United States has also assumed responsibility for coping with the foremost threat to contemporary international security, the spread of nuclear weapons to "rogue" states and terrorist organizations. The U.S.-sponsored Cooperative Threat Reduction program is designed to secure nuclear materials and weapons in the former Soviet Union. A significant part of the technical and human assets of the American intelligence community is devoted to the surveillance of nuclear weapons-related activities around the world. Although other countries may not always agree with how the United States seeks to prevent proliferation, they all endorse the goal, and none of them makes as significant a contribution to achieving that goal as does the United States.

America's services to the world also extend to economic matters and international trade. In the international economy, much of the confidence needed to proceed with transactions, and the protection that engenders this confidence, comes from the policies of the United States. For example, the U.S. Navy patrols shipping lanes in both the Atlantic and Pacific oceans, assuring the safe passage of commerce along the world's great trade routes. The United States also supplies the world's most frequently used currency, the U.S. dollar. Though the euro might one day supplant the dollar as the world's most popular reserve currency, that day, if it ever comes, lies far in the future.

Furthermore, working through the International Monetary Fund (imf), the United States also helps to carry out some of the duties that central banks perform within countries, including serving as a "lender of last resort." The driving force behind imf bailouts of failing economies in Latin America and Asia in the last decade was the United States, which holds the largest share of votes within the imf. And Americans' large appetite for consumer products partly reproduces on a global scale the service that the economist John Maynard Keynes assigned to national governments during times of economic slowdown: The United States is the world's "consumer of last resort."

Americans purchase Japanese cars, Chinese-made clothing, and South Korean electronics and appliances in greater volume than any other people. Just as national governments have the responsibility for delivering water and electricity within their jurisdictions, so the United States, through its military deployments and diplomacy, assures an adequate supply of the oil that allows industrial economies to run. It has established friendly political relations, and sometimes close military associations, with governments in most of the major oil-producing countries and has extended military protection to the largest of them, Saudi Arabia. Despite deep social, cultural, and political differences between the two countries, the United States and Saudi Arabia managed in the 20th century to establish a partnership that controlled the global market for this indispensable commodity. The economic well-being even of countries hostile to American foreign policy depends on the American role in assuring the free flow of oil throughout the world.

To be sure, the United States did not deliberately set out to become the world's government. The services it provides originated during the Cold War as part of its struggle with the Soviet Union, and America has continued, adapted, and in some cases expanded them in the post-Cold War era. Nor do Americans think of their country as the world's government. Rather, it conducts, in their view, a series of policies designed to further American interests. In this respect they are correct, but these policies serve the interests of others as well. The alternative to the role the United States plays in the world is not better global governance, but less of it—and that would make the world a far more dangerous and less prosperous place. Never in human history has one country done so much for so many others, and received so little appreciation for its efforts.

Inevitable Ingratitude

Nor is the world likely to express much gratitude to the United States any time soon. Even if they privately value what the United States does for the world, other countries, especially democratic ones, will continue to express anti-American sentiments. That is neither surprising nor undesirable. Within democracies, spirited criticism of the government is normal, indeed vital for its effective performance. The practice is no different between and among democracies.

Anti-Americanism has many domestic political uses. In many parts of the world, the United States serves as a convenient scapegoat for governments, a kind of political lightning rod to draw away from themselves the popular discontent that their shortcomings have helped to produce. That is particularly the case in the Middle East, but not only there. Former German Chancellor Gerhard Schröder achieved an electoral victory in 2002 by denouncing the war in Iraq. Similarly, it is convenient, even comforting, to blame the United States for the inevitable dislocations caused by the great, impersonal forces of globalization.

But neither the failure to acknowledge America's global role nor the barrage of criticism of it means that the officials of other countries are entirely unaware of the advantages that it brings them. If a global plebiscite concerning America's role in the world were held by secret ballot, most foreign-policy officials in other countries would vote in favor of continuing it. Though the Chinese object to the U.S. military role as Taiwan's protector, they value the effect that American military deployments in East Asia have in preventing Japan from pursuing more robust military policies. But others will not declare their support for America's global role. Acknowledging it would risk raising the question of why those who take advantage of the services America provides do not pay more for them. It would risk, that is, other countries' capacities to continue as free riders, which is an arrangement no government will lightly abandon.

In the end, however, what other nations do or do not say about the United States will not be crucial to whether, or for how long, the United States continues to function as the world's government. That will depend on the willingness of the American public, the ultimate arbiter of American foreign policy, to sustain the costs involved. In the near future, America's role in the world will have to compete for public funds with the rising costs of domestic entitlement programs. It is Social Security and Medicare, not the rise of China or the kind of coalition that defeated powerful empires in the past, that pose the greatest threat to America's role as the world's government.

The outcome of the looming contest in the United States between the national commitment to social welfare at home and the requirements for stability and prosperity abroad cannot be foreseen with any precision. About other countries' approach to America's remarkable 21st-century global role, however, three things may be safely predicted: They will not pay for it, they will continue to criticize it, and they will miss it when it is gone.

POSTSCRIPT

Is U.S. Global Dominance Destructive?

The United States was one of the two dominant countries in the world from the end of World War II in 1945 to the collapse in 1991 of the other superpower, the Soviet Union. Since then, it has been the lone hegemonic power, a country that has an extraordinary amount of influence over how the international system operates. For an exploration of the background and extent of this power that puts it in the context of the superpowers of bygone eras, see Charles S. Maier, *Among Empires: American Ascendancy and Its Predecessors* (Harvard University Press, 2006). That the United States is powerful is not controversial; the consequences of that power are very controversial. Some scholars contend that the world needs a hegemonic power or coalition of powers to maintain stability. From this perspective, an eclipse of U.S. hegemonic power without the rise of another state to keep control would bring disaster. For this view and a relatively benign sense of U.S. hegemony akin to Mandelbaum's view, read Niall Ferguson, *Colossus: The Price of America's Empire* (Penguin, 2004). A longer exposition of Mandelbaum's views are in his book, *Case for Goliath: How America Acts As the World's Government in the Twenty-first Century* (Public Affairs, 2005)

Of course, others differ dramatically with this view. Some scholars reject the notion that a dominant power is necessary for global peace and prosperity. Others focus on the role of the United States in the world and, as Janowski does, find it destructive. One such book is Robert Merry, *Sands of Empire: Missionary Zeal, American Foreign Policy, and the Hazards of Global Ambition* (Simon & Schuster, 2005).

One restraint on U.S. power is the tendency of lesser powers to try to escape dominance by the hegemonic power. That reaction is explored in Stephen Walt's study, *Taming American Power: The Global Response to U.S. Primacy* (W.W. Norton, 2005). As Mandelbaum points out, a second factor that could markedly restrain the U.S. global presence is the American public. Polls show that a solid majority of Americans favor the United States being active in the world. A 2005 poll recorded only 10 percent of Americans favoring the United States play no leadership role in the world. But this does not mean most Americans want to dominate the world. The same poll found only 12 percent of Americans wanting their country to be the "single world leader," while 74 percent wanted it to play "a shared leadership role," with 4 percent uncertain.

Internet References . . .

Country Indicators for Foreign Policy (CIFP)

Hosted by Carlton University in Canada, the Country Indicators for Foreign Policy project represents an ongoing effort to identify and assemble statistical information conveying the key features of the economic, political, social, and cultural environments of countries around the world.

http://www.carleton.ca/cifp/

U.S. Department of State

The information on this site is organized into categories based on countries, topics, and other criteria. "Background Notes," which provide information on regions and specific countries, can be accessed through this site.

http://www.state.gov/index.cfm

http://www.state.gov/countries/

WorldAtlas.com

The world may be "getting smaller," but geography is still important. This organization's site contains a wide variety of maps and a range of other useful information.

http://www.worldatlas.com/aatlas/world.htm

UNIT 2

Regional and Country Issues

*T*he issues in this section deal with countries that are major regional powers. In this era of interdependence among nations, it is important to understand the concerns that these issues address and the actors involved because they will shape the world and will affect the lives of all people.

- Has Russia Become Undemocratic and Antagonistic?

- Will China Soon Become a Threatening Superpower?

- Would It Be an Error to Establish a Palestinian State?

- Should All Foreign Troops Soon Leave Iraq?

- Are Strict Sanctions on Cuba Warranted?

ISSUE 4

Has Russia Become Undemocratic and Antagonistic?

YES: Tucker Herbert and Diane Raub, from "Russian Geopolitik," *The Stanford Review* (June 2, 2006)

NO: Eugene B. Rumer, from Testimony during Hearings on "Developments in U.S.–Russia Relations" before the Subcommittee on Europe and Emerging Threats, Committee on International Relations, U.S. House of Representatives (March 9, 2005)

ISSUE SUMMARY

YES: Tucker Herbert and Diane Raub, both of whom are on the staff of the *Stanford Review,* an independent, student-run newspaper at Stanford University, argue that under President Vladimir Putin, Russia has fallen from the ranks of democracies and is engaged in a foreign policy that pits U.S. interests against those of Russia.

NO: Eugene B. Rumer, a senior research fellow at the National Defense University's Institute for National Strategic Studies in Washington, D.C., recognizes that Russian democracy falls short of full scale and that Russian policy sometimes clashes with the United States, but argues that compared to the history of Russian democracy, which was zero before the 1990s, the country is not doing poorly and that Russia's pursuit of its own interests should not be construed as necessarily antagonistic.

Russia has experienced two momentous revolutions during the twentieth century. The first began in March 1917. After a brief moment of attempted democracy, that revolution descended into totalitarian government, with the takeover of the Bolshevik Communists in November and the establishment of the Union of the Soviet Socialist Republics.

The second great revolution arguably began in 1985 when reform-minded Mikhail S. Gorbachev assumed leadership in the USSR. The country's economy was faltering because of its overcentralization and because of the extraordinary amount of resources being allocated to Soviet military forces. Gorbachev's reforms unleashed strong forces within the USSR. The events of the next six years were complex, but suffice it to say that the result was the collapse of the Soviet Union. Of the former Soviet republics (FSRs), Russia is by far the largest, has the largest population, and is in reality and potentially the most powerful. Russia retained the bulk of Soviet Union's nuclear weapons and their delivery systems.

When Russia reemerged in the aftermath of the collapse of the USSR, its president, Boris Yeltsin, seemed to offer the hope of strong, democratic leadership that would economically rejuvenate and democratize Russia internally and that, externally, would work to make Russia a peaceful and cooperative neighbor. However, these prospects soon faded amid Russia's vast problems. The country's economy fell more deeply into shambles, leaving 22 percent of all Russians below the poverty level. Russia's economic turmoil also caused a steep decline in Russia's military capabilities. To make matters even worse, the rekindling of an independence movement by the Chechens, a Muslim nation in the Caucuses Mountains region, led to savage fighting.

Yeltsin's ill-fated presidency ended when he resigned on December 31, 1999. His elected successor and current president, Vladimir Putin, is an individual who spent most of his professional career in the KGB (*Komitet Gosudarstvennoi Bezopasnosti*/Committee for State Security), the Soviet secret police, and who headed its successor, Russia's FSB (*Federal'naya Sluzhba Bezopasnosti*/Federal Security Service).

For good or ill, Putin has brought a level of stability to Russia. Slowly, Russia's economy has steadied itself. Moreover, with a well-educated populace, vast mineral and energy resources, and a large (if antiquated) industrial base, Russia has great economic potential. Similarly, while Russian military forces fell into disarray in the 1990s, the country retains a potent nuclear arsenal. Furthermore, its large population, weapons manufacturing capacity, and huge land mass make it likely that the breakdown of Russia's conventional military capabilities and geostrategic importance will only be temporary.

Putin was reelected by an overwhelming margin to a second term in March 2004, but Russia is less democratic than it once was. Putin has used the various challenges facing his country as a reason to consolidate Moscow's power. Much of the independent new media is gone, local authorities have lost much of their power, and the country's largest company has been seized and its leader jailed on charges of corruption.

There are also numerous issues that divide Russia from the United States. For example, Moscow believes that it is threatened by the the U.S. drive to deploy a ballistic missle defense system and by the expansion of the North Atlantic Treaty Organization to even include some FSRs.

The question, then, is, Wither Russia? What are the chances it will once again become antagonistic toward the United States and its allies? In the first of the following readings, Tucker Herbert and Diane Raub are somewhat pessimistic about the future. They fret that old thinking among Russia's foreign and security policy elites has caused the country to return to a strategic posture that is both prickly and at times anti-United States. Eugene Rumer is more optimistic in the second reading. He contends that Russia is neither as undemocratic nor hostile as its critics charge.

YES

**Tucker Herbert
and Diane Raub**

Russian Geopolitik

Today's Russia is a strange political animal. It emerged from decades-long Soviet isolation in 1991 with the prospect of beginning a new era. Many hoped that Russia would finally join the ranks of the G8 [seven wealthy industrialized countries plus Russia] as a Western-style democracy. The yoke of authoritarianism, however, is not easily broken. Democracies are not created overnight, and the Russian Federation is no exception. Over the past fifteen years, both [President] Boris Yeltsin and his successor Vladimir Putin have made a great show of some democratic reforms, and the world has seen Russia undergo considerable changes. But the Russia that is emerging is not a Western-style liberal democracy.

Russia under President Putin holds fundamentally different values from the U.S., and operates under different assumptions. Justice, liberty, and equality have entirely different meanings in Putin's democracy. Regardless of arguments that Putin uses to claim that he governs a free society, Russia receives a Freedom House ranking of 168th of 192 countries in terms of political rights. The World Economic Forum places it 84th out of 102 countries in independence of the judicial system, and Transparency International places it 126th out of 169 countries in terms of corruption.

Just how serious is this divide between Russian and American political values? The short answer is very serious. The long answer can be found in a two-pronged analysis: first, an analysis of the handling of some salient international issues facing both the U.S. and Russia; and second, a glimpse into recent Russian domestic trends which offer insight into Russian motivations and values. The Russians may pose no immediate threat to U.S. interests—but they are still sitting on the opposite side of the chess board. Some day, an issue will arise which could induce Russia to start the game: and Russia has few qualms about exerting her power against U.S. democratic interests.

Foreign Policy

Russia's foreign policy towards its neighbors is often characterized as domineering and brusque. There is little respect for democratically elected leaders. The Kremlin keeps no secret of their preferred victor in the elections of states which they consider within their sphere. When a former-Soviet ally elects pro-Western democratic leadership, the Kremlin claims the CIA must be involved. Russia tacitly supports break-away republics in both Georgia and Moldova. Most recently, Russia has barred exports of Georgian wines and bottled water because of "health concerns" which Russian officials have failed to validate—again, Russia does not approve of Georgia's democratically elected leader. They affirmed their endorsement of President Islam Karimov of Uzbekistan following the massacre he ordered of hundreds of political demonstrators, despite swift condemnation from the U.S. and European Union. Putin is one of the only allies of the Belarusian dictator Alexander Lukashenko.

With regard to the Middle East, Russia is at times pragmatic while at other times blatantly opportunistic. Their reception of the newly-elected Hamas leadership of the Palestinian Territories was a calculated and measured response that sought to contrast the reactions of the United States and the European Union, while gaining favor in the eyes of other Arab states. Although Russia is making efforts to prevent a nuclear-armed Iran, Russia does not fear for the security of Israel in the same way that the West does. Russia's proposed sale of truck-loaded missiles to Syria is just absurd. Russia will support America's war on terrorism, so long as it fulfills its own ends. By labeling certain groups as terrorists, Putin has justified the use of intensive force against the Chechnyans [a separatist ethnonational group in southern Russia]. Russia's participation in the War on Terror has served as validation of its military buildup.

Military Might

Russian defense officials are making a concerted effort to revamp the Russian military. Most recently, Defense Minister Sergei Ivanov announced widespread cuts in the number of conscripts and officers as part of an effort to make the army more efficient and professional. Moscow is also pouring resources into making the remainder of the army more powerful. So far these resources have helped to deploy a strategic missile regiment of a quality "unmatched by world rivals"; to develop a new nuclear-powered submarine armed with sea-launched ballistic missiles; and to significantly increase the number and level of large-scale military exercises. In a January letter to the Wall Street Journal, Ivanov outlines the motivations behind Russia's "profound and comprehensive modernization" of their armed forces. He emphasizes that Russia intends to use these new forces to thwart any political processes that carry the potential to "change the geopolitical reality in a region of Russia's strategic interest". He condemns "interference in Russia's internal affairs by foreign states—either directly or through structures that they support" and specifies that "our top concern is the internal situation in some members of the Commonwealth of Independent States, the club of former Soviet republics, and the regions around them." Although Ivanov insists that he is not "saber-rattling," his words are chillingly reminiscent of Cold War rhetoric. Russia has also contributed to military buildup in other regimes. Most notable is Hugo Chavez's

Venezuela, which has purchased $54 million worth of Russian assault rifles, ammunition, and other light weapons in the past year alone.

China and Russia

A strong Sino-Russo alliance has gradually emerged over the past ten years. Russia and China have made clear their joint desire to achieve a world order that does not orbit around the American superpower. Joint military exercises have demonstrated the possibility that such an order may be reached through means other than peace. Indeed, Russia and China seem to get along better now than they did during the Cold War when they were purportedly comrades allied against the capitalist bastards of the West. In 2005, Russia and China signed a pact ending 40 years of negotiations over centuries-old border disputes. Both nations are pursuing a military buildup in the name of defense of sovereignty; desire to limit U.S. intervention in their spheres of influence; and have established their willingness to support sketchy regimes.

Nevertheless, the two powers remain in competition economically, politically, and militarily. Much of Russia's industrial sector has been replaced by more efficient Chinese manufacturers. China has gained entrance to the World Trade Organization, while Russia has been left in the cold. China may be moving closer to the West on UN security initiatives. The world seems more patient with China's human rights abuses than with those of Russia. Relative to Russia, China places more emphasis on its economic dominance than its military might. China has devoted vast amounts of resources to investment in infrastructure and human capital, while remaining tight-lipped about their military developments and insisting upon the peaceful nature of their rise. The future of this Sino-Russian alliance remains to be seen. Judging from recent developments, however, the two neighbors are more than willing to put aside resource squabbles in favor of good old-fashioned anti-American ideology.

Oil Politics

Russia is the world's largest exporter of natural gas and the second-largest international oil exporter. In the past year, Putin has demonstrated that he is not skittish of using Russia's abundant resource exports as a tool of political manipulation. For a few days in early January, Russia cut off natural-gas deliveries to the Ukraine after a dispute over an extreme price hike. Many believe this was a form of punishment directed at Ukrainian president Viktor Yushchenko for his Westward orientation. Border explosions in gas pipelines running to similarly democratic Georgia have also raised suspicions. The E.U. draws 25% of its natural gas from Russia. E.U. member states are watching Russian oil politics with apprehension while scrambling to diversify their foreign suppliers.

The domestic structure of the Russian oil industry is another cause for concern. In recent years, Putin has cozied up to state-run energy giants, while building an environment increasingly less friendly to the private energy industry. Russia's oil has played a significant role in fueling 6% growth rates since 1998. Oil wealth is a double-edged sword; if international oil prices fall once again they can drag Russia's economy with them. But for now prices are high and Russia is reaping the benefits.

"Managed Democracy"

Though Putin has continued to lower taxes and increase pro-market incentives that encourage consumer spending, some of his policies look dangerously similar to state centralization. In December 2005, one of President Putin's economic advisors resigned in protest over declining political and economic freedom; and the heads of pro-democracy Russian NGOs [transnational nongovernmental organizations] complain routinely of government harassment and efforts to silence them. The government has passed legislation that declares certain international NGOs illegal in Russia. The Duma [Russia's national parliament] has given Putin the authority to appoint regional governors. Corruption is such that bribes regularly determine the outcomes of court cases. The lack of freedom in the press stifles accountability and calls into question the legitimacy of this democracy.

Russia is no longer the rival superpower it used to be. In the past two decades, Russia has suffered considerable losses to its military clout and political influence. From a Russian perspective, Putin can be seen as a great leader who has restored Russian pride. The economy has rebounded and boomed since he took office in 1999. His economic reforms have coincided with increased investment and consumer confidence. Russia justifies its own interference in the surrounding region by citing cases of U.S. "intervention," despite the more democratically-inclined nature of the approach used by the United States. This belies the fact that the two states have fundamentally different political systems and values. The emerging Russia, in some ways, is as diametrically opposed to U.S. values as the Soviet Union was during the Cold War. Putin is playing a different game than his Soviet predecessors, but it is still a game which pits U.S. interests against Russian. Putin has made clear that he does not attach the same value to liberty, democracy, and peaceful rule that the U.S. does. The U.S. must beware of these differences and understand the Russian psyche when forming U.S. foreign policy.

Developments
in U.S.–Russia Relations

In 2005, two decades after a little-known Communist Party functionary named Mikhail Gorbachev was selected to the leadership of the Soviet Union, Russia presents an elusive target for students of its foreign policy and domestic affairs, both critics, of whom there are growing numbers, and admirers, whose ranks have been dwindling lately. True to the old adage, Russia is neither as strong as its sheer size and geopolitical heft suggest, nor as weak as it appears relative to other continental giants—China and Europe. No longer capable of projecting its power far beyond its borders as it aspired to do a generation ago, Russia remains the critical variable on the map of Eurasia position on the balance sheet of partners vs. adversaries can make or break most, if not all U.S. design on the continent.

Is Russian Democracy Dying?

Any discussion of modern day Russia inevitably turns to the country's uncertain domestic political situation and what many observers, both Russian and foreign, have lamented as retreat from democracy. Critics point to greater consolidation of government control over major media outlets, marginalization of democratically-oriented political parties, use of law enforcements against Kremlin political opponents and abolition of gubernatorial elections as signs of Russia's abandonment of democracy and possible return to its undemocratic past. Major human rights organizations have been critical of Russia's internal developments; Freedom House, a highly regarded human rights advocacy and monitor of freedom worldwide considers Russia as "not free" with the overall rating of 6, with 7 being the least free.

The facts cited by these human rights organizations are not in dispute. The Russian government directly or indirectly controls major media outlets. The most biting programs mocking leading Russian politicians, including presidents Boris Yeltsin and Vladimir Putin can no longer be seen on Russian TV.

However, contemporary Russian media, although more restrained than during the 1990's, is a far cry from what it was during the Soviet era or from what is implied in the short phrase "retreat from democracy." Russian newspapers, sold freely and available on the Internet, are full of diverse opinions;

Testimony during hearings on "Developments In U.S.-Russia Relations" before the Subcommittee on Europe and Emerging Threats of the Committee on International Relations (March 9, 2005).

public opinion polls are freely disseminated; news reports ranging from Kremlin infighting to developments in Iraq are published in print and electronic media.

Russian media are certainly not as free-wheeling as they were during the 1990's. But any claim of Russian retreat from democracy ignores the fact that Russia in the 1990's was not a democracy either. Does increased control of the media by the Russian government represent a bigger blow to democracy in Russia than ownership or control of major TV and print outlets by powerful businessmen who did not shy away from editorial interference when their business or political interests so required? Who bears greater responsibility for many Russians' cynical attitudes toward freedom of the press-President Vladimir Putin who has sought to consolidate his control over major media, or those oligarchs who used their media holdings as a tool of their business and political pursuits?

The issue of freedom in Russia too deserves a more nuanced consideration. There is little doubt that a number of steps by the Kremlin toward greater centralization of power and authority in the hands of the federal government is at odds with its stated commitment to greater democracy and open society. But does Russia deserve its "Not Free" rating in 2005 more than it did in 1996, when it held a rather unfair and unbalanced presidential election? Or 1994 and 1995, when it waged a brutal war in Chechnya? Or in 1993, when the Yeltsin government shelled the parliament building in an effort to resolve a constitutional crisis? During all those years, Russia was rated as "Partially Free."

The notion that Russian democracy is dead or dying ignores widespread grass-roots unrest triggered in recent months by the Russian government's unpopular social welfare reforms. People have been organizing and marching in the streets to protest government policies. After months of protests that have confronted the Russian government with a crisis like no other in recent years, Russian democracy is no less alive than it was when Boris Yeltsin was reelected to his second term in an election that was anything but fair.

Rumors of Russian democracy's demise are not only premature, but ignore the impact of such factors as the ever-expanding access to the Internet in many Russian cities in towns; cell phone use; ability to travel abroad; ability by foreigners to travel deep into the Russian heartland. Russia is no longer cut off from the outside world by the Iron Curtain. All this is having impact in many, often immeasurable ways—from the emergence of hundreds of civic organizations at the grass-roots level to academic debates about globalization and its impact on Russia, to the emergence of new independent candidates in the 2008 election to succeed—or challenge, whatever the case may be—President Vladimir Putin. None of these phenomena promise quick change, but they are signs that changes are taking place.

When the Soviet Union dissolved in 1991, it was universally recognized that Russian democracy-building would be a difficult and ambitious generational project. 15 years into that project one thing is clear: the future of Russian democracy will remain uncertain for a long time to come. Any judgment about its quality or condition at this point is premature and inaccurate at best.

Is Russia Moving toward Authoritarianism?

As a corollary to debates about Russian democracy, students of Russian domestic politics have raised the question of whether Russia is moving toward a more authoritarian system of government.

Surface signs have definitely pointed in the direction of a system that places greater power and authority, as well as greater control over resources, into the hands of the federal executive at the expense of regional governors, legislature and even courts. This has manifested itself in the reform of the Federation Council, which diminished the power and authority of popularly elected governors, reform, which was followed by subsequent elimination of gubernatorial elections altogether.

This was further manifested in the emergence of the pro-Kremlin "party of power" and the federal government's domination of the Duma [the dominant house in Russia's parliament] with its help, marginalization of other political parties and proliferation of electoral techniques that while certainly not invented in Russia and imported into Russian political life well before Vladimir Putin's tenure, were put to frequent and widespread use in multiple election campaigns on his watch. Other manifestations of authoritarian tendencies in Russian domestic affairs have taken the form of attempts by the Kremlin to establish greater control over the business community and its role in the nation's political life.

However, this trend, which began soon after President Putin's rise to the presidency of Russia, has progressed against the background of disasters and setbacks that have highlighted the shortcomings and failures of the Russian government and its inability to act in a crisis, respond to new challenges and cope with their aftermath. The Kursk submarine disaster [after it sank with all hands in 2000], the failure to put an end to the war in Chechnya [a rebellious province], the growing threat of domestic terrorism, the hostage dramas in Moscow [where in 2002 Chechen terrorists seized a crowded theater, with 129 hostages and all 42 Chechens eventually killed] and Beslan [where in 2004, 186 children and almost 200 civilians were killed by Chechen terrorists], and most recently the political and social crisis triggered by the welfare reform, have brought to light the fact that far from being authoritarian, the Russian state is dangerously close to being chaotic.

To the people of Russia this comes as no surprise. Public opinion polls consistently demonstrate low confidence on the part of the Russian people in their government's ability to perform the most basic functions—protect the nation's wealth, sovereignty and territorial integrity; provide for the poor and the weak; and protect citizens against crime and violence.

An authoritarian system may be the goal pursued by President Vladimir Putin and his political advisors. Having concentrated a great deal of decision-making authority and resources under its control, the Kremlin should be omnipotent. Yet, real power, the ability to formulate and execute policies, to produce results, to deal with crises and their aftermath, to effect change-all that so far has proven elusive to the degree that various branches of the Russian government and the country's far-flung provinces appear out of control, driven not by a vision of national interest and will imposed from the center, but narrow, parochial concerns or corporate interests of local elites. In

December 2004, two percent of participants in a public opinion survey feared introduction of a "dictatorship based on force;" 15 percent feared anarchy and government incompetence; and 16 percent feared the breakup of Russia.

What Is to Be Done about Russian Democracy?

How should the United States react to developments in Russia? As policy experts and leaders on both sides of the Atlantic debate policy toward Russia, calls to expel Russia from G–8 [Group of 8: the 7 leading developed countries plus Russia] have been heard with increased frequency. The most frequently cited reason for it is that Russia does not deserve a seat at the table of the world's most advanced industrialized democracies, especially in the light of its retreat from democracy in recent years.

Indeed, on the one hand, the state and direction of Russia's democratic transformation is uncertain. Russian democracy is not of the same variety as that of the United States, Great Britain or Germany. That is not subject to serious debate.

But on the other hand, to many observers of Russian democracy inside and outside of Russia, the notion that Russia should be kicked out of G–8 now is just as counterintuitive as the notion that Russia belonged among the crème de la crème of industrialized democracies in the 1990's, when it gradually became accepted there as a full member of that select group.

Russian acceptance into G–8 was based on the principle, embraced by several U.S. Administrations of both political parties, that Russia's integration into major international institutions would secure Russia's constructive posture abroad and promote positive change at home. In shaping relations between Russia and the G–7, the leaders on both sides of the Atlantic and Japan took the long view of Russia's transformation. Excluding Russia from that group now would mark a departure from that view, ignore important developments in Russia and abandon the vision the West put in place as the foundation of its relations with Russia at the end of the Cold War—a vision of Russia integrated into the Atlantic and Pacific economic, political and security structures—and abandon it prematurely with the most adverse consequences for both Russia and its G–8 partners themselves.

How should the United States then respond to developments in Russia? As a constructive observer and partner who is fully aware of the complexity of the task ahead, of the national sensitivities and peculiarities due to Russia's historical and cultural preferences and traditions; as an interlocutor who understands that his own record of engagement on this issue has at times lacked consistency and impartiality; and, of course, as a candid critic in those instances where he feels his core interests and principles are at stake.

Russia and Her Neighbors

Russia's pattern of behavior toward her neighbors has been the other major area of recent criticism of Russian international behavior. Russian meddling in Ukraine, Georgia and Moldova has generated further calls for expelling

Russia from G–8 and a more confrontational stance toward Russia on the part of its G–8 partners in the international arena.

Once again, the facts are not in dispute. Russian heavy-handed interference in its neighbors' affairs is well documented. However, this is an area where once again Russian behavior is more apt to be interpreted as a sign of weakness, rather than strength.

The public record of Russian involvement in Ukraine's "Orange Revolution," Georgia's "Rose Revolution," recent elections in Moldova and breakaway Georgian province of Abkhazia suggests that Russian influence in the former provinces of the Soviet Union is on the wane. Russia appears to be so unpopular and its interference so heavy-handed that it often produces the opposite effect from what is presumably intended. The results of recent elections in Moldova suggest that a candidate could be well served by Russian interference *against* him, for such interference is likely to help one's credentials as an independent-minded leader.

However, in areas other than politics, Russia plays an important and at times positive role. This may not be the result of its deliberate policies, but Russia, especially as its coffers swell from the flood of petrodollars, remains an important market for excess labor and goods from some of the neighboring countries, where access to Russian market is a matter of critically important remittances, export revenues and as a result social stability and even survival in some of the poorest areas. It is these flows of goods, people, services and money, often undetected or overlooked by the policy community, that comprise many ties that continue to bind Russia to its neighbors.

Perhaps, the biggest problem that Russia poses in relation to its neighbors is in the area of the so-called "frozen conflicts"—in Abkhazia, Moldova, South Ossetia and Nagorno-Karabakh. Russian involvement with a number of these breakaway regimes is a long-standing irritant in Moscow's relations with some of its neighbors, the United States and other countries.

The dilemma facing U.S. policymakers in this area is whether to confront Russia more forcefully or stay the course of patient, albeit unproductive dialogue. The balance of arguments appears to favor dialogue, though one that needs to be intensified if we are to achieve our stated objective of "unfreezing" these conflicts.

Additional arguments favoring dialogue include changes in Russian attitudes toward these conflicts. Increasingly, Russian interlocutors have acknowledged that developments in the South Caucasus have an impact on the situation in the North Caucasus, where Russian authorities face a growing prospect of destabilization. Some Russian analysts have begun to come to terms with the realization that they lack the capabilities to address the problem of security and stability in the Caucasus alone and that they will need to deal with other parties involved in the region, especially as the United States and Europe carry on with greater involvement there.

The discussion of "frozen conflicts" is bound to come to the fore of the trans-Atlantic agenda for one more reason: the final status of Kosovo. As Europe and the United States approach that thorny issue, as the option of independence for Kosovo looms large in discussions on both sides of the

Atlantic, the Abkhaz, the Ossetians and others will ask: if independence is OK for Kosovo, why not for us? It is equally likely to be an issue of considerable importance for Russia, which will be torn between its preference for client-regimes in Abkhazia and Ossetia and its fear that Kosovo's independence may be the harbinger of the international community's attitudes toward Chechnya. A preventive dialogue with Russia on this subject is essential to avoid a crisis in relations over this issue.

Chechnya   One of the thorniest problems on the U.S.-Russian agenda will have to be discussed as well. Long treated as a major human rights concern for the United States, this issue has acquired new dimensions—sovereignty vs. self-determination in the context of Kosovo, as discussed in preceding paragraphs; regional stability and security because of spillover into the South Caucasus; and counterterrorism in the aftermath of hostage-takings in Moscow and Beslan, as well as other terrorist incidents. Recognizing the complex and multi-faceted nature of the problem is the first step toward addressing our respective concerns.

Demands and ultimatums, as well as criticism of Russian crisis response, as was the case in the aftermath of Beslan, can only lead to Russian intransigence on this issue. There are no certain answers or solutions to this problem in advance. However, recognizing Russian sensitivities in times of national tragedies such as Beslan, being honest and realistic about our own ability to advise and to help in very difficult circumstances is the first step toward honest dialogue, possibly shared interests and even solutions.

Iran   In looking at Russia in the context of Iran's WMD ambitions, there is both good news and bad: Russia is neither *the* problem nor is it the solution. On the one hand, Presidents Putin and Bush have jointly stated that Iran should not be allowed to obtain a nuclear weapon. On the other hand, Russia continues to provide equipment for Iranians' nuclear energy program.

From Moscow's perspective, Iran's program represents a major export opportunity for its nuclear industry that has few domestic or international markets. It perceives Iran as a major political player in the region; an Islamic country that has been largely deferential to Russian interests in the past; and a key partner in the Gulf region.

For the Russians, the Iranian issue is not high enough on their list of the most pressing security concerns. While Moscow would prefer the status quo and considers the prospect of a nuclear-armed Iran to be an unwelcome one, the threat it would pose is not so great as to move the Russian Government to jeopardize other Russian interests in Iran in order to resolve this issue. At the same time, Moscow would not want to be cut out of any scheme to solve the issue put together by Europe and the United States.

Russian officials and analysts understand that it is an important issue for the international community, one that is high on the agenda of its (Russia's) principal interlocutors—the United States, United Kingdom, Germany and France. Russian policymakers would most likely view their involvement in solving the Iranian nuclear crisis as a great power prerogative, as well as a function of their interests in that country.

When discussing Iran's nuclear ambitions, Russian analysts appear to be more concerned about a US intervention than about Iran's ambitions as such. US intervention, they fear, would jeopardize Russian commercial interests; complicate relations with the United States, Israel, and others; cause further regional destabilization; and set off other ripple effects that Russia may be ill-equipped to handle. Some in Russia view the Iranian nuclear program as chiefly aimed at the U.S. and therefore a positive in countering growing U.S. "adventurism."

That is not to say that Russia is cavalier about Iranian intentions; they continue to monitor Tehran's behavior for signs of greater ambition and possible mischief. Generally though, while Russia might object to solutions that rely on use of force, it is unlikely to become a true obstacle to U.S. policy in the region. It is unlikely that Russia will ever become a major player in dealing with an Iranian nuclear program and would probably be more reactive than proactive.

At the same time, Russia could play a useful role in the general framework of the international community's response to the crisis. In doing so, Russia is more likely to use the international legal framework than adopt position that could leave senior policymakers vulnerable to domestic charges of caving in to U.S. pressure. For example, Russia's agreement with Iran on spent nuclear fuel ran against U.S. policy preferences, but instead emphasized compliance with Russian obligations under the NPT Treaty. Perhaps, one collateral benefit of the agreement is that it underscores the point that Iran does not need to develop its own full nuclear fuel cycle.

Russian behavior in the run up to OIF [Operation Iraqi Freedom, the U.S.-led intervention in Iraq beginning in 2003] could be indicative of Russian behavior in a future crisis involving Iran. Unwilling to jeopardize its bilateral relations with the United States or Europe, Russia would likely adopt a "wait-and-see" attitude and watch the debate unfold among allies on both sides of the Atlantic. Russia would likely shy away from a leadership position in that debate, leaving that role to others, while insisting on keeping the tensions confined to the UN–NPT framework, which would give it a major decision-making role, shield its equities vis-à-vis the United States and Europe, as well as maximize its leverage vis-à-vis Iran and neutralize domestic anti-U.S. sentiments.

Summing up   U.S.–Russian relations are neither as bad as critics charge, nor as good as optimists hope they can be. It is indeed a relationship that has fallen far short of its potential. At the same time, it is a relationship that has avoided many very real downturns and certainly avoided the worst. For the United States, it remains a relationship that could facilitate enormously U.S. pursuit of its geopolitical and strategic objectives—stability and peace in Europe, balanced relations with China, global war on terror, counterproliferation and energy security. It is a relationship that if it turns sour and adversarial, could seriously complicate U.S. pursuit of these objectives and the prosecution of the war on terror in Eurasia, as well as elsewhere in the world. It is a relationship that was founded at the end of the Cold War on the realization that the road ahead would be long, difficult and involve change that would be nothing short of generational. It is also a relationship that has paid off in a number of key areas—NATO [North Atlantic Treaty Organization] and EU [European Union] enlargement, Cooperative Threat Reduction, cooperation in the war on terror, etc. It has paid off for the United States through perseverance and adherence to the long view. There is little in the balance of Russia's domestic trends or international behavior to warrant a fundamental reassessment of U.S. commitment to that relationship, let alone a radical departure from it.

And while on the subject of radical departures, anyone considering a fundamental change in this relationship ought to consider the implications and costs of the alternative—a policy of neo-containment of Russia. They would be enormous, ranging from the added burden of military encirclement of Russia to political, involving a new rift in trans-Atlantic relations, for such a radical turnaround is unlikely to be endorsed by Europe. To paraphrase an old-fashioned Soviet phrase, the correlation of factors favors staying the course.

POSTSCRIPT

Has Russia Become Undemocratic and Antagonistic?

The debate over the future of Russia is not a matter of idle speculation. There are two very real policy considerations. The first involves the fact that the direction Russia takes in the future is likely to have important consequences for the world. Both the ultranationalist right and communist/socialist left wings of Russian politics favor a much more aggressive foreign policy. Under President Yeltsin and during the earlier years of President Putin's first term, the Russian government sometimes strongly criticized such U.S.-favored actions as the expansion of NATO's expansion, but Moscow's weakness constrained it from trying to block U.S. preferences.

There is still not a great deal that Russia can do, but it has gotten somewhat more assertive. Russia opposed the U.S. invasion of Iraq in 2003 and has helped block Washington's effort to get sanctions on Iran for its Nuclear Development Program passed by the UN Security Council, on which Russia has a permanent seat and a veto. Russia cannot stop the U.S. efforts to build and deploy a ballistic missile defense (BMD) system, but Putin's government has countered by beginning to deploy mobile intercontinental ballistic missiles (ICBM) with improved in-flight maneuverability meant to limit the ability of a BMD system to intercept them. New issues continue to emerge, including the friction between Washington and Moscow over Russia's interference on the elections in the Ukraine in 2004. For the view that there are consistencies in the foreign policies of historic Russia, the USSR, and modern Russia, see Robert H. Donaldson and Joseph L. Nogee, *Foreign Policy of Russia: Changing Systems, Enduring Interests* (M. E. Sharp, 2005). Steven Rosefielde, *Russia in the 21st Century: The Prodigal Superpower* (Cambridge University Press, 2004), contends that Russia will try to restore its position as a full-fledged superpower within the next decade.

There are also doubts about whether democracy can survive in a country that is in such poor condition and that has no democratic tradition. The increasing curbs on a free press and other essential democratic elements that have occurred in Russia led U.S. Vice President Dick Cheney to warn publically in 2006 that in Russia "opponents of reform are seeking to reverse the gains [in democracy] in the last decade." This concern with Russian democracy arguably has important implication for foreign policy. Many scholars contend that democracies generally do not go to war with one another, which means that the collapse of democracy in Russia might increase the potential for clashes between it and the Western democracies. Since much will depend on President Putin, worth reading are Andrew Jack, *Inside Putin's Russia* (Oxford University Press, 2005) and Katheryn Stoner-Weiss, *Resisting the State* (Cambridge University Press, 2006) on the struggle of Putin's central government to get control of Russia often resistent provinces.

It is too early to accurately predict what course Russia and its foreign relations will take in the decade ahead. What can be said is that Russia has seemed to be down and out financially and military at more than one juncture in its history, and it has always recovered, as it seems to be doing now. If the trend continues, Russia will regain the economic and military muscle necessary to play an important role in global affairs. A number of outstanding policy disputes still divide Moscow from Washington. How those are managed by both sides will be an important determinant of the general tone of future relations. A recent discussion of U.S. policy toward Russia is Roderic Lyne, Strobe Talbott, and Koji Watanabe, *Engaging with Russia: The Next Phase* (The Trilateral Commission, 2006).

ISSUE 5

Will China Soon Become
a Threatening Superpower?

YES: Robert T. McLean, from "The Pentagon Gets China Right," http://FrontPageMagazine.com (June 7, 2006)

NO: Alice Lyman Miller, from "China: A Superpower? No Time Soon," *Hoover Digest* (Spring 2005)

ISSUE SUMMARY

YES: Robert T. McLean, a research associate at the Center for Security Policy in Washington, D.C., contends that the U.S. Defense Department is correct in its view that China is an expanding danger based on its expansive aspirations in the economic and political arenas coupled with an equally bold foreign policy.

NO: Alice Lyman Miller, editor of the Hoover Institution journal, *China Leadership Monitor*, projects that it will be a long time before China acquires the global political, strategic, and economic reach of a superpower.

China has a history as one of the oldest and at times most powerful countries (and empires) in the world. During the Yuan dynasty (1271–1368) and most of the Ming dynasty (1368–1644), China was also arguably the world's most powerful empire, dominating most of Asia.

However, China's power compared to Europe began to ebb with the Industrial Revolution beginning in Europe in the mid-1700s playing a major role. By the 1800s, the European powers, joined by the United States in the last years of the century, came to increasingly dominate China. The Chinese consider these years a period of humiliation, emblemized by a park in a European enclave in Shanghai that bore the sign, "Dogs and Chinese Not Allowed."

China's road back began in 1911 when Nationalist forces under Sun Yat-sen overthrew the last emperor. Internal struggles and the invasion by Japan (1931–1945) blocked much advance in China's economic and political power until the Communists under Mao Zedong defeated the Nationalists under Chiang Kai-shek who fled and set up the remnants of the Nationalist government on Formosa (Taiwan) as the Republic of China.

Gradually, Communist China (the People's Republic of China, PRC), built up its strength. Military power came first. China's military was saddled by obsolete weapons, but it was the world largest military force, numbering as many as 4.2 million troops in the 1980s. China also sought to acquire nuclear weapons and delivery capability, and succeeded in that quest by the mid-1960s.

Fundamental changes in China's status began in the 1970s. In 1971, the United Nations changed the rightful owner of China's seat, including its position as a permanent member of the Security Council, from the Nationalist government on Taiwan to the PRC. The following year, the United States relaxed its hostility, and President Richard Nixon visited China. In 1979, President Jimmy Carter shifted U.S. diplomatic recognition of the "legitimate" government of China from the Taiwan government to the PRC government. Domestically, the two great leaders of the Communist Revolution and government, Premier Zhao Enlai and Communist Party Chairman Mao Zedong both died in 1976. This opened the way for a less ideological approach to improving China's economy.

Since then, China has changed rapidly. It retains a communist government, but it has adopted many of the trappings of a capitalist economy. Where once China rejected global trade and other international economic organizations, it has now embraced them.

Economically, it is possible to argue that China is still a poor country, one whose 2005 per capita gross domestic product (GDP) of about $1,700 was less than one-twentieth the per capita GDP of the United States. But China has also become one of the largest economies in the world. China's 2005 GDP was $2.2 trillion. That makes it the fourth largest economy in the world, still far behind the United States ($12.5 trillion), but about equal to Great Britain. China has also become a major global trader, with its $1.3 trillion in exports and imports placing it third among countries after only the United States and Germany. China is also the fastest growing large economy, expanding by an annual average of over 8 percent since 1975. Much of this is industrial growth, and China is the world's fourth largest producer of automobiles and commercial vehicles and third greatest steel manufacturer.

China's growing economy and industrialization has allowed it to upgrade its military technology. The country's 2005 official defense budget was only $29 billion dollars, but there is little doubt that actual spending is higher than that. Still the amount, whatever it is, falls far short of the 2005 U.S. defense budget ($419 billion).

What all this portends is the issue here. In the first reading, Robert T. McLean reacts to a Pentagon report warning that China's growing power represents a significant threat by arguing that the military's viewpoint is correct. Alice Lyman Miller takes a much more restrained view of China's power and intentions in the second reading.

YES

Robert T. McLean

The Pentagon Gets China Right

In late May [2006] the Department of Defense issued its annual report to Congress on the "Military Power of the People's Republic of China." While not a perfect document, this assessment of the expanding danger emanating from Beijing displays that the Pentagon not only understands the implications of a Chinese challenge to the American primacy in Asia, but is also bold enough to confront Beijing about Washington's concerns. At face value the Defense Department's document is not unlike those released in previous years; however, a close examination of the report and its surrounding reactions demonstrate that the situation has become all the more serious.

Beijing's expansive aspirations in the economic and political arenas are beginning to pave the way for an equally bold foreign policy. As this year's report notes, "China's foreign policy is now global." This is a consequential development whose process has been highlighted in previous reports, yet it was deemed premature to label China as a world power until now. Just as the dawn of the nineteenth century when Thomas Jefferson realized that in order to become an economic power, the United States must trade all over the world, Beijing has reached the conclusion that their economic growth is increasingly dependent on foreign markets and natural resources. In Jefferson's eyes, American commerce would have to be protected and "paid for by frequent war." Beijing has drawn similar conclusions as the Pentagon's report prefigures: "As China's economy expands, so too will its interests and the perceived need to build a military capable of protecting them." Such parallels may draw some to become empathetic of China's current course and accept the People's Republic's rise to great power status as not only inevitable, but legitimate. This, however, is exceedingly perilous.

A balance of power in Asia and the Pacific is neither to the advantage of the United States nor the region. Prior to his influence in promoting the Monroe Doctrine as Secretary of State, John Quincy Adams deemed that it was imperative for the young American republic to expand across the continent to the Pacific because a North America plagued by a security environment predicated on the power balancing structure that consumed Europe would inevitably lead to an "eternal war" for possessions as insignificant as "a rock or a fish pond."

Such a state of affairs in the latter half of the twentieth century led to the endless series of proxy wars that defined the Cold War era. Today, as the Defense Department's report states, "The rapid growth of the PRC's [People's Republic of China] economy, coupled with its military expansion, has propelled China's emergence as a regional power." Therefore, [Secretary of Defense Donald] Rumsfeld's Pentagon has correctly made it a priority to maintain the preservation of America's relative power in Asia rather than preparing for a stage of balance of power.

Reaction from Beijing to the report has been unusually docile for a regime that throws fits every year after the State Department releases its "Annual Country Reports on Human Rights." There are several possible explanations for the PRC's conspicuously composed response. The most obvious is that the leadership in Beijing wants to avert a rise in tensions with Washington over an issue that is relatively insignificant. Strong denunciations of the Pentagon's report could have the adverse effect of giving the perceivably hawkish Department of Defense legitimacy in their claims. And whereas human rights reports undermine the regime's credibility at home, references to an increasingly assertive and powerful China are unlikely to stir such domestic dissent.

There is another reason, however, that the regime's propaganda machine—the government has virtually absolute control of information flows in China—toned down its customary criticisms of America. On May 22, the day before the Pentagon's report, the Chinese official news agency *Xinhua* reported that the "U.S. [was] likely to increase hi-tech exports for civilian use to China." This is something that the regime in Beijing has long strenuously advocated, and it is imperative that Undersecretary of State for Commerce David H. McCormick abides by his words of ensuring that dual-use [peaceful and military] technologies do not wind up in the hands of the Chinese military establishment.

A chapter on force modernization in the DOD's report quoted Chinese President Hu Jintao's statement earlier this year that a comprehensive system of research and development should "create a good structure under which military and civilian high technologies are shared and mutually transferable." Thus, there is a reason tight export control of dual-use technology has prevailed. Whereas this year's assessment of the advancement of China's technological components notes that foreign investment in China's civilian industrial sector "has increased the prospect for spin-off with military dual-use industries," the June 2000 report was more dismissive of the dangers of Beijing's technological improvements. The 2000 report claimed: "Even if the PLA [People's Liberation Army] were to acquire the modern weaponry it seeks, integrating those systems and training commanders and troops to employ them will remain a difficult task and will inhibit the PLA's maturation into a world-class military force."

Unfortunately, it seems that the Chinese were underestimated. Just six years later the Pentagon notes not only the technological improvements by the PLA, but also the number of highly trained Chinese citizens capable of developing, maintaining, and operating the country's increasingly modern defense capabilities. For instance, the report notes that a growing number of Chinese nationals are being trained abroad in the sciences and engineering, including the nearly 36,000 that were granted student or exchange visas in the United States in 2004. The Defense Department understands the dangers here and has no intention of permitting the PRC to challenge for future technological dominance.

That is not how many see it, however. To some, the Pentagon's report represents a deceitful exaggeration in order to justify future defense spending. The Chinese Communist Party's *Renmin Ribao* wrote on May 26: "The American society has become one big interest group since World War II. . . . Just imagine, if there is not one bit of tension, if there is no 'opponent,' how could the Defense Department attain more budget from Congress." These sentiments were largely echoed by Fred Kaplan in *Slate* when he imprudently stated: "Every day and night, hundreds of Air Force generals and Navy admirals must thank their lucky stars for China."

Adding that the Pentagon's report "adds up to diddly," Kaplan stipulates that the Chinese are no threat at all. Perhaps, these China doves should ask Beijing's neighbors how they feel about that dictatorship's increasing military power and regional muscle flexing. Assistant secretary of defense for international security affairs Peter Rodman noted that one of the biggest changes articulated in this year's report is that "China is beginning to develop the capacity to project power." Just one year earlier, the 2005 report assessed that "China's ability to project conventional military power beyond its periphery remains limited." Thus, it is clear that within the last year Beijing has made considerable strides towards constituting a military threat to the United States, its allies, and its interests far beyond a conflict over Taiwan.

Further evidence of this development—although regrettably not mentioned or adequately addressed in the report—are several instruments of force projection that have and will enable Beijing to increase its global influence. Chinese intelligence agents are active at both points of entry of the Panama Canal as the country's corporations control much of vital sectors of the canals management. China is also assisting their allies in Pakistan to develop the Gwadar Port giving them access to the Gulf of Oman and the potential ability to project power in the Persia Gulf. The report also glossed over the Beijing and Moscow led Shanghai Cooperation Organization. The SCO is an increasingly powerful military alliance that frequently works to counter American interests. This organization delivers both allies and natural recourses to the Chinese in Russia and Central Asia.

Thus, the Defense Department is hardly guilty of overstating the threat posed by a rising China. One reason for this is that Beijing is not only increasing its military capacity and global influence, but gauging their intentions remains a fretful affair. A noteworthy element in the 2006 report is the Pentagon's accurate assessment of the PRC's dangerously unpredictable strategy. Sighting former paramount Chinese leader Deng Xiaoping's words from the early 1990's, Rodman noted: "The phrase that strikes me, of course is 'hide our capacities and bide our time." The assistant secretary added, "I think this encapsulates what China's strategy is. They are very patient." What many fail to understand, and something the Defense Department understands well, is that just like the al-Qaeda forces we are battling now, the Chinese think beyond the immediate and plan for the long-term.

The United States' use of force in first Kosovo and then Iraq was greatly troubling to the Chinese leadership because these instances not only displayed that the United States had the ability to effectively project power anywhere in the world, but that the will was there as well. Thus, whereas the Pentagon's original report to Congress in 2000 stated that the Chinese military force structure planning was a principal concern as it seemed to be designed for a cross-strait conflict with Taiwan, and perhaps the United States; the 2006 report highlights the increasing capabilities of the Chinese forces as the "PLA Second Artillery is fielding mobile, more survivable missiles capable of targeting the United States, Japan, India, Russia, and other targets in Asia and the rest of the world" with nuclear weapons.

The Soviet Union had this capability, and combined with their concurrent efforts—much like the Chinese—to counter the United States around the world, the result was half a decade of Cold War with conflicts springing up the world over to satisfy the relative balance of power that no corner of the Earth was able to escape. Tens of thousands of Americans died fighting in Soviet initiated and facilitated struggles. This is not something the generals and admirals are wishing every day and night will reemerge. The Pentagon has got it right on China, and unlike its many critics, the Defense Department is working tirelessly to ensure that will not happen again.

Alice Lyman Miller  **NO**

China: A Superpower? No Time Soon

People have been predicting China's emergence as a superpower since the days of Napoleon, who purportedly appreciated China's potential as a world power and cautioned against waking the sleeping dragon. China's subordination into the Western international system in the 1839–42 Opium War, and its decline as the "sick man" of East Asia for the rest of the nineteenth century and the first half of the twentieth century, dulled but never extinguished the expectation that, sooner or later, China would again dominate the world.

Several recent events have provoked the latest announcements of China's looming ascent to superpower stature and suggest that these long-held expectations are, at long last, coming true. In December 2003 China launched its first human into space, joining the United States and the former Soviet Union as the only countries to have done so. American media have recently taken notice of China's efforts to expand and diversify its access to sources of oil in the Middle East, Africa, Latin America, and—unsettlingly close to home—Canada. The world's industrial economies, including the United States, have inferred from the giant sucking sound created by lost manufacturing jobs and from the flood of Chinese exports into their markets that China is becoming the world's manufacturing hub. Meanwhile, analysts ponder the implications for global security of China's military modernization effort, now two decades old.

The term *superpower* is often used loosely in popular discourse, so let us define it as a country that has the capacity to project dominating power and influence anywhere in the world, sometimes in more than one region of the globe at a time, and so may plausibly attain the status of global hegemon. By this measure, in modern times we have as benchmarks only the historical examples of Britain and the Soviet Union and the yardstick of continuing American power today. The basic components of superpower stature may be measured along four axes: economic, military, political, and cultural (or "soft"). Let us examine China's stature along each of these four measures.

Economic Power

The expanding range of China's economic interactions has provoked the most recent attention to China as an emerging superpower. American media have

From *Hoover Digest*, Spring 2005, no. 2—Spring. Copyright © 2005 by Hoover Institution Press. Reprinted by permission.

taken note of recent Chinese diplomacy in search of long-term sources of oil, and the growth of China's oil imports has had an impact on gasoline prices that American consumers notice at the pump. China's enormous trade surplus with the United States is now the largest of any American trading partner, including Japan. China's leading place in heavy industries such as steel and shipbuilding reflects the dramatic advances that China's economy has made in the past two decades. And China's low labor costs are making it the manufacturing hub of the world, contributing to the hollowing out of the traditional American manufacturing base.

These important trends signal China's arrival as a major player in the international economy and underscore China's rise over the past 25 years as a competitor for world markets and resources. But they do not lead inexorably to the conclusion that China is an emerging economic superpower.

For one thing, the size of China's GDP makes it a member in the cast of industrialized economies, but it is still a long way from economic superpower stature. In 2003, China's GDP (by exchange-rate measures) totaled $1.159 trillion and ranked sixth in the world, behind France, Britain, Germany, Japan, and the United States ($10,065 trillion). For another thing, China has indeed become an important trading nation, but it still ranks well behind other major economies. In 2003, China ranked ninth, supplying 3.5 percent of the world's exports. By comparison, the United States in 2003 accounted for 14.7 percent of the world's export volume, and the European Union accounted for 16.8 percent. Although Chinese acquisition of foreign assets has attracted attention recently, its overall foreign investment is negligible in comparison with other major economies. China is nowhere close to becoming a world financial center.

China's economic successes are impressive and deserve attention. They reflect China's late entry into the international economy—China was effectively shut out of interactions in the international economy until 1971—and the revision of its development policies begun by Deng Xiaoping in 1978. Over the two decades after 1978, China's economic growth rates approached 10 percent annually.

But China's further rise depends on the continuation of such growth rates, and one wonders how long the spectacular rates of the past 25 years can continue. The high proportion of China's economy occupied by its exports makes it sensitive to the ups and downs of the international economy generally and to the engine of American consumption in particular. China lacks a genuine central bank and national banking system, and the accelerating growth of its energy demands places uncertainties on long-term economic growth. Meanwhile, China's population is graying, as the bulge of people born during Mao's heyday ages and places heavy burdens on the smaller generations of Chinese born in the 1980s and after. In some measure, China's current wave of industrialization replicates the industrial cycle pioneered by the United States, followed by Japan, South Korea, and Taiwan, as they shifted away from heavy industry toward lighter, more efficient, and environmentally less intrusive industries and services. And China faces competition from other rising centers, including India.

Military Muscle

Since 1985, China has pursued a concerted program of military modernization that has attracted attention and, since the mid-1990s, generated controversy. Since 1989, defense allocations in China's public state budget have risen at double-digit rates. China is developing a new generation of strategic and tactical missiles, some of which are deployed on the Chinese coast facing Taiwan. China is building a much more capable navy and has bought advanced aircraft from Russia.

But these modernization efforts are best understood as an effort targeted at the needs of specific conflict scenarios in China's immediate periphery. They do not appear to reflect an effort to acquire the strategic and power-projection capacities of a superpower. Specifically, China's military modernization programs appear focused on several priorities:

- Acquiring "green water" naval and air support capacities to defend China's coastal provinces, now the geographic backbone of China's industrial economy
- Establishing credible military capacities to win conflicts quickly and decisively on China's long land borders in Asia, where China still has several unresolved boundary disputes
- Defending China in what is arguably the most heavily militarized region in the world, which includes five of the world's seven declared nuclear states (as well as South Korea, Japan, and Taiwan, all of which could rapidly develop nuclear weapons, and North Korea, which may already have them)
- Compelling resolution of the Taiwan question either politically or by outright military force—even in the event of American intervention on Taipei's behalf—as well as Chinese claims in the South China Sea (the Spratly Islands) on terms acceptable to Beijing
- Preserving the credibility of China's second-strike nuclear deterrent against a strategic first strike

Most of China's military modernization programs appear to be addressed to these priorities. To meet its aims with respect to Taiwan, for example, Beijing is seeking to develop enhanced submarine capacities to blockade the island; buying advanced Su-27 fighters from Russia to establish control of the skies over the Taiwan Strait; and exploring asymmetric information warfare capacities to paralyze Taipei's capacities to resist. Beijing has bought Russian *Sovremenniy* destroyers primarily because they carry the SSN-22 Sunburn—a supersonic, low-altitude anti-ship missile designed to attack aircraft carriers, the instrument of choice should the United States choose to intervene in a Strait conflict.

What Beijing does *not* appear to be doing is acquiring the elements of global power projection characteristic of a superpower. China's navy during the last two decades has increasingly shown its flag in foreign ports around the world, but there is as yet no decision to build aircraft carriers, the premier contemporary mode of naval power projection (the U.S. Navy has 12). Neither is there a clear effort to build a strategic force on the scale of American forces or those of the former Soviet Union. China has no long-range bomber force. China has demonstrated a capacity since the early 1980s to deploy a ballistic missile submarine and fire a missile from it, but China's single such submarine reportedly has serious seaworthiness problems and has not left port since 1988. Likewise, China's small land-based missile force is aging and increasingly vulnerable to a first strike, especially with the advent (however notional at this point) of American missile defense. Beijing has given no evidence that it is aiming to establish the kind of massive strategic force of thousands of deliverable warheads possessed for decades by the United States and, still, by Russia.

China's military modernization has made significant strides, but it remains handicapped by China's weak defense industrial base, a reality underscored by Beijing's readiness to buy weapons from foreign suppliers. After two decades of concerted efforts, China's military modernization has so far created what the U.S. secretary of defense's annual report to Congress calls "pockets of excellence" within a larger picture of obsolescence.

From this perspective, Chinese military developments deserve vigilance, in the broader context of ongoing military modernization efforts throughout Asia, but not alarm. For China to change the balance of military power in Asia decisively, a number of things must happen. First, China's dramatic economic growth must continue indefinitely, a prospect about which there are grounds for skepticism. Second, China's neighbors must stand still in their own defense modernization efforts, which so far has not been true. Third, Russia must continue to be willing to sell advanced weapons systems and military technology to China; sooner or later, however, one might expect Moscow to reconsider how much further it can aid the advance of China's military capacities without jeopardizing Russia's own security interests. Finally, the United States would need to draw down from its security commitments in the region, a development that does not appear likely.

Political and Soft Power

Undeniably, China's political influence has grown during the past three decades. In part, this rise in political influence simply reflects the reversal in its position in the international order. For the first two decades of its existence, the People's Republic of China was an outsider, shut out of the international political and economic community by the effective American containment policies of embargo and ostracism. On entry into the United Nations in 1971, Beijing at last acquired legitimate standing in the international community and could begin to use the instruments of conventional diplomacy and access to the international economy to pursue its national interests abroad. China's international prestige and political influence grew as Deng Xiaoping's reforms in the 1980s transformed China's economy and its relationship to the world. But it suffered dramatically as a consequence of the brutal suppression of the 1989 Tiananmen demonstrations, of the revolutions in Eastern Europe in the same year, and of the collapse of the Soviet Union in 1991, making China appear a reactionary political fossil in the perceived tide of democratization elsewhere. Since then, it has worked to translate its continued economic success into political influence and to overcome international perceptions of it as an atrocious abuser of human rights.

China's seat as a permanent member of the United Nations Security Council is perhaps its asset of greatest leverage in international politics. But since taking its seat in 1971, China has used it to mediate and balance, not to disrupt or displace American leadership and initiatives in international affairs. During the 1990–91 Persian Gulf crisis, for example, Beijing voted in favor of all U.N. resolutions sanctioning Iraq and calling for its withdrawal from Kuwait except the two authorizing the use of military force. Although voicing its reservations about those two resolutions, however, Beijing did not veto them but merely abstained. Similarly, in the diplomatic maneuvering preceding the 2003 Iraq war, Beijing played up French, German, and Russian opposition to resolutions explicitly authorizing an American-led use of force against Baghdad and attempted to broker that opposition with the Americans and British. But it was also clear that Beijing was unlikely to go it alone in vetoing such a resolution had Paris, Berlin, and Moscow folded.

More broadly, Beijing has preached the gospel of "multipolarity" in international politics and sought to promote strategic partnerships with other centers of power to balance American hegemony. But these efforts have been largely unsuccessful, frequently because Beijing's potential partners, like China itself, depend on cooperative relationships with the United States, much as they may chafe at American dominance in the international system. A case in point was the joint declaration signed by then Chinese president Jiang Zemin and Russian president Vladimir Putin in 2001 insisting on the sanctity of the 1968 ABM treaty. When the Bush regime disavowed the treaty in 2002, neither Moscow nor Beijing responded with much more than mild criticism, underscoring the limits of their strategic collaboration against the United States.

In other respects, Beijing's political influence and soft power abroad are comparably limited. No other country seeks to emulate China's political model. Instead, Beijing is accommodating itself, with each passing leadership generation, to the discourse of democracy associated with the West and the United States and striving to sustain the power of the Chinese Communist Party—itself vastly transformed. China rightly complains that Washington and other Western capitals do not appreciate the progress China has made on human rights issues during the past two decades, Tiananmen notwithstanding. And, with some justification, it points out that American concern about human rights in China was virtually absent during Mao's heyday, when human rights abuse was at its height in China, and in the 1970s and 1980s, when China served important American strategic interests in collaborating against the Soviet Union. Since the end of the Cold War, China has had some political success in collaborating with other Asian countries that bristle at what they regard as overweening American preachiness and hypocrisy. But Beijing has yet to dissolve the cloud of skepticism and opprobrium that shadows it on human rights in international politics.

China's culture has long fascinated the West, and China today has become a major tourist attraction. Tokens of this fascination abound in the United States. I am reminded of this when I see my son, now a Seattle resident and long a consumer of "alternative" counterculture, who has a tattoo of the Chinese word *heping* ("peace"). More and more American students are studying Chinese rather than French as their second language and are taking time out for study in China itself, a decision that undoubtedly reflects growing perceptions of China as a land of opportunity. But the numbers of American students studying Chinese—as laudable as they are—are far short of the numbers of Chinese students who study English or who come to the United States and other Western countries. Nor is Chinese likely to displace English as the language of international politics anytime soon.

Prospects

By all these measures, China is not now a superpower, nor is it likely to emerge as one soon. It is establishing itself as a great power, on a par with Great Britain, Russia, Japan, and, perhaps, India. China is today a serious player in the regional politics of Asia but just one of several. In global affairs, its stature and power are growing, but in most respects it remains a regional power, complementing the cast of other great powers under the overarching dominance, however momentary, of the United States.

China's rise over the past two decades has been spectacular from any perspective and deserves attention and respect, especially in view of the difficult course of China's attempt to adapt to the modern world since the nineteenth century. From the perspective of realist geopolitics, however, it does not merit the alarm and trepidation that the announcement of a rival superpower might conjure. Napoleon, in that regard, may be right, but not yet and not soon.

POSTSCRIPT

Will China Soon Become a Threatening Superpower?

One of the reasons that Richard Nixon sought to begin the process of normalizing relations with China more than three decades ago was that he believed China was not only on the road to becoming a superpower but also that it might become the predominant country in the twenty-first century. While it remains unclear if Nixon was correct or not, there can be no doubt that China's power continues to develop. It still has the world's largest military (about 2.3 million troops), and its array of nuclear weapons and delivery systems, while still smaller than those of the United States and Russia, is substantial. Preliminary data for 2006 indicate that China's economy and its defense spending continue to grow rapidly.

How to react to the growth of China is one of the hottest topics in national security circles. To a degree, it is only natural for China to seek a military capability to protect itself and to promote its interests in Asia and perhaps globally. That is what the United States does and, to a lesser degree, other countries do as well. Certainly China has come a long way toward that goal, but the Chinese began from a very low military technology point and their weaponry remains far behind U.S. standards. Still, China's military technology has improved substantially, and it is most likely to use its military muscle in Asia, where it has a geographical advantage over the far distant United States. Moreover, China's forces are concentrated in Asia; those of the United States are dispersed globally.

For a view that China and the United States are on a collision course over China's eventual goal of reincorporating Taiwan, read Ted Galen Carpenter's *America's Coming War with China: Collision Course over Taiwan* (Palgrave/Macmillan, 2006). A less worried assessment is offered by C. Fred Bergsten, Bates Gill, Nicholas R. Lardy, and Derek Mitchell, *China The Balance Sheet: What the World Needs to Know Now About the Emerging Superpower* (PublicAffairs, 2006).

One key to China's intentions will be not only how much weaponry it acquires, but the configuration of those weapons. Those "power projection" weapons systems, such as aircraft carriers or amphibious landing capabilities, which would allow China to apply military power far from its own territory, are the most likely to signal expansive Chinese diplomatic ambitions. There are numerous sources to keep track of China's weapons and military policy. Since many have a point of view, it is better to consult more than one. Three such sites are the Project on Defense Alternatives' "Chinese Military Power" Web page at http://www.comw.org/cmp/; that of GlobalSecurity.org at http://www.globalsecurity.org/military/world/china/index.html, and that of China Defense Today at http://www.sinodefence.com/.

Whatever China's long-term intentions and prospects to be a global superpower may be, there is no doubt that the country is becoming increasingly important in the regional balance of power in Asia, a status explored by David Shambaugh in *Power Shift: China and Asia's New Dynamics* (University of California Press, 2006).

There are numerous articles and books with policy prescriptions for the United States related to the future role of China. One good study is Avery Goldstein, *Rising to the Challenge: China's Grand Strategy and International Security* (Stanford University Press, 2005). Also good to read is the January/February 2005 issue of the journal *Foreign Policy*, which was devoted to the symposium topic, "China Rising." For China's view of itself and its relations with the United States, visit the embassy Web site of China's embassy in Washington, D.C., at http://www.china-embassy.org/eng/.

ISSUE 6

Would It Be an Error to
Establish a Palestinian State?

YES: Patricia Berlyn, from "Twelve Bad Arguments for a State of Palestine," An Original Essay Written for This Volume (2006)

NO: Rosemary E. Shinko, from "Why a Palestinian State," An Original Essay Written for This Volume (October 2006)

ISSUE SUMMARY

YES: Patricia Berlyn, an author of studies on Israel, primarily its ancient history and culture, refutes 12 arguments supporting the creation of an independent state of Palestine, maintaining that such a state would not be wise, just, or desirable.

NO: Rosemary E. Shinko, who teaches in the department of political science at the University of Connecticut, contends that a lasting peace between Israelis and Palestinians must be founded on a secure and sovereign homeland for both nations.

T he history of Israel/Palestine dates to biblical times when there were both Hebrew and Arab kingdoms in the area. In later centuries, the area was conquered by many others; from 640 to 1917 it was almost continually controlled by Muslim rulers. In 1917 the British captured the area, Palestine, from Turkey.

Concurrently, a Zionist movement for a Jewish homeland arose. In 1917 the Balfour Declaration promised increased Jewish immigration to Palestine. The Jewish population in the region began to increase slowly, then it expanded dramatically because of refugees from the Holocaust. Soon after World War II, the Jewish population in Palestine stood at 650,000; the Arab population was 1,350,000. Zionists increasingly agitated for an independent Jewish state. When the British withdrew in 1947, war immediately broke out between Jewish forces and the region's Arabs. The Jews won, establishing Israel in 1948 and doubling their territory. Most Palestinian Arabs fled (or were driven) from Israel to refugee camps in Gaza and the West Bank (of the Jordan River), two areas that had been part of Palestine but were captured in the war by Egypt and

Jordan, respectively. As a result of the 1967 Six Day War between Israel and Egypt, Jordan, and Syria, the Israelis again expanded their territory by capturing several areas, including the Sinai Peninsula, Gaza, the Golan Heights, and the West Bank. Also in this period the Palestine Liberation Organization (PLO) became the major representative of Palestinian Arabs. True peace was not possible because the PLO and the Arab states would not recognize Israel's legitimacy and because Israel refused to give up some of the captured territory.

Since then, however, continuing violence, including another war in 1973, has persuaded many war-exhausted Arabs and Israelis that there has to be mutual compromise to achieve peace. Perhaps the most serious remaining sore point between the Arabs and Israelis is the fate of the Palestinians, who live primarily in the West Bank and Gaza.

In 1991 Israelis and Palestinians met in Spain and held public talks for the first time. Israeli elections brought Prime Minister Yitzhak Rabin's liberal coalition to power in 1992. This coalition was more willing to compromise with the Arabs than had been its more conservative predecessor. Secret peace talks occurred between the Israelis and Palestinians in Norway and led to the Oslo Agreement in 1993. Palestinians gained limited control over Gaza and parts of the West Bank and established a quasi-government, the Palestinian authority led by Yasser Arafat.

The peace process was halted in 1995 when Prime Minister Rabin was assassinated by a Jewish fanatic opposed to Rabin's policy of trying to compromise with the Palestinians. Soon thereafter, conservative Prime Minister Benjamin Netanyahu came to power. He dismissed any possibility of an independent Palestine, made tougher demands on the PLO, and moved to expand Jewish settlements in the West Bank. With some 200,000 Jews already in the West Bank and East Jerusalem, these actions compounded the difficult issue of the fate of those people in a potentially Palestinian–controlled area.

Pressure from a number of quarters, including the United States, have kept the government of Israel and the Palestinians talking, at least at times. President George W. Bush announced his support of a Palestinian state, declaring in 2003, "A two-state solution to the Israeli-Palestinian conflict will only be achieved through an end to violence and terrorism." At times there has been optimism in the region. Arafat died in late 2004 and was succeeded by a seeming moderate, Mahmoud Abbas. Then Israel withdrew the last of its troops from Gaza in 2005, leaving it under full Palestinian control. Just a few months later, though, much of the world was appalled when the Palestinians gave representatives of Hamas, a terrorist organization, control of the Palestinian parliament. Matters worsened in June 2006 when Palestinian gunmen entered Israel and seized an Israeli soldier. The Israelis responded with a sharp military attack on Gaza. The next month, members of the militant Muslim group Hezbolla based in south Lebanon captured two other Israeli soldiers in a cross-border raid. The incident set off a major Israeli military response, which pummeled Lebanon for weeks, destroying a good part of the country infrastructure. It is at this juncture that Patricia Berlyn wrote her essay arguing that creating an independent Palestinian state would be a grave error and Rosemary E. Shinko wrote her reply contending that there is no hope for peace without a Palestinian state.

YES

Patricia Berlyn

Twelve Bad Arguments for a State of Palestine

In 1991, during the administration of President George H. W. Bush, the government of the United States officially pledged to the government of Israel:

> In accordance with the United States' traditional policy, we do not support the creation of an independent Palestinian state. . . . Moreover, it is not the United States' aim to bring the PLO into the [peacemaking] process or to make Israel enter a dialogue or negotiations with the PLO.

A decade later, President George W. Bush announced his administration's "vision" of establishing an Arab State of Palestine west of the Jordan River. The vision was quickly ensconced in a U.N. Security Council Resolution.

This reversal of policy is based on the supposition that the pesky Israel-Palestine-Arab problem can be solved via a Two-State Solution (Israel and Palestine). Actually, it would be a Three-State Solution, because both Israel and Jordan are states within the bounds of Mandate Palestine (see Argument 3).

The necessity of an additional division of that very small area is promoted with twelve arguments that have become a kind of mantra.

1. Israel's Occupation of Palestinian Territory is the Cause of an Islamic Jihad That Spreads Much Discomfiture Across Several Continents. Only the End of Occupation and the Proclamation of a State of Palestine Can Relieve the World of this Discomfiture

On the contrary There is no Israeli occupation and no Palestinian Territory. Rather, there is Israeli administration of a section of Mandate Palestine that still has no assigned sovereignty. The right to this land may be debated, but it should not be dictated with a foregone conclusion based on casual assumptions.

This sliver of land, viewed as an issue of prime and urgent global importance, is hard to find on a map of the world without a magnifying glass. Israel knows it by its biblical name of Judea-Samaria. Jordan dubbed it the West Bank. It is not the crux of the Palestine problem and its growing international repercussions, and transforming it into a State of Palestine will exacerbate not solve that problem.

A realistic view depends on understanding the Muslim belief that the world is divided into two sections: *Dar al-Islam* [House of Islam] and *Dar al-Harb* [House of War]. Any land once acquired by Dar al-Islam must remain within it forever and ever. If it is lost—as in Spain—it must one day be regained. Dar al-Harb will eventually be conquered by *jihad* [struggle for the faith], military or otherwise.

"Palestine" was once part of the Ottoman Turkish Caliphate, and thus Dar al-Islam. It must never be yielded to any infidel, least of all to Jews, those despised and downtrodden *dhimmis*, the "sons of apes and pigs." Thus, Israel's existence as a sovereign nation is permanently intolerable, and will be so wherever its borders are set. The goal, whether declared or disguised, is the total obliteration of Israel. [Note: *Dhimmis*, an Arabic word, are non-Muslims living in a country government by the sharia, Muslim religious law.]

The current half-and-half approach to the Palestine problem is futile. It will not satisfy Israel's foes nor lead them toward genuine peace. Rather, it will dilute Israel's ability to defend itself against those foes and thereby encourage them to go to war. Policymakers who grasp the real issue have two options: (1) Facilitate the destruction of Israel, in hopes that it will mollify Dar al-Islam and postpone jihad against Dar al-Harb. (2) Strengthen, not weaken, Israel because it is the frontline of defense against jihad, and if the jihadis can overcome so staunch a nation they will be emboldened to move on to other prey.

2. The United States Will Benefit from Establishing a State of Palestine, and Win Arab Support for Its War on Terror

On the contrary   A Palestine-Arab State will be an enemy of the United States, not a friend or ally. The "vision" of a State of Palestine that is a democracy, has leaders untainted by terror, and wants to live peacefully side-by-side with Israel is not a vision but a mirage.

Under the Oslo Accords of 1993, Israel put much of Judea-Samaria under the control of the PA [Palestine Authority], and it quickly became a terrorist entity. In advance of Israel's withdrawal from Gaza in 2005, President Bush stated: "I can understand why people think this decision is one that will create a vacuum into which terrorism will flow. [. . . .] I think this will create an opportunity for democracy to emerge. And democracies are peaceful." The Hamas/Fatah regime that was soon elected in Gaza quickly demonstrated that terrorism flows and democracy does not emerge.

The Palestine-Arabs for whom the U.S. administration evinces much sympathy are fiercely anti-American. They admire and side with every enemy of the United States: Nazi Germany, the Soviet Union, Saddam Hussein, Al-Qaeda. They rejoice at events that bring pain and loss to the American people, and celebrate them with cheering, singing, dancing, and distributing sweets. The official religious leaders of the Palestine Authority curse America and pray for its destruction.

Israel, in contrast, is strongly and sincerely pro-American, and shares its values, many of them rooted in a shared biblical heritage. The American people sense this affinity, and strongly oppose the notion of a State of Palestine imposed on the Land of Israel.

If the Administration compulsively pursues its vision, it will create a dysfunctional terrorist entity that is both hostile to the United States and a perpetual dependent of the American taxpayers who have already been made to waste billions of ill-spent dollars on the Palestinian experiment.

3. It Will Rectify an Historic Injustice to the Palestine-Arabs

On the contrary   Of all that Arabs have demanded for themselves since the end of World War I, they have been given 99.5 percent. They were given 22 states, with a combined area of 6,145,389 square miles. Israel has 8,000 square miles of sovereign territory and 2,000 square miles of disputed territory.

Judea was conquered by Rome 2000 years ago, and renamed "Palastina." It was not again a nation or sovereign state until 1948. In the interval, it was a province of one foreign empire or another; usually a backward, neglected, and misgoverned province. In recent centuries Western travelers to the Holy Land found the Land of Milk and Honey now desolate, barren, decayed, uncultivated, and almost empty of population.

From the late nineteenth century onward, Jewish pioneers came to restore the land of their fathers, bringing it back to life by clearing rocks, draining swamps, carrying water, planting crops, and building villages and towns.

After World War I and the collapse of the Ottoman Turkish Empire, Great Britain governed Palestine under a League of Nations Mandate that covered the area that is now Israel, Jordan, the West Bank, and Gaza. The terms of the Mandate repeated those proclaimed by Great Britain itself in the Balfour Declaration, issued by Foreign Secretary Arthur Balfour in 1917: Palestine was to be developed as a "Jewish National Home," open to "close Jewish settlement."

If Britain had honored these terms, there might never have been a Palestine problem. Instead, the British government violated them.

First, it detached all the land east of the Jordan River, more than three-quarters of Mandate Palestine, to provide a kingdom for a protégé Arab emir who had been expelled from Saudi Arabia. There was no historic name suitable for this kingdom so it was called after a river: Trans-Jordan and later Jordan.

In the remaining sector west of the Jordan River, Jewish immigration and settlement were progressively restricted and then banned. There was a rigid blockade against Jews trying to escape the hell-fires of Nazi Europe that consigned an incalculable number of them to death. At the same time, Britain allowed massive immigration of Arabs into Mandate Palestine, filling up the empty places meant for but denied to the Jews.

The offspring of these recent Arabs migrants and those who had preceded them by a few decades are today's "Palestinians" who claim the Land of Israel as their ancient ancestral heritage. Neither the name nor the claim predates the year 1967. Until then, Arab spokesmen and scholars insisted that there was not and never had been any such place as Palestine—only Southern Syria.

In 1948, the United Nations undertook a second partition of the Jewish National Home to create a second Arab state therein. Had the Arabs accepted the offer, they would have had 83 percent of Mandate Palestine. Instead, they went to war to get 100 percent of it. The series of wars that the Arab states launched were for the destruction of Israel and for their own aggrandizement. There was no interest in a state for the Palestine-Arabs.

The failure of the concerted Arab attack on Israel in the Six-Day-War of 1967, led to a revision in Arab rhetoric. The fight against Israel would continue, but it would win more sympathy if it were fought in the cause of "Falastin." This name is an Arabic mispronunciation of the Greco-Roman Palastina. The would-be-nation that claims to have held this land since the dawn of history has no name of its own. The ploy was so successful, that soon most of the world's governments, media, and academics adopted and disseminated with precipitate enthusiasm the fabrication of a Palestine unjustly stolen and unlawfully occupied by the Jews.

It is not unjust that the Arab world should have to make do with 22 states instead of 23. It is not unjust that there should be only one Arab state in Mandate Palestine instead of two. The injustice would be to deprive Israel of the heartland of its historic homeland, an erstwhile wilderness that it toiled to rebuild and restore.

4. It Will Satisfy the Demands of the Palestine-Arabs, Who Will Give Up Terrorism and War and Settle Down to Building a Society

On the contrary   The charters of Fatah, Hamas and Hezbollah define their goal as the destruction of Israel and they cling to that goal even when they fight each other for control of the areas that Israel gives up.

Hamas does not disguise its bloody intentions. Fatah's Mahmoud Abbas/ Abu Mazen, chairman of the PA, speaks literally in two tongues: In English he professes a willingness to recognize Israel and co-exist with it; in Arabic he says the opposite. He is a lifelong terrorist, former second-in-command to Yasser Arafat, but if he says the right word in at least one language, Western policymakers can embrace him without violating their own rule of not dealing with terrorists, and demand that Israel jeopardize its own most vital interests to strengthen him in the interests of the Peace Process.

A plurality of the Palestine-Arab population has demonstrated through both election polls and opinion polls that it prefers the Hamas line, approves of suicide bombings and murder of Israelis, and believes that a prospective State of Palestine should keep up such attacks until Israel disappears.

Where the Palestine Authority is in power, maps show Palestine as an all-Arab entity with Israel obliterated. In the year 2006 it is declared that the Israeli Occupation has been going on for 58 years—dating it back to Israel's Declaration of Independence in 1948, not the loss of territory in 1967. In schools and summer camps, children are taught to aspire to martyrdom by killing Jews. None of this suggests that Palestine-Arabs plan ever to co-exist with Israel on any terms.

The PLO (Palestine Liberation Organization) in 1974 formally adopted a plan to be carried out in two stages: (1) Take whatever territory Israel can be persuaded or forced to yield. (2) Use that territory as a base for the future war to take all of Israel. Stage 1 was achieved with the Oslo Accords and the empowerment of the PA. Yet one of its top ministers and spokesmen, Faisal al-Husseini, defined the forthcoming Stage 2 as: "Whatever we get now, cannot make us forget this supreme truth. If we agree to declare our state over . . . the West Bank and Gaza, our ultimate goal is the liberation of all historic Palestine from the River [Jordan] to the Sea [Mediterranean]."

This purpose and intent has never been changed.

5. It Will Bring Peace and Stability to the Middle East

On the contrary   It will establish a sovereign national base for violent jihad. This can be deduced from the evidence of experience.

Every area from which Israel withdrew its administration and security patrols is now a base for terrorism and/or preparation for military attack: In Ramallah and other PA enclaves, bombings are planned and perpetrators dispatched to their targets. In the border zone of Lebanon, the Iranian-sponsored Hezbollah installed missile bases and launchers, whence they have so far fired some 4,000 deadly Katyusha missiles into Israel and brought devastation to Lebanon. In Gaza, Fatah and Hamas steadily shoot Kassam rockets into Israeli towns. When Israel relinquishes control, it opens the way for massive imports of weapons and explosives, and infiltration by Al-Qaeda. These are consequences of withdrawal, and no measures to prevent or counter them have any effect.

There is no reason to suppose that a State of Palestine will deviate from this pattern. It will be a base for terror and jihad, in a location where it can imperil both Israel and Jordan. Secretary of State Condoleeza Rice has said, "There can be no peace without a Palestinian state." That forecast can be amended by cutting a mere three letters: "There can be no peace with(out) a Palestinian state."

6. A State of Palestine Will Be Demilitarized and Not a Danger to Israel

On the contrary   A State of Palestine cannot be kept demilitarized. If it signs an agreement or treaty to that effect it will be worthless because promises to infidels are not binding. Arafat compared the Oslo Accords to a treaty Muhammad made with an Arabian tribe that he then attacked and annihilated.

The PA was bound by signed agreement to have only a police force of no more than 8,000 with no heavy weapons. It acquired a military force of at least 50,000 with heavy weapons. Nothing was done about this violation because neither Israel nor any other nation demands that Arabs adhere to agreements. It is prudent to anticipate that a State of Palestine will not be subject to any effective restrictions on its doings. As in Gaza and the Lebanese border zone there will be a massive influx of heavy weapons and trained fighters.

The strategic danger to Israel of a Palestine-Arab state was analyzed by the U.S. Joint Chiefs of Staff, who reported that Israel must at the very least keep control of the highlands of Judean Hills and the Jordan valley. Without them, Israel at its narrowest point is only nine miles wide. "Palestine" holding the adjacent highlands can bombard much of Israel with missiles and rockets and shoot down civilian aircraft. Foreign troops can sweep in across the Jordan Valley without hindrance.

An administration that forces Israel out of these vitally strategic points rejects the counsel of its own highest-ranking military men. As though this were not ill-advised enough, it also demands that a State of Palestine must have "contiguity." That is: Judea-Samaria and Gaza must be linked together. It is geographically impossible to satisfy this demand without splitting Israel in half.

To render Israel so vulnerable is an invitation to massive military attack upon it.

7. If a State of Palestine Commits Aggression Against Israel, Then Israel Can Take Back the Land it Gave Away

On the contrary   The supporters of the Oslo Accords said. "If they [the PLO] do not keep their commitment to peace, we will just take the land back." No commitment was kept, and nothing was taken back.

Regaining the forfeited land would require a military campaign, difficult, perhaps long, and costly in casualties. It would be carried out against a background chorus of denunciations and demands to cease and desist. In the past, when the Israel Defense Force has gone into PA-held areas even briefly, to close down terrorist bases and weapons factories and depots, there were international howls for Israel to "get out of Palestinian territory immediately." Any such defensive move against a State of Palestine would be branded as aggression against a sovereign state, perhaps even with a threat of sanctions against Israel and/or intervention by foreign troops.

In the event of a full-scale military attack on Israel, it might be granted some right of self-defense, but even that would be limited. If Palestine were on the verge of crumbling, the United Nations would likely save it with an imposed ceasefire. If Israel were to regain any or all of its forfeited land, there would be international pressure for it to yield the land to the defeated aggressor, just as there has been with territories won in the Six-Day War.

8. If Israel Does Not Cut Away from Regions With Large Arab Populations, the Arabs Will Soon Become a Majority and Rule Over the Jews

On the contrary   This argument, sometimes dubbed "The Demographic Time-Bomb," rests on erroneous statistics and unsound projections.

The calculations are based on a census by the Palestine Authority. An examination of the statistics and the methods of compiling them found that the number of Arabs was over-estimated by one million or more. Estimates of population growth depend on an inflated anticipated Arab birthrate.

More precise calculations yield both a smaller Arab population and an ongoing drop in the Arab birthrate. Furthermore, there is little if any immigration to PA areas, and indeed a high percentage of the residents say they would like to emigrate if they had the means. In Israel, in contrast, the birthrate is steady or rising, and there is ongoing immigration.

9. It Will Secure the Human Rights of the Palestinian Arabs and Solve the Arab Refugee Problem

On the contrary   The PA regime in areas of Judea-Samaria and with full sway in Gaza has nothing to its credit in human rights.

Wherever Fatah and/or Hamas rules, there are no human or civil rights or rule of law. Those under their rule are subject to oppression, extortion, and brutality. Those accused of offenses have no right of fair trial, and at times are lynched without trial. Christians are especially vulnerable to harassment and abuse, and desecration of their churches. Their communities, which long pre-date the Muslim incursion into the region, are shrinking and dwindling away. There would not be a live Jew anywhere in a State of Palestine.

To the Arab refugees, whose plight the United Nations has deliberately perpetuated for almost 60 years, a State of Palestine would bring no relief. The chieftains of Fatah and Hamas, along with the rulers of Saudi Arabia and other Arab states, insist on a Right of Return. That is: Israel itself must take in the massive population of the United Nations camps for Palestine refugees and their descendants, who are taught and trained to loathe it and dedicate them-selves to destroying it. This impossible demand is designed to evade solving a problem deliberately perpetuated for propaganda.

10. It Will Encourage Civic and Economic Development, Raise the Standard of Living and Bring Contentment to the People

On the contrary   In areas under PA control, the standard of living drops and hardship increases.

When the disputed territories were entirely under Israeli administration, there was economic growth, a rise in the standard of living, improved health care, and the establishment of the first universities. Since administration was turned over the PA, there has been a slide backwards. Economic development is strangled by graft and corruption, and revenues are squandered. The devel-opment of an economy and a civic infrastructure are not a priority.

The United States and the European Union have subsidized the PA so lav-ishly that the Palestine-Arabs have received per capita more donations than any other group in the world. The bulk of the money melted away, ended up in private foreign bank accounts, or was spent on buying weapons and train-ing terrorists. Some individuals have gotten very rich, but little benefit has seeped down to the working-class or the unemployed-class.

In civil society, schools are for the indoctrination of martyrs-to-be; radio and television stations are for propaganda, recruitment of terrorists, and curses upon Israel and America; streets are for gang-warfare. There is water and electricity only because Israel still provides it.

As the standard of living sinks, international agencies cry "Humanitarian Crisis!" and blame it on Israel—especially in Gaza, where there has been no Israeli presence or control since August 2005.

11. Israel Must Comply With United Nations Resolutions

On the contrary The United Nations is a world epicenter of corruption engaged in active hostility against Israel. It has made itself a foe and should be treated as such.

Israel has never been granted the rights and protections due to a member state. Since 1948, Arab states that are U.N. members have perpetrated every form of aggression against Israel, without interference or even rebuke. There is a built-in anti-Israel majority that churns out anti-Israel resolutions, while no resolution with even a shade of balance can pass.

The Secretariat that is the administrative branch of the United Nations celebrates an annual Day of Solidarity with the Palestinian People, and the Secretary-General poses in front of a map of Palestine from which Israel has been obliterated. Peacekeeping troops aid and abet Arab terrorists in the kidnapping and murder of Israelis. Demands for Israeli compliance focus on the obsolete Security Council Resolution 242, passed in the wake of the Six Day War of 1967. The Council did nothing to hinder the Arab states in their openly announced intent of launching a war to exterminate Israel. When they had lost the war and along with it control of Judea-Samaria [West Bank], East Jerusalem, Gaza, the Sinai Peninsula, and the Golan Heights, the Council presumed to dictate the terms of a future peace settlement: Israel should withdraw from unspecified "territories" to "agreed and secure borders." The United States and Great Britain, who wrote the resolution, gave official and unequivocal assurances that it did not mean Israel's return to the pre-war frontiers, which were merely the ceasefire lines of the War of Independence of 1948–1949. This Resolution is widely misquoted in a falsified version that requires Israel's full and unconditional withdrawal from all of the land the Arabs lost in 1967, and the establishment of a Palestinian state. This is not true.

The United States and Great Britain, the authors of Resolution 242, have since reneged on the words of their own past governments and call for Israel's full or near-full surrender of the disputed territories to a Palestine-Arab state-to-be. This flip-flop demonstrates that if Israel makes any sacrifice in deference to the United Nations there will be more demands for more severe sacrifices.

12. It Will Win the Respect of World Opinion for Israel

On the contrary Honest and informed opinion does not need to be bought. Dishonest and ignorant opinion is not worth buying.

Some holders and makers of opinion are fair-minded or even friendly toward Israel. Their views can include reasonable disagreements and criticisms made without malice.

Some are automatically hostile to Israel because of Judeophobia, or ideology, or financial interests in the Arab world, or a desire to curry favor with Israel's foes, or simply because it is a fad. They do not make their judgments according to anything Israel does or does not do, and Israel cannot affect them.

Some judge only by what they hear from teachers—many of whom fit into the "automatically hostile" category—and the popular news media, whose practitioners have slipped from slanting news against Israel to complicity in lies and hoaxes.

Israel can and should do more to bring accurate facts and explanations to public attention. It should never compromise its own best interests and jeopardize its own security to oblige distant opinion-makers.

Conclusion

Giving up Judea-Samaria would cut the Jewish People off from the heart of the land to which they have been bound for almost 4,000 years. Arabs would destroy ancient Jewish sites and relics, as they have already done in Jerusalem. There would be no chance for scholars and archeologists to make new discoveries, and much knowledge of the past would be lost. And all this loss would be on behalf of an ill-advised political experiment.

Even so, it may be said "It is useless to oppose a State of Palestine—it is inevitable." Such passive submission is moral indolence, a limp acceptance of a plan regardless of the harm it is bound to do.

For 2000 years, the Jewish people did not despair of restoration to their land. When the restoration has at last come, those who toss it away betray both their ancestors and their descendants.

Rosemary E. Shinko  **NO**

Why a Palestinian State

A Two State Solution

On July 8, 1937, the Palestine Royal Commission (Peel Commission) offered its recommendations to the British government regarding the disposition of the Palestinian question. The commission expressed serious reservations about the possibility of reconciliation between Arabs and Jews and thus concluded; "only the 'surgical operation of partition' offers a chance of ultimate peace. The commission proposed the establishment of two separate states—a sovereign Arab State and a sovereign Jewish State.

President, Bill Clinton reiterated these same sentiments in a speech he delivered on January 7, 2001. "I think there can be no genuine resolution to the conflict without a sovereign, viable, Palestinian state that accommodates Israel's security requirements and the demographic realities." Any settlement, he continued, must ultimately be "based on sovereign homelands, security, peace and dignity for both Israelis and Palestinians." In 2002 the UN Security Council adopted a US supported resolution supporting the establishment of an independent Palestinian state. The current Bush administration has also expressed support for statehood as part of its roadmap for peace in the Middle East.

Why is it then that Patricia Berlyn argues that the creation of a 23rd Arab state would be unwise, unjust and undesirable? Her arguments revolve around the following five main assertions: (1) there is no such thing as a 'Palestinian territory' (2) nor do the Arabs constitute a 'Palestinian people,' (3) if such a state were established the Arabs would be unable to fulfill the rights and duties associated with statehood, (4) it would not be in the self-interest of the State of Israel because its [the Palestinian state's] aim would be Israel's demise, and finally it would betray the sacrifices of the past and the promises of the future of the Jewish people.

Berlyn's arguments follow an all too familiar pattern, one which seeks to denigrate the 'other,' in this case the Palestinian other, at the expense of constituting an Israeli identity that encircles itself with all of the admirable qualities, distances itself from any responsibility for the plight of the Palestinians, and claims the moral high ground of victimization at the hands of an illegitimate, infidel other. For instance she equates all Palestinians with former and current enemies of the United States; the Nazis Communists, Saddam Hussein and al-Qaeda. Jewish settlements in the late 19th century are characterized as making profitable and industrious use of land that was otherwise wasted, uncultivated, and barren. These characterizations bear a striking resemblance to [English philosopher John] Locke's arguments in his fifth chapter on property in the *Second Treatise of Government* [1689], which were a carefully crafted argument intended to justify European colonization and deny the consent of the wasteful, non-industrious indigenous inhabitants whose land was taken from them.

What is a 'state' and why does the possibility of the creation of a Palestinian state; in particular, provoke such a strong, emotional response from Berlyn? What does the term 'state' signify? According to [German philosopher Georg Wilhelm Friedrich Hegel [1770–1831], "only those peoples that form states can come to our notice" because it is the state that provides the foundation for "national life, art, law, morality, religion, [and] science." The political identity of most peoples is inextricably bound up with the notion of statehood. According to an international relations text, *International Politics on the World Stage*, written by John Rourke and Mark Boyer, "States are territorially defined political units that exercise ultimate internal authority and that recognize no legitimate external authority over them." The political implications of legitimacy that would flow from the establishment and recognition of a Palestinian state are extremely significant in this particular instance.

As scholar Malcom Shaw notes in his 1999 Cambridge University Press book *International Law*, a state is recognized as having a 'legal personality,' which includes the capacity to possess and exercise certain rights and to perform specific duties. These rights and duties encompass the attributes of independence, legal equality, and peaceful coexistence. Thus a Palestinian State would claim the right to exercise jurisdiction over its population and territory, as well as, the right to self-defense. Such a state would also have a concomitant duty not to intervene in the internal affairs of another state and a duty to respect the territorial integrity and sovereignty of other states.

The Palestinians have been denied anything that has even remotely resembles an independent sovereign existence that is not determined by and ultimately reliant upon Israeli dictates. Israeli settlements have served to cut the West Bank in half, isolating East Jerusalem, and carving the economic heart out of the Palestinian territories, according to Jeff Halper in the *Catholic New Times* on April 24, 2005. The patchwork of Palestinian designated areas currently resembles apartheid inspired Bantustans, which serve to further isolate and impoverish their residents. [Note: Bantustan was one of the segregated, theoretically autonomous enclaves in South Africa in which white South Africans once forced many of the country's blacks (who speak Bantu and other languages) to live.]

Legitimacy and Equality

The establishment and recognition of a Palestinian state would confirm the political legitimacy and legal equality of the Palestinian people. Historically they have been denied recognition as a people, and the legitimacy of their claims to the territory of Palestine has been dismissed. Berlyn's arguments are designed to foster the sense of Palestinian illegitimacy with her intimations that the Arabs have 'no roots and no history' in Palestine and that there is 'no such thing as a Palestinian territory'. To round out her argument, she employs the [traditional Hebrew] term 'Judea-Samaria' when referring to the territory that would constitute a Palestinian State in order to historically delegitmate and rupture Palestinian connections to their homeland, while attempting to privilege the historical primacy and unbroken continuity of Israeli claims. Only a state troubled by its own legitimacy would find it necessary to work so hard to represent their historical lineage in the form of an unbroken line from the dim mists of the past to the clarity of the present.

All states are man-made creations; all states are reflective of the political, legal, social, and economic conditions which led to their rise. All states, even the State of Israel, are current and ongoing political creations of contemporary men and women. But more importantly, she attempts to cover over the fact that states are not divinely sanctioned nor guaranteed by claims to lineage alone, but instead created out of hard fought political struggles, compromises, and bargains. Berlyn's arguments, which are framed to effect the dismissal of a Palestinian presence and history, are an extension of earlier Zionist attempts to portray Palestine as a 'land without people for a people without land'. Such a perception promotes the view that the territory of Palestine was 'empty' and that its only inhabitants were uncivilized, backward nomads.

Demographic realities, however, prove otherwise. "There were always real, live Palestinians there; there were census figures, land-holding records, newspaper and radio accounts, eyewitness reports and the sheer physical traces of Arab life in Palestine before and after 1948," according to Edward W. Said, and Christopher Hitchens in their 1988 study, *Blaming the Victims, Spurious Scholarship and the Palestinian Question*. In 1947 when the United Nations Committee on Palestine (UNSCOP) made its recommendation that Palestine be portioned into two separate states, there were 1.2 million Arabs as compared to 570,000 Jews living in the territory. Clearly the Arabs formed the majority of the population in Palestine. On what basis then can it be maintained that the Palestinians had no history, had no roots, and had no presence in Palestine? "The fact is that [when] the people of Israel . . . came home, the land was not all vacant," President Clinton commented in 2001. Statehood confirms presence, establishes legitimacy, confers recognition, and provides a focal point for a peoples' identity.

Recognition and Self-Determination

David Shipler in an October 15, 2000 article in the *New York Times* commented astutely that "Recognizing the authenticity of the other in that land comes hard in the midst of the conflict. Yet the conflict cannot end without that recognition." Ultimately legitimacy and recognition are the keys to the end of conflict and to the establishment of peace in the Middle East. Peace cannot occur without the recognition of the Palestinian people's right to self-determination and without their consent to a government that exercises authority within a territorial sovereign entity of their own. "The six wars with the Arabs created a situation in which 3 million Jews came to control territories that contained nearly 2 million Arabs," scholar John G. Stoessinger observed in his 2001 book, *Why Nations Go to War*. The United Nations General Assembly also concluded that without "full respect for and the realization of these inalienable rights of the Palestinian people," namely the right to self-determination and the right to national independence and sovereignty, there would be no resolution of the question of Palestine.

Statehood implies the capacity to maintain certain rights and the performance of specific duties. Berlyn maintains that even if the Palestinians were granted their own state they would not live up to the duties of a state because a Palestinian State would be committed to the destruction of Israel and would merely serve as a base for further acts of terror. In her estimation a Palestinian State would not respect the territorial integrity and sovereignty of the State of Israel. Furthermore, she even questions the ability of such a state to be able to fulfill the requirements of statehood, including civic and economic development and the promotion of human rights. Fundamentally such a negative assessment rests on conjecture and an underlying sense of distrust born of conflicting claims of legitimacy to the same parcel of land.

No one can claim to profess the future, and not even Berlyn can with any certainty predict the actions of a State of Palestine, much less characterize an entire people as terrorists. One thing does however appear to be foreseeable, and that is the continued agitation of the Palestinians for recognition, self-determination and legitimacy. As Professor Stoessinger concluded in *Why Nations Go to War*, "The shock inflicted on the Arab consciousness by the establishment of Israel and the resulting homelessness of a million native Palestinians grew more, rather than less, acute as Arab nationalism gathered momentum." The Arabs perceive Israel as the ever-expanding and ever-growing threat to their survival, thus a state is the only way to insure their continued existence as a people. Declaring that a Palestinian State would be unable to fulfill the requirements of statehood is merely a thinly veiled ethno-centric critique, which smacks of patronization and cultural superiority. What precisely do the Palestinians lack that would deem them ill suited to exercise self-rule and incapable of founding a government that rests on consent which would secure their rights to life, liberty and property? The Lockean assertion that the only legitimate form of government is that which rests on consent is as true for the Jews as the Arabs of Palestine.

Equivalence and Justice

Israel feels exposed and vulnerable as a direct result of the Palestinians unrelenting quest for legitimacy and recognition. Israel's economic strength and military power dwarfs that of the Palestinians, yet despite all of the material aspects of power, the Israeli quest for security remains more elusive than ever. Berlyn's arguments reiterate the mantra that Israel will never be secure unless the Palestinians are erased via absorption into neighboring Arab states. The very existence of the Palestinians serves as a constant reminder of the ongoing exclusionary colonization practices carried out in furtherance of Israel's quest for ethnic and religious homogeneity. Thus a case can be made that Israel ultimately wishes to expunge the Palestinians and obliterate any traces of their existence.

However, Israel's self-interest may ultimately rest with the establishment of a separate Palestinian state in order to diffuse the longstanding animosities and hatreds that have arisen between the two peoples. Walid Khalidi, in a 1978 article in *Foreign Affairs*, forcefully argued that a sovereign Palestinian state would end their "anonymous ghost-like existence as a non-people" because their own state could serve as "a point of reference, a national anchorage, a center of hope and achievement." We have seen where the denial of legitimacy has taken us, and it has not nurtured the seeds of peace. In a spasm of frustration in January 2006 the Palestinians elected a Hamas-dominated leadership to the Palestinian Legislative Council. In a setting in which all of the really significant political decisions are made by Israel, moderation has no chance to prevail when desperation is the defining attribute of life itself within the occupied territories. Peace can only be established in the wake of the recognition of legitimacy and equality between the two peoples.

Berlyn offers us 12 justifications why a Palestinian state is a bad idea; however, the Palestinian case rests on only one singular point; that justice demands equivalence. In order to secure the national character and the cultural identity of the Israelis, the national character and the cultural identity of the Palestinian Arabs must likewise be secured. This can only occur with the establishment of a separate, sovereign Palestinian State.

POSTSCRIPT

Would It Be an Error to Establish a Palestinian State?

The Middle East's torment is one of the most intractable problems facing the world. In addition to the ancient territorial claims of Jews and Palestinian Arabs, complexities include long-standing rivalries among various religious and ethnic groups and countries in the region. To learn more about the history of the current conflict, consult Bernard Wasserstein, *Israelis and Palestinians: Why Do They Fight? Can They Stop?* (Yale University Press, 2004).

Complicating matters for Israel is the fact that the country is divided between relatively secular Jews, who tend to be moderate in their attitudes toward the Palestinians, and Orthodox Jews, who regard the areas in dispute as land given by God to the Jewish nation and who regard giving up the West Bank and, especially, any part of Jerusalem as sacrilege. Furthermore, there are some 200,000 Israelis living in the West Bank, and removing them would be traumatic for Israel. The issue is also a matter of grave security concern. The Jews have suffered mightily throughout history; repeated Arab terrorism represents the latest of their travails. It is arguable that the Jews can be secure only in their own country and that the West Bank (which cuts Israel almost in two) is crucial to Israeli security. If an independent Palestine centered in the West Bank is created, Israel will face a defense nightmare, especially if new hostilities with the Palestinians occur. Additional material on a prospective Palestinian state is available in David Gompert, *Building a Successful Palestinian State* (Rand, 2004).

Thus, for the Israelis the "land for peace" choice is a difficult one. Some Israelis are unwilling to cede any of what they consider the land of ancient Israel. Other Israelis would be willing to swap land for peace, but they doubt that the Palestinians would be assuaged. Still other Israelis think that the risk is worth the potential prize: peace.

Palestinians do not march in political lockstep any more than do Israelis. As noted in the Introduction, the Palestinians chose a moderate, Mahmoud Abbas, as their president in 2005 but then in the parliamentary elections gave Hamas enough votes to make one of its leaders, Ismail Haniya, prime minister. Further complicating matters, Palestinian-Israeli relations do not exist in a vacuum, and actions like the Hamas kidnapping of two Israeli soldiers and launch of hundreds of missiles into Israel from Lebanon and the devastating Israeli response on Lebanon poisoned the atmosphere in the Middle East, at least for now. Symbolic of the turmoil in the region, the Palestinian National Authority used to have a Web site, but it no longer operates. However, one source of the viewpoint of Palestinians is the Palestine Media Center at http://www.palestine-pmc.com/. The government of Israel's home page is at http://www.gov.il/firstgov/english. A somewhat pessimistic view of the immediate future is in Casimir A. Yost, "Hamas, Israel, and the Prospects for Peace," *Georgetown Journal of International Affairs* (Fall 2006).

ISSUE 7

Should All Foreign Troops Soon Leave Iraq?

YES: William E. Odom, from "Cut and Run? You Bet," *Foreign Policy* (May/June 2006)

NO: Richard B. Cheney, from "Remarks on the War on Terror," Speech Delivered at the American Enterprise Institute (November 21, 2005)

ISSUE SUMMARY

YES: William E. Odom, senior fellow at the Hudson Institute in New York City; retired lieutenant general, U.S. Army; and former director of the National Security Agency, argues that the United States cannot be successful in Iraq and that withdrawing quickly will end or ameliorate all the negative effects of having U.S. troops in the country.

NO: Richard B. Cheney, vice president of the United States, tells an audience that in light of the commitments our country has made, and given the stated intentions of the enemy, those who advocate a sudden withdrawal from Iraq are advocating a course that will bring disaster.

In August 1990 after Iraq overran Kuwait, President George H. W. Bush sent U.S. troops to protect Saudi Arabia. Later, working through the United Nations, the United States built a coalition that sponsored a Security Council resolution demanding that Iraq soon withdraw from Kuwait and, if Iraq refused, authorizing UN members to use "all necessary means" to expel Iraq from Kuwait. The U.S.-led attack in January 1991 quickly defeated Iraqi forces. There were calls for President Bush to continue on to Baghdad and to overthrow Iraqi president and dictator Saddam Hussein, but Bush rejected that option. In the aftermath, huge stocks of Iraqi chemical weapons were uncovered. Security Council Resolution 687 (1991) spelled out the terms of peace for Iraq. Among these were that Iraq was barred from possessing, producing, or seeking to acquire any weapons of mass destruction (WMDs) and that UN arms inspectors would have unhindered access anywhere in the country to ensure that Iraq was complying. During the following dozen years, a cat-and-mouse game ensued. Iraq claimed to be complying with Resolution 687, but Baghdad often blocked or delayed UN inspections, and in 1998 it even expelled the inspectors. In response, economic sanctions continued, and there were periodic attacks by U.S. warplanes and cruise missiles under President Bill Clinton. The U.S. attitude hardened even more once George W. Bush became president, especially after the terrorist attacks of September 11, 2001. In Iraq, UN inspectors found no hard evidence of Iraqi WMDs, but they also reported repeated barriers to their inspections. In this tense atmosphere, the U.S. Congress authorized (October 2002) the use of U.S. force against Iraq if necessary. In November, Washington began to seek a Security Council resolution authorizing force if Iraq continued to impede inspections, but U.S. diplomacy was blocked by French, Russian, and Chinese veto power and could not even get majority Council support. Frustrated and claiming that intelligence reports indicated that Iraq was seeking to acquire nuclear weapons and supporting terrorism, President Bush in March 2003 "issued an ultimatum to Iraq demanding that Saddam Hussein and his sons leave the country and that Iraqi forces surrender their arms." Iraq refused, and another U.S.-led invasion ensued. Iraq's forces were soon vanquished, and Saddam Hussein was later captured. Securing the peace proved much more difficult. No weapons of mass destruction were ever found. Terrorist-style operations began against occupying U.S. and other coalition troops, civilians, and any-one, including Iraqis, who cooperated with them. Soon coalition casualties exceeded the number killed and wounded during invasion. Americans were also frustrated by the cost of the war, which by late 2006 was approaching $300 billion. Also disheartening to many Americans was the fact that trying to bring Iraqis together proved maddening. The country had been ruled by Sunni Moslems led by Saddam Hussein, who dominate in the central and western provinces. Shiite Muslims are a majority in the southern and eastern part of the country, and non-Arab Kurds (also Muslims) are a majority in the North. Under U.S. pressure a unity government was formed through elections, but its ability to control Iraq remained problematic at best. Officials in Washington and Baghdad both pointed to many successes in the country, including the fact that violence was rare in many provinces. However, in some places, especially near Baghdad, violence continued to mount into 2006 and by mid year over 2,300 U.S. and coalition troops had been killed in combat and another 20,000 wounded. Perhaps 40,000 Iraqi civilians had also died, and about 1,000 a month were being added to that toll in the first half of 2006.

These grim statistics set the stage for the debate that follows. In the first reading, Vice President Cheney takes the position that the United States must stay the course in Iraq, keeping troops there until a stable and united Iraq is able to take over its own security. Former lieutenant general and National Security Agency director William Odom replies that U.S. troops will never be able to achieve the goals that Cheney sets out and may even be counter-productive to them. Therefore, Odom advocates a speedy withdrawal.

YES

William E. Odom

Cut and Run? You Bet

Withdraw immediately or stay the present course? That is the key question about the war in Iraq today. American public opinion is now decidedly against the war. From liberal New England, where citizens pass town-hall resolutions calling for withdrawal, to the conservative South and West, where more than half of "red state" [a state which is apt to elect Republicans] citizens oppose the war, Americans want out. That sentiment is understandable.

The prewar dream of a liberal Iraqi democracy friendly to the United States is no longer credible. No Iraqi leader with enough power and legitimacy to control the country will be pro-American. Still, U.S. President George W. Bush says the United States must stay the course. Why? Let's consider his administration's most popular arguments for not leaving Iraq.

If we leave, there will be a civil war   In reality, a civil war in Iraq began just weeks after U.S. forces toppled Saddam. Any close observer could see that then; today, only the blind deny it. Even President Bush, who is normally impervious to uncomfortable facts, recently admitted that Iraq has peered into the abyss of civil war. He ought to look a little closer. Iraqis are fighting Iraqis. Insurgents have killed far more Iraqis than Americans. That's civil war.

Withdrawal will encourage the terrorists   True, but that is the price we are doomed to pay. Our continued occupation of Iraq also encourages the killers—precisely because our invasion made Iraq safe for them. Our occupation also left the surviving Baathists [members of Saddam Hussein's political party] with one choice: Surrender, or ally with al Qaeda. They chose the latter. Staying the course will not change this fact. Pulling out will most likely result in Sunni groups' turning against al Qaeda and its sympathizers, driving them out of Iraq entirely.

Before U.S. forces stand down, Iraqi security forces must stand up   The problem in Iraq is not military competency; it is political consolidation. Iraq has a large officer corps with plenty of combat experience from the Iran-Iraq war. Moktada al-Sadr's Shiite militia fights well today without U.S. advisors, as do Kurdish pesh merga units. The problem is loyalty. To whom can officers and

From *Foreign Policy*, May/June 2006. Copyright © 2006 by the Carnegie Endowment for International Peace. Reprinted with permission. www.foreignpolicy.com.

troops afford to give their loyalty? The political camps in Iraq are still shifting. So every Iraqi soldier and officer today risks choosing the wrong side. As a result, most choose to retain as much latitude as possible to switch allegiances. All the U.S. military trainers in the world cannot remove that reality. But political consolidation will. It should by now be clear that political power can only be established via Iraqi guns and civil war, not through elections or U.S. colonialism by ventriloquism.

Setting a withdrawal deadline will damage the morale of U.S. troops   Hiding behind the argument of troop morale shows no willingness to accept the responsibilities of command. The truth is, most wars would stop early if soldiers had the choice of whether or not to continue. This is certainly true in Iraq, where a withdrawal is likely to raise morale among U.S. forces. A recent Zogby poll suggests that most U.S. troops would welcome an early withdrawal deadline. But the strategic question of how to extract the United States from the Iraq disaster is not a matter to be decided by soldiers. Carl von Clausewitz [a 19th century German military thinker] spoke of two kinds of courage: first, bravery in the face of mortal danger; second, the willingness to accept personal responsibility for command decisions. The former is expected of the troops. The latter must be demanded of high-level commanders, including the president.

Withdrawal would undermine U.S. credibility in the world   Were the United States a middling power, this case might hold some water. But for the world's only superpower, it's patently phony. A rapid reversal of our present course in Iraq would improve U.S. credibility around the world. The same argument was made against withdrawal from Vietnam. It was proved wrong then and it would be proved wrong today. Since Sept. 11, 2001, the world's opinion of the United States has plummeted, with the largest short-term drop in American history. The United States now garners as much international esteem as Russia. Withdrawing and admitting our mistake would reverse this trend. Very few countries have that kind of corrective capacity. I served as a military attaché in the U.S. Embassy in Moscow during Richard Nixon's Watergate crisis. When Nixon resigned, several Soviet officials who had previously expressed disdain for the United States told me they were astonished. One diplomat said, "Only your country is powerful enough to do this. It would destroy my country."

Two facts, however painful, must be recognized, or we will remain perilously confused in Iraq. First, invading Iraq was not in the interests of the United States. It was in the interests of Iran and al Qaeda. For Iran, it avenged a grudge against Saddam for his invasion of the country in 1980. For al Qaeda, it made it easier to kill Americans. Second, the war has paralyzed the United States in the world diplomatically and strategically. Although relations with Europe show signs of marginal improvement, the trans-Atlantic alliance still may not survive the war. Only with a rapid withdrawal from Iraq will Washington regain diplomatic and military mobility. Tied down like Gulliver in the sands of Mesopotamia [the ancient name for the region between the

Tigris and Euphrates Rivers in what is now Iraq], we simply cannot attract the diplomatic and military cooperation necessary to win the real battle against terror. Getting out of Iraq is the precondition for any improvement.

In fact, getting out now may be our only chance to set things right in Iraq. For starters, if we withdraw, European politicians would be more likely to cooperate with us in a strategy for stabilizing the greater Middle East. Following a withdrawal, all the countries bordering Iraq would likely respond favorably to an offer to help stabilize the situation. The most important of these would be Iran. It dislikes al Qaeda as much as we do. It wants regional stability as much as we do. It wants to produce more oil and gas and sell it. If its leaders really want nuclear weapons, we cannot stop them. But we can engage them.

None of these prospects is possible unless we stop moving deeper into the "big sandy" of Iraq. America must withdraw now.

Remarks on the War on Terror

My remarks today concern national security, in particular the war on terror and the Iraq front in that war. Several days ago, I commented briefly on some recent statements that have been made by some members of Congress about Iraq. Within hours of my speech, a report went out on the wires under the headline, "Cheney says war critics 'dishonest,' 'reprehensible.'"

One thing I've learned in the last five years is that when you're Vice President, you're lucky if your speeches get any attention at all. But I do have a quarrel with that headline, and it's important to make this point at the outset. I do not believe it is wrong to criticize the war on terror or any aspect thereof. Disagreement, argument, and debate are the essence of democracy, and none of us should want it any other way. For my part, I've spent a career in public service, run for office eight times—six statewide offices and twice nationally. I served in the House of Representatives for better than a decade, most of that time as a member of the leadership of the minority party. To me, energetic debate on issues facing our country is more than just a sign of a healthy political system—it's also something I enjoy. It's one of the reasons I've stayed in this business. And I believe the feeling is probably the same for most of us in public life.

For those of us who don't mind debating, there's plenty to keep us busy these days, and it's not likely to change any time soon. On the question of national security, feelings run especially strong, and there are deeply held differences of opinion on how best to protect the United States and our friends against the dangers of our time. Recently my friend and former colleague [Representative] Jack Murtha [D-PA] called for a complete withdrawal of American forces now serving in Iraq, with a drawdown to begin at once. I disagree with Jack and believe his proposal would not serve the best interests of this nation. But he's a good man, a Marine, a patriot—and he's taking a clear stand in an entirely legitimate discussion.

Nor is there any problem with debating whether the United States and our allies should have liberated Iraq in the first place. Here, as well, the differing views are very passionately and forcefully stated. But nobody is saying we should not be having this discussion, or that you cannot reexamine a decision made by the President and the Congress some years ago. To the contrary,

Speech delivered at the American Enterprise Institute by Richard B. Cheney (November 21, 2005).

I believe it is critical that we continue to remind ourselves why this nation took action, and why Iraq is the central front in the war on terror, and why we have a duty to persevere.

What is not legitimate—and what I will again say is dishonest and reprehensible—is the suggestion by some U.S. senators that the President of the United States or any member of his administration purposely misled the American people on pre-war intelligence.

Some of the most irresponsible comments have come from politicians who actually voted in favor of authorizing the use of force against Saddam Hussein. These are elected officials who had access to the intelligence materials. They are known to have a high opinion of their own analytical capabilities. And they were free to reach their own judgments based upon the evidence. They concluded, as the President and I had concluded, and as the previous administration had concluded, that Saddam Hussein was a threat. Available intelligence indicated that the dictator of Iraq had weapons of mass destruction, and this judgment was shared by the intelligence agencies of many other nations, according to the bipartisan Silberman-Robb Commission [The Commission on the Intelligence of the United States Regarding Weapons of Mass Destruction chaired by Laurence H. Silberman and Charles S. Robb]. All of us understood, as well, that for more than a decade, the U.N. Security Council had demanded that Saddam Hussein make a full accounting of his weapons programs. The burden of proof was entirely on the dictator of Iraq—not on the U.N. or the United States or anyone else. And he repeatedly refused to comply throughout the course of the decade.

Permit me to burden you with a bit more history: In August of 1998, the U.S. Congress passed a resolution urging President [Bill] Clinton take "appropriate action" to compel Saddam to come into compliance with his obligations to the Security Council. Not a single senator voted no. Two months later, in October of '98—again, without a single dissenting vote in the United States Senate—the Congress passed the Iraq Liberation Act. It explicitly adopted as American policy supporting efforts to remove Saddam Hussein's regime from power and promoting an Iraqi democracy in its place. And just two months after signing the Iraq Liberation law, President Clinton ordered that Iraq be bombed in an effort to destroy facilities that he believed were connected to Saddam's weapons of mass destruction programs.

By the time Congress voted to authorize force in late 2002, there was broad-based, bipartisan agreement that the time had come to enforce the legitimate demands of the international community. And our thinking was informed by what had happened to our country on the morning of September 11th, 2001. As the prime target of terrorists who have shown an ability to hit America and who wish to do so in spectacular fashion, we have a responsibility to do everything we can to keep terrible weapons out of the hands of these enemies. And we must hold to account regimes that could supply those weapons to terrorists in defiance of the civilized world. As the President has said, "Terrorists and terror states do not reveal . . . threats with fair notice, in formal declarations—and responding to such enemies only after they have struck first is not self-defense, it is suicide."

In a post-9/11 world, the President and Congress of the United States declined to trust the word of a dictator who had a history of weapons of mass destruction programs, who actually used weapons of mass destruction against innocent civilians in his own country, who tried to assassinate a former President of the United States, who was routinely shooting at allied pilots trying to enforce no fly zones, who had excluded weapons inspectors, who had defied the demands of the international community, whose regime had been designated an official state sponsor of terror, and who had committed mass murder. Those are the facts.

Although our coalition has not found WMD stockpiles in Iraq, I repeat that we never had the burden of proof; Saddam Hussein did. We operated on the best available intelligence, gathered over a period of years from within a totalitarian society ruled by fear and secret police. We also had the experience of the first Gulf War—when the intelligence community had seriously underestimated the extent and progress Saddam had made toward developing nuclear weapons.

Finally, according to the Duelfer report, Saddam Hussein wanted to preserve the capability to reconstitute his weapons of mass destruction when sanctions were lifted. And we now know that the sanctions regime had lost its effectiveness and been totally undermined by Saddam Hussein's successful effort to corrupt the Oil for Food program. [Note: the Duelfer report is the Comprehensive Report of the Special Adviser to the Director of Central Intelligence on Iraq's Weapons of Mass Destruction, submitted September 30, 2004 by Charles S. Duelfer.]

The flaws in the intelligence are plain enough in hindsight, but any suggestion that prewar information was distorted, hyped, or fabricated by the leader of the nation is utterly false. Senator John McCain [R-AZ] put it best: "It is a lie to say that the President lied to the American people."

American soldiers and Marines serving in Iraq go out every day into some of the most dangerous and unpredictable conditions. Meanwhile, back in the United States, a few politicians are suggesting these brave Americans were sent into battle for a deliberate falsehood. This is revisionism of the most corrupt and shameless variety. It has no place anywhere in American politics, much less in the United States Senate.

One might also argue that untruthful charges against the Commander-in-Chief have an insidious effect on the war effort itself. I'm unwilling to say that, only because I know the character of the United States Armed Forces—men and women who are fighting the war on terror in Iraq, Afghanistan, and many other fronts. They haven't wavered in the slightest, and their conduct should make all Americans proud. They are absolutely relentless in their duties, and they are carrying out their missions with all the skill and the honor we expect of them. I think of the ones who put on heavy gear and work 12-hour shifts in the desert heat. Every day they are striking the enemy—conducting raids, training up Iraqi forces, countering attacks, seizing weapons, and capturing killers. Americans appreciate our fellow citizens who go out on long deployments and endure the hardship of separation from home and family. We care about those who have returned with injuries, and who face the long, hard road of recovery. And our nation grieves for the men and women whose lives have ended in freedom's cause.

The people who serve in uniform, and their families, can be certain: that their cause is right and just and necessary, and we will stand behind them with pride and without wavering until the day of victory.

The men and women on duty in this war are serving the highest ideals of this nation—our belief in freedom and justice, equality, and the dignity of the individual. And they are serving the vital security interests of the United States. There is no denying that the work is difficult and there is much yet to do. Yet we can harbor no illusions about the nature of this enemy, or the ambitions it seeks to achieve.

In the war on terror we face a loose network of committed fanatics, found in many countries, operating under different commanders. Yet the branches of this network share the same basic ideology and the same dark vision for the world. The terrorists want to end American and Western influence in the Middle East. Their goal in that region is to gain control of the country, so they have a base from which to launch attacks and to wage war against governments that do not meet their demands. For a time, the terrorists had such a base in Afghanistan, under the backward and violent rule of the Taliban. And the terrorists hope to overturn Iraq's democratic government and return that country to the rule of tyrants. The terrorists believe that by controlling an entire country, they will be able to target and overthrow other governments in the region, and to establish a radical Islamic empire that encompasses a region from Spain, across North Africa, through the Middle East and South Asia, all the way to Indonesia. They have made clear, as well, their ultimate ambitions: to arm themselves with weapons of mass destruction, to destroy Israel, to intimidate all Western countries, and to cause mass death in the United States.

Some have suggested that by liberating Iraq from Saddam Hussein, we simply stirred up a hornet's nest. They overlook a fundamental fact: We were not in Iraq on September 11th, 2001—and the terrorists hit us anyway. The reality is that terrorists were at war with our country long before the liberation of Iraq, and long before the attacks of 9/11. And for many years, they were the ones on the offensive. They grew bolder in the belief that if they killed Americans, they could change American policy. In Beirut [Lebanon] in 1983, terrorists killed 241 of our service men. Thereafter, the United States withdrew from Beirut. In Mogadishu [Somalia] in 1993, terrorists killed 19 American soldiers. Thereafter, the U.S. withdrew its forces from Somalia. Over time, the terrorists concluded that they could strike America without paying a price, because they did, repeatedly: the bombing at the World Trade Center in 1993, the murders at the Saudi National Guard Training Center in Riyadh in 1995, the Khobar Towers in 1996, the simultaneous bombings of American embassies in Kenya and Tanzania in 1998, and, of course, the bombing of the USS Cole in 2000.

Believing they could strike us with impunity and that they could change U.S. policy, they attacked us on 9/11 here in the homeland, killing 3,000 people. Now they are making a stand in Iraq—testing our resolve, trying to intimidate the United States into abandoning our friends and permitting the overthrow of this new Middle Eastern democracy. Recently we obtained a message from the number-two man in al Qaeda, Mr. [Ayman al] Zawahiri [a top Al Qaeda leader], that he sent to his chief deputy in Iraq, the terrorist [Abu Musab al] Zarqawi. The letter makes clear that Iraq is part of a larger plan of imposing Islamic radicalism across the broader Middle East—making Iraq a terrorist haven and a staging ground for attacks against other nations. Zawahiri also expresses the view that America can be made to run again.

In light of the commitments our country has made, and given the stated intentions of the enemy, those who advocate a sudden withdrawal from Iraq should answer a few simple questions: Would the United States and other free nations be better off, or worse off, with Zarqawi, [Osama] bin Laden, and Zawahiri in control of Iraq? Would we be safer, or less safe, with Iraq ruled by men intent on the destruction of our country?

It is a dangerous illusion to suppose that another retreat by the civilized world would satisfy the appetite of the terrorists and get them to leave us alone. In fact such a retreat would convince the terrorists that free nations will change our policies, forsake our friends, abandon our interests whenever we are confronted with murder and blackmail. A precipitous withdrawal from Iraq would be a victory for the terrorists, an invitation to further violence against free nations, and a terrible blow to the future security of the United States of America.

So much self-defeating pessimism about Iraq comes at a time of real progress in that country. Coalition forces are making decisive strikes against terrorist strongholds, and more and more they are doing so with Iraqi forces at their side. There are more than 90 Iraqi army battalions fighting the terrorists, along with our forces. On the political side, every benchmark has been met successfully—starting with the turnover of sovereignty more than a year ago, the national elections last January, the drafting of the constitution and its ratification by voters just last month, and, a few weeks from now, the election of a new government under that new constitution.

The political leaders of Iraq are steady and courageous, and the citizens, police and soldiers of that country have proudly stepped forward as active participants and guardians in a new democracy—running for office, speaking out, voting and sacrificing for their country. Iraqi citizens are doing all of this despite threats from terrorists who offer no political agenda for Iraq's future, and wage a campaign of mass slaughter against the Iraqi people themselves— the vast majority of whom are fellow Arabs and fellow Muslims.

Day after day, Iraqis are proving their determination to live in freedom, to chart their own destiny, and to defend their own country. And they can know that the United States will keep our commitment to them. We will continue the work of reconstruction. Our forces will keep going after the terrorists, and continue training the Iraqi military, so that Iraqis can eventually take the lead in their country's security and our men and women can come home. We will succeed in this mission, and when it is concluded, we will be a safer nation.

Wartime conditions are, in every case, a test of military skill and national resolve. But this is especially true in the war on terror. Four years ago,

President Bush told Congress and the country that the path ahead would be difficult, that we were heading into a long struggle, unlike any we have known. All this has come to pass. We have faced, and are facing today, enemies who hate us, hate our country, and hate the liberties for which we stand. They dwell in the shadows, wear no uniform, have no regard for the laws of warfare, and feel unconstrained by any standard of morality. We've never had a fight like this, and the Americans who go into the fight are among the bravest citizens this nation has ever produced. All who have labored in this cause can be proud of their service for the rest of their lives.

The terrorists lack any capacity to inspire the hearts of good men and women. And their only chance for victory is for us to walk away from the fight. They have contempt for our values, they doubt our strength, and they believe that America will lose our nerve and let down our guard. But this nation has made a decision: We will not retreat in the face of brutality, and we will never live at the mercy of tyrants or terrorists.

None of us can know every turn that lies ahead for America in the fight against terror. And because we are Americans, we are going to keep discussing the conduct and the progress of this war and having debates about strategy. Yet the direction of events is plain to see, and this period of struggle and testing should also be seen as a time of promise. The United States of America is a good country, a decent country, and we are making the world a better place by defending the innocent, confronting the violent, and bringing freedom to the oppressed. We understand the continuing dangers to civilization, and we have the resources, the strength, and the moral courage to overcome those dangers and lay the foundations for a better world. Thank you very much.

POSTSCRIPT

Should All Foreign Troops Soon Leave Iraq?

One thing to beware of in this debate is accepting as a given the argument by some people that since the U.S. invasion of Iraq was a mistake in the first place, it follows that the United States should quickly withdraw its troops. The problem with that argument is that the equation changed dramatically once the invasion occurred and that action cannot be undone. For example, Iraq was a brutal dictatorship, but it was a relatively stable country. When the U.S.-led coalition toppled Saddam Hussein, it created a power vacuum in Iraq that has yet to be filled by the Iraqi government. In that atmosphere, a rapid withdrawal might well lead to a bloodbath among Kurds, Shiites, and Sunnis and even among factions within those groups. An uncertain, but probably very high, number of innocent Iraqis would be killed in a civil war. Also, the country might fall apart. That could lead to a nearly independent Kurdish area, a Kurdistan, which might set off a war with Turkey trying to prevent its own sizeable Kurdish minority from seceding and joining its territory to Iraqi Kurdistan. Some also fear that an autonomous Shiite segment of Iraq would ally itself with Shiite Iran, an outcome that would dismay most U.S. policy planners (see Debate 6). U.S. credibility would also be diminished and the effort to spread democracy dealt a heavy blow. Yet there is also no point to pouring money and lives into Iraq if General Odom is correct. Perhaps the damage was done in March 2003, and nothing the United States can do now can undo it. If the United States will inevitably have to deal with civil war in Iraq and perhaps its dissolution, then arguably sooner is better than later. Well symbolizing the "damned if you do, damned if you don't" conundrum was a national intelligence estimate (NIE) that leaked to the press in September 2006. Those wanting a speedy withdrawal seized on the reports finding that "The Iraq conflict [has been] . . . breeding a deep resentment of U.S. involvement in the Muslim world and cultivating supporters for the global jihadist movement." Yet the very next sentence arguably supported staying the course by predicting that if the jihadists fail to force the United States out of Iraq, "fewer fighters will be inspired to carry on the fight" and implying that jihadist success would embolden the terrorist movement.

For an overview of a very complex situation, start with William R. Polk, *Understanding Iraq: The Whole Sweep of Iraqi History, from Genghis Khan's Mongols to the Ottoman Turks to the British Mandate to the American Occupation* (Perennial, 2006). Current information on the situation in Iraq, including casualties, is available from CNN at www.cnn.com/SPECIALS/2003/iraq/forces/casualties/. The National Priorities Project has a counter for its up-to-the-minute estimate of the monetary cost of the war is at http://nationalpriorities.org/index.php?option=com_wrapper&Itemid=182. Vice President Cheney mentioned two important reports. The Duelfer report can be found at: https://www.cia.gov/cia/reports/iraq_wmd_2004/. The Silberman-Robb report is available at: http://www.wmd.gov/report/index.html.

ISSUE 8

Are Strict Sanctions on Cuba Warranted?

YES: Commission for Assistance to a Free Cuba, from "Hastening Cuba's Transition," *Report to the President: 2004* (May 6, 2004)

NO: William Ratliff, from "The U.S. Embargo Against Cuba Is an Abysmal Failure. Let's End It," *Hoover Digest* (Winter 2004)

ISSUE SUMMARY

YES: The Commission for Assistance to a Free Cuba, which President George W. Bush established on October 10, 2003, and charged with making recommendations about how to hasten a transition to democracy in Cuba, argues in its report to the president that the U.S. government should take stronger measures to undermine the Castro regime and to promote conditions that will help the Cuban people hasten the end of President Fidel Castro's dictatorial regime.

NO: William Ratliff, a research fellow at the Hoover Institution, argues that sanctions on Cuba only hurt the Cuban people because nothing the United States is doing today contributes significantly to the achievement of any change in the Castro regime.

U.S. concern for Cuba goes back to the origins of the Monroe Doctrine of 1823. President James Monroe declared that the Western Hemisphere was not subject to "further colonization" and that any attempt by a power outside the hemisphere aimed at "oppressing . . . or controlling by any other manner" part of the so-called New World would be viewed as "the manifestation of an unfriendly disposition toward the United States." The Monroe Doctrine created in American minds the notion that they have the right to exercise some special authority over the hemisphere, especially Central America and the Caribbean. From early on, Cuba was a central focus of this self-declared sphere of influence. For example, President James K. Polk considered trying to purchase Cuba from Spain for $100 million in 1848.

The tensions over slavery and the ensuring Civil War precluded any attempt to acquire Cuba, but the island remained an issue. The outbreak of an independence movement in Cuba in 1870 spurred more American interest.

Americans sympathized with the Cuban revolutionaries. Lurid stories about the treatment of Cubans by Spanish authorities filled the American press, and hostility toward Spain reached a fever pitch after the U.S. battleship *Maine* blew up in Havana's Harbor and the press accused (incorrectly) the Spanish of attaching a mine to it. The ensuing Spanish-American War of 1898 was a lopsided U.S. victory, and Cuba and Puerto Rico in the Caribbean, as well as the Philippines and Guam in the Pacific, came under U.S. control. In 1904, President Theodore Roosevelt declared the Roosevelt Corollary to the Monroe Doctrine, which asserted a U.S. right to intervene in the affairs of other countries in the Western Hemisphere to stop actions that Washington deemed unacceptable. American intervened repeatedly in the region, including occupying Cuba (1895–1922), among other countries.

Cuba was frequently controlled by dictators, and they were supported or tolerated by Washington as long as they did not contravene U.S. interests. This situation changed in 1959 when rebels led by Fidel Castro toppled right-wing dictator Fulgencio Batista. In the atmosphere of the Cold War, Americans were alarmed by Castro's leftist leanings, and tensions grew worse when Castro aligned Cuba with the Soviet Union. A U.S.-sponsored but ill-supported attempt of expatriate Cubans to land at the Bay of Pigs in 1961 and topple Castro was an utter failure. The following year, the U.S.-U.S.S.R. confrontation over the placement of Soviet nuclear weapon–armed missiles in Cuba was resolved when the Soviets withdrew the missiles and Washington secretly pledged not to use military force to try to overthrow Castro.

This left the United States unable to try to remove Castro by force, so it continued a policy of stringent economic sanctions against Cuba. During the 1990s, several factors worked to ease tension. The end of the Cold War did away with images of Cuba as part of a global communist threat. Also, President Bill Clinton was less antagonistic toward the Castro government than had been his immediate predecessors. Castro further helped relations by pledging in 1992 to no longer provide weapons or advisors to leftist revolutionary movements in the hemisphere.

Yet these moderating influences were offset by other factors. The Castro government remained staunchly communist and undemocratic. Periodic floods of refugees from Cuba brought protests from Americans, particularly those in Florida. Given the state's importance in the electoral college, U.S. presidents were wary of appearing "soft" on Castro, and this sentiment was furthered by the voting importance of the ardently anti-Castro Cuban-American community in Florida. An incident in 1998 in which Cuban fighters shot down a small American plane from which Cuban Americans were dropping anti-Castro leaflets over Cuba sparked Congress to pass the Helms-Burton Act that strengthened sanctions even further.

During his presidency, George W. Bush has resisted pressures to ease the sanctions on Cuba by various groups, including business groups that want to trade with and invest in Cuba. Indeed, Bush appointed the Commission for Assistance to a Free Cuba, whose report is featured in the first reading to investigate how to speed the end of the Castro regime. The commission recommended even stronger sanctions, an approach opposed by William Ratliff in the second reading.

Hastening Cuba's Transition

Fidel Castro continues to maintain one of the world's most repressive regimes. As a result of Castro's 45-year strategy of co-opting or crushing independent actors, Cuban civil society is weak and divided, its development impeded by the comprehensive and continuous repression of the Castro regime.

Yet despite decades of suppression, degradation, and deprivation, the aspiration for change is gathering momentum and growing in visibility on the island. Brave Cubans continue to defy the regime and insist that it recognize their fundamental rights, as guaranteed by the Universal Declaration on Human Rights, which Cuba signed, but to which Cuba now outlaws any reference. The March-April 2003 crackdown on peaceful opposition activists was only the most recent and brutal high-profile effort by the regime to eliminate democratic civil society. While these actions set back the consolidation of that movement, they did not end the Cuban people's quest for freedom.

The Castro regime continues to be a threat not only to its own people, but also to regional stability, the consolidation of democracy and market economies in the Western Hemisphere, and the people of the United States. The Castro regime harbors dozens of fugitives from U.S. justice, including those convicted of killing law enforcement officials. It aggressively conducts espionage against the United States, including having operated a spy network, one of whose members was convicted of conspiring to kill U.S. citizens. The Castro regime also has engaged in other hostile acts against its neighbors and other democracies in the Hemisphere. On several occasions, Castro has threatened and orchestrated mass sea-borne migrations to Florida of tens of thousands of Cubans in an effort to intimidate and harm the United States.

This dictatorship has every intention of continuing its stranglehold on power in Cuba and is pursuing every means at its disposal to survive and perpetuate itself, regardless of the cost to the Cuban people. In furtherance of this goal, the regime ruthlessly implements a strategy to maintain the core elements of the existing political and repressive structure to ensure that leadership passes from Fidel Castro to his selected successor, Raul Castro. Under this "succession strategy," the core governmental and Communist Party elite would survive the departure of Fidel Castro and would seek to effect a new relationship with the United States without undergoing fundamental political

Report to the President: 2004, May 6, 2004.

and economic reform. An element that is critical to the success of the regime's strategy is its repressive security apparatus, which instills fear in the Cuban people and uses their impoverishment as a means of control.

This strategy cannot succeed without the continued flow of resources to the regime from outside Cuba. To this end, the Castro regime has built an economic structure on the island designed specifically to exploit all outside engagement with Cuba. One of the regime's central goals is to obtain additional sources of income from the United States, especially through tourism receipts. Overall, these efforts annually subsidize the regime in the amount of more than $3 billion in gross revenues. Specifically, the tourism sector has been developed to generate hard currency as well as to contribute to an image of "normalcy" on the island and to promote international acceptance of the regime.

The Castro regime also cynically exploits U.S. humanitarian and immigration policies, primarily remittances and "family visits," to generate millions in hard currency flows from its victims: those seeking freedom and the Cuban diaspora. Further, Cuba maintains a beneficial arrangement with the sympathetic government of Hugo Chavez in Venezuela, whereby Castro receives up to 82,000 barrels of oil per day on preferential terms; this arrangement nets more than $800 million in annual savings to Cuba (mirrored by an identical amount of lost revenues to Venezuela). Cuba continues to exploit joint economic ventures with third-country investors, who enter these arrangements despite the absence of the rule of law or neutral dispute resolution mechanisms and despite Cuba's lack of respect for basic labor rights. Under these ventures, international employers pay hard currency to the Castro regime for each Cuban worker, who is in turn paid in worthless Cuban pesos.

Another facet of the regime's survival strategy is to control information entering, circulating within, and coming from the island. The regime seeks to minimize the information available to the Cuban people, as well as to manipulate what the outside world knows about the Castro dictatorship and the plight of the average Cuban citizen.

Cuba presents itself internationally as a prime tourist destination, as a center for bio-technological innovation, as a successful socialist state that has improved the standard of living of its people, and as a model for the world in terms of health, education, and race relations. This image belies the true state of Cuba's political, economic and social conditions and the increasingly erratic behavior of its leadership.

Despite the aggressive internal and international propaganda effort by the regime, there is a growing international consensus on the need for change in Cuba. This consensus has been strengthened by the regime's March-April 2003 suppression of peaceful pro-democracy activists, the summary executions of three Afro-Cubans attempting to flee the island, and the courageous effort by many peaceful activists to continue to reach out to the Cuban people and the international community. This flagrant repression, along with the continued work of pro-democracy groups in Cuba, has caused the international community to again take stock of the Castro regime and condemn its methods.

This re-evaluation provides an opportune moment to strengthen an evolving international consensus for democratic change in Cuba. America's commitment to support the Cuban people against Castro's tyranny is part of our larger commitment to the expansion of freedom. In furtherance of this commitment, President George W. Bush mandated that the Commission for Assistance to a Free Cuba identify additional means by which the United States can help the Cuban people bring about an expeditious end to the Castro dictatorship.

This comprehensive framework is composed of six inter-related tasks considered central to hastening change. . .

Empower Cuban Civil Society

The Castro dictatorship has been able to maintain its repressive grip on the Cuban people by intimidating civil society and preventing the emergence of a credible alternative to its failed policies. . . . Now, the tide of public opinion has turned and Castro's loyalists must constantly work to restrain the Cuban people from organizing and expressing demands for change and freedom. . . . Cuban civil society is not lacking spirit, desire, or determination; it is hampered by a lack of materials and support needed to bring about these changes. [The Commission report goes on to recommend a series of efforts to support dissident individuals, groups and organizations in Cuba and of Cuban expatriates]. . . .

Break the Information Blockade

The Castro regime controls all formal means of mass media and communication on the island. Strict editorial control over newspapers, television, and radio by the regime's repressive apparatus prevents the Cuban people from obtaining accurate information on such issues as the Cuban economy and wide-scale and systematic violations of human rights and abridgement of fundamental freedoms. It also limits the ability of pro-democracy groups and civil society to effectively communicate their message to the Cuban people. . . . This blockade on information must be broken in order to increase the availability to the Cuban people of reliable information on events in Cuba. [The Commission report goes on to recommend a series of efforts to facilitate the flow of outside information and viewpoints into Cuba]. . . .

Deny Revenues to the Cuban Dictatorship

A. Undermine Regime-Sustaining Tourism

"Flooding the island with tourists" is part of the Castro regime's strategy for survival. Since 1992, it has been aggressively developing and marketing a tourism infrastructure, including a cynically-orchestrated campaign to make Cuba attractive to U.S. travelers. The estimated annual total number of international travelers is in the 1.8 to 2 million range. Of this global figure, some

160,000 to 200,000 legal and illegal travelers have come from the United States on an annual basis over the past decade. Since the October 10, 2003 implementation of increased U.S. enforcement efforts, there has been a decrease in the number of U.S. travelers, reducing the total to about 160,000.

The regime has a target of hosting 7.5 million international tourists by 2010 and 10 million by 2025. Currently, tourism is Cuba's largest single source of revenue, generating some $1.8–$2.2 billion in annual gross revenues. Of this amount, it is estimated that the regime nets 20 percent, although its take may be greater given the Cuban regime's routine failure to pay creditors or honor contracts with foreign investors. . . .

Tourism & travel-related exports   Central to the marketing of Cuba as a tourist destination, including to U.S. nationals traveling for licensed activities, is its "sand, sun, rum, and cigars" image. Closely related to tourism is the marketing and export of alcohol and tobacco products, a significant revenue-generating activity. Under current U.S. Department of Treasury regulations, licensed U.S. travelers to Cuba can import up to $100 worth of Cuban goods as accompanied baggage. In practice, these goods are almost exclusively Cuban rum and tobacco. In 2003, such imports by licensed travelers could have generated as much as $20 million in revenues to the regime through sales. . . . Revenue gained from the sale of Cuban state-controlled commodities and products strengthens the regime. . . .

Educational travel   Under current regulations, accredited academic institutions receive specific licenses, usually valid for up to two years, to permit students to travel to Cuba for certain educational activities. . . . In practice, while there are well-meaning participants who use this license category as intended, other travelers and academic institutions regularly abuse this license category and engage in a form of disguised tourism. . . . Moreover, the regime has often used the visits by U.S. education groups to cultivate the appearance of international legitimacy and openness to the exchange of ideas. Requiring that educational licenses be granted only to programs engaged in full-semester study in Cuba would support U.S. goals of promoting the exchange of U.S. values and norms in Cuba, would foster genuine academic study in Cuba, and would be less prone to abuse than the current regulations. . . .

Recommendations   Continue to strengthen enforcement of travel restrictions to ensure that permitted travel is not abused and used as cover for tourism, illegal business travel, or to evade restrictions on carrying cash into Cuba. . . [Among other changes:]

- Eliminate the regulatory provision allowing for the import of $100 worth of Cuban goods produced by Cuban state entities, including cigars and rum, as accompanied baggage. . . .
- Eliminate abuses of educational travel by limiting educational travel to only undergraduate or graduate degree granting institutions and only for full-semester study programs, or for shorter duration only when the program directly supports U.S. policy goals. . . .

- Eliminate the general license provision for amateur or semi-professional athletic teams to travel to Cuba to engage in competitions and require that all such travel be specifically licensed.
- Eliminate the specific license provision for travel related to clinics and workshops in Cuba. . . .

B. Limit the Regime's Manipulation of Humanitarian U.S. Policies

To alleviate the hardships of a portion of the Cuban population, the United States has implemented various measures by which those with family members in Cuba can send cash remittances to them; travel to Cuba carrying gifts; and ship "gift parcels." Castro has exploited these policies by effectively shifting burdens that ought to be assumed by the Cuban state and by profiting enormously from these transactions. Not only has he benefited from the pacifying effects of these humanitarian outreaches within the population—relying on the exile community to provide the Cuban people what he refuses to—but he attaches high fees to the various transactions involved. Whether sending remittances or care packages or traveling to the island, the costs to the exile community far exceed market rates and translate into a significant cash windfall to the regime. The Commission found that more than $1 billion annually in funds and goods are sent to Cuba from those living outside the island. . . .

Recognizing the humanitarian need in Cuba as a basis for U.S. policies on remittances, gift parcels, and family travel, the Commission recommends a tightening of current policies to decrease the flow of resources to the regime. [Among recommended actions:]

- Permit individuals to send remittances only to immediate family (grandparents, grandchildren, parents, siblings, spouses, and children) in Cuba.
- Limit gift parcels to medicines, medical supplies and devices, receive-only radios, and batteries, not to exceed $200 total value, and food (unlimited in dollar amount).
- Limit gift parcels to one per month per household, except for gift parcels exclusively containing food, rather than the current policy of allowing one gift parcel per month per individual recipient.
- Limit family visits to Cuba to one trip every three years; . . . [l]imit the definition of "family" for the purposes of family visits to immediate family (including grandparents, grandchildren, parents, siblings, spouses, and children); [and l]imit the length of stay in Cuba for family visitation to 14 days. . .

C. Deny Other Sources of Revenue to the Regime Foreign Investment in Cuba

Starting in the early 1990s as part of its effort to replace lost Soviet subsidies, the Castro regime has pursued an aggressive effort to attract third-country investors for joint ventures. A number of these ventures involve properties expropriated by the regime without adequate and effective compensation. The Castro regime continues to promote foreign investment opportunities in Cuba, including in confiscated properties, claims to which are owned by U.S. nationals. An unfavorable investment climate, a hostile Cuban bureaucracy, and unwieldy and frequently changing laws have limited the levels and types of foreign investment in recent years. In 2003, for example, the number of foreign joint ventures in Cuba dropped by 15 percent, the most notable decline in recent years and a sign of the Castro regime's failed economic and investment policies. However, it continues to actively seek foreign investment, especially from Europe, Canada, and Latin America, in its drive to reap more hard currency.

The Cuban Liberty and Democratic Solidarity (LIBERTAD) Act provides measures to discourage foreign investments in Cuba that involve confiscated property, claims to which are owned by U.S. nationals. Implementation of these laws must address the legitimate desire of U.S. citizens to seek redress for the confiscation of their property, an objective consistent with efforts to implement a comprehensive strategy to deny hard currency to the Castro regime. For those U.S. nationals who hold an ownership claim to property wrongfully confiscated by the Castro government, . . . the LIBERTAD Act provides that U.S. nationals the right to bring an action in U.S. federal court against foreign nationals benefiting from that property. Furthermore, . . . [the act] provides authority to impose visa sanctions against foreign nationals who benefit from properties wrongfully confiscated when a claim to the property is owned by a U.S. national. The U.S. Government should seek to deter investment in Cuba by devoting additional personnel and resources to implementation and enforcement.

Cuban government front companies The Cuban government is believed to operate a number of front companies in the United States, Latin America, and Europe that are used to circumvent travel and trade restrictions and to generate additional hard currency. These front companies are believed to be involved in efforts to encourage illegal tourism and the sending of illegal remittances and gift parcels to Cuba, as well as helping the regime acquire high-end computer equipment and other sensitive technologies. These front companies provide another source of currency and technological information for the regime and function as a base for economic espionage.

Venezuelan oil Cuba maintains an extremely favorable oil arrangement with Venezuelan President Hugo Chavez, whereby up to 82,000 barrels of oil per day is received on preferential terms, a portion of which is then sold on the spot market. This arrangement nets more than $800 million in annual savings to Cuba, mirrored by an identical amount of lost revenues to Venezuela. In exchange, according to his own accounts, Castro has provided Chavez with an army of up to 12,000 Cubans, including doctors, medical personnel, and other technicians to bolster Chavez's popularity with the poorer segments of Venezuelan society, as well as more senior political and military advisors to help Chavez strengthen his authoritarian grip on the nation. Reports from Venezuela also indicate that Cuban doctors are engaging in overt political activities to boost Chavez's popularity. Cheap Venezuelan oil is vital to keeping the Cuban economy functioning, generates additional hard currency, and enables Cuba to postpone much needed economic reforms.

Recommendations   [Among the commissions recommendations are:]

- To deter foreign investment in Cuba in confiscated properties, claims to which are owned by U.S. nationals, aggressively pursue sanctions against those foreign nationals trafficking in (e.g., using or benefiting from) such property . . .
- Neutralize Cuban government front companies by establishing a Cuban Asset Targeting Group. . . . [to] work to identify and close Cuban government front companies.

Illuminate the Reality of Castro's Cuba

The current survival of the regime is in part dependent upon its carefully crafted international image. Cuba presents itself internationally as a prime tourist destination, as a center for bio-technological innovation, and as a successful socialist state that has improved the standard of living of its people. This image belies the true state of Cuba's economic and social conditions and the increasingly erratic behavior of its leadership. [The Commission goes on to recommend a series of efforts to counter Cuba's public diplomacy effort.]

Encourage International Diplomatic Efforts to Support Cuban Civil Society and to Challenge the Castro Regime

There is a growing international consensus on the nature of the Castro regime and the need for change. This consensus was brought about, in part, by the March–April 2003 crackdown on peaceful pro-democracy activists, the valiant effort by these same activists to continue to reach out to the Cuban people and the international community, and Castro's political attacks against the European Union and other nations. Many of those who once stood by Castro have now begun to speak out publicly against the regime's abuses. This same international consensus has limits. All too frequently, moral outrage and international condemnation have not translated into real actions that directly assist the Cuban people in their quest for freedom and basic human rights. On the positive side, the European Union and its member states have denounced the Cuban regime, curtailed assistance and, in some cases, stepped up contacts with Cuban dissidents. However, much more needs to be done. Encouraging international solidarity, challenging the regime in international organizations where appropriate, and strengthening international proactive support for pro-democracy groups in Cuba form a cornerstone of our policy to hasten an end to the Cuban regime and the transition to a free Cuba. [The Commission goes on to recommend a series of efforts to support this goal.]

Undermine the Regime's Succession Strategy

Approaching his 78th birthday, Fidel Castro has conspicuously deteriorated physically and probably mentally as well. His decline over the last few years has been apparent on several occasions at public events in Cuba and abroad. The quality of Castro's decision-making has declined along with his physical condition. . . . The senior Cuban leadership is now faced with the reality that Fidel Castro's physical end is at hand and is making preparations to manage a "succession" of the regime that will keep the senior leadership in power. The regime's survival strategy is to maintain the core elements of the existing political structure in passing eventual leadership of the country from Fidel to Raul Castro and others currently in the senior leadership. U.S. policy must be targeted at undermining this succession strategy by stripping away layers of support within the regime, creating uncertainty regarding the political and legal future of those in leadership positions, and encouraging more of those within the ruling elite to shift their allegiance to those pro-democracy forces working for a transition to a free and democratic Cuba. To these ends, attention and pressure must be focused on the ruling elite so that succession by this elite or any individual is seen as what it would be: an impediment to a democratic and free Cuba. Targeting current regime officials for U.S. visa denials is one instrument available to the United States to hold them accountable for human rights abuses against the Cuban people and others, including the torture by Castro regime officials of American POWs in South East Asia, or for providing assistance to fugitives in Cuba from U.S. justice. [The Commission goes on to make a series of efforts to undermine any Castro-connected succession regime.]

William Ratliff  **NO**

The U.S. Embargo Against Cuba Is an Abysmal Failure. Let's End It

More and more Americans are asking how the United States can come up with a realistic policy toward Cuba during the remainder of Fidel Castro's seemingly interminable lifetime. [Castro has led Cuba since 1959.] The underlying problem with our policy today is that while its objectives are desirable, they cannot be realized with the resources we are willing to commit. That means that no matter how much we and the Cuban people want Castro out, and no matter how much we support democracy, human rights, market reform, and a peaceful transition, in reality nothing we are doing today contributes significantly to the achievement of any of these outcomes. In fact, since the end of the Cold War our policy has been about as effective as our earlier comical efforts to make the dictator's beard fall out. Our policy is a plodding example of how a legitimate lobby (militant Cuban-Americans, especially in Miami) and its political target (U.S. political parties seeking money and votes, especially in Florida) can to some degree reach their own goals at the expense of the general populations of two countries.

Decades of Soviet and U.S. policies toward Cuba have shown that Castro is his own player and will not change his game more than temporarily to suit even a big foreign bidder. Therefore, unless we are willing to force regime change violently, we will just have to endure Castro until he dies. That is what the vast majority of the Cuban people have decided to do. No one likes such a passive policy, but the alternatives, such as what we have been doing or greater intervention, are worse. With this in mind, rather than seeking to heighten tensions across the strait, as we do now, we should try to reduce conflict in order to make life a little easier for the Cuban people in the interim and actually improve the prospects of a more peaceful transition in the post-Castro period. The easiest way to move in this direction is to increase personal and other contacts between the two countries. At very long last, in late 2003 a substantial majority of legislators from both parties in both houses of Congress voted to do just that by easing travel restrictions. But, alas, a clique of Republican legislators in conference committee, contemptuous of the popular will, struck out the provision, which the president had vowed to veto in any

From *Hoover Digest,* Winter 2004. Copyright © 2004 by Hoover Institution Press. Reprinted by permission.

event. This is the kind of political skullduggery that gives the political profession its bad image. The good news, however, is that the majority of the American people and their legislators now support change, and in time they undoubtedly will rout the minority.

From the beginning, we must recognize three things: (1) We still do have legitimate concerns about what Castro is up to; (2) our misguided policy is bipartisan; and (3) the embargo causes us and the Cuban people more problems than it does Castro. Beginning with number one, the issues that warrant attention include whether Castro is obstructing the war on terrorism, involved in the trans-shipment of drugs and money-laundering, developing a germ warfare capacity, and nurturing anti-Americanism across Latin America. To the extent that he is doing some or all of these things, we would be able to monitor and counter them better with more rather than fewer people of all sorts on the island. An embargo targeting the entire country is a blunt instrument against the possible activities of a tiny elite. We should instead bomb Havana with Big Macs, that is, increase the American presence there in every possible way.

Second, our current policy is bipartisan. The most militant spokesman for the embargo today is President George W. Bush, but during the 1990s it was President Bill Clinton. In 1992 it was presidential candidate Clinton who got our post–Cold War policy going in the wrong direction by supporting the legislation of former New Jersey senator Robert Torricelli that tightened the embargo, a policy then-president George H.W. Bush had wisely opposed. And in 1998–99, toward the end of his time in office, it was Clinton again who killed the proposed Presidential Bipartisan Commission on Cuba. The idea of a commission to review U.S. policy was conceived by former undersecretary William Rogers and endorsed by former secretaries of state Henry Kissinger, George Shultz, and Lawrence Eagleburger, along with many members of Congress and others.

Finally, since the end of the Cold War the embargo has been largely a vote-getting, feel-good stunt rather than a serious international policy. It has not caused Cuba's main political, economic, or other problems. Cuba's problems are the entirely predictable consequences of Castro's own flawed and self-serving decisions. Today almost every country in the world has political and economic relations with Cuba, but Cuba produces almost nothing anyone abroad wants to buy and has very little money to buy what others produce. Ironically, according to polls conducted in the Miami area by Florida International University (FIU), only slightly more than 25 percent of Cuban-Americans themselves think the embargo really works, though a majority wants to continue it nonetheless. A character in Cuban novelist Pedro Juan Gutierrez's *Dirty Havana Trilogy* remarks that she is "pained to witness so much poverty and so much political posturing to disguise it." One should only add that the embargo is also sustained by massive moral posturing and that although Gutierrez was speaking of posturing in Cuba, this same quality pervades support for sanctions in the United States. To the degree that the embargo does have a real impact, however, it is mainly negative on the lives of ordinary Cuban people and on our international stature.

Why the Embargo Doesn't Work

In the post–Cold War period, the embargo has become a strategic liability. Even though most embargo supporters say the sanctions are intended to promote a peaceful transition, in fact they heighten tensions and hardships for the Cuban people and exacerbate differences among Cubans in Cuba and with those in exile. Our policy encourages conflict and instability and, to the degree that it succeeds, could promote a violent uprising or even civil war. (A few embargo supporters quietly admit they want war to clean out the flotsam and jetsam of the Castro period.) But if the democratic forces do rise up against Castro, which is unlikely in the foreseeable future, and are in danger of being crushed by Castro's repressive apparatus, which is highly probable, the U.S. government would be under heavy pressure to intervene militarily to rescue the reformers. FIU polls show 61 percent of Cuban-Americans want U.S. military intervention, as do a few militant gringo politicians. Most Americans, however, emphatically including officers of the U.S. armed forces I have talked to at many levels, wisely oppose this course of action.

The Helms-Burton Law, the heart of our current policy, is destructive of U.S. interests because it makes demands on the current *and future* governments of Cuba that are imperialistic, logically inconsistent, and counter-productive. [Helms-Burton is the common name for the Cuban Liberty and Democratic Solidarity Act of 1996, which imposed stringent limits on interactions with Cuba and which was sponsored by Senators Jesse Helms (R-NC) and Representative Dan Burton (R-IN).] Helms-Burton is a new Platt Amendment, 100 years after the first. Mark Falcoff of the American Enterprise Institute has noted correctly that the original Platt Amendment—the 1901 agreement that in important respects made Cuba a U.S. dependency—planted "seeds of a long smoldering resentment" in Cuba and that Helms-Burton is doing the same.

Cuba is no military or economic threat to the United States, but our policy there is destructive of what Joseph Nye has called our "soft power" worldwide, that is, the international goodwill that persuades other nations to cooperate with us in matters of real importance, such as the war on terrorism. International polls, confirmed by my recent personal experiences on four continents, tell us that America's image around the world today is low and that hostility toward us is rising. Much of the hostility results from what foreigners consider our bullying of other nations, exemplified in particular by Bill Clinton's bombing of Yugoslavia in 1999 and George W. Bush's invasion of Iraq in 2003. Thus although Cuba is not a major cause of our current reputation, it fits what critics consider to be our objectionable and dangerous style. A unilateral lifting of the embargo should relax tensions on the island and improve our image, especially in Latin America, where regard for the United States is plummeting.

Some embargo supporters say lifting the embargo now would reward Castro for his stubbornness and brutal repression in early 2003. No. We must announce that Castro simply has been dumped from our "most wanted" to our "least relevant" list. His international admirers would shout *"Viva Fidel!*

Hasta la Victoria Siempre," ["to victory always"] but the rest, or at least those few who notice, would just say, "Good Lord, it's about time."

On the other hand, the embargo feeds Castro's soft power. It gives him a scapegoat for his repression and economic failures, and it also refurbishes his image as the enduring scourge of American imperialism, the central drive and purpose of his entire career. If we take this scapegoat from him, it will be a major step toward killing him while he is still alive. One of the tragic and bitter ironies of the embargo is that those who most hate Castro are the ones who most relentlessly and effectively feed his insatiable ego and sustain his international image.

Many embargo supporters note that the dollars Cuba draws from investments, trade, and tourism support repression and therefore should be kept from the island. Yes, some do, but many also pass through the hands and lives of millions of Cubans, giving them hope for survival in a destitute economy. If that isn't so, why do so many Cubans dig so hard to find any kind of freelance work to earn a few greenbacks? Even Cuban-Americans know this is true when they set their passions aside for a moment, which is why they are the main ones who shatter the spirit of the embargo by using a legal loophole that allows them to send remittances to family and friends on the island. Cuban-Americans now send an estimated $1 billion per year to Cuba. All of these dollars, the island's main source of foreign currency, also funnel into Castro's hands, and many support the repressive apparatus. Therefore a really honest embargo would forbid the sending of *any* dollars to Cuba. Cutting *all* dollars to the island would reduce almost everyone to serious poverty and, more than anything we can do short of an invasion, might indeed spark an uprising against Castro. In my judgment, the remittances are humanitarian acts that should continue, but they shatter the logic of the sanctions regime. One important result of the general tourism industry is that it makes at least some dollars available to many Cubans who have no family abroad, thus reducing somewhat the increasingly explosive divide between classes of Cubans, namely those who have dollars and those who do not.

Finally, has the embargo improved human rights? Embargo supporters say they champion human rights, thus trying to seize the moral high ground in the debate over the embargo. In fact there is more evidence to the contrary. Embargo supporters say the arrests, trials, and executions of March and April 2003, which I witnessed firsthand while leading educational tours (now banned) of the island, prove that the moderate engagement line of the Europeans has failed. But if anything the repression proves that *our* policy of assisting the dissidents has backfired. The arrests and imprisonments were a severe blow to the pro-democracy movement. For almost 45 years Castro has shown that neither threats nor enticements, from the former Soviet Union in the past or from Europe or us today, will move him more than temporarily closer to policies he does not support. Castro is like T. S. Eliot's Rum Tum Tugger, if we paraphrase thusly: "Fidel Castro *will* do, as Fidel Castro *do* do, and there's no doing *anything* about it." So unless the United States is prepared to go in and take Castro out, Cubans must just find a way to survive his rule, as they have already done for decades, and so must we.

Constructive Engagement

Two years ago I spent a long evening with Cuban dissidents Elizardo Sanchez, Oscar Espinosa Chepe, Mirian Leyva, and Hector Palacios. (Chepe and Palacios are now serving decades-long prison terms.) Palacios, who had recently polled dissidents on the island, found that 90 percent wanted the embargo lifted. Why? Because, as Sanchez said, "isolation is oxygen to totalitarians." And yet the United States is not only maintaining the embargo but cutting back on the number of Americans who can visit the island legally, thus increasing the isolation that is the oxygen to Castro's totalitarian regime.

One might ask, who knows better how to deal with Fidel Castro? A few Cuban-American legislators who have lived in the United States for decades and represent militantly anti-Castro constituencies with their own understandable (but misguided) agendas and their declining supporters around the country? Or the people of Cuba, including the dissidents on the front lines and in jail? The latter, of course, and Cubans generally and the dissidents in particular want to see more Americans, not fewer, on the island. Embargo supporters, however, promise fewer visitors but more moral and material support for the dissidents. Two years ago, Palacios told me that dissidents are very uncomfortable with aid from abroad, particularly from Washington, even when they take it, because it "burns." It certainly "burned" the 75 dissidents arrested in early 2003 because the Castro regime used contacts with the U.S. government and receipt of support from Americans to "prove" democratic advocates were agents of American imperialism.

Embargo supporters are quick to proclaim support for dissidents, or democratic reformers, when they condemn Castro's repression or call for peaceful reform. The dissident most lauded by Americans today is Oswaldo Paya, who in 2002 won the European Union's top human rights award (the Sakharov Prize) and in December 2003 published a detailed peaceful transition program for Cuba. Paya approved the United Nations General Assembly's condemnation of the embargo in November 2003 (while fruitlessly calling upon the world body to simultaneously condemn Castro's repression). If we Americans really admire courageous men and women like Paya, Palacios, and many others who stand up to Castro to demand a little more freedom, why don't we show them the ultimate respect of doing what they ask of us? Why don't we open the doors wider to Americans who want to visit Cuba or, better yet, lift the embargo altogether?

POSTSCRIPT

Are Strict Sanctions on Cuba Warranted?

The Commission for Assistance to a Free Cuba reported to President Bush on May 6, 2004. The following day he imposed most of the increased sanctions on Cuba proposed the commission. Bush praised the commission's recommendations as "strategy that says 'we're not waiting for the day of Cuban freedom, we are working for the day of freedom in Cuba'." Differing sharply, Wayne Smith of the Center for International Policy called Bush's policy "a farce, pure political theater," and predicted, "It will be a nuisance, but it's not going to have a significant effect." A general overview of current Cuba–U.S. relations is found in Chris McGillion and Morris H. Morley, eds., *Cuba, the United States, and the Post–Cold War World: The International Dimensions of the Washington-Havana Relationship* (University Press of Florida, 2004). A good site for the U.S. government view is at the unofficial embassy in Cuba, the U.S. Interests Section, Havana http:havana.usinterestsection.gov. The English version of the Web site of the government of Cuba is at http://www.cubagob.cu/ingles/default.htm.

Of the proposed measures, the most important one that Bush did not follow was the recommendation to reduce the funds that Cuban Americans could send to relatives still in Cuba. Reportedly, the White House felt that doing so might anger Cuban Americans. This would have been politically unwise given the impending presidential election, the fact that Cuban Americans make up 5 percent of Florida's population, and that the state casts 27 electoral college votes—the fourth largest total in the country. Indeed, electoral politics may have a great deal to do with U.S. policy toward Cuba. While supporters of President Bush point to his well-established aversion to leftist governments and his repeated pronouncements in favor of encouraging democracy as reasons for imposing the sanctions, critics attribute his anti-Castro stand to the president's desire not to upset the many Cuban Americans who are both passionately anti-Castro and vote in U.S. elections. This political factor was captured in a quip published in the *Miami Herald*: "What irony! Cubans can't elect their president in Cuba, but they elect one in the United States." For a generally pro-sanction Cuban American group, visit the Web site of the Cuban American National Foundation at http://www.canf.org/2004/principal-ingles.htm. A Cuban American group that views sanctions as harmful is the Cuban American Alliance at http://www.cubamer.org/index.asp?Lang=Eng.

Whatever the U.S. government does or does not do, the most likely end to the Castro regime will come with his death. Born in 1926 and in power since 1959, Castro is old and is in increasingly poor health. In July 2006,

Castro suffered an illness so severe that he temporarily handed over power to his bother, Minister of Defense Raul Castro, who is 5 years younger than Fidel. The elder Castro had still not resumed his duties as of mid-October, and there were stories circulating that he had terminal cancer. A study of Castro is in Leycester Coltman, *The Real Fidel Castro* (Yale University Press, 2005). The Bush administration reacted to Castro's ill-health by creating a task force to tighten enforcement of its sanctions against Cuba and crack down on Americans who violate them, As one U.S. official put it, the intent of the Cuban Sanctions Enforcement Task Force is to "isolate" the Cuban government economically and "speed up" its end. For a view of the possibilities in a post-Castro Cuba, see Brian Latell, *After Fidel: The Inside Story of Castro's Regime and Cuba's Next Leader* (Palgrave Macmillan, 2005).

Internet References . . .

IPE Net

The International Political Economy Network hosted by the University of Arizona and sponsered by the IPE section of the International Studies Association is a good starting point to study the intersection of politics and economics globally.

http://www.isanet.org/sections/ipe/

United Nations Development Programme (UNDP)

This United Nations Development Programme (UNDP) site offers publications and current information on world poverty, the UNDP's mission statement, information on the UN Development Fund for Women, and more.

http://www.undp.org

Office of the U.S. Trade Representative

The Office of the U.S. Trade Representative (USTR) is responsible for developing and coordinating U.S. international trade, commodity, and direct investment policy and leading or directing negotiations with other countries on such matters. The U.S. trade representative is a cabinet member who acts as the principle trade adviser, negotiator, and spokesperson for the president on trade and related investment matters.

http://www.ustr.gov

The U.S. Agency for International Development (USAID)

This is the home page of the U.S. Agency for International Development (USAID), which is the independent government agency that provides economic development and humanitarian assistance to advance U.S. economic and political interests overseas.

http://www.usaid.gov/

World Trade Organization (WTO)

The World Trade Organization (WTO) is the only international organization dealing with the global rules of trade between nations. Its main function is to ensure that trade flows as smoothly, predictably, and freely as possible. This site provides extensive information about the organization and international trade today.

http://www.wto.org

Third World Network

The Third World Network (TWN) is an independent, nonprofit international network of organizations and individuals involved in economic, social, and environmental issues relating to development, the developing countries of the world, and the North-South divide. At the network's Web site you will find recent news, TWN position papers, action alerts, and other resources on a variety of topics, including economics, trade, and health.

http://www.twnside.org.sg

Economic Issues

*I*nternational economic and trade issues have an immediate and personal effect on individuals in ways that few other international issues do. They influence the jobs we hold and the prices of the products we buy—in short, our lifestyles. In the worldwide competition for resources and markets, tensions arise between allies and adversaries alike. This section examines some of the prevailing economic tensions.

- Is World Trade Organization Membership Beneficial?

- Should the United States Take a Hard-line with China About Its International Economic Policies?

- Is Immigration an Economic Benefit to the Host Country?

ISSUE 9

Is World Trade Organization Membership Beneficial?

YES: Peter F. Allgeier, from Testimony during Hearings on "The Future of the World Trade Organization," before the Subcommittee on Trade, Committee on Ways and Means, U.S. House of Representatives (May 17, 2005)

NO: Lori Wallach, from Testimony during Hearings on "The Future of the World Trade Organization," before the Subcommittee on Trade, Committee on Ways and Means, U.S. House of Representatives (May 17, 2005)

ISSUE SUMMARY

YES: Peter F. Allgeier, Deputy U.S. Trade Representative, Office of the U.S. Trade Representative, describes the World Trade Organization as beneficial to U.S. strategic and economic interests and argues that there is overwhelming value to be gained through continued U.S. participation in the organization.

NO: Lori Wallach, director of Public Citizen's Global Trade Watch, part of Public Citizen, a Washington, D.C.–based advocacy group, maintains that Congress should demand a transformation of WTO trade rules because they have failed to achieve the promised economic gains and have also undercut an array of nontrade, noneconomic policies and goals advantageous to the public interest in the United States and abroad.

The debate here is an extension of the controversy over economic globalization found in Issue 1. A key component of the growth of interaction and interdependence among the countries of the world has been the expansion of international trade through the lowering of tariffs and nontariff barriers to trade, such as quotas on imports and government subsidies for domestic producers. On the global level, the World Trade Organization (WTO) is at the center of the drive to continue to remove trade barriers and the resolution of disputes among countries over trade policy.

The origins of the WTO extend back to the General Agreement on Tariffs and Trade (GATT), an organization confusingly named after the treaty that established it in 1947 to promote free trade. The confusion was ended in 1995 when the treaty was amended to change the name of the organization to the World Trade Organization. One mark of the WTO's importance is that from an initial 23 countries, almost all countries are now either a member (149 countries) or an observer (32 countries) on the path to membership.

Since the GATT/WTO began, there have been nine "rounds" of trade talks among its members aimed at further reducing trade barriers. The eighth and most recently completed round, the "Uruguay Round" named after the site of the initial meeting, was begun in 1986 and concluded in 1994. This complex agreement is about 26,000 pages long and covers not just exporting and importing raw materials and manufactured goods, but also buying and selling services abroad, protecting copyrights and patents, and virtually everything else that impacts the flow of goods and services among countries.

Hoping to build on the Uruguay Round, the WTO launched its ninth round at a meeting in Doha, Qatar, in 2001. The Doha Round has floundered. One issue is between the economically less developed countries (LDCs) and economically developed countries (EDCs). The LDCs believe that the EDCs have created trade rules that have benefited themselves and disadvantaged the LDCs. There are also disputes between the EDC, especially pitting the United States versus the European Union. Several meetings to negotiate new revisions to the GATT have failed to make progress, and the success of the Doha Round is doubtful.

Adding to the LDCs' criticism of the rules under the WTO are a wide range of other complaints about the organization and even the very concept of free trade. Critics argue, for example, that WTO rules prevent countries from refusing to import goods that are produced in low-wage "sweatshops" or in a manner that damages the environment. Labor unions, among others, argue that free trade is undermining employment in their country by allowing low-cost imports to undercut domestic production. U.S. trade unions, for example, are very skeptical of free trade. Other groups oppose it because they do not believe that all countries abide by the rules. American software, movie, and music producers, for example, complain that their copyright-protected "intellectual property" is pirated in other countries with at least the passive complicity of the government. Yet another issue concerns national sovereignty. Treaties legally bind countries, and, for example, a country that believes another is not living up to the WTO treaty can file a suit against the offending country in what amounts to a WTO court. The fact that an international organization can, in effect, find a country wrong and direct it to change its policy is an affront to those who defend absolute sovereignty for their country. Without denying that there is a range of important concerns that face the WTO, Peter F. Allgeier argues in the first reading that the WTO has contributed to American and world prosperity and indicates U.S. support for even further reductions in trade barriers. Lori Wallach does not argue for withdrawing precipitously from the WTO, but depicts it and the GATT as deeply flawed and in need of major repair.

YES

Peter F. Allgeier

Supporting the World Trade Organization

Introduction

I am pleased to be here to discuss the World Trade Organization (WTO) and the WTO Agreements, the relationship to the strategic and economic interests of the United States, and the overwhelming value of continued U.S. participation in the WTO. . . .

My testimony today provides an opportunity to look back at the creation of the WTO and our participation over the last 10 years and, equally important, to focus on our agenda for the next several months leading up to the Sixth WTO Ministerial in Hong Kong this December and head toward a successful conclusion of the Doha Development Agenda negotiations in 2006.

Historical Context for the WTO

The creation of the WTO represented the culmination of a decades-long bipartisan U.S. commitment to lead the world away from economic isolationism and toward the imperative of an open, rules-based global trading system. The GATT [General Agreement on Tariffs and Trade] had been created in 1947—drawn up in an unsteady post-war world that collectively was determined to strengthen global security and peace through economic opportunity and growth in living standards.

Today, we continue to exercise our leadership in a world that faces new challenges to maintaining global security and stability, underscoring the continuing important strategic interest of the United States in an open global trading system governed by the rule of law. The United States is fully engaged in the WTO work under the Doha Development Agenda [DDA], and the United States aggressively uses the existing WTO machinery to effectively enforce our rights.

WTO membership now stands at 148. Accession to the WTO carries more stringent requirements than what was used in the GATT. Key entries during the past decades include not only China, but also a wide array of other countries that each carry their own strategic and economic importance, such as Jordan, Cambodia, and several former Soviet Republics. Negotiations toward

Testimony before the Subcommittee on Trade, Committee on Ways and Means, Peter F. Allgeier (May 17, 2005).

entry into the WTO are ongoing at various stages for more than 25 countries, ranging from Russia and Vietnam, to Iraq, Ukraine, Saudi Arabia, and Afghanistan. Each effort underscores the importance attached to membership in the WTO, and the importance of moving forward with a member-driven, rules-based approach to the global trading system.

Commercial Significance for the United States of Uruguay Round and the WTO

During the five years since the last review under the Uruguay Round Agreements Act, unprecedented growth in trade and global economic integration has continued—led by continuing advances in technology, communications, manufacturing, and logistics. Five years ago we did not have ubiquitous cell phones that captured and transmitted photos miles away, nor was it yet routine to use the Internet to order overnight delivery of a product from thousands of miles away. Advances such as these demonstrate that the trade environment is always changing, the citizens of the United States—like the rest of the world—are being presented with new products, new services and, most important, new economic opportunities that did not exist in 1995, or 2000. At the same time, globalization also undoubtedly presents new issues, new competitive challenges and new economic pressures.

Simply put, the WTO exists as the most important vehicle to advance U.S. trade interests, and is critical to America's workers, businesses, farmers, and ranchers. Many are dependent and all are affected by a global trading system that must operate with predictability and transparency, without discrimination against American products, and providing for actions to address unfair trade practices. The United States remains the world's largest exporter. During the first 10 years of the WTO—from 1994 to 2004—U.S. exports of goods and services have risen 63 percent, from $703 billion to over $1.1 trillion.

To ensure equal opportunities for U.S. businesses, farmers, ranchers, and other exporters, the United States has brought more WTO dispute settlement cases than any other member. Since establishment of the WTO, the United States has initiated 74 cases. Examples of cases include those focusing on: dairy, apples, biotechnology, telecommunications, automobiles, apparel, unfair customs procedures, and protecting intellectual property rights. Of those, we have won 23 on core issues, lost four, and settled 23 before decision. The remaining 24 are "in process" (in panel, in consultations, or monitored for progress or otherwise inactive). In the last five years, our record to-date in cases—both offensive and defensive—is 16 wins and 14 losses. From 1995 to 2000, the U.S. record was 18 wins and 15 losses. The United States represents roughly 17 percent of world trade, yet has brought nearly 22 percent of the WTO disputes between January 1, 1995 and December 31, 2004.

This year marks the full implementation of many key Uruguay Round agreements, such as completion of the 10 year phased implementation of global tariff cuts on industrial and agricultural goods and reductions in trade-distorting agricultural domestic support and export subsidies; elimination of quotas and full integration of textile trade into the multilateral trading system; and improvements in patent protection in key markets such as India. The Uruguay Round was highlighted by the negotiating results being adopted in a "single undertaking" by all members, who together rejected any notion of a two or three-tier global trading system.

The WTO also provides opportunities on a day-to-day basis for advancing U.S. interests through the more than 20 standing WTO committees—not including numerous additional Working Groups, Working Parties, and Negotiating Bodies—which meet regularly to administer agreements, for members to exchange views, work to resolve questions of members' compliance with commitments, and develop initiatives aimed to improve the agreements and their operation.

The United States has advocated greater transparency and openness in WTO proceedings. The WTO has taken important steps to increase the transparency of its operation across the board, from document availability to public outreach. WTO members continue to set the course for the organization, and the members themselves remain responsible for compliance with rules.

Responding to U.S. leadership, during the past 10 years the WTO has shown itself to be a dynamic organization, one where our interests are advanced toward achievements with concrete positive effect. We have seen to it that the substantive agenda has provided the path for significant market-opening results over the past decade, such as concluding the Information Technology Agreement (ITA) to eliminate tariffs worldwide on IT products, and bringing the Basic Telecommunications Agreement into effect, which opened up 95 percent of the world's telecommunications markets. Both are achievements that continue to contribute to the ability of citizens around the globe to take advantage of the Information Age.

The 1997 Agreement on Trade in Financial Services has achieved fair, open and transparent practices across the global financial services industry, fostering a climate of greater global economic security. The agreement helps ensure that U.S. banking, securities insurance, and other financial services firms can compete and invest in overseas markets on clear and fair terms.

In a world where over 95 percent of consumers live beyond our borders, the WTO is an essential tool for U.S. interests. Increasingly, small businesses are important players in the global economy and an important stake holder in advancing U.S. interests in the WTO agenda. Between 1992 and 2002, U.S. exports from small and medium-sized enterprises rose 54 percent, from $102.8 billion to $158.5 billion—a faster pace than the rate of growth for total U.S. exports during the same time.

Falling trade barriers—many of which reflect the 10 year implementation of the results of the Uruguay Round—have helped rapidly increase the value of trade relative to the U.S. economy. U.S. goods and service trade (exports plus imports) reached the levels of 18 percent of the value of U.S. GDP in 1984, 21.7 percent in 1994 and 25.2 percent in 2004. Both U.S. manufacturing exports and U.S. agricultural exports have grown strongly during our 10 years in the WTO. Between 1994 and 2004, they were up 65 percent and 38 percent, respectively. U.S. exports of high technology products grew by 67 percent during the past 10 years and accounted for one-quarter of total goods exports.

During this time period, U.S. exports to Mexico more than doubled, while exports to Canada and the EU grew by 66 percent and 56 percent, respectively. Among major countries and regions, exports to China exhibited the fastest growth, nearly quadrupling over the past 10 years. China's entry into the WTO in December 2001 locked in improved market access opportunities, committing to reduce its tariffs on industrial products, which averaged 24.6 percent, to a level that averages 9.4 percent. The growth in services exports between 1994 and 2004 (69 percent) slightly exceeded that of goods (61 percent). Nearly all of the major services export categories have grown between 1994 and 2004.

Development

The United States has been the engine of economic growth for much of the world economy. Strong growth of the U.S. economy and openness to trade assisted the recovering countries involved in the Asian financial crisis of the late 1990s and further helped pull the global economy back from the brink of severe recession in the early part of the current decade. The completion of the Uruguay Round and creation of the WTO have figured prominently in helping our nation to sustain not only our own domestic economic strength but also our leadership role within the global economy.

The United States continues to be second to none in actively working with developing countries to encourage trade liberalization that will boost economic growth and development. Trading partners with strong economies make good allies and provide important consumers for US goods and services. Study after study shows that the WTO's rules-based system promotes openness and predictability leading to increased trade and improved prospects for economic growth in member countries. By promoting the rule of law, the WTO fosters a better business climate in developing country members, which helps them attract more foreign direct investment and helps to increase economic growth around the globe, while also helping to lift the least developed countries out of poverty. Economic literature confirms that countries that have more open economies engage in increased international trade and have higher growth rates than more closed economies. Several World Bank studies in 2004 found that trade and integration into the world economy lead to faster growth and poverty-reduction in poor countries. The developing countries that were most open to trade over the past two decades also had the fastest growing wages.

Looking Ahead: Advancing the Doha Development Agenda

Two months after the events of September 11th, 2001, U.S. leadership played a critical role in the launch of a new round of multilateral trade negotiations, the first to be conducted under the WTO. The negotiations under the Doha Development Agenda reflect the dynamic complexities of today's economic world, and present new opportunities to make historic advancements on the idea of open markets and a respect for the rule of law.

The main focus of the negotiations is in the following areas: agriculture; industrial market access; services; trade facilitation; WTO rules (i.e., trade remedies, regional agreements and fish subsidies); and development. In addition, the mandate gives further direction on the WTO's existing work program and implementation of the Agreement. The goal of the DDA is to reduce trade barriers so as to expand global economic growth, development and opportunity.

The market access related negotiations of the DDA offer the greatest potential to create high-quality jobs, advance economic reform and development, and reduce poverty worldwide. We recognize that the national economic strategies of our developing country partners include many important issues, but at the same time we believe that the focus of the WTO should be concentrated on reducing trade barriers and providing a stable, predictable, rules-based environment for world trade.

The DDA provides us with historic opportunities to achieve agriculture reform and greatly diminish current market distortions that present barriers to American farmers and ranchers. We are also aiming to achieve significant new market access for our manufactured goods through broad tariff cuts while working to reduce non-tariff barriers. We are also pressing for ambitious global market opening for our services industries. The WTO negotiations on trade facilitation will result in less red tape and more efficiency and predictability for moving goods across borders. And less corruption in customs activities.

The WTO's Doha Development Agenda is part of President Bush's strategy to open markets, reduce poverty, and expand freedom through increased trade among all countries in the global trading system, developed and developing. The U.S. role in the WTO is at the core of this strategy.

Dismantling trade barriers multilaterally holds immense potential. From 1994 to 2003, the world economy expanded at an average rate of about 2.5 percent, but exports have grown at more than double that pace—about 5.5 percent, a harbinger of accelerating globalization.

Obstacles to the free flow of commerce undermine our ability to maximize this potential and its benefits. We need to move toward a system that provides incentives for innovation and growth in the most competitive aspects of our productive sectors. The best way to do this is successfully to complete the WTO Doha Development Agenda negotiations.

Last August, we made a crucial step forward by adopting negotiating frameworks. Much of our work this year has been on fleshing out the technical details to set the negotiating table. Looking ahead, the next major challenge for the WTO will be preparations for the 6th Ministerial Conference in Hong Kong, China, December 13–18, 2006, where Ministers will be providing direction and guidance as to how to bring the Doha negotiations to a successful conclusion. Final negotiations need to be underway, with offers on the table in the first quarter of 2006. Once we agree on modalities, we have tough bargaining ahead.

One important lesson we drew from the meetings in Seattle and Cancun is that such meetings only succeed if they are well prepared. Simply put, most of the work needs to be done before arriving at the Ministerial meeting. This gives all of us the necessary time at home, and with our partners to build the needed consensus among the wider WTO membership on any given issue.

For Hong Kong, we clearly need to have an agreement on the modalities for negotiation in agriculture and non-agricultural market access, prospects in hand for a significant result in services, directions for how to ensure that WTO rules remain effective and in some cases are strengthened (e.g., by adding new disciplines to subsidies to deal with over fishing) and the outlines of an agreement on Trade Facilitation.

If we are to secure such results in Hong Kong, we will need to be very far along in the process before the August recess in Geneva, and have an outline of the agreements to be affirmed at Hong Kong. To meet this timetable, we believe that there is an urgent need to reinvigorate the negotiations Doha provides us an opportunity we cannot afford to waste. We can set a vision for the global economy for the next decades and make a major contribution to development.

We will conclude in 2006 only if we achieve a balanced outcome with results that will benefit all members. That's why agriculture, non-agricultural market access (NAMA), services, rules and development are the major issues for the negotiations. We have learned that while agriculture may be the engine for negotiations, success requires us to secure strong results across the broad range of issues in the Round. We believe we can secure results that provide new opportunities for America's workers, farmers, ranchers, service providers, and consumers. And, at the same time secure a result that strengthens the rules of the global trading system to meet America's trade interests.

On agriculture, we have work to do in all three pillars of agriculture: market access, export competition and domestic support. The 2004 Geneva framework envisions reforms in global agricultural trade: the complete elimination of export subsidies by a date to be negotiated; a framework for negotiating substantial reductions in domestic agricultural supports, including a significant down payment up front in the form of a 20 percent cut in the allowable level of domestic supports; and a commitment to making substantial improvements in agricultural market access.

Until last week, the negotiations were blocked on a technical issue. It is clear that how deeply and broadly tariffs are cut will determine the level of ambition for the agriculture negotiations overall. The World Bank recently reported that the 92% of the welfare gains from liberalization in agriculture will come from improvements in market access, compared to 6% from reduction of domestic subsidies and 2% from the elimination of export subsidies. So, the stakes are high, and highest for our partners in the developing world.

On non-agricultural market access, the key standard of success will be increased market access in manufactured goods, which account for nearly 60 percent of all global trade. The mandate from Doha lays the groundwork for broad cuts in tariffs through a formula that would make deeper cuts in higher tariffs, and it provides the possibility of complete tariff elimination in key sectors.

Negotiations now are focused on the technical details of how we get a big result. We need to find common ground on the centerpiece of the proposal—the Swiss formula—combined with appropriate forms of flexibility for developing countries in order to proceed. Other issues—work on sectoral initiatives and non-tariff barriers—must also be addressed. There are concerns and sensitivities—we all have them—and we need to understand one another. We have a big opportunity to open markets for the future—particularly for developing countries—but we need to find a way to ensure that all contribute fairly to the outcome.

We cannot afford to be anything but ambitious and ensure that we are looking to markets of the future. We did so in the Uruguay Round with great success—we accomplished a number of sectoral initiatives where growth has been substantial (e.g., chemicals, medical equipment, pharmaceuticals). We want to look at the most aggressive ways to create market opportunities. As a result of the market openings in the Uruguay Round on the sectoral initiative on medical equipment, that sector grew nearly 165% in global exports (U.S. exports grew 89.2%).

On services, in July 2004 WTO members agreed to intensify the negotiations on opening markets and made clear that services are definitely on par with agriculture and manufacturing as a "core" market access area. Services are playing an increasing role in both developed and developing economies. Indeed, the World Bank recently reported on the force multiplier effect of open services markets: developing countries with open telecommunication and financial services markets grew 1.5 percent faster than countries where those two markets remained closed. Services, investment and trade go hand-in-hand, and liberalization in services will be a powerful engine for growth and job creation—especially in higher value added and therefore higher paying jobs.

This month, members are expected to table revised market access offers, according to the timetable established for negotiations. The process is slower than we would like, but we are encouraged that governments are beginning to see the important role that services plays in development. For developing countries, for example, over 55% of GDP comes from services trade—and much of this trade is done with other developing countries. Working with industry, we want to build out the negotiations and supplement the current process to ensure that the degree of openness and liberalization now provided by the United States is matched by others.

On rules, negotiations are underway on subsidies and antidumping. We have found convergence with our trading partners on a number of issues, notably the importance of creating greater transparency, certainty and predictability in the ways in which the rules are administered—and we have vigorously questioned any proposal that would undermine the effectiveness of our trade laws. We have also seen that there is enormous interest in building out the subsidy disciplines further to address new and emerging issues, including those that challenge the environment. . . .

WTO members are currently negotiating clarifications and improvements to the WTO Dispute Settlement Understanding. The United States recognizes that an effective dispute settlement system advantages the United States not only through the ability to secure the benefits negotiated under the agreements, but also by encouraging the rule of law among nations. The DSU negotiations offer members the opportunity to assess the strengths and weaknesses of the WTO dispute settlement system and to work together to improve the system.

In those negotiations, the United States has taken an active role. The United States has tabled proposals that would provide greater flexibility and member control in the dispute settlement process, including the ability to more effectively address errant or unhelpful panel reasoning. Moreover, the United States has tabled proposals to open up the dispute settlement process to the public—there is no reason the public should not be able to see the briefs filed or the panel and Appellate Body hearings.

After substantial delay, in July last year we managed to have an agreement to launch negotiations on trade facilitation. These negotiations are aimed at updating and improving border procedures to be more transparent and fair, and to expedite the rapid release of goods. The goal will be to overhaul 50 year-old customs rules that no longer match the needs of today's economy, much less tomorrow's. This work on trade facilitation will round out the market access elements of the overall Doha negotiating agenda and present the opportunity for true win-win results for every WTO member—developed and developing country alike.

This leads me to the question of development. It is clear that the biggest gains to development will be in the core areas of goods, services and agriculture. I am pleased to report that many of our trading partners see the issue in the same way. Liberalizing trade among developing countries is an essential part of this effort. Some 70 percent of the duties collected on developing country trade are due to tariffs imposed by developing countries. This is significant.

In addition to the negotiations, the United States will continue to contribute in various ways to development. On the technical assistance and capacity building side, I am pleased to announce that the United States will contribute an additional $1 million this year to the WTO's DDA Trust Fund. The appropriation by Congress for this purpose is something that we appreciate, as yet another example of our working together to support our overall strategic efforts. In this regard, I would also note that our total trade capacity building activities last year were close to $1 billion ($903 million).

In sum, the Doha negotiations hold the potential to make an important contribution to global growth and development. The Uruguay Round was launched in 1986, finalized in 1994, and we are just now seeing the final implementation of results. With care and attention, we can use the WTO to make a further substantial contribution to global growth and development. The United States is prepared to lead by example, but we need to ensure that we secure real gains and market opportunities in the decades ahead.

Conclusion

The first 10 years of the WTO have demonstrated why the United States must continue its active participation and leadership role. A turn away from the work of the past six decades to bring about a rules-based liberalized global trading system would bring certain closure of markets to those American workers and farmers dependent on continued trade liberalization and would ignite persistent trade conflicts that would distort the global economy beyond anything imaginable today. A world where the United States steps away from a rules-based global trading system would be a world where trade no longer would be a positive contribution toward solving broader international tensions; instead, trade issues would simply act as an additional dimension exacerbating larger strategic conflicts.

We know that the global trading system is not perfect, and remains—and perhaps always will remain—a work in progress. But through American leadership within the WTO, the core U.S. trade agenda of promoting open markets and the rule of law remains the core agenda of the global trading system. The work toward these objectives is complex and often difficult, especially in a dynamic global economy unfolding as never before. But this work is no less vital today than it was in those first decades after a catastrophic world war. The participation and leadership of the United States in the global trading system remains a critical element for ensuring America's continued prosperity, and for meeting the new challenges in seeking a more stable and secure world.

Problems with World Trade Organization Membership

On the basis of the ten-year record of the WTO [World Trade Organization] in operation, Public Citizen urges Congress to demand a transformation of the current global 'trade' rules which have not only failed to achieve the economic gains we were promised when Congress debated the establishment of the WTO in 1994, but have resulted in unacceptable reversals in an array of non-trade, non-economic policies and goals which promote the public interest in the United States and abroad. While this hearing is focused on the WTO's record, I urge this committee to hold a future hearing about ideas for transforming the current system to one that is more economically and environmentally sustainable and democratically accountable. Unfortunately the Bush administration's March annual trade report to Congress, which was also to be understood as fulfilling its statutorily required five-year report on the WTO, did not satisfy the statutory language by answering the specific questions set forth there which were designed to measure both the positive and negative results of the WTO on the United States. Rather, the March 1 report only touted the administration's view of the WTO's benefits for the United States.

We have spent the last ten years closely monitoring and documenting the outcomes of numerous trade agreements. Beginning in 2001, we compiled these findings for a book released in 2003, entitled *Whose Trade Organization? A Comprehensive Guide to the WTO*. This book is unique in its examination of the effect of WTO rules on economic well-being and development, agriculture and food safety, the environment, public health, and democratic policy-making. This testimony summarizes and updates the major findings of the book.

During the Uruguay Round negotiations of the General Agreement on Tariffs and Trade (GATT) which established the WTO and over a dozen new substantive agreements it would enforce, Public Citizen raised concerns about the implications of establishing such broad global rules on non-trade matters in the context of an international regime whose goal was expanding trade. While expanded trade has the ability to bring benefits to consumers, workers, and farmers, setting broad non-trade rules in a body whose aim was trade expansion, threatened to undermine an array of consumer, environmental and human rights goals, the implementation of which, sometimes limits trade, such as in food containing banned pesticides. Effectively our concern was that

Testimony before the Subcommittee on Trade, Committee on Ways and Means, Lori Wallach (May 17, 2005).

the WTO did not mainly cover 'trade,' but rather served to implement a much more expansive corporate globalization agenda that required countries to change their domestic policies worldwide to meet the needs and goals of the world's largest multinational business interests.

We also raised deep concerns about the WTO's threat to citizen-accountable, democratic policy-making processes—in which the people who would live with the results participate in making decisions and are able to alter policies that do not meet their needs. While some problems require a global approach—such as transboundary environmental problems or weapons proliferation—others, such as setting domestic food or product safety standards or developing policies to ensure a countries' inhabitants have access to affordable medicine or basic services such as healthcare, education, transportation, water or other utilities do not require global redress and moreover, setting global rules on these matters can undermine democratic policy making that reflects the needs and desires of different countries' inhabitants at different times.

We sought to alert Congress as to what a dramatic shift WTO would affect in how and where non-trade policy would be set. Yet even in this hearing, much of the focus remains on the important, but not singular implications of the WTO on trade flows. While the GATT covered only traditional trade matters, such as tariffs and quotas, with respect only to trade in goods, the WTO included agreements setting terms on the service sector; food, environmental and product safety standards; patents and copyrights; investment policy; and even the terms by which countries could make procurement decisions regarding their domestic tax dollars. The operative term of the WTO requires that "all countries shall ensure conformity of their domestic laws, regulations and administrative procedures" to all of these broad WTO requirements. As well, the WTO's Dispute Settlement Understanding (DSU) provided for a stringent enforcement mechanism, subjecting countries who fail to conform their domestic policies to the WTO dictates to trade sanctions after a tribunal process that does not guarantee the basic due process protections afforded by U.S. law, such as open hearings, access to documents, conflict of interest rules for tribunalists, or outside appeals.

In 1990 when Public Citizen began working on the Uruguay Round, we were not particularly focused on the potential implications for poor country development or on U.S. wages, income inequality or jobs. However, over 15 years of working on the GATT and then WTO, our relationships with developing country economists and policy experts, as well as our tracking of economic trends, has expanded the scope of our focus.

Now, after a decade of tracking the WTO's actual outcomes, Public Citizen's concerns about the WTO have grown dramatically. We have worked internationally with civil society and governments to promote a transformation of the existing global "trade" rules contained in the WTO and oppose the expansion of the scope of the WTO. Yet, even as the negative consequences of the current rules and the model they represent increase, the current Doha Round WTO negotiations fail to address the existing problems and instead are designed to expand the WTO's jurisdiction into yet greater non-trade matters.

The WTO's Controversial Dispute Settlement Procedure

Unlike the GATT, which required consensus to bind any country to an obligation, the WTO is unique among international agreements in that its panel rulings are automatically binding and only the unanimous consent of all WTO nations can halt their implementation. These rulings are backed up by trade sanctions which remain in place until a WTO-illegal domestic policy is changed. Among our analysis of WTO decisions between 1995 and 2003 are the following findings:

- **U.S. Domestic policies from gambling regulations to tax policies have been repeatedly ruled against by run-away WTO panels.** The recent WTO gambling case is the most recent demonstration that when expansive 'trade' rules come up against public interest laws before WTO tribunals, nondiscriminatory, democratically-created domestic policies can be undercut. Among the WTO panel's outlandish decisions in that case, where the Caribbean nation of Antigua challenged various U.S. state and federal anti-gambling laws, were the following: The *entire* U.S. gambling sector is covered by provisions within the WTO's General Agreement on Trade in Services (GATS) irrespective of the intention of U.S. trade negotiators. As such, the ability of the U.S. government to regulate not only Internet but ALL forms of gambling at the federal, state and local level is limited by the rules of GATS. The panel also announced that GATS rules forbidding numerical restrictions on covered services means that a *ban* on an activity in a GATS-covered sector, even if applied to domestic and foreign service providers alike, is a "zero quota" and thus a violation of GATS rules—with broad implications for bans on an expansive range of pernicious activity. These two elements of the ruling mean that the U.S. is exposed to future WTO challenges in light of limits on gambling common in many states, as well as assorted exclusive supplier arrangements, such as with Indian tribes, and state monopoly gaming, such as the 43 U.S. states and territories which use lotteries to raise revenues. Thus, the WTO panel, in this case, interpreted that a GATS exception for "laws necessary to protect public morals," could be applied if the U.S. eliminates discrepancies between the way in which it regulates domestic and foreign providers, including through the U.S. Interstate Horseracing Act, which waives the three laws challenged by Antigua for certain domestic firms. A week later, a WTO tribunal issued a ruling on the same necessity text within the GATS exceptions clause in a case having to do with the Dominican Republic's alcohol distribution system which explicitly contradicted the inclusive reading in the gambling case. At a minimum this conflict in rulings shows that the lenient decision in the gambling case with regards to the necessity test is not a settled WTO standard. Some WTO observers wonder if the sudden switch back to the past, narrow ruling on the necessary test points to the political nature of the WTO dispute process and an attempt to avoid an explosive WTO ruling just before the U.S. Congress takes up the WTO ten year review.

- **With only two exceptions, every health, food safety or environmental law challenged at the WTO has been declared a barrier to trade.** The exceptions have been the highly-politicized challenge to France's ban on asbestos and a WTO compliance panel's determination that after losing a WTO case on the Endangered Species Act turtle protection regulations, the U.S. had weakened the law to sufficiently comply with the WTO's orders.

- **In most WTO cases, the country that launches the challenge wins.** As a result, mere threats of WTO action now cause many nations to change their policies. The challenging country at least partially prevailed in an astonishing 102 out of 118 completed WTO cases—a success rate of 86.4 percent.

- **Important U.S laws ruled illegal at the WTO.** In 42 out of 48 cases brought against the United States in which a WTO panel has made a ruling, or 85.7 percent of the time, the WTO has labeled as illegal policies ranging from sea turtle protections and clean air regulations to tax and antidumping policies. The United States also lost two high-profile cases that it brought against EU computer tariff classifications and Japan's film policies.

- **U.S. trade safeguard laws have been successfully challenged numerous times in the WTO.** One of the most politically sensitive aspects of Congress' 1994 consideration of the WTO was the degree to which U.S. trade safeguard law would have to be changed to conform to the related WTO agreements. Congress was promised that our laws would remain effective, yet, a decade later, the United States has not been able to successfully defend any of our safeguard laws in 14 out of 14 completed cases brought by other countries against our safeguards on products ranging from steel to lamb to wool shirts. Furthermore, the United States has lost 11 out of 15 anti-dumping or countervailing duties cases. Additionally, Doha Round "Rules" negotiations are poised to translate these WTO cases against the U.S. into new, more expansive limits on U.S. domestic trade safeguard laws. Meanwhile despite promises that other U.S. trade laws, such as Section 301, would remain operational under a WTO regime, the U.S. withdrew a case against Japan regarding anticompetitive practices in film trade after it became clear that use of Section 301 sanctions would be prohibited under WTO rules.

- **The process is closed, narrow and unbalanced.** Our concerns about the WTO dispute resolution process have born out. Complaints are typically filed at the request of business interests with no opportunity for input from other interested parties. The WTO Secretariat selects panel members from a roster formed using qualifications that ensure a bias towards the WTO's primacy. Panelists' identities are not disclosed and there is no requirement that they disclose conflicts of interest they might have in deciding cases. Tribunals meet in closed sessions and proceedings are confidential unless a government voluntarily makes its submissions public. Far from being a neutral arbiter, the singular and explicit goal of the dispute settlement process is to expand trade in goods and services. Increasingly, WTO panels have rewritten WTO provisions with their broad interpretations, a situation that can find no remedy as there is no outside appeal.

The WTO Decade and the U.S. Economy: Exploding U.S. Trade Deficits, Increased Income Inequality, Stagnant Real Wages, and the Loss of 1 in 6 U.S. Manufacturing Jobs

In the early 1990s, many economists argued that the opening of foreign markets for U.S. exports under WTO (and NAFTA) would create U.S. jobs and increase income for U.S. workers and farmers. When Congress was preparing to vote on WTO in 1994, the President's Council of Economic Advisers informed Congress that approval of the package would increase annual U.S. GDP by $100–200 billion over the next decade. Others claimed that the WTO's adoption would lead to a decline in the U.S. trade deficit. President [Bill] Clinton even went so far as to promise that the average American family would gain $1,700 in income annually from the WTO's adoption, which would have meant that the U.S. real median family income would have been upwards of $65,000 in 2005, or a nearly 35 percent increase since 1995. These growth projections have been shown to be wildly off the mark.

- **U.S. Median Income Growth Meager:** U.S. median income grew only 8 percent to $52,680 in 2003—the latest numbers available. There is little reason to think that this has improved in 2004–05, since median real wages have not grown since that time. In fact, the U.S. real median wage has scarcely risen above its 1970 level (only 9 percent), while productivity has soared 82 percent over the same period, resulting in declining or stagnant standards of living for the nearly 70 percent of the U.S. population that does not have a college degree.
- **Trade Deficit Soars as Imports Boom**: During the WTO era, the U.S. trade deficit has risen to historic levels, and approaches six percent of national income—a figure widely agreed to be unsustainable, putting the U.S. economy at risk of lowered income growth in the future. Soaring imports during the WTO decade have contributed to the loss of nearly one in six U.S. manufacturing jobs.
- **U.S. Has Suffered a Good-Job Export Crisis:** Another factor contributing to this job loss is the shift in investment trends, with China overtaking the United States in 2003 as the leading target for FDI [foreign direct investment: the purchase of realty property abroad or a controlling interest in a foreign business]. WTO Trade Related Investment Rules, (TRIMs), limit the ability of countries to set conditions on how foreign investors operate in other countries, making it more appealing for manufacturers to seek lower wages by relocating. Meanwhile, WTO terms guaranteed low tariff access for products made in low wage countries back into wealthy markets while forbidding rich countries from setting labor or other standards such products must meet. The type and quality of jobs available for workers in the U.S. economy has dramatically shifted during the WTO decade, with workers losing to imports or offshoring [hiring people abroad to do a job] their higher wage manufacturing jobs (which often also provided health care and other benefits) and finding reemployment in lower wage jobs. Labor Department data shows that such workers lose up to 27 percent of their earnings in such shifts.
- **U.S. Income and Wage Inequality Have Jumped:** During the WTO decade these trends have resulted in U.S. income and wage inequality

increasing markedly. In 1995, the top five percent of U.S. households by income made 6.5 times what the poorest 20 percent of households made, while this gap grew by nearly 10 percent by 2003. In wages, the situation was comparable. In 1995, a male worker that ranked at the 95th percentile in wages earned 2.68 times what a worker at the 20th percentile earned. By 2003, that gap had widened nearly 8 percent. Nearly all economists agree that increased trade has partially driven this widening inequality. One study by the non-partisan Center for Economic and Policy Research found that trade liberalization has cost U.S. workers without college degrees an amount equal to 12.2% of their current wages. For a worker earning $25,000 a year, this loss would be slightly more than $3,000 per year. William Cline, at the pro-WTO Institute for International Economics, estimates that about 39 percent of the actually observed increase in wage inequality is attributable to trade trends.

- **Job Export Crisis Is Expanding from Manufacturing to High Tech and Services:** While some commentators, such as Nike CEO Phil Knight, have famously argued that this decline in assembly-line U.S. manufacturing is a result of "Americans simply not wanting to make shoes for a living," job loss and wage stagnation is increasingly affecting workers in those sectors where the United States is understood to have a comparative advantage, such as professional services and high technology. Studies commissioned by the U.S. government have shown that as many as 48,417 U.S. jobs—including many in high-tech sectors—were offshored to other countries in the first three months of 2004 alone. This trend does not appear to be slowing down, as 3.3 million high-end service sector jobs—including physicians, computer programmers, engineers, accountants and architects—are all forecast to be outsourced overseas in the next decade. Another study by the Progressive Policy Institute, a think-tank associated with the pro-WTO faction of the Democratic Party, found that 12 million information-based U.S. jobs—54 percent paying better than the median wage—are highly susceptible to such offshoring.

    This manufacturing and high-tech job loss has had direct impact on workers' ability to bargain for higher real wages. Studies commissioned by the U.S. government show that as many as 62 percent of U.S. union drives face employer threats to relocate abroad, with the factory shut-down rate following successful union certifications tripling in the years after WTO relative to the years before.

    In short, few of the claims made about the U.S. economic benefits that would flow from greater trade liberalization can be shown to have been close to accurate. This, however, has not stopped another round of WTO expansion from being launched, accompanied by a new set of promises. The WTO and the Developing World: Do As We Say, Not As We Did

    The WTO's failure to deliver the promised economic gains in the United States has also been mirrored abroad. Despite a paucity of evidence, think tanks, public opinion-makers and newspapers editorials have continued to relentlessly promote the notion that developing countries are the primary beneficiaries of WTO globalization. After a decade of the WTO, few if any of the promised economic benefits have materialized for developing countries. For many, poverty and inequality have worsened, while nearly all countries have experienced a sharp slowdown in their rates of economic growth.

- **Poverty on the Rise.** The number and percentage of people living on less than $1 a day (the World Bank's definition of extreme poverty) in the regions with some of the worst forms of poverty—Sub-Saharan Africa and the Middle East—have increased since the WTO went into effect, while the number and percentage of people living on less than $2 a day has gone up in the same time for these regions, as well as for Latin America and the Caribbean. The number of people living in poverty has gone up for South Asia, while the rate of reduction in poverty has slowed nearly worldwide—especially when one excludes China, where huge reductions in poverty have been accomplished, but not by following WTO-approved policies given China only became a WTO member in 2001.
- **Slowdown in global growth rates under WTO model.** The per-capita income growth rates of developing regions before the period of structural adjustment and WTO liberalization are higher than the growth rates after the countries implemented the WTO—International Monetary Fund (IMF) model, many aspects of which are locked in through the WTO's services, investment, intellectual property and other agreements. For low and middle-income countries, per capita growth between 1980 and 2000 fell to half of that experienced between 1960 and 1980. Latin America's per-capita GDP grew by 75% between 1960–1980; however, between 1980–2000—the period during which these countries adopted the package of economic policies required by the WTO and IMF—it grew by only six percent. Even when one takes into account the longer 1980–2005 period, there is no single 25-year window in the history of the continent that was worse in terms of rate of income gains. Sub-Saharan Africa's per-capita GDP grew by 36% between 1960–1980 but declined by 15% between 1980–2000. Arab states' per-capita GDP declined between 1980–2000, after it grew 175% between 1960–1980. South Asia, South East Asia and the Pacific all had lower per-capita GDP growth, subsequent to 1980 than in the previous 20 years. (Only in East Asia was this trend not sustained, but only because China's per-capita GDP quadrupled during this period prior to China joining the WTO).
- **Developing countries that did not adopt the package fared better:** In sharp contrast, nations like China, India, Malaysia and Vietnam, that chose their own economic mechanisms and policies through which to integrate into the world economy had more economic success. These countries had among the highest growth rates in the developing world over the past two decades—despite ignoring the directives of the WTO, IMF or World Bank.
- **Gap between rich and poor widens.** Instead of generating income convergence between rich and poor countries, as WTO proponents predicted, the corporate globalization era of the 1990s exacerbated the income inequality between industrial and developing countries, as well as between rich and poor within many countries. According to one United Nations study, "in almost all developing countries that

have undertaken rapid trade liberalization, wage inequality has increased, most often in the context of declining industrial employment of unskilled workers and large absolute falls in their real wages, on the order of 20–30% in Latin American countries." According to another, the richest 5 percent of the world's people receive 114 times the income of the poorest 5 percent, and the richest one percent receives as much as the poorest 57 percent. This trend is widening over time, not closing, with the 20 richest countries earning per-capita incomes 16 times greater than non-oil producing, less developed countries in 1960, and by 1999 the richest countries earning incomes 35 times higher, signifying a doubling of the income inequality.

The track record of the IMF and WTO—condoned policies—which have failed to reduce poverty and inequality or increase growth—are falling into greater ignominy. A recent study by the Inter-American Development Bank found that, of a total of 66 presidential and 81 legislative elections in 17 Latin American countries during the 1985–2002 period, incumbent parties that pursued trade liberalization and privatizations while in office lost between 25 to 50 percent of their previous votes when pursuing reelection. If anything, voter discontent in Latin America, a region widely seen as having most fully implemented the standard "neo-liberal" policies, has increased since 2002.

Even policy-makers who once pursued such liberalization policies, such as former Venezuelan economic minister Ricardo Hausmann and SAIS [school of Advanced International Studies, Johns Hopkins University] economist Riordan Roett, have now advocated a move away from the Washington Consensus policies, due to their utter failure to generate growth and rising living standards. Such a reversal is not surprising, given that no developed country, including the United States, England, or even Korea developed on the basis of "free trade," without managing foreign investment or without government intervention in providing basic services and infrastructure. Indeed, many commentators have observed that developed country's advocacy of WTO liberalization policies is akin to "kicking away the ladder" to development for the poor countries, once the rich countries have already climbed up.

U.S. Becomes Net Food Importer Under WTO, While Poor Countries Face Increased Food Insecurity

The WTO's approach to agriculture is to treat food as if it were any other commodity, like steel or rubber, not something on which every person's life depends. WTO rules on agriculture, both under the Agreement on Agriculture (AoA) and the Trade Related Aspects of Intellectual Property (TRIPS), have led to devastating outcomes for developing countries, while farm income in the wealthy countries has declined as food trade volumes have risen. These WTO rules have forced the elimination of domestic policies aimed at ensuring food sovereignty and security in developing countries, and of policies aimed at balancing power between producers and grain traders and food processors in rich countries. These changes have greatly benefited multinational commodity trading and food processing companies who, in the absence of government price and supply management programs, have been able to manipulate the markets to keep prices paid to farmers low, while at the same time keeping the prices paid by consumers steady or rising. Farmers in rich and poor countries have only seen their incomes decline, with many losing farms and livelihoods under the decade of the WTO regime. In the developing world, the combination of sharply lower prices and the effects of WTO rules regarding the patenting of seeds and plants under TRIPS have led to increased hunger.

- **United States to become net food importer.** According to a U.S. Department of Agriculture (USDA) write-up of the topic, 2005 may be the first time since 1959 that the United States will be a net food importer, thanks to a flood of imports and declining export growth. That the report blames the increased appetite of U.S. consumers for foreign products for this projected deficit is nonsensical given that much of the flood of imports is in the products in which the United States was once considered the leading exporter, such as beef and poultry, while U.S. exports of cotton, soy, red meat have declined dramatically in recent years.
- **Under the AoA, export prices for key U.S. crops have fallen to levels substantially below the cost of production, while consumer prices increased.** Since 1996, U.S. crop prices have generally declined about 40 percent, while the cost of running a farm has risen by as much. The overall tilt of U.S. government farm policy, in line with the WTO's AoA, has been to remove the last vestiges of production management and price support, while topping off the dips in gross farm income through government payments. According to government data, however, real prices for food eaten at home in the U.S. rose by 30% during the WTO era (1994 and 2004), even as prices paid to farmers plummeted.
- **A similar long-term trend holds in the developing world**, where falling real prices for the agricultural commodity exports on which poor countries depend have fallen 50 percent relative to the 1960s, while wild price swings of up to 25 percent off of price trends make planning and subsistence difficult. At the same time, many of the very poorest countries are increasingly reliant on grain imports to meet their food needs, with the share of food imports in national income tripling since the 1960s. This trend has been particularly felt in Mexico, where the consumer price of the staple food corn tortillas has only risen since NAFTA, despite a flood of cheap corn imports into Mexico that have collapsed much of Mexico's domestic small-scale corn production.
- **A dramatic loss of U.S. family farms accompanies sharp falls in income for the poorest farmers under the WTO.** The United States lost 226,695 small and family farms between 1994 and 2003, while average net cash farm income for the very poorest farmers dropped to an astounding −$5,228.90 in 2003—a colossal 200 percent drop since the WTO went into effect.
- **Displacement and hunger the norm in developing countries.** Following the decade of the WTO and NAFTA, over 1.5 million Mexican *campesino* farmers were thrown from their land. The agricultural sector, traditionally a major source of employment in Mexico, was

devastated by the dumping of U.S. and foreign agricultural products into their markets. Likewise, the Chinese government projects that as many as 500 million of China's peasants will be made surplus, as the country continues the rapid acceleration of industrial development of its agriculture sector under WTO rules. In country after country, displaced farmers have had little choice but to join swelling urban workforces where the oversupply of labor suppresses wages and exacerbates the politically and socially destabilizing crisis of chronic under- and unemployment in the cities of the developing world.

- **By dramatically expanding legal definitions of what can be patented under the TRIPS Agreement, the WTO has endangered food sovereignty and security in poor countries.** In most developing countries, the majority of the population lives on the land and feeds itself by replanting saved seeds. Yet over 150 cases have already been documented of research institutions or businesses applying for patents on naturally-occurring plants, some of which have been farmed for generations. After the WTO TRIPS Agreement becomes fully binding for developing countries in 2006, governments that fail to enforce patents on seeds—by pulling up crops or by forcing subsistence farmers who can not afford to do so to pay royalties—will face trade sanctions.

These trends and the policies underpinning them are not expected to be improved upon in the current WTO Doha Round negotiations. Increasingly, even pro-trade academics such as Jagdish Bhagwati are arguing that the proposed agricultural reforms will not benefit most poor countries, characterizing claims to the contrary as "dangerous nonsense" and a "pernicious fallacy." The liberalization-led fall in prices has had a negative effect on producers in rich and poor countries alike, as a recent National Bureau of Economic Research study concluded when it found that middle income corn farmers in Mexico saw their incomes fall by more than 50 percent after NAFTA / WTO implementation. After a decade of failed policies, it is clear that the WTO's "one size fits all" approach to agriculture and food security issues has failed at delivering its promised results.

The WTO's Coming to Dinner and Food Safety is Not on the Menu

The WTO's relentless drive toward the "harmonization" of food, animal and plant regulations based on low, industry-preferred international standards, endangers human health and sharply curtails the ability of elected governments to protect the health of their citizens in this critically important area. WTO-approved standards are generally set in private-sector bodies which do not permit consumer or health interests to participate and which make decisions without complying with domestic regulatory procedures for openness, participation or balance. Even if a country's domestic food safety laws treat domestic and foreign products identically, if the policy provides greater consumer protection than the WTO-named international standard, it is presumed to be a WTO violation and must pass a series of WTO test established in the Sanitary and Phytosanitary Agreement that have proved impossible to meet. Some of our key findings include:

- **As required under WTO "equivalency determination" rules, the U.S. declared that dozens of countries ensure their meat inspection systems are "equivalent" to that of the U.S. even though the countries' standards and performance violated U.S. law and regulation.** Many nations maintain their equivalency status and this right to ship meat to the U.S. despite documented violations of U.S. policy. For instance, Argentina's meat inspection system maintains its U.S. equivalency status despite well-documented problems that include contamination of meat with oil, hair and feces. Similarly, the Brazilian system, which allowed companies to pay meat inspectors in violation of U.S. law requiring independent government inspection, was declared "equivalent." USDA [U.S. Department of Agriculture] labeling of imported products makes them indistinguishable to the consumer.
- **Time and time again, WTO tribunals have refused to permit any regulatory action based on the "Precautionary Principle."** Governments have long relied on this principle to shield their populations from uncertain risks from new or emerging products. Previous "precautionary" actions by the U.S. government to ban the morning sickness drug Thalidomide in the 1960s and to prevent the outbreak of Mad Cow disease in the 1980s and 90s helped avert the substantial human and agricultural devastation that occurred in other countries due to these and other policies. Yet the U.S. has used the WTO to systematically attack other countries' precautionary regulations such as those dealing with beef hormones, genetically modified organisms (GMOs), invasive species and agricultural pests.
- **Any domestic standard that provides more health protection than a WTO-approved standard, is presumed to be a trade barrier,** unless the higher standard is supported by extensive scientific data and analysis that clearly shows a specific and significant risk associated with the lower standard. No nation has yet been able to demonstrate the need for higher standards, much to the WTO's satisfaction, despite several lengthy and costly attempts by developed countries to perform WTO-required risk assessments on the dangers posed by artificial hormones in beef, invasive species, pest contamination of native salmon populations, and more.

The WTO's Environmental Impact: First, Gattzilla Ate Flipper

Public Citizen has documented a systematic pattern of WTO attacks on member nations' vital environmental concerns and policy priorities, as well as a series of biases built into WTO rules that promote unsustainable uses of natural resources. Over its ten years of operation, the WTO's anti-environmental rhetoric has been replaced by more political pronouncements, even as WTO tribunals have systematically ruled against every domestic environmental policy challenge that has come before it, and eviscerated whatever GATT Article XX exceptions that might have been used to safeguard such laws. Instead of seeking to resolve conflicts between commercial and environmental goals, the WTO's largely ineffectual Committee on Trade and the Environment has become a venue mainly for identifying green policies that violate WTO rules. Key findings include:

- **To date, all GATT/ WTO dispute panel decisions on environmental laws have required that the challenged domestic laws and measures be weakened**—even when the challenged policy treats domestic and foreign goods the same, or when it implements a country's obligations under a Multilateral Environmental Agreement (e.g. the U.S. Endangered Species Act regulations implementing the Convention on International Trade in Endangered Species (CITES)). When the WTO ruled against U.S. Endangered Species Act rules protecting CITES-listed sea turtles from shrimpers' nets, the U.S. complied with the WTO order by replacing the requirement that all countries seeking to sell shrimp in the United States had to ensure that their shrimpers used turtle exclusion devices. The new U.S. regulations were approved several years later, but Thailand and other shrimp exporting countries continue to put pressure on the United States to weaken the rule's enforceability.
- **WTO rules have consistently been interpreted to mean that products cannot be treated differently according to how they were produced or harvested.** This interpretation, for which there is no legal basis in the actual rules, requires, for example, that clear-cut tropical timber cannot be treated differently from sustainably-harvested timber, that fish caught with damaging drift nets cannot be distinguished from sustainably-caught fish, and that products made using child labor or extreme cruelty toward animals must be given the same trade treatment as products made under more humane and ethical conditions.
- **Because WTO panels have systematically ruled against challenged environmental policies, now mere threats of challenges often suffice.** For example, after years of sustained trade law challenges, the Bush administration decided to quietly implement a change to a "dolphin safe" labeling policy which Mexico had demanded as necessary for implementation of a GATT ruling. (Mexico had threatened a new WTO case if their demands were not met). On New Years Eve 2002, when few U.S. citizens were focused on policy matters, the Bush administration announced that it would change the "Flipper-friendly" tuna policy and allow the "dolphin-safe" label to be used on tuna caught using deadly purse seine nets and dolphin encirclement. While this policy was eventually overturned in a challenge brought by environmentalists to federal court, Mexico and other countries continue to make noises about a possible WTO challenge. Another case involved Hong Kong's WTO complaint about U.S. anti-invasive species laws. In this case, U.S. regulatory efforts to fight the costly infestation of the Asian Longhorned Beetle (which is devastating maple and other trees throughout the United States) are being classified as violating WTO rules. The mere threat of a challenge in

this regard has provoked the USDA to considering watering down regulations requiring treatment of raw wood packing material to comply with a weaker, WTO-sanctioned "international" standard.

Warning: The WTO Can be Hazardous to Public Health

The WTO's wide-ranging rules have consistently troubled public health advocates, who have found that many policies which have little to do with trade, are being threatened by WTO mandates. The following are some examples:

- **Access to and safety of medicines.** The creation of a worldwide pharmaceutical patenting system under the WTO's TRIPS agreement has raised pharmaceutical costs in the U.S. and further restricted the availability of lifesaving drugs in developing countries. A 1995 study on the overall impact of the TRIPS agreement on U.S. consumers "conservatively estimated" $6 billion in higher U.S. drug prices due to windfall patent extensions under the WTO. Why a business protection scheme guaranteeing monopoly markets would be inserted into a trade 'liberalization' agreement has outraged consumer groups worldwide. Poor country governments and health officials note with fury that even though the current patent and licensing regime has only recently been accepted in developed countries (Switzerland for example, did not recognize drug patents until the 1960s), under WTO rules developing nations around the world are required to adopt monopoly patents on medicines. Concern about public health has grown around the world, with many Members of Congress taking a lead in opposing trade agreements that restrict access to essential medicines. Unfortunately, the U.S. government has often been on the wrong side of this issue, WTO challenging Brazilian and threatening Thai and South African laws on compulsory licensing of pharmaceutical products and pushing to undermine in its new Free Trade Agreements a 2001 WTO Declaration reiterating countries' ability to issue compulsory licenses for medicines. Yet the U.S. itself used the power it seeks to deny other nations in WTO when it threatened a compulsory license after the 2001 anthrax scare.
- **Downward harmonization for drug testing.** In order to fulfill its harmonization obligations under the WTO, the Food and Drug Administration (FDA) in 1996 proposed changes to its guidelines for testing the potential carcinogenicity of medicines being approved for U.S. use. The FDA had previously required companies to test drugs on two species (typically mice and rats) because tests on rats alone often failed to produce evidence of carcinogenicity where it was subsequently found in mice. The new WTO "harmonized" testing standard approved by the FDA, however, allows drug companies to drop long-term mice tests and substitute them with less reliable short-term second species tests.
- **Threatening developing countries with WTO challenges to pressure them into reducing public health protections.** American Gerber Products Company refused to comply with Guatemalan infant

formula labeling laws that implemented the WHO/UNICEF "Nestlé's Code" on the grounds that the laws violated trademark protections provided in the WTO's TRIPS agreement. The Guatemalan law forbid pictorial depictions of healthy babies aimed at inducing illiterate people to replace breast feeding with formula which, when mixed with unsanitary water, was causing an epidemic of avoidable infant deaths. Gerber refused to remove its trademark "Gerber Baby" from its labels. The law might have withstood the threatened WTO challenge. However, to avoid the prohibitive cost of mounting an uncertain defense, Guatemalan authorities instead exempted imported formula from this important public health law, whose success in saving babies' lives had led to Guatemala previously being held up as an example by UNICEF.

Conclusion: The WTO Must Shrink or Sink in Order for the Public Interest to be Served

The WTO, far from being a win-win proposition, has been a lose-lose affair for most people in the United States and abroad, threatening people's livelihoods, the environment, public health, and the right of people around the world to enjoy democratic policy-making processes that allow them to decide what is best for themselves.

The recent WTO gambling ruling and other controversial rulings are widening the coalition of groups questioning U.S. trade policy. Groups such as the Association of State Supreme Court Justices, U.S. League of Cities, National Conference of State Legislatures, National Association of Counties, and National Association of Towns and Townships all have expressed concerns that current and proposed trade rules may undermine our nation's system of federalism and the integrity of our domestic courts. Groups typically considered bedrocks of the "pro-trade" alliance, such as the National Association of State Departments of Agriculture and other agricultural groups, are expressing concerns about depressed commodity prices, lowered farm income, and the United States' "net food importer" status. Associations of immigrant-descended groups such as the League of United Latin American Citizens are expressing concerns that Hispanics and people of color are not sharing in the gains from trade. And high-tech workers and inventors are arguing that the drive to make ever-more protectionist trade law favoring the largest high-tech corporations like Pfizer and Microsoft is cheating workers whose jobs are being offshored, inventors who are seeing few gains for their innovations, and consumers in rich and poor countries alike, who face lessened access to essential medicine and restrictions on legitimate uses of copyrighted items.

Opposition to the WTO's rules is increasingly coming from governments themselves, as the organization's ever-growing crisis of legitimacy bursts into public view again with the collapse of the WTO's Cancun Ministerial. In particular, these countries—led by Brazil, India, South Africa and other nations— demanded that the WTO should not establish one-size-fits all, anti-democratic rules over investment, government procurement, and competition policy, proposed rules that were subsequently dropped from WTO discussion. It is extremely ironic that while the Bush Administration argues that one of its top priorities is promoting democracy worldwide, the status quo WTO and U.S. positions regarding the WTO's future course push in the opposite direction.

We no longer have to guess what might happen under the WTO: we now know. A decade of WTO policy has led to stagnant real national and family incomes around the world, increased poverty in the poorest regions, and undemocratic WTO attacks on national sovereignty and public policy. Based on this evidence, Public Citizen finds it highly unlikely that continuation or expansion of this model will reverse these failures.

Thus, Public Citizen works with a global movement calling for transformation of the current WTO system. While we believe that a system of global trade rules is vital, the current rules are not serving us well. We propose that certain non-trade aspects be eliminated from the WTO. We also propose that the trade rules that would remain be altered so as to better meet the goals of providing sustainable livelihoods to people in rich and poor countries alike, fighting for the elimination of poverty, ensuring sustainable use of natural resources and providing food sovereignty, the essential tool in fighting hunger. For details on these proposals, we [urge] you to review their summary at "WTO—Shrink or Sink! The Turnaround Agenda International Civil Society Sign-On Letter," or for a more thorough review, *Alternatives to Economic Globalization: A Better World is Possible*, which is an edited anthology with contributions from Public Citizen.

To maintain, much less expand, a global 'trade' regime that to date has worsened the economic situation in rich and poor countries alike, threatened food sovereignty and access to essential medicines, and that undermined democratic governance is a recipe for growing economic, social and political instability. At a minimum, the real life outcomes of a continuation of the expansive status quo corporate globalization agenda as implemented by the WTO poses an enormous risk to the legitimacy of trade itself.

POSTSCRIPT

Is World Trade Organization Membership Beneficial?

There can be no doubt that there are winners and losers in globalization, including free trade, both among countries and within them. Moreover, it is much easier to see the negative consequences of free trade and its central organization, the World Trade Organization, than it is to see the positive aspects. Low or no tariffs on imported fabrics and clothing has, for example, meant that most of these commodities sold in the United States are imported from China and elsewhere. Tens of thousands of American workers in fabric mills and clothing manufacturing plants have lost their jobs, and it is easy to empathize with them. Yet it is also the case that imports mean that Americans pay less for their shirts, pants, and other garments than they would have if they were made in the United States given the differing wages and other production costs with China. It is also easy to be offended when a WTO hearing finds that your country has violated trade rules. Yet the WTO's rules, which all member countries have agreed to follow, also mean that your country can file a case against another country when it violates trade law. It is axiomatic that if your country is free to ignore the rules and the WTO that other countries are also free to do so, even if that negatively impacts your country. It is also the case that almost every country thinks that it is disadvantaged in one way or another by their WTO membership, yet almost all countries are either members of the organization or aspire to membership. The best way to evaluate the WTO, then, is to decide, on balance, whether it is performing well or not.

As the matter stands, the Doha Round remains stalled. Top-level negotiations in Cancun, Mexico, in 2003 and in Hong Kong in late 2005 both collapsed. Another try to move the negotiations forward held in July 2006 at WTO headquarters in Geneva, Switzerland, also ended in stalemate. As a result, WTO Director-General Pascal Lamy recommended that talks be suspended until members are ready to negotiate more flexibly. "If the political will really exists [to reach an agreement], there must be a way," Lamay told the WTO Council. "But it is not here today," Lamay lamented. "And let me be clear: there are no winners and losers in this assembly. Today there are only losers." Challenging the WTO members, Lamay concluded, "The ball is clearly in your court."

To further explore the WTO, good places to start is the Web site of the WTO at www.wto.org, and the overview the organization, its history, and the current issues related to it found in John H. Barton, Judith L. Goldstein, Timothy E. Josling, and Richard H. Steinberg, *The Evolution of the Trade Regime: Politics, Law, and Economics of the GATT and the WTO* (Princeton University Press, 2006). More on the WTO's dispute resolution system is available in Giorgio Sacerdoti, Alan Yanovich, and Jan Bohanes, eds., *The WTO at Ten: The Contribution of the Dispute Settlement System* (Cambridge University Press, 2006). The best location to look into the U.S. government's perspective on the WTO and the Doha Round is at the Web site of the U.S. Trade Representative at http://www.ustr.gov/. B. S. Chimni, "The World Trade Organization, Democracy and Development: A View From the South," *Journal of World Trade* (February 2006) takes the view that the WTO is an instrument of capitalism used by the United States and other developed countries to continue to dominate and disadvantage the developing countries.

ISSUE 10

Should the United States Take a Hard-line with China About Its International Economic Policies?

YES: Robert Baugh, from "Currency Manipulation and Labor Violations as Illegal Industrial Subsidies," Testimony during Hearings on "China's World Trade Organization Compliance: Industrial Subsidies and the Impact on U.S. and World Markets," before the U.S.–China Economic and Security Review Commission (April 4, 2006)

NO: John Frisbie, from "U.S.–China Business Council Advocates Balanced Approach to China Trade," Testimony during Hearings on "U.S.–China Economic Relations Revisited," before the Finance Committee, U.S. Senate (March 29, 2006)

ISSUE SUMMARY

YES: Robert Baugh, executive director, Industrial Union Council, AFL-CIO, asserts that the litany of China's failures to meet its trade obligations is extensive and that the failure of the U.S. government to respond strongly has put the country on a dangerous path.

NO: John Frisbie, president of the U.S.–China Business Council in Washington, D.C., concedes that there are some difficult issues to resolve with China but argues that jeopardizing the U.S. economy with tariffs or other protectionist measures is not an acceptable way to inform China that it must change some of its policies.

To a degree, the debate in Issue 9 on the World Trade Organization (WTO) extended the debate in Issue 1 on economic globalization by focusing on one of the major international financial institutions, the WTO, and its primary function, facilitating free trade. Now Issue 10 takes the process of evaluating economic globalization yet another step by narrowing the focus even more. In this case, the topic is trade and other aspects of the economic relationship between China and the United States. Also note that the topic here is connected to the debate in Issue 5 over whether China's growth should be a source of alarm.

Only a little more than a quarter century ago, trade and other forms of economic interchange between the United States and China were almost nil. Washington recognized the long-ousted (1949) Nationalist Chinese government on Taiwan as the legal government of all China and regarded the Chinese government in Beijing as an illegal usurper. The shift in U.S. recognition from Taipei to Beijing in 1979 and the more pragmatic economic approach of China's government after Mao Zedong died in 1976 were the key elements that ended the three-decade-long economic freeze between the two countries.

Trade is the cornerstone of the rapidly expanding relationship. As recently as 1986, U.S.–China bilateral annual trade was only $8 billion. By 1995, total trade between the two countries came to $57 billion and by 2005 it had quintupled during the decade to $285 billion. The problem is that U.S.–China trade was already out of balance in 1995 and has grown markedly more so since then. In 1995, China sold $46 billion in goods to the United States but bought only $12 billion in U.S. products. Thus, China's exports to the United States exceeded its imports by $34 billion. Data for 2005 shows that China sold $244 billion in goods to the United States but bought only $42 billion in U.S. products. Thus, the U.S. trade deficit with China worsened between 1995 and 2005 both in terms of the ratio (from 3.8:1 to 5.8:1) and the amount (from –$34 billion to –$202 billion). Even more troublesome is the fact that this adds significantly to the overall U.S. trade deficit, which grew 747 percent from –$96 billion in 1995 to –$717 billion in 2005.

The image that China mostly sends low-tech items to the United States and buys high-tech items in return is largely a myth. In 2005 the most common category of goods that each country exported to the other was the same: electrical machinery and equipment. What was different was that China's exports of these products to the United States amounted to $53 billion, while China's imports of U.S. electrical machinery and equipment came to $7 billion. Another quasi-myth about the economic relationship is that the flow of U.S. trade dollars to China is offset by profits earned from U.S. investments (foreign direct investment, FDI) in China's manufacturing plants and other enterprises. However, total U.S. earnings on its FDI in China came to only about 1 percent of U.S. global FDI earnings in 2005.

In the first reading by Robert Baugh, critics of China accuse it of any number of practices that violate WTO trade rules. One of these is the charge that China has discouraged imports by keeping the exchange rate of its currency, the yuan, artificially high—at 8.3 yuan to the dollar at a time when the U.S. dollar weakened against most other currencies. Among other reactions, Congress considered the (Hunter-Ryan bill H.R. 1498), which would have imposed a 27.5 percent increase in the U.S. tariff on Chinese goods unless Beijing devalued its currency. In July 2005, China agreed to devalue the yuan by 2 percent and to let it fluctuate further within a narrow range. That concession and the White Houses pressure on Congress not to force an economic confrontation to China kept H.R. 1498 and other retaliatory legislation from passage. Instead, the U.S. administration who argued that there were improvements in China's policy advocated a role of diplomacy and quiet pressure on China to change. This approach is much the same as the one advocated by John Frisbie in the second reading.

YES

Robert Baugh

Currency Manipulation and Labor Violations as Illegal Industrial Subsidies

The litany of China's failures to meet its trade obligations is extensive—loans from state banks to industry that are never repaid, extensive currency manipulation, illegal dumping, rampant intellectual property violations, environmental degradation, and massive human rights, religious, and workers' rights abuses. Compounding these problems is a complete lack of transparency within China. It remains difficult and dangerous to obtain information on workers' or human rights problems, and the banking and financial systems are closed to outsiders. Additionally, the government of China implements stringent regulations making it a criminal act to reveal information deemed to be a "state secret." Unfortunately, "state secret" seems to apply to almost anything, including reporting on labor disruptions.

This hearing is particularly important, as Chinese President Hu [Jintao] plans a visit to Washington, D.C., later this month. While currency manipulation appears to be on the agenda for discussion at that meeting, we urge policymakers and the [Bush] administration not to neglect the ongoing humanitarian and economic issues raised by the Chinese government's repressive policies toward its own workers.

Our country is on a dangerous and unsustainable path, one that encourages and rewards irresponsible corporate policies, while leaving American workers, family farmers, domestic producers, and communities devastated. Growing debt in both the private and public sectors is powering American consumption, which in turn is driving global growth. This debt-driven growth masks underlying weaknesses and cannot be a sustainable solution.

The current situation serves the short-term interests of the multinational corporate elite around the globe, but is already failing working families here and abroad.

Falling real wages, negative savings, and growing inequality in the United States are clear signs that working families are paying the price today for these failed policies. We are mortgaging our children's future to pay for unsustainable debt and consumption today. And if we do not take dramatic

Testimony during hearings on "U.S.–China Economic Relations Revisited" before the Finance Committee, Robert Baugh (March 29, 2006).

steps soon to reverse this unsustainable trend, then the resulting collapse could be devastating to global economic prosperity and stability.

Trade Deficit and Job Loss

The U.S. bilateral trade deficit with China hit $201 billion last year [2005]. This is the largest bilateral trade deficit between any two countries in history. The Economic Policy Institute estimates this trade deficit has cost us 410,000 jobs and job opportunities in the past two years alone.

It is a sad but true fact that empty cargo containers are our largest export to China. Our imports from China continue to outstrip our exports by more than five to one, making this by far our most imbalanced trade relationship with any major trading partner. Meanwhile, the United States has lost almost three million manufacturing jobs since 2001.

While many factors contributed to this devastating job loss, it is clear that the Chinese government's manipulation of its currency, violation of international trade rules, and egregious repression of its citizens' fundamental democratic and human rights are key contributors to an unfair competitive advantage. The Chinese government is flouting its international obligations, and no one is holding them accountable.

Unfortunately, to date, the U.S. government has failed to act effectively to stem the job losses resulting from the burgeoning U.S. trade deficit with China. The Bush administration has refused concrete action to ensure that the Chinese government lives up to its international obligations on trade, currency manipulation and human rights. President Bush has denied American businesses and workers the import relief they are entitled to under the law, and he has taken positions at the World Trade Organization (WTO) that will only worsen our trade relationship with China.

Over the past five years, China has repeatedly and consistently failed to comply with WTO rules. The Bush Administration, rather than take advantage of the WTO's formal dispute settlement mechanism to address these violations, has preferred to rely on prolonged discussions and informal consultations in its failed attempts to guarantee China's compliance. Nothing has been accomplished.

Illegal Subsidies and Transparency

Currency manipulation may be the most visible violations of trade law by the Chinese government but there are many other forms of illegal subsidies. The violations of workers' rights are the most egregious and costly of all.

Failure to Act on Currency Manipulation

Since last summer the Chinese yuan is no longer technically pegged to the dollar. However, China's currency has barely moved from the rate established in 1994, and it is estimated to be undervalued by as much as 40 percent. This gives China an enormous competitive advantage in the U.S. market and creates an inherently unstable and unsustainable situation.

The Chinese government must allow the yuan to reflect underlying economic and market forces. It must revalue its currency to reflect true value, then adopt flexibility for the yuan and cease its accumulation of U.S. dollar reserves. While the Chinese government's reluctance to take this action is perhaps understandable, the Bush Administration's failure to act more forcefully in this regard is not.

We believe Congress should take action by passing HR 1498, the Hunter-Ryan bill, and use its mechanisms to send a clear message to the Chinese government that the current situation is unacceptable and will not be tolerated. It is now clear that simple diplomacy and lackluster negotiations have failed.

China Misrepresents Actual Trade Surplus Figures

The China Currency Coalition in a 2005 study found that China's global surplus is more than 325 percent higher than China's trade statistics claim, according to its partner trading data.

China is "hiding the ball" by deliberately reporting incorrect trade statistics. The China Currency Coalition maintains the figure reported by import partners more accurately reflects China's net income from trade. The problem of incorrect trade statistics underscores a much larger transparency problem across government agencies.

Free Money: China's Non-Performing Loan Practice

The deliberate extension of billions of dollars in non-performing loans by China's central banks has given China another unfair advantage. Simply put, state banks make loans to industry with little expectation those loans will be repaid. Most of these free loans have been transferred to four government-owned asset management corporations (AMCs), so the government budget, rather than the banking system, will bear the costs.

According to IMF reports, bad loan ratios for the major commercial banks in China have fallen from about 24% of loans in 2002 to about 13% in September 2005. This apparent decline results from questionable accounting practices—they only report the bank share of the debt, and not the government-owned share.

Due to the lack of transparency in the Chinese banking and financial system, it is difficult to calculate the total amount of these illegal non-performing loans. However, IMF economists reported in 2005 that these bad loans may have amounted to as much as 30 percent of China's GDP in 2003.

It is further estimated that 40% of all loans in 2002 were non-performing, and that previous non-performing loans (some now in the form of government debt) might total $400 billion. Other estimates place the figure higher, at a whopping $650 billion.

Either way, it is clear that over the past decades, the Chinese have illegally subsidized business development through non-performing loans—unfairly subsidizing industry to the tune of hundreds of billions of dollars.

Direct and Indirect Subsidies: Free Land, Labor and Facilities

Non-performing bank loans are just the tip of the iceberg when it comes to illegal subsidies by the Chinese government. Here too transparency is an issue because it is difficult to obtain accurate and complete data about these practices but it is clear from the information available these practices are widespread.

The U.S. government is aware of these violations, and our trade delegation in Geneva has actively used the WTO Transitional Review Mechanism (TRM) to scrutinize China's ongoing compliance with its WTO commitments and obligations. Last fall the U.S. used the TRM to question the Chinese government's failure to provide a comprehensive accounting of its subsidy program. The Chinese government continues to administer programs that are thought to be illegal. The U.S. government also questioned the Chinese government's Northeast Revitalization Industrial Policies, an industrial policy designed to help companies located in the north-eastern region of the country compete in global markets. Among other things, the policy provides export credits and carries out strategic restructuring of key enterprises in the oil, petrochemical, iron and steel, automotive, shipbuilding, and aircraft products manufacturing sectors.

The concerns over China's industrial policy and illegal subsidies are well placed. Senator Joseph Lieberman [D-CT] in an article, "The U.S. Must Act Quickly to Maintain Vital Defense Technology" [*Signal*, November 2003] outlined how illegal subsidies and industrial policy come together to capture manufacturing and technology in one critical industry:

> The migration of research and design capabilities to China is of particular concern. Chinese policy has resulted in a sharp upsurge in construction of fabrication facilities in that country, with plans for a great many more. To ensure that they develop the ability to build the next-generation fabrication facilities, the Chinese central government, in cooperation with regional and local authorities, has undertaken a large array of direct and indirect subsidies to support their domestic semiconductor industry . . .

The immediate and most powerful incentives for a highly leveraged industry are the direct and indirect subsidies, including the infrastructure needed for state-of-the-art fabrication plants, offered by the government. For example, the Chinese central government has undertaken indirect subsidies in the form of a substantial rebate on the value-added tax (VAT) charged on Chinese-made chips. While many believe this is an illegal subsidy under the General Agreement on Tariffs and Trade (GATT) rules, the impact of the subsidy on the growth of the industry may well be irreversible before—and if—any trade action has taken place. China also systematically undervalues its currency, often by as much as 40 percent, which gives its goods a major price advantage. This practice also may violate trade rules.

The development of special government-funded industrial parks, the low costs of building construction in China as compared with the United States, and China's apparent disinterest in the expensive pollution controls required of fabrication facilities in the United States all represent further hidden subsidies. . . . These actions reflect a strategic decision by the Chinese government to capture the benefits of this enabling, high-technology industry and become a monopoly supplier, and thus control pricing and supply levels."

The cost of construction is also underwritten by continuing violations of labor standards. The April 4, 2006 report by the International Confederation of Free Trade Unions for the WTO General Council Review of the Trade Policies of the Peoples Republic of China found that "over 94 million private sector migrant workers are owed more than $100 billion yuan in back wages . . . the problem is most severe in the construction industry, which accounts for 70 percent of the total amount owed."

Lack of Environmental Regulation Lowers Cost of Production

Another unfair competitive advantage for manufacturers in China comes from lax environmental regulations and failure to enforce existing laws. Because China does not effectively regulate pollution, dumping, and emissions, corporations often fail to effectively employ even basic environmental protections. Cheaper goods, ruined communities, and sick workers are the result.

According to the Environmental Sustainability Index, an initiative by the Yale Center for Environmental Law and Policy (YCELP) and the Center for International Earth Science Information Network (CIESIN) of Columbia University, in collaboration with the World Economic Forum and the Joint Research Centre of the European Commission, China ranks a lowly 133 out of 146 nations. Its environmental sustainability rating, at 38.6 percent, is just below Iran, and just above Tajikistan.

A recently published study from the *Environment, Science, and Technology Journal* entitled, *Modeling Study of Air Pollution Due to the Manufacture of Export Goods in China's Pearl River Delta*, found that exported goods from China are cheaper to produce due to low or non-existent emission controls.

According to David Sheets, a policy analyst at Argonne National Laboratory and lead author of the report, "We in the West take advantage of cheap goods manufactured in China and other developing countries, and one reason they're cheap is because there aren't a lot of environmental controls. So we get the benefits of the cheap goods, and they absorb the air pollution; there's something not quite right about that."

Violations of Workers' and Human Rights

In addition to the unfair competitive advantage gained through currency manipulation and illegal subsidies, the Chinese government's systematic repression of fundamental workers' rights is a key contributor to the undue advantage Chinese exports enjoy in the U.S. market. Chinese workers' most basic rights are routinely repressed, and they do not enjoy the political freedom to criticize, let alone change, their government.

Enforcement of wages, hours, and health and safety rules is lax or non-existent in many areas of the country. These abuses allow producers in China to operate in an environment free of independent unions, to pay illegally low wages, and to profit from the widespread violation of workers' basic human rights. For example, Chinese mineworkers face conditions that rival or surpass some of the worst labor abuses in American history. Research indicates that more than 10,000 people die in Chinese mines each year. Coal mines in China may be the most dangerous places in the world to work. But unlike American mineworkers, Chinese mineworkers are denied the right to organize and bargain collectively.

Rates of illness and injury have never been higher in China's manufacturing sector—as officials of China's own Work Safety Administration conceded as recently as February, 2006. Aggregate unpaid wages have risen to record levels, setting off thousands of illegal demonstrations, labor shortages, and increased child labor—as adult workers increasingly refuse to accept such injustice. Workers who merely petition for payment of their wages are increasingly met with violence by security police and other local officials.

There are as many as ten to twenty million child workers in China—from one-eighth to one-quarter the number of factory workers. The problem of child labor has increased in recent years. China's minimum working age standard is very widely violated, and the Chinese government does little to enforce the standard. As the U.S. State Department stated in its 2005 Report on China, "The government continued to maintain that the country did not have a widespread child labor problem." As reported in CSR—Asia Weekly last November local officials rushing to compete for manufacturing investments local are reticent to enforce child labor regulations.

China oversees a system of forced labor, not prison labor. The precise number of forced prison laborers is unknown but estimates range from 1.75 million to 6 million and higher. Independent researchers, the Congressional-Executive Commission on China, and the U.S. House of Representatives confirmed that goods produced in China by forced labor continued to be exported to the United States in 2005. In its 2005 resolution condemning China's forced labor, the House of Representatives detailed the appalling working conditions, hours of work, and that the "Chinese Government has continuously encouraged the export of goods produced through the Laogai prison system and relies on forced labor as an integral part of its economy.

Chinese policies amount to a deliberate and artificial suppression of wages below what a freely bargained wage would be, and even below what would be efficient in the Chinese context. This exploitation impacts American workers and domestic producers, as well as those in other developing countries, and artificially lowers the price of Chinese exports in the U.S. market.

In China, the result has been "labor shortages," wildcat strikes, and massive protests. According to *Time Magazine* ("Inside the Pitchfork Rebellion," by Hannah Beech), "Violent local protests are convulsing the Chinese countryside with ever greater frequency—and Beijing has proved unable to quell the unrest. By the central government's own count, there were 87,000 'public order disturbances' in 2005, up from 10,000 in 1994."

That is an average of 238 protests every day last year.

President Bush did not demand any specific improvements in human rights when he met with China's President Hu in the summer of 2003. Instead, the Bush Administration has only engaged in an ambiguous and ineffective "cooperative dialogue."

The Administration's failure to take concrete actions on human rights and workers' rights in China allows rampant violations to continue. Workers in China, the United States, and around the world pay the price for this inaction, while companies producing in China enjoy the profits.

ICFTU Report to WTO on China's Failure to Meet Labor Rights Commitments

The People's Republic of China has ratified four of the eight, core ILO [International Labour Organization] labor Conventions. In view of restrictions on the trade union rights of workers and continuing problems with discrimination, child labor and forced labor, major policy changes are required to comply with the commitments WTO Members have accepted in Singapore and at Doha, in the WTO Ministerial Declarations over 1996–2001, and in the ILO Declaration on Fundamental Principles and Rights at Work. [Note: the ICFTU is the International Confederation of Free Trade Unions]

- China has not ratified the ILO core Convention on the Right to Organize and Collective Bargaining, nor the Convention on Freedom of Association and Protection of the Right to Organize. Workers are deprived the right to organize freely, to form independent trade unions, and to engage in collective bargaining. The right to strike is not recognized. The state and government use a variety of anti-union tactics to control workers, including repression of industrial action and imprisonment of those fighting for workers' rights.
- China has ratified the core ILO Convention on Equal Remuneration and the Convention on Discrimination. Discrimination is prohibited by law but does occur in practice. Legislation requires equal pay but wage differences continue to exist between men and women and among different ethnic groups.
- China has ratified the ILO core Convention on the Worst Forms of Child Labor and the Convention on Minimum Age. Child labor,

however, remains a problem in China, in particular in rural areas and in some industrial sectors, where regulations are applied lightly and where children, thus, are exposed to hazardous working conditions.

- China has not ratified the Convention on the Abolition of Forced Labor or the Convention on Forced Labor. Forced labor exists in such forms as prison labor, legal punishment in the form of "re-education-through-labor", and forced prostitution of women.

Chinese policies amount to a deliberate and artificial suppression of wages below what a freely bargained wage would be. This exploitation impacts American workers and domestic producers, as well as those in other developing countries, and artificially lowers the price of Chinese exports in the U.S. market.

Workers' Rights Section 301

Over two years ago, the AFL-CIO filed an unprecedented petition with the United States Trade Representative under Section 301 of the Trade Act of 1974. The petition asked the Trade Representative to take action to end the Chinese government's repression of the human rights of its factory workers.

It marked the first time in the history of Section 301 that a petition invoked the violation of workers' rights as an unfair trade practice, although it is common for corporations or the government to use Section 301 to challenge commercial unfair trade practices, such as illegal subsidies or violations of intellectual property rights.

Section 301(d)(3)(B)(iii) of the Trade Act provides that acts, policies, or practices of a trading partner are unreasonable if they constitute "a persistent pattern of conduct" that—

(I) denies workers the right of association,
(II) denies workers the right to organize and bargain collectively,
(III) permits any form of forced or compulsory labor,
(IV) fails to provide a minimum age for the employment of children, or
(V) fails to provide standards for minimum wages, hours of work, and occupational safety and health of workers.

The petition showed that the Chinese government was engaged in a "persistent pattern" of denying the fundamental rights of its factory workers. Second, it demonstrated that China's violation of workers' rights artificially reduces wages and production costs in China and, as a result, displaces hundreds of thousands of manufacturing jobs in the United States.

The petition also showed that workers in China are being forced to work for wages 47 to 86 percent below what they should be, often as bonded laborers, with few workplace health and safety protections and no right to join or form free trade unions. The cost-advantage of this worker repression is staggering. If the Chinese government enforced workers' rights and its own minimum wage and workplace standards, manufacturing costs there would rise between 12 and 77 percent, or an average of 44 percent.

This unfair cost advantage, continues to add to the stunning bilateral trade deficit with China.

Under the terms of Section 301, we argued that this clearly "burdens and restricts" U.S. commerce.

In the model of development embodied in section 301(d), the global integration of labor markets, capital markets, and markets in goods and services is not intrinsically a bad thing. If workers' rights are vigorously enforced, then the impoverished and underemployed—whether in China, India, Indonesia, Mexico, or the United States—may improve their standard of living and generate new domestic demand in a virtuous cycle of equitable development, while providing new markets for overseas investors and workers, including those in the United States.

If, however, the workers' rights of one-quarter of the world's workforce are radically suppressed—as they in fact are, in China—then labor conditions for the world's unskilled and semiskilled workers are worsened; domestic and global demand is depressed; excess productive capacity is created; and a path of inequitable, unsustainable development is promoted.

Failure to address the systematic, egregious, and institutionalized repression of workers' rights in China costs hundreds of thousands of good jobs here, creates conditions of desperation and exploitation in China, and fundamentally alters the nature of global labor competition in the rest of the world.

The AFL-CIO's 301 petition sought to ensure that our government would give this issue the priority it deserves in its economic dialogue with the Chinese government.

China Denies Workers' Rights

The overwhelming evidence that the Chinese government denies the workers' rights covered by the Section 301 petition in 2004 has only become stronger in the two years since the case was filed. The petition amassed evidence from the U.S. State Department, the International Labour Organization (ILO), labor unions, academics, newspaper accounts, and human rights groups. The AFL-CIO and other organizations continue to track the Chinese government's violations. Rather than showing signs of improvement, all reports indicated conditions are worsening.

China denies freedom of association and the right to bargain collectively. The Chinese government relentlessly represses attempts to organize unions that are independent of the government-controlled All-China Federation of Trade Unions (ACFTU). The ACFTU is officially and legally subservient to the Communist Party and to local officials who profit from export enterprises. Workers who attempt to strike or organize unions independent of the ACFTU have been arrested, imprisoned, beaten, and tortured. Even workers who have spoken out against corrupt managers, who have had the temerity to demand that wage arrears be paid, or who have attempted to publicize workplace problems have been subject to severe reprisals and arrest.

Conditions of forced labor are widespread. Many of the workers in China's export sector are temporary migrants from the countryside, who work under a repressive system of internal controls. Factory workers arriving from the countryside must pay substantial fees to local government officials and to employers to obtain the residence and work permits required by the "hukou" system, often leaving them heavily indebted. They lose their deposit if they quit without the employer's consent. In addition, employers frequently withhold one month to several months' pay, which workers lose if they quit or assert their rights. They are thereby essentially turned into bonded laborers who cannot leave their employment without incurring large and disproportionate penalties. The wages, conditions of work, and hours often turn out to be quite inferior to what is promised upon arrival, meaning that workers have clearly not entered into a free labor market, with fairly enforced rules.

China does not enforce its own laws with respect to minimum wages, maximum hours, and workplace safety and health. Many manufacturers in China, including multinational corporations, pay their workers much less than the minimum wage standards set by the central and provincial governments. It is apparently common for companies to keep double and triple sets of books, to hide this practice. Workplace safety and health practices are atrocious, and China has the highest rate of industrial deaths and accidents in the world. Government officials simply do not enforce their own laws on wages, hours, and safety and health.

The AFL-CIO's petition did not challenge China's right to compete in the global economy on the basis of low wages. It is natural for a developing country with an excess supply of poorly educated rural workers to have low wages. We fully understand that even if China fully enforced its workers' rights, the wage gap between Chinese and American workers would not disappear. But it would surely narrow. The AFL-CIO challenge was specifically targeted to the *incremental* cost advantage that comes from the brutal and undemocratic repression of workers' human rights. That increment was then and remains today illegitimate advantage under universal norms of human rights. And it is illegitimate under U.S. trade law as well.

Workers and Currency: No Action Then, No Action Now

Between China's brutal repression of workers' rights and its continuing currency manipulation, the Chinese government has a one-two punch that is destroying American manufacturing jobs and critically endangering our national security.

While the Bush Administration conceded there were serious concerns with regard to China's workers' rights abuses, it nonetheless denied the AFL-CIO's petition. Seven months after the President rejected the AFL-CIO's first petition, the Chinese government abruptly cancelled an international conference on the monitoring of workplace conditions.

In its 2005 Annual Report, the Congressional-Executive Commission on China (CECC) concluded "the Chinese government has avoided discussions with the international labor community on Chinese workers' rights." The CECC also found in 2005 that:

> The Commission finds no improvement overall in human rights condi- tions in China over the past year. . . . The Chinese government does not recognize the core labor rights of freedom of association and collective bargaining. The government prohibits independent labor unions and pun- ishes workers who attempt to establish them. Wage and pension arrears are among the most important problems that Chinese workers face . . . Chinese workers continue to struggle to collect wages and benefits because relevant agencies do not enforce the regulations. Workplace health and safety con- ditions are poor for millions of Chinese workers . . . Forced labor is an integral part of the Chinese administrative detention system, and child labor remains a significant problem in China, despite being prohibited by law. . . .

Similarly, the State Department's 2004 Country Report on Human Rights in China concludes "The [Chinese] Government continued to deny internationally recognized worker rights, including freedom of association"— the identical conclusion reached in the State Department's 2003 Report.

The just-released 2005 State Department Country Report on Human Rights in China is much the same, finding that China denies basic worker rights, including freedom of association, workplace health and safety, pay- ment of wages, rights against forced labor, and rights against trafficking in children. Peaceful labor protestors are subject to police violence, imprison- ment, and torture. This report by the Administration itself concedes that these fundamental facts have not changed since the President's assertion in 2004 that he would undertake measures to remedy China's noncompliance. Accord- ing to the State Department, regulations aimed at suppressing autonomous labor organizations grew harsher in 2005.

Following the denial of the Section 301 workers' rights petition, the China Currency Coalition, an organization representing business and labor, including the AFL-CIO, submitted a Section 301 petition on Chinese currency manipulation on September 9, 2004. The Administration denied the petition the day it was filed. A third 301 petition, again addressing the currency issue, was filed by 35 United States Representatives and Senators. It too was sum- marily rejected.

In all instances, the Administration's excuse was an ambiguous response that some unspecified action would be taken. The *modus operandi* has been and remains to talk little and do less. The President consistently sides with multinational corporate interests that manufacture in China over American working families and America's manufacturing industries.

The results in the U.S. have been devastating: hundreds of thousands of lost jobs, countless bankrupt businesses and ruined communities. Unsafe and exploitative working conditions remain for uncounted Chinese workers.

Time to Act

The administration has clearly abdicated its duty to protect American workers and industry. The onus now falls upon Congress and the U.S. China Economic and Security Review Commission to help guide our nation to swift action. We simply cannot afford another year of inaction and empty promises. We cannot afford another year of watching working conditions in China worsen and good jobs continue to leave the United States.

The AFL-CIO will continue to support measures to address currency manipulation, such as H.R. 1498, the bipartisan Ryan-Hunter China Currency Act of 2005; as well as S.295, the Schumer-Graham bill, which would impose a 27.5 percent tariff on Chinese goods if the Chinese government fails to revalue its currency in a timely fashion. And we will support legislation to address other illegal subsidies raised in this testimony. Most of all we will continue to work in every forum possible to improve workers' rights in China.

U.S.–China Business Council Advocates Balanced Approach on China Trade

Introduction

The U.S.–China Business Council (USCBC) favors a balanced approach to our trade policy toward China. This involves recognizing the significant benefits trade and investment with China have provided U.S. companies and the American economy, while also understanding the challenges experienced by some sectors. A balanced approach also requires addressing the barriers still faced by U.S. companies doing business with China, while expanding the opportunities created by the opening of China's economy.

These themes were addressed in our written statement submitted for last June's Senate Finance Committee hearing on China. Since then, China and Hong Kong combined have become our third-largest export market, passing Japan and trailing only our free-trade-area neighbors, Canada and Mexico. Moreover, China continues to be the fastest growing of our top fifteen export markets. Our exports to China have grown 150 percent over the past five years since China joined the World Trade Organization (WTO); the second fastest growing major market for American products during that time was Belgium, with a cumulative growth of 33 percent.

At home, U.S. trade and investment with China will by 2010 result in an annual 0.7 percent increase in U.S. gross domestic product and an annual 0.8 percent decrease in U.S. prices—the combined effect of which will be an annual increase of up to $1,000 in real disposable income per U.S. household. At the same time, however, it must be acknowledged that China's expanding role in the international economy has likely contributed to the decades-long shift in U.S. employment from manufacturing to service sectors, even as our manufacturing output continues to rise.

Most of the USCBC's approximately 250 member companies are focused primarily on either exporting to, or manufacturing and selling in, China. This focus is reflected in the annual survey results of our membership regarding its China business. For USCBC member companies, the top concerns include improving the protection of intellectual property rights (IPR); fully utilizing

Testimony during hearings on "U.S.–China Economic Relations Revisited" before the Finance Committee, John Frisbie (March 29, 2006).

newly granted distribution rights; increasing government transparency; finding and retaining local management staff; lowering market access barriers in various service sectors; and ensuring that Chinese technical, safety, and health standards do not hinder U.S. companies' ability to sell in China. With the exception of IPR, companies using China as an export platform would not be concerned with these issues.

Before going further, it is important to understand the global dynamics of trade and investment affecting the U.S.-China economic relationship. Increases in the U.S. trade deficit with China are generally not the result of specific Chinese policies. Rather, they mainly reflect the ballooning U.S. global trade deficit and shifts in patterns of trade and investment within Asia. Over the last ten years, China's share of the total U.S. trade deficit remained fairly constant, increasing from 23 percent to 26 percent (even though it has grown significantly in real terms). During the same period, the rest of East Asia's share of our global trade deficit declined significantly, from 42 to 18 percent. Why has this happened? During that period, East Asian economies invested heavily in China, thereby shifting much of their manufacturing capacity—and therefore their trade surpluses with the United States—to China.

Furthermore, when taken as a whole, China and East Asia's share of the U.S. global trade deficit actually has dropped from 67 percent to 44 percent over ten years. In contrast, our trade deficit with the rest of the world has grown across the board and now makes up 56 percent of our global trade deficit. Some of this increase is from petroleum imports. But even when the effects of petroleum are stripped out the growth of the U.S. trade deficit with East Asia including China ($225 billion) is roughly matched by the growth in our trade deficit with the rest of the world ($205 billion) during this time. The U.S. economy may have a trade deficit problem, but if so its causes extend beyond simply our trade with China. On this basis, I would like to turn to key developments since last June's Senate Finance Committee hearing on China.

USTR's Top-To-Bottom Review

The USCBC welcomed the findings and recommendations of the Office of the U.S. Trade Representative's (USTR) "top-to-bottom" review of U.S. trade policy toward China released in February of this year. As the Committee is aware, the report proposed enhancing USTR's enforcement capabilities, increasing staff both in China and in Washington, and improving coordination with our other trading partners on China issues—all of which we believe are essential to addressing the concerns of the U.S. business community. The review demonstrates USTR's commitment to working on the key issues in our trading relationship and it highlights the balanced approach we describe above. While China is our fastest growing major export market and our commercial relationship with China is vital to the strength of the U.S. economy, we also must take steps to resolve problems in that relationship.

USCBC member companies, like most businesses operating in China, agree that these key issues must be addressed. IPR protection and enforcement remain inadequate. China's regulatory process still remains too opaque.

Market access for foreign companies operating in China remains inconsistent. China's financial sector reforms are unfinished. Resolution of these problems is best pursued through the type of constructive engagement that USTR described in the top-to-bottom review. We support the refocusing of resources and anticipate tangible results from stepped-up engagement.

China's Currency

One issue more than any other has captured the attention of Congress and much of the American public: the exchange rate between the U.S. dollar and the Chinese yuan. Many say that China's government keeps the value of its currency artificially low in order to boost its exports and that this is the main cause of the bilateral trade deficit between China and the United States. As we noted in our submitted testimony last year, China should indeed adopt a market-determined exchange rate. Toward this end, our focus should be on encouraging China to undertake the broader financial sector reforms that will enable China to remove capital controls at the appropriate time and allow market forces to determine fully the value of its currency.

These include opening the financial sector to more private companies, introducing more financial market products such as currency futures, requiring greater commercial accountability from existing financial sector companies, and, of course, allowing more foreign participation in China's capital and credit markets. We understand that the Treasury Department has made these reforms a central part of its engagement with China's government and we fully support this dialogue. In the meantime, China should move more quickly to allow market influences from trade flows to be reflected in the exchange rate between the dollar and the yuan. Last July's change in China's currency policy was welcomed by all. Movement since then to allow market influences a greater role in setting the exchange rate has been slow, although the pace has increased during the past month. Many economists and the local press in China expect gradual appreciation to continue for the balance of this year.

It should be noted, however, that the effect of China's exchange rate policy on bilateral trade is likely overstated. USCBC member companies generally do not cite the exchange rate as a key business issue affecting their competitiveness in China. Many are concerned, though, about potential repercussions should the political dispute between the two countries over the exchange rate worsen. More broadly, recent research indicates that even a 25 percent revaluation of the yuan against the dollar—far greater than expected—would decrease the total U.S. trade deficit, which was $766 billion in 2005, by $20 billion. Even so, any benefit China gains from an undervalued currency—even if its actual impact on the U.S. economy is not great—should be addressed. The best way to eliminate any such unfair advantage is to continue to push for greater market influences to be reflected in the exchange rate now, and for broader financial reforms that will lead to the removal of capital controls at the appropriate time and a truly market based currency in the future.

Joint Commission on Commerce and Trade

As the members of this committee are aware, the Joint Commission on Commerce and Trade (JCCT) will meet on April 11, 2006 in advance of PRC President Hu Jintao's visit to the United States later in the month. Before I note some of the issues that the USCBC's members hope will be addressed at this year's meeting, I want to highlight a concern about the process in general. The JCCT originally was created as a means to promote commercial opportunities. In recent years, the JCCT has focused solely on resolving trade problems.

There are, of course, many more issues of concern between our two countries than can be resolved in a single annual meeting. As one would expect, negotiators on both sides frequently begin to plan for the JCCT several months in advance with extensive lists of possible topics that may be included in the final JCCT agenda. As the list of issues is reduced to a manageable number, unresolved issues are put aside until the next opportunity for resolution—frequently, the following year's JCCT.

Given the breadth of the issues, U.S. government and industry need to see engagement with the PRC in the areas of concern on a more regular basis. The current, irregular, schedule of the JCCT and its limited scope of coverage are not adequate to make continued, meaningful progress. For instance, issues affecting U.S. media companies are, for the most part, outside of the portfolio of China's JCCT team. A mechanism for broader and more frequent engagement is necessary if we hope to resolve the irritants in our economic relationship with China. Until such a mechanism is established, however, the JCCT remains the best means to achieve progress on the greatest number of issues. China has done moderately well in following through on the commitments it has made as part of the JCCT process, though some issues remain unresolved.

Two areas that the USCBC believes must be central in this year's meeting should be highlighted. First and foremost is IPR enforcement, the top problem cited by our membership in our most recent survey. USCBC continues to regularly lobby the PRC government on the need for improved IPR enforcement. We will be submitting recommended regulatory changes directly to the PRC government this spring. And we are providing American companies with "best practice" tools so that they can do the maximum to reduce their exposure in a difficult environment. Intellectual property piracy simply cannot be tolerated. At the same time, this far-reaching problem will not be solved overnight. The key is for China to show steady progress in reducing piracy—that effective steps are being made toward the goal. The challenge for us is to identify specific measures for adoption in the JCCT process that, if implemented, would lead to such tangible progress. Last July's JCCT IPR measures were a good step in this direction; we need to continue this approach in April. And, China needs to bring greater transparency to its enforcement efforts so that all can assess if progress is being made.

China published just recently its 2006 IPR Work Plan. The plan suggests that many of the July 2005 JCCT actions are being implemented and additional measures are being taken. We encourage USTR and the Department of

Commerce to evaluate this plan's effectiveness and identify additional specific measures that could be incorporated in this year's JCCT that would encourage further progress on IPR enforcement in China. We hope these measures would include China's favorable response to the request for case information under Article 63.3, which would bring more transparency to the enforcement effort.

A second issue that the USCBC believes must be addressed in this year's JCCT is subsidies. If we are to seek a level playing field for U.S. companies operating in China, as well as for American companies facing Chinese competition at home and in other markets, we need to devote more effort and resources to better understanding this aspect of China's economy. While China's economy continues to evolve, it is transitioning from a state-run, command economy that directly subsidized much activity in the past. There may be remnants of the old system still in place that are benefiting Chinese companies at the expense of foreign competitors. China's WTO accession required it to file a report on its subsidies upon accession in December 2001. That deadline was missed. At the 2005 JCCT, China agreed to submit the report by the end of the year. It still has not been submitted. The report must be completed and submitted now. It will not likely provide the detail or complete picture needed, but it is a necessary first step to getting at this important aspect of the level playing field.

Beyond these issues, we hope the JCCT will successfully address other issues, such as: establishing a start date for negotiations on China's accession to the WTO Government Procurement Agreement; resolving the auto parts customs classification issue; addressing several air express delivery concerns with China's draft Postal Law; and allowing direct selling companies to practice their internationally accepted model in China. We also hope to see progress on several other issues that USTR and the Department of Commerce are discussing with their PRC counterparts.

A Bigger Framework?

The USCBC hopes that President Hu's visit will provide additional incentive for resolution of bilateral concerns. The main goal for the United States, however, should be to reinforce at the highest level China's continued commitment to implement fully its WTO obligations and to participate in the global economy as a mature trading partner.

One of China's goals is recognition by the United States as a market economy. U.S. law clearly lays out the criteria for market economy status, one of which is the extent to which a country's currency is convertible into other currencies. Given the need for tangible progress on that and other issues, it may be time to provide China with a clearer roadmap of how to meet those criteria. As further encouragement, perhaps we should also consider the steps China could take to become a member of what would then become the "G9." Setting positive, mutually beneficial goals and outcomes may help facilitate progress in China on the reforms and market openings needed to get there, including resolution of issues adversely affecting American companies and the American economy.

Conclusion

Since the Senate Finance Committee hearing on China last June, we have seen progress in a number of important areas:

- A JCCT meeting took place in July, at which several specific IPR-related measures were included. China has enacted several of those measures. China announced a 2006 IPR Work Plan in March that incorporates many of these measures, plus additional actions.
- Other, non-IPR measures agreed to at last July's JCCT have also been implemented, including a meeting under the U.S.-China Insurance Dialogue in December to address regulatory issues; a meeting of the Information Technology Working Group in January to work on capitalization requirements and other issues; and a delay in issuing regulations on PRC government procurement of software.
- China revised its currency policy in July, along with a 2.1% revaluation of the exchange rate, and has allowed the yuan to appreciate slowly since then.
- U.S. exports grew 20% last year, making China our fourth-largest export market, or third largest when combined with Hong Kong.
- USTR released its top-to-bottom review of China trade policy, offering a comprehensive approach to addressing trade concerns.

However, we also need to see more progress in some of these same as well as other areas:

- IPR protection is still a significant problem for U.S. (and other foreign and Chinese) companies. While the IPR problem cannot be solved overnight, we have to see progress toward reaching that goal, with more transparency needed from China in its enforcement effort.
- China should allow market influences to be reflected in its exchange rate at a faster pace. We should keep in mind that broader financial reforms and market openings are also needed to get to the eventual goal of a fully market-based exchange rate.
- The bilateral trade deficit grew to just over $200 billion in 2005. While our bilateral trade balance needs to be put into the context of our shifting trade pattern with East Asia as a whole and with the rapid growth in our trade deficit with the world, we nonetheless need to make a more fact-based assessment of the "level playing field," including subsidies that may give Chinese enterprises an unfair competitive advantage. On our side, we need to boost our exports by continuing to engage the PRC on removing market barriers and by devoting more resources to helping American companies—especially small- and medium-sized enterprises—enter and succeed in the China market.
- Insurance licensing, telecommunications capitalization requirements, and government software procurement questions remain, despite the

limited progress noted above. Further attention to these issues is required to ensure progress continues to be made.

- China needs to start accession negotiations to the WTO Government Procurement Agreement by the middle of this year; allow direct selling firms market access based on internationally accepted practices; ensure that its standards setting process does not exclude foreign competition; and engage in meaningful discussions with the U.S. government to eliminate or reduce numerous other market access barriers.

In closing, we feel it is important to comment on the call for protectionist policies from some quarters in response to the challenges of trade. As noted in our statement submitted to the Senate Finance Committee last June, the US-China Business Council is very much aware that the benefits and costs of international trade do not distribute to all Americans evenly. We recognize that some sectors of our economy struggle with the challenges brought by trade with China and the rest of the world. We must also remember, however, that our large global trade deficit is not caused solely or, perhaps, even mainly by Chinese policies.

In addition, the benefits of trade, in the form of substantial exports, a lower cost of living, and less inflation, are large and clearly outweigh the challenges. Business and government should work to guarantee that all Americans have the opportunity to enjoy these benefits. Part of this work requires us to press China to abide by its international trade agreements and to enforce our trade remedy laws to ensure a level playing field, but jeopardizing the U.S. economy with tariffs or other protectionist measures is not an acceptable way to inform China that it must change some of its policies. Rather, we should also focus on policies to correct a trade deficit that has grown remarkably with all regions—not just China—such as reducing our large fiscal deficit and enhancing the competitiveness of our economy.

POSTSCRIPT

Should the United States Take a Hard-line with China About Its International Economic Policies?

The U.S. trade deficit with China has continued to worsen. Based on data through July 2006, the year's totals will be approximately $314 billion in exports from China to the United States, with only $51 billion in goods traveling in the other direction. This amounts to (–)$263 billion U.S. deficit, up 30 percent from 2005 and 774 percent since 1995. Similarly, the trade ratio grew to 6.2:1 (up from 5.8:1 in 2005 and 3.8:1 in 1995). China allowed the yuan to ease versus the dollar, but only slightly. From 8.3 yuan = $1 in 2005, the exchange rate fell only about 5 percent to 7.9 yuan = $1 in October 2006, far short of the 40 percent drop to 4.5 yuan = $1 that some experts thought would occur if the yuan was fairly valued.

Several factors are important in deciding what to do. One is what is causing the massive trade deficit. Certainly, it is easy to blame China's policies, and the country is clearly not living up to all its WTO obligations. Even those who favor not taking strong action against China concede that. Yet it may be that the largest part of the problem is not Chinese policy but American spending habits. Remember that Americans have a huge and growing trade deficit with the world. A significant part of that is because Americans save less than people in any other developed country. Moreover, the U.S. personal savings rate fell from an average of about 10 percent of net income (income after taxes) during the 1970s, to 7 percent in the 1980s, to 3 percent in the 1990s. In 2006 through October Americans were actually spending more than their net income, for a minus (–)0.5-percent personal savings rate. Thus, the greatest cause of the deficit may be lack of economic discipline among Americans, and their seemingly insatiable drive to acquire material goods. For this view, read Chad P. Bown, Meredith Crowley, Rachel McCulloch, and Daisuke J. Nakajima, "The U.S. Trade Deficit: Made in China?," *Economic Perspectives* (Fall 2005).

Another consideration, and one that John Frisbie did not delve into, is the wider impact of how China might react to strong sanctions by the United States. The two countries have a complex strategic relationship, and the United States needs China's help in many areas. For example, China is one of the few countries with any influence in North Korea, and Chinese participation is important to the effort to resolve the ongoing confrontation with North Korea over its nuclear weapons program. China also has a veto in the UN Security Council and could block U.S. efforts there on such matters as getting sanctions or even military action authorized against Iran and North Korea in response to their nuclear program (see Issues 14 and 15). Therefore, the costs of a trade war with China cannot be calculated only in dollars and cents.

None of this means, however, that the United States should do nothing. A recent book advocating strong corrective measures is Senator Byron L. Dorgan (D-ND), *Take This Job and Ship It* (Thomas Dunne Books, 2006). For the view that U.S. dependence on China threatens U.S. national security, read Barry C. Lynn, "War, Trade and Utopia," *National Interest,* (Winter 2005/2006). As for the official U.S. position, go to the Web site of the U.S. Trade Representative at http://www.ustr.gov. One source there is the report, "U.S.–China Trade Relations: Entering a New Phase of Greater Accountability and Enforcement" (February 2006), which can be accessed through the "Document Library" hyperlink.

ISSUE 11

Is Immigration an Economic Benefit to the Host Country?

YES: Dan Siciliano, from Testimony during Hearings on "Immigration: Economic Impact," before the Committee on the Judiciary, U.S. Senate (April 24, 2006)

NO: Barry R. Chiswick, from Testimony during Hearings on "Immigration: Economic Impact," before the Committee on the Judiciary, U.S. Senate (April 24, 2006)

ISSUE SUMMARY

YES: Dan Siciliano, executive director, Program in Law Business and Economics and research fellow with the Immigration Policy Center at the American Immigration Law Foundation, Stanford Law School, contends that immigration provides many economic benefits for the United States.

NO: Barry R. Chiswick, UIC Distinguished Professor, and program director, Migration Studies IZA—Institute for the Study of Labor, Bonn, Germany, takes the position that legal immigration is having a negative impact on the U.S. economy and that illegal immigration increases the problems.

Part of the saga of human history is the migration of people ranging from individuals to entire populations migrating from their homes in search of a better life. Indeed, there are some countries, such as the United States, whose origins and growth are very substantially based on the flow of outsiders into its territory. Sometimes such influxes have gone fairly smoothly. At other times they have met significant opposition within the country of destination. Such is the case currently, with the global tide of refugees and immigrants, both legal and illegal, facing increasing resistance. A poll that asked people in 44 countries whether immigrants were having a good or bad impact found that a plurality in 28 countries said bad, with a plurality answering good in just 13 countries, and 3 countries evenly divided. Moreover, a lopsided 72 percent of the respondents favored stricter controls on immigration. Support for this position averaged 76 percent in the wealthiest countries such as the United States, Canada, and Western Europe. But opposition was even slightly higher in Latin America (77 percent) and sub-Saharan Africa (79 percent) and also strong among East Europeans (67 percent), Asians (61 percent), and Middle Easterners (66 percent).

Opposition to immigration comes from several sources. One is prejudice based on race, ethnicity, religion, or some other characteristic. More legitimate in the view of many is worry that immigrants are diluting the host country's language and other aspects of its national culture. Security concerns are a third source of opposition to immigration. Some critics of immigration argue that crime is higher among immigrant populations, and in recent years the possibility of immigrants being terrorists has increased this worry for some. Economic concerns are a fourth source of opposition to immigrants. One economic argument is that immigrants work for low wages, thereby undercutting the wage of native-born workers. Another charge is that immigrants are an economic burden, requiring far more in terms of welfare, medical care, education, and other services than the migrants return to the economy in terms of productivity and taxes. These charges are met by counterarguments that depict immigrants as providing needed workers and otherwise giving a boost to their new country's economy.

Immigration into the United States has changed markedly in recent decades. One difference is that it has increased significantly, with legal immigration growing almost 300 percent from a yearly average of 330,000 in the 1960s to an annual average of 971,000 between 1990 and 2005. A second difference is that immigrants are more likely to be people of color from Africa, Asia, and Latin American. European-heritage whites made up more than 70 percent of all immigrants as late as the 1950s. Now, due to changes in U.S. immigration law, only 48 percent of legal immigrants are from Latin America and the Caribbean, 32 percent are from Asia, and 4 percent are from Africa. Adding to both the overall number of immigrants and the percentage who are not from Europe, Canada, and other European-heritage countries is an estimated 400,000 to 500,000 illegal (undocumented, unauthorized) immigrants who arrive in the United States yearly. There are perhaps 11 million such immigrants currently in the United States, with approximately 80 percent of them from Central America, especially Mexico.

The presence of so many undocumented immigrants has become a major political issue in the United States. At one level, it is question unto itself. It also relates to the general concerns about immigration that many Americans have regarding culture and security. Certainly, American attitudes are different for legal and illegal immigrants, but there is also an overlap, illustrated by the fact that polls find that most Americans favor decreasing immigration overall. When Americans are asked what bothers them about illegal immigration, about the impact of unauthorized immigrants on wages, job availability, and the cost of social and educational services. Taking up this concern, Dan Siciliano examines the economic impact of both documented and undocumented immigrants on the United States in the first reading and finds that the country benefits. Barry Chiswick disagrees in the second reading, finding economic damage from legal and illegal immigration alike.

YES

Dan Siciliano

Immigration: The Positive Impact

Today's hearing on U.S. immigration policy and its impact on the American economy comes at a critical time. Efforts are underway in the House and in the Senate to repair a system that is generally acknowledged to be broken. I suggest that any reform to immigration policy should be evaluated by considering how immigrants directly, and as the evidence now seems to indicate, positively impact our nation's economic prosperity.

Much of the public debate over immigration in the United States has focused on the rapid growth of the undocumented population over the past decade and a half. However, undocumented immigration is just one symptom of the larger disconnect between U.S. immigration policy and the reality of our economy's fundamental reliance on a diverse and, hopefully, growing pool of available labor. The U.S. economy has become increasingly reliant on immigrant workers to fill the growing number of less-skilled jobs for which a shrinking number of native-born workers are available. Yet current immigration policies offer very few legal avenues for workers in less-skilled occupations to enter the country. Undocumented immigration has been the predictable result of the U.S. immigration system's failure to respond effectively to actual labor demand.

Many critics of immigration point to economic arguments that the presence of immigrants, particularly undocumented immigrants, has broad negative consequences for the native-born workforce. Some claim that immigration reduces employment levels and wages among native-born workers. This is generally not true. These arguments are largely the result of an over-simplified economic model used to measure the impact of immigration on the workforce, while ignoring the role that immigrants play in expanding the economy and stimulating labor demand through their consumer purchases and investments. Moreover, the empirical evidence indicates that businesses expand through the investment of more capital when the labor supply is not artificially constrained. Careful analysis and more recent studies add a dynamic component to the economic analysis of immigration by treating immigrants (both documented and undocumented) as real economic agents: earning, spending, and investing in the economy. Businesses, in turn, are

Committee on Judiciary, U.S. Senate, Dan Siciliano (April 24, 2006).

considered dynamic as well: adjusting to the available resources and expanding accordingly. Or, if this issue should be mishandled, rediverting resources and shrinking accordingly.

Few argue with the notion that immigration provides many benefits to the United States. As a nation of immigrants, our culture, customs, and traditions reflect the diverse backgrounds of the millions of individuals who have made their way to America over time. But more than cultural benefits, recent economic analysis, including work by Giovanni Peri of the University of California, shows that the United States sees real economic benefits from immigration. Native-born wages increased between 2.0 and 2.5 percent during the 1990s in response to the inflow of immigrant workers. Overall annual growth in the Gross Domestic Product is 0.1 percentage point higher as a result of immigration—a misleadingly small number that represents billions of dollars in economic output and, when compounded across a generation, represents a significant improvement in the standard of living of our children and grandchildren.

The positive impact of immigration results in part from the fact that immigrants help to fill growing gaps in our labor force. These gaps develop as aging native-born workers, in larger numbers than ever before, succeed in attaining higher levels of education and subsequently pursue higher-skill, higher-wage jobs. If the United States were to reform the immigration system to better address the demand for foreign-born labor, largely through ensuring that such workers were a part of the transparent and competitive "above ground" economy, the economic benefits of immigration could be even greater than what we have already experienced. Immigrants and their employers would likely benefit from a more predictable workforce environment and less time and resources would be spent addressing the dysfunction that is a result of a strong demand for a labor force that our laws do not accommodate.

Undocumented immigration is largely the result of two opposing forces: an immigration policy that significantly restricts the flow of labor and the economic reality of a changing native-born U.S. population. The extent to which the U.S. economy has become dependent on immigrant workers is evident in the labor force projections of the Bureau of Labor Statistics (BLS). According to BLS estimates, immigrants will account for about a quarter of labor force growth between 2002 and 2012. Given that roughly half of immigrants now arriving in the United States are undocumented, this means that 1 in 8 workers joining the U.S. labor force over the coming decade will be undocumented immigrants. Many of the jobs that would be harder to fill without this labor supply are already associated with immigrant labor: construction, agriculture, meatpacking, and hospitality. A growing number of immigrants, however, are also filling jobs in fields that are vitally important to serving America's aging population, such as home healthcare. This indicates that while policymakers debate the relative merits of various immigration reform proposals, immigration beyond current legal limits has already become an integral component of U.S. economic growth and will likely remain so for the foreseeable future.

The Impact of Immigrants on Native-Born Wages

Despite the critical role that immigration plays in preventing labor shortages that might impede economic growth, many critics of immigration argue that foreign-born workers reduce the wages of native-born workers with whom they compete for jobs. However, this argument relies on an overly simplistic understanding of labor supply and demand that fails to capture the true value that immigrants bring to the economy. If you are to gauge accurately the economic impact of immigration, the role that immigrants play in creating jobs is just as important as the role they play in filling jobs.

To analyze the impact of immigration on the U.S. economy as a whole, particularly in the studies relied upon in this debate, economists typically use one of two models: "static" or "dynamic." The static model is the simplest and most frequently used by critics of immigration, yet it is the least realistic because it fails to account for the multi-dimensional role that immigrants play as workers, consumers, and entrepreneurs. The dynamic model, on the other hand, offers a more nuanced portrait of immigrants as economic actors. The net economic benefits of immigration are apparent in both models, but are larger in the dynamic model.

Under the static model, economists assume that immigrant workers serve only to increase the labor supply, which results in slightly lower wages and thus higher profits for the owners of capital. In other words, if there are more workers competing for a job, an employer might pay a lower wage for that job and pocket the difference. For instance, under a popular version of the analysis that utilizes the static model, the 125 million native-born workers in the United States in 1997 would have earned an average of $13 per hour if not for the presence of immigrants. However, the 15 million immigrant workers who were actually in the country increased the labor force to 140 million and, under the static scenario, thereby lowered average wages by 3 percent to $12.60 per hour. Nonetheless, the net benefit to the U.S. economy of this decline in wages would have amounted to about $8 billion in added national income in 1997.

Despite the seeming simplicity of this logic (more workers competing for jobs results in lower wages for workers and higher profits for businesses), the assumptions underlying the static model bear little resemblance to economic reality. Recent evidence supports the contention that the impact of immigration on wages is not as simple, or negative, as the static model would suggest. A 2004 study found that, despite the large influx of immigrants without a high-school diploma from 1980 to 2000, the wages of U.S.-born workers without a diploma relative to the wages of U.S.-born workers with a diploma "remained nearly constant." More importantly, [research shows] . . . that the dynamic response of small and medium sized businesses to this phenomena means that nearly all U.S. born workers, especially those with a high school education or better, have benefited from higher wages due to the presence of this low skilled, often undocumented, immigrant labor.

The inability of the static model to explain this finding rests in part on the fact that the model incorrectly assumes immigrant and U.S.-born workers are perfectly interchangeable; that is, that they substitute for each other rather than complement each other in the labor force. Common sense alone suggests that this is not always the case. For example, less-skilled foreign-born construction laborers enhance the productivity of U.S.-born carpenters, plumbers, and electricians, but do not necessarily substitute for them. More broadly, the different educational and age profiles of foreign-born and native-born workers indicate that they often fill different niches in the labor market.

More importantly, the static model fails to account for the fact that immigrants spend money or invest capital, both of which create jobs and thus exert upward pressure on wages by increasing the demand for labor. This amounts to more than a minor omission given the scale of immigrant purchasing power and entrepreneurship. For instance, in 2004, consumer purchasing power totaled $686 billion among Latinos and $363 billion among Asians. Given that roughly 44 percent of Latinos and 69 percent of Asians were foreign-born in that year, the buying power of immigrants reached into the hundreds of billions of dollars.

The dynamic model accounts for many of these additional economic contributions by immigrants. In the dynamic scenario, immigrant workers spend some of their wages on housing and consumer goods, which in turn increases the demand for labor by creating new jobs. Rising labor demand then increases wages relative to what would have existed if immigrant workers had not been present in the labor market. Businesses in turn invest more capital, expand, and hire more workers across the spectrum of skill levels. The result is a larger economy with higher employment.

The Impact of Immigrants on Native-Born Employment Levels

An IPC research report released in November of 2005 provides strong demographic evidence that the impact of immigrants on native-born employment levels is extremely limited or, in some cases, positive. The report examines the significant differences between the native-born workforce and the immigrant workforce and finds that immigrants are largely complementary to the native-born in education, age and skill profile. The complementary nature of immigrant labor makes it unlikely that immigrants are replacing a significant number of native-born workers, but are instead moving into positions that allow native-born workers to be more productive.

As the number of less-skilled jobs continues to grow, it will become increasingly difficult for employers to find native-born workers, especially younger workers, with the education levels that best correspond to those jobs. In this sense, immigrant workers are a vital complement to a native-born labor force that is growing older and better educated. On average, foreign-born workers tend to be younger than their native-born counterparts and a larger proportion have less formal education. In addition, immigrants participate in the labor force at a higher rate. As a result, immigrants provide a needed source of labor for the large and growing number of jobs that do not require as much formal education.

Immigrant Workers are More Likely to Have Less Formal Education

Immigrants comprise a disproportionate share of those workers who are willing to take less-skilled jobs with few or no educational requirements. In 2004, 53.3 percent of the foreign-born labor force age 25 and older had a high-school diploma or less education, compared to 37.8 percent of the native-born labor force. Immigrant workers were more than four times as likely as native workers to lack a high-school diploma. In contrast, immigrant workers were nearly as likely to have a four-year college degree or more education, amounting to more than 30 percent of both the native-born and foreign-born labor force.

In general, foreign-born workers are more likely to be found at either end of the educational spectrum, while most native-born workers fall somewhere in the middle. Roughly three-fifths of the native-born labor force in 2004 had either a high-school diploma or some college education short of a four-year degree, whereas three-fifths of the foreign-born labor force either did not have a high-school diploma or had at least a four-year college degree. Given their different educational backgrounds, most native-born workers are therefore not competing directly with foreign-born workers for the same types of jobs.

Immigrant Workers Tend to be Younger

Immigrants also include a large number of younger workers, particularly in the less-skilled workforce. In 2004, 67 percent of the foreign-born labor force with a high-school diploma or less education was between 25 and 45 years old, as opposed to 52 percent of the native-born labor force with no more than a high-school diploma. While relative youth is not a requirement for many jobs, it is an asset in those less-skilled jobs that are physically demanding or dangerous.

Given the different age and educational profiles of foreign-born and native-born workers, it is not surprising that immigrants comprise a disproportionately large share of younger workers with little education. In 2004, immigrants made up more than a quarter of all workers 25–34 years old with a high-school diploma or less, and more than half of workers 25–34 years old without a high-school diploma. Employers searching for younger workers in less-skilled positions therefore often find that a large portion of prospective hires is foreign-born.

The Fiscal Costs of Immigration

Critics of immigration often focus on the fiscal costs of immigration instead of the economic benefits. These costs are often exacerbated by the undocumented status of many immigrants. An immigration policy that acknowledged the economic need for and benefits of immigration would significantly reduce these costs. To support the contention that immigrants are a net fiscal drain, critics cite studies indicating that immigrants contribute less per capita in tax revenue than they receive in benefits. However, these studies fail to acknowledge that this has more to do with low-wage employment than with native-born status. Native-born workers in low-wage jobs similarly receive benefits in excess of the level of taxes paid. However, net tax revenue is not the same as net economic benefit. Generally accepted analysis reveals that the net economic benefit compensates for and exceeds any negative fiscal impact. The "fiscal only" analysis ignores the fact that in the absence of sufficient immigrant labor, unfilled low-wage jobs, regardless of the relative tax implications, hurt the economy.

Conclusion

Immigration is a net positive for the U.S. economy and the presence of immigrants does not generally harm the native-born workforce. Studies that purport to demonstrate a negative impact on native-born wages and employment levels rely on an overly simplistic economic model of immigration and the economy. The most recent demographic analysis in conjunction with more sophisticated economic analysis reveals that most immigrants, including undocumented immigrants, do not compete directly with native-born workers for jobs. Instead, these immigrants provide a critical element of our nation's economic success and continued resiliency: a relatively young, willing, and dynamic supply of essential workers in areas such as healthcare, construction, retail, and agriculture. These are jobs that, once filled, enable our economy to continue the cycle of growth and job creation.

Indeed, this makes clear that the implication of the government's own BLS data cannot be ignored. To prosper, our economy desperately needs workers at both ends of the spectrum: young and less skilled as well as more educated and highly skilled. As a nation, we are in the midst of a slow-motion demographic cataclysm unlike any we have previously experienced. Immigration is not the only tool for seeing our way clear of the coming storm—but it is one without which we will not prosper. Without a continued and normalized flow of immigrant labor our workforce will fall well short of the numbers needed to meet the emerging demand for labor. The result will be an erosion of both the growth and increased standard of living that our citizenry has come to expect and to which future generations are entitled. Until the United States adopts a more articulated and thoughtful immigration policy that accommodates these economic realities, the insufficiency of current immigration and the problematic nature of undocumented immigration, in particular, will continue to hobble the economy.

Barry R. Chiswick

 **NO**

Immigration:
The Negative Economic Impact

When I am asked the question "What is THE economic impact of immigration?" where the tone indicates the emphasis on the word "the," I respond that this is not the best way to couch the question. There are two fundamental questions. One is: "What is the optimal size of the immigrant population?" The other is: "What are the different impacts of immigrants that differ in their productivity-related characteristics?"

Impacts on Relative Wages

Let us begin with a discussion of the second question. Conceptually, it is best to think in terms of two types of immigrants, which for simplicity we will call high-skilled and low-skilled, with the same two skill groups represented in the native-born population. High-skilled immigrants will have some characteristics in common, without regard for their country of origin. They tend to have high levels of schooling, which means they tend to have a high degree of literacy, perhaps also numeracy, critical thinking or decision-making skills. Many, but not all, will have a high degree of scientific or technical knowledge, and in the modern era a high comfort level with computer technology. Many, but certainly not all, will either have a degree of proficiency in the destination language (in this case, English) or the ability to acquire proficiency in that language shortly after arrival. These are all characteristics that have been shown to improve the earnings of immigrants and to facilitate their economic adjustment in the host country.

Although particular individuals may differ, low-skilled immigrants generally have little formal schooling, limited literacy proficiency in their mother tongue (the language of their origin country), and limited scientific and technical knowledge. These are characteristics associated with low earnings in the destination.

High-skilled and low-skilled immigrants will, in general, have different impacts on the host economy and labor market. Labor markets behave in a manner similar to other markets, in that a greater supply of a given type of labor tends to depress the market wage of workers with similar characteristics.

Committee on the Judiciary, U.S. Senate, by Barry R. Chiswick (April 24, 2006).

An increase in the supply of a given type of worker also increases the productivity of the complementary factors of production with which it works, including other types of labor and capital. To give a simple example, an increase in the supply of low-skilled restaurant kitchen help will result in more competition for this type of job and lower wages for ordinary kitchen workers. Yet this will increase the productivity (and hence wages) of the master chefs because with more help for the menial kitchen chores they can spend their time on the highly specialized tasks for which they have trained. By the same token, an increase in the supply of high-skilled chefs would raise the productivity of low-skilled restaurant kitchen workers since they would have more master chefs for whom to work.

The result of high-skilled immigration tends to be an increase in the wages of all low-skilled workers (and reduce their use of public income transfers) and a decrease in the wages of high-skilled natives. This reduces income inequality, which we generally view as a good development. Like high-skilled natives, the taxes paid by high-skilled immigrants tend to be greater than the costs they impose on the public treasury through the income transfers they receive, the schooling received by their children, and the publicly subsidized medical care that they receive. High-skilled immigrants are also more likely to bring with them the scientific, technical and innovative skills that expand the production capabilities of the economy. As a result, the population as a whole tends to benefit from high-skilled immigration, although with some benefiting more than others.

Now consider the impacts of low-skilled immigration. While these immigrants tend to raise the earnings of high-skilled workers, their presence in the labor market increases competition for low-skilled jobs, reducing the earnings of low-skilled native-born workers. This not only increases income inequality, which is rightly considered to be undesirable, it also increases the need among low-skilled natives for public assistance and transfer benefits. Because of their low earnings, low-skilled immigrants also tend to pay less in taxes than they receive in public benefits, such as income transfers (e.g., the earned income tax credit, food stamps), public schooling for their children, and publicly provided medical services. Thus while the presence of low-skilled immigrant workers may raise the profits of their employers, they tend to have a negative effect on the well-being of the low-skilled native-born population, and on the native economy as a whole. These points are not purely theoretical arguments. In the past two decades the real wages of low-skilled workers have remained stagnant even as the real earnings of high-skilled workers have risen. As a result, income inequality has increased. Several factors have been responsible for this development, but one of them has been the very large increase in low-skilled immigration.

The "Need" for Low-Skilled Immigrants

"But," I am often asked, "don't we need low-skilled immigrant workers to do the jobs that native workers are unwilling to do?" I respond: "At what wage will native workers decline to take these jobs?" Consider the following thought experiment: What would happen to lettuce picking or the mowing of suburban lawns if there were fewer low-skilled workers? Earlier this month on ABC's Nightline program a winter lettuce grower in Arizona provided the answer. He acknowledged that he would pay higher wages to attract native-born workers and he would speed up the mechanization of lettuce harvesting. The technology is there, but with low wages for lettuce pickers there is no economic incentive for the growers to mechanize or invest in other types of new technology. If the supply of low-skilled immigrant workers decreased substantially, mechanical harvesting would replace many of them with capital (machines) and more highly paid native workers. How would suburban lawns get mowed if there were fewer low-skilled immigrant workers? Wages for lawn care workers would surely rise. The result would be that more teenagers and other low-skilled native workers would find it worth their while to make themselves available for this work.

In addition to this substitution of one type of labor (youthful and low-skilled natives) for another (low-skilled immigrants), there would be other adjustments to the higher cost of lawn mowing. One would be letting the grass grow longer between mows—say, every ten days instead of weekly. Another would be the substitution of grass that grows more slowly, or the substitution of ground cover or paving stones for grass, etc. The point is that there would be many ways for consumers and employers/producers to respond to the higher wages of low-skilled workers to mitigate the adverse effects of having fewer low-skilled immigrants.

A Century Ago

At this point in the conversation, someone usually points to the period of mass immigration of unskilled workers from the 1880s to the 1920s: If these arguments are valid now, wouldn't they have applied at that time as well?—and we know that immigration was a tremendous net benefit to the United States at that time. The answer is both yes and no. The economy and economic institutions of 100 years ago were quite different from those of today in ways that are both important and relevant to our discussion. Then, rapid industrialization of the American economy generated a very large demand for unskilled workers in mines and in factories producing everything from steel to shirts. This is no longer the case. Technological change, the increased cost of even low-skilled labor (wages plus fringe benefits and employment taxes), the falling cost of capital equipment, and globalization/international trade have sharply reduced the demand for low-skilled workers in U.S. manufacturing, mining, agriculture, and even service occupations and industries. Moreover, 100 years ago income inequality and income distribution issues were not a matter of public policy concern. If there were poor people in the United States—so be it. If private individuals and charities helped the poor—fine, but there was nothing like the tax-funded income transfer system in place today.

Yet in some ways the mass immigration from Europe 100 years ago had a similar impact as the one we are facing today. By holding down the wages of low-skilled workers in the industrializing centers of the economy, especially in the Northern states, rural-urban and South-North migration was slowed. Rural and Southern poverty persisted longer than they might have otherwise, and it was only after war (WWI) and immigration restrictions (in the 1920s) had effectively stopped the European migration that these poverty-reducing internal migrations resumed. While there is no question that there were long-term benefits from the massive wave of immigrants for the country as a whole, it is also true that the low-skilled native-born workers of that time paid a price.

Fallacies in Estimating Immigrant Impacts

In the course of these hearings on the economic impact of immigration, you may receive testimony regarding a body of literature that attempts to estimate this impact. In this literature a statistical technique, regression analysis, is used to show how the wages of native workers (or low-skilled natives in particular) in a state or metropolitan area are affected by the extent to which there are immigrants (or low-skilled immigrants) in the same area. These studies tend to find no relation, or sometimes a very small relation, between the presence of immigrants and wage levels.

There is nothing wrong with regression analysis per se as a statistical technique, but its application in this case is flawed. This application of regression analysis requires us to assume that each state or metropolitan area is a self-contained economy, with little or no in-and-out movement of workers, of capital, or even of goods and services. We know, however, that this is not the case. Labor, capital and goods are highly mobile across state boundaries and metropolitan areas. What we learn from these studies is not that immigrants have no effect on wages, but that these wage effects—whatever they may be—have spread throughout the country. Although it does provide evidence that markets in the United States function quite efficiently, the impacts of immigration can not be detected by this statistical technique.

At the aggregate level, many analyses consider immigrants as an undifferentiated whole without distinguishing between high-skilled and low-skilled workers. These also provide misleading implications, often to the effect that immigrant impacts on wages and income distribution are small. When the positive economic benefits of high-skilled immigration are lumped together with the more negative consequences of low-skilled immigration, they appear to cancel each other out because there are both gains and losses. In the real world, however, the penalty paid by low-skilled natives because of high levels of low-skilled immigration is not so easily cancelled out by the positive impacts of high-skilled immigration.

Does Country of Origin Matter?

To this point I have not said anything about country of origin. That is because country of origin per se is not really relevant for an analysis of economic impacts. What is most relevant is the skills that immigrants bring with them.

Immigration Law and Low-Skilled Immigrants

I have also not said anything yet about legal status. For various reasons, most individuals working in the United States in violation of immigration law are low-skilled workers. But most low-skilled workers are not "undocumented" aliens. Most low-skilled workers were born in the United States and hence are citizens by birth.

Current U.S. immigration law, however, encourages the legal immigration of low-skilled workers. This encouragement comes through the kinship preferences for various relatives built into our legal immigration system and to the smaller diversity visa program. Our immigration law permits a "snowball effect" where even immigrants granted a visa for the skills they bring to the U.S. labor market can sponsor low-skilled relatives who will then legally work in the U.S.

Of the 946,014 people who received Permanent Resident Alien visas in 2004, 65.6 percent entered under one of the several kinship categories, 8.8 percent entered as refugees or asylees, 5.3 percent entered under "diversity" visas, and 3.5 percent had a cancellation of deportation order. The 155,330 employment-based visas represented only 16.4 percent of the total. However, only about half of those who received an employment-based visa were themselves skill-tested (less than 73,000), while the remainder of these visas were received by their spouses and children. Thus, only about 7.6 percent of the nearly one million visa recipients were asked a question about their skills. . . .

The 1986 Immigration Reform and Control Act (IRCA) was sold to the American public as having two major features—amnesty which was to "wipe the slate clean" of undocumented workers, and employer sanctions which was to "keep the slate clean"—along with some increased border enforcement of the immigration law. Employer sanctions were intended to cut off the "jobs magnet" that attracted undocumented workers to the United States. Half of the political bargain was fulfilled. Under its two major amnesty provisions legal status was granted to nearly 3 million undocumented individuals, nearly all of whom were low-skilled workers, and millions more have subsequently been able to immigrate as their relatives. It is noteworthy that while in 1986 the word "amnesty" was used outright, in the current political debate the "A" word is anathema to the proponents of what is euphemistically called "earned legalization." This by itself is testimony to public perception of the failures of the 1986 Act.

Border and Interior Enforcement

Border enforcement, both at land borders and at airports, is a necessary element in the enforcement of immigration law. Border enforcement by itself has not, can not, and will not work in controlling illegal entry of undocumented immigrants. If a potential immigrant is unsuccessful in penetrating the border on the first try, success may be had on the second or third try. This may be done by "entry without inspection" (i.e., sneaking across the border) or by using "fraudulent documents" at a border crossing point. Alternatively, a "visa abuser" enters into illegal status by violating a condition of a legally obtained visa—by working while on a tourist visa, for example, or by overstaying the time limit permitted on a temporary visa.

Thus, border enforcement must be complemented with "interior enforcement." The 1986 Act focused on "employer sanctions," penalties for employers who knowingly hire people who do not have the legal right to work in this country. There has, however, been no serious effort over the past two decades to enforce employer sanctions. Modern technology makes it easier to create fraudulent documents, but it also makes it easier to develop more stringent identity checks. There are two major failings in the current system. Employers are not given a "foolproof" mechanism to readily identify those with a legal right to work, and the Federal authorities show no interest in enforcing the law, except for an occasional "show raid."

It is not obvious that new enforcement legislation (e.g., to criminalize an illegal status) is called for. What is obvious is that illegal immigration can not be controlled without a political will to enforce current immigration law. This includes providing employers with a simple and "foolproof" mechanism for identifying workers with a legal right to work in the U.S. along with more stringent enforcement of employer sanctions.

The Current Immigration System

The current legal immigration system is not serving the best economic interests of the United States. Only a small percentage of the immigrants who enter the U.S. legally in any year (less than 8 percent) are screened for their likely economic contribution to this economy. The vast majority enter under a nepotism system (the kinship preferences), with a smaller group entering under a lottery (diversity visas). To enhance the competitiveness of the U.S. economy in this increasingly globalized world, where efficient competitors are emerging across the world, the U.S. needs to change the basic question from "To whom are you related?" to "What can you contribute to the U.S. economy?"

Other highly-developed democratic countries—Canada, Australia, New Zealand—introduced "skills-based" immigration policies several decades ago. More recently, some countries in Western Europe have done the same. Some, like Canada and Australia, use a "points system" in which points are awarded based on characteristics that research has shown to enhance the earnings of immigrants such as age, schooling, technical training, and proficiency in the host country's language. Those with more than the threshold number of points receive a visa for themselves, their spouse and their minor accompanying children. This shift in emphasis in the rationing of visas would increase the skill level of immigrants and provide greater economic benefits to the U.S. economy than the current system.

A points system has many advantages over the current targeted employment-based visas. Under the current system a complex and very expensive bureaucratic process is required for employers to demonstrate to the U.S. Department of Labor not only that the visa applicant is qualified for a specific job but also that there is no qualified person with a legal right to work in the U.S. who will take the job at "prevailing wages." Even then, the worker who obtains a visa through this process is not obliged to remain on that job or with that employer.

Other proposals would use market mechanisms to "close the gap" between the large demand for visas and the much smaller supply that the U.S. is willing to make available. One possibility would involve auctioning visas; another involves charging a large market-clearing "visa fee." Among other advantages of these market mechanisms is that people in the U.S. can express their preferences for bringing relatives and friends by contributing to the price of their visa. Nor does there need to be only one mechanism—a skill-based system and a market-based system could both be used.

How Many Immigrants?

This returns us to a question posed early in this testimony: "What is the optimal size of the immigration flow?" The optimal immigration policy is neither a completely open door nor a completely closed one. There is no magic number or proportion of the population. Currently, legal immigration is running at approximately one million immigrants per year. This is on a par with the peak period of immigration from 1905 to 1914, when immigration also averaged one million per year. Yet, relative to the size of the U.S. population, current legal immigration is about one-fourth of the ratio in this earlier period. There is no clear evidence that the U.S. has exceeded—or even reached—its absorptive capacity for immigration. The U.S. economy and society exhibits a remarkable adaptability to immigrants, and thus far immigrants continue to show considerable adaptability to the U.S. economy and society. This adaptability means that the U.S. economy can absorb a continuous stream of immigrants without fracturing the system.

The demand for visas to enter the U.S. is very strong and, if anything, it seems to be increasing. This is a credit to the U.S. economy, society, and political system. The number of visas the U.S. political process is willing to supply is not immutable. The greater the economic benefits of immigration, the larger the optimal number of visas and the greater the willingness of the American public to provide them.

A comprehensive immigration policy reform would reduce undocumented migration by more stringent enforcement of existing law. It should also include the adoption of a skill-based points system and/or market mechanisms to ration visas, while limiting kinship migration to the immediate relatives of U.S. citizens (spouse, minor children, aged parents). These policies would increase the benefits of immigration for the American public, providing economic incentives to increase the supply of visas and hence the annual total number of immigrants entering the country legally.

POSTSCRIPT

Is Immigration an Economic Benefit to the Host Country?

During 2005 and 2006, the American public and its politicians debated what to do about immigration, especially illegal immigration. Some wanted stronger security measures to keep illegal immigrants out and deport those already in the United States. Others favored a guest-worker program that would permit those undocumented immigrants in the country to remain for a period of years as temporary workers but that would also require them to eventually leave the country. Yet others supported a program that would allow unauthorized immigrants already in the country to get a work permit and eventually to apply for citizenship. One poll found 20 percent of Americans favoring the first option, 14 percent supporting the second, and 63 percent preferring the third option, with 3 percent unsure. In the narrow realm of Washington, D.C., opinions were more evenly split, and, as a result, Congress enacted some piecemeal legislation dealing with immigration security, but failed to enact a comprehensive plan.

Although this issue focused on the United States, it is well to remember that this provided an example of a debate going on in many countries. Whatever views about legal and illegal immigrants may be, one certainty is that the pressure on people to abandon their homelands and seek new ones will persist as widespread poverty and violence exist in many of the world's countries. Border barriers can impede, but not stop, the flow of those desperately seeking physical and economic security. Therefore, it might be wise to address the cause of immigration and also to avoid annually spending of huge amounts on immigration control to help Mexico, Central America, and other developing countries to achieve greater prosperity so that the people in those countries would no longer be willing to experience the dislocation and danger that leaving home and slipping into the United States or some other developed country entails.

An overview of the the history of U.S. immigration and policy is found in Aristide R. Zolberg, *A Nation by Design: Immigration Policy in the Fashioning of America* (Harvard University Press, 2006). A group that says it welcomes immigrants, but argues that there are way too many of them is the Center for Immigration Studies at http://www.cis.org/. Taking a distinctly positive view of immigration and immigrants is the National Immigration Forum at http://www.immigrationforum.org/. The view that immigrants pose a challenge to American culture is expressed by Samuel P. Huntington in *Who We Are: The Challenges to American National Identity* (Simon & Schuster, 2004). To avoid any doubt about the main source of the problem in Huntington's view, see his "The Hispanic Challenge," *Foreign Policy* (March/April 2004). Huntington's thesis evoked numerous challenges including, Luis R. Fraga and Gary M. Segura, "Culture Clash? Contesting Notions of American Identity and the Effects of Latin American Immigration," *Perspectives on Politics* (June 2006). For the impact of immigration beyond the United States, read Craig A. Parsons and Timothy M. Smeeding (eds.), *Immigration and the Transformation of Europe* (Cambridge University Press, 2006).

Internet References . . .

Disarmament Diplomacy

This site, maintained by the Acronym Institute for Disarmament Diplomacy, provides up-to-date news and analysis of disarmament activity, with a particular focus on weapons of mass destruction.

http://www.acronym.org.uk

The Center for Security Policy

The Web site of this Washington, D.C.–centered "think tank" provides a wide range of links to sites dealing with national and international security issues.

http://www.centerforsecuritypolicy.org

National Defense University

This leading center for joint professional military education is under the direction of the Chairman of the U.S. Joint Chiefs of Staff. Its Website is valuable for general military thinking and for material on terrorism.

http://www.ndu.edu/

Office of the Coordinator for Counterterrorism

This worthwhile site explores the range of terrorist threats and activities, albeit from the U.S. point of view, and is maintained by the U.S. State Department's Counterterrorism Office.

http://www.state.gov/s/ct/

Centre for the Study of Terrorism and Political Violence

The primary aims of the Centre for the Study of Terrorism and Political Violence are to investigate the roots of political violence; to develop a body of theory spanning the various and disparate elements of terrorism; and to recommend policy and organizational initiatives that governments and private sectors might adopt to better predict, detect, and respond to terrorism and terrorist threats.

http://www.st-ANDREWS.ac.uk/academic/intrel/research/cstpv/

Issues About Violence
and Arms Control

*W*hatever we may wish, war, terrorism, and other forms of physical
coercion are still important elements of international politics. Countries
calculate both how to use the instruments of force and how to implement
national security. There can be little doubt, however, that significant
changes are under way in this realm as part of the changing world system.
Strong pressures exist to expand the mission and strengthen the security
capabilities of international organizations and to gauge the threat of
terrorism. This section examines how countries in the international system
are addressing these issues.

- Is Preemptive War an Unacceptable Doctrine?

- Does the United States Have a Sound Strategy for the War on Terrorism?

- Is Patient Diplomacy the Best Approach to Iran's Nuclear Program?

- Is North Korea an Aggressive Rogue State?

ISSUE 12

Is Preemptive War an Unacceptable Doctrine?

YES: High Level Panel on Threats, Challenges, and Change, from "A More Secure World: Our Shared Responsibility," A Report to the Secretary General of the United Nations (December 2, 2004)

NO: Steven L. Kenny, from "The National Security Strategy Under the United Nations and International Law," Strategy Research Project, U.S. Army War College (March 19, 2004)

ISSUE SUMMARY

YES: The High Level Panel on Threats, Challenges, and Change, which was appointed by United Nations Secretary-General Kofi Annan in response to the global debate on the nature of threats and the use of force to counter them, concludes that in a world full of perceived potential threats, the risk to the global order posed by preemptive war is too great for its legality to be accepted.

NO: Colonel Steven L. Kenny argues in a research report he wrote at the U.S. Army War College, Carlisle Barracks, Pennsylvania, that substantial support from the acceptability of preemptive war results from such factors as the failure of the UN to enforce its charter, customary international law, and the growing threat of terrorists and weapons of mass destruction.

In September 2002 President George W. Bush issued "The National Security Strategy of the United States of America," an annual report to Congress required by the National Security Act of 1947. Seldom has one ignited the sort of fiery debate that the 2002 report sparked.

Undoubtedly the most controversial part of the president's policy, as noted in the introduction to Issue 2 in this volume, was his assertion that the United States had the right to strike enemies before they attacked Americans. Bush argued that the growing threat of terrorism and weapons of mass destruction had extended the meaning of self-defense to include preemptive action. As Bush put it in his report:

> . . . Our enemies have openly declared that they are seeking Weapons of mass destruction. . . . As a matter of common sense and self-defense, America

will act against such emerging threats before they are fully formed. . . . History will judge harshly those who saw the coming danger but failed to act. In the new world we have entered, the only path to peace and security is the path of action.

This claimed right to strike first and do so unilaterally was at the heart of what was soon dubbed the Bush Doctrine. As a statement of principle, the Bush Doctrine set off an intense debate, but it reached a crescendo when the United States applied the doctrine as part of its rationale for war against Iraq. When Bush addressed the nation on March 19, 2003 to announce the beginning of military operations against Iraq, he explained:

The people of the United States . . . will not live at the mercy of an outlaw regime that threatens the peace with weapons of mass murder. We will meet that threat now, with our [military forces] so that we do not have to meet it later with armies of fire fighters and police and doctors on the streets of our cities.

As you will see in the following articles by the UN-based High Level Panel on Threats, Challenges, and Changes and by Steven L. Kenny, the doctrine of preemption is debated at both a practical level and legal level. At the pragmatic level it is important to consider both near-term and long-term consequences. Certainly, attacking an enemy country or terrorist organization before it attacks you has its obvious attractions. But what if your sense of threat is wrong, and people on both sides are killed and wounded? Additionally, the "golden rule" has to be considered, and asserting the right to preemptive war means that others also have the right to strike first if they feel threatened.

Legally, there are two main points to consider. One is the traditional "just war" theory that holds in part that *jus ad bellum* (just cause of war) exists only when war is (1) a last resort, (2) declared by legitimate authority, (3) waged in self-defense or to establish/restore justice, and (4) fought to bring about peace. Some might dismiss these standards a mere philosophy, but the United States applied them as part of the charges against Japanese and German leaders after World War II, tried those individuals in international tribunals, and imprisoned and even executed them after they were convicted. Moreover, just war theory is part of what underpins the definitions of illegal warfare that is subject to the newly established International Criminal Court (see Issue 18). The legal aspect of preemptive war also involves the obligations of all countries, including the United States, that signed the UN Charter. Under Article 2 of that treaty, signatories pledge to "refrain in their international relations from the threat or use of force against the territorial integrity or political independence of any state." And while Article 51 stipulates, "Nothing in the present Charter shall impair the inherent right of individual or collective self-defense if an armed attack occurs," Article 39 specifies that in all other cases, the "Security Council shall determine the existence of any threat to the peace, breach of the peace, or act of aggression and . . . decide what measures shall be taken . . . to maintain or restore international peace and security."

205

Collective Security and the Use of Force

What happens if peaceful prevention fails? If none of the preventive measures so far described stop the descent into war and chaos? If distant threats do become imminent? Or if imminent threats become actual? Or if a non-imminent threat nonetheless becomes very real and measures short of the use of military force seem powerless to stop it?

We address here the circumstances in which effective collective security may require the backing of military force, starting with the rules of international law that must govern any decision to go to war, if anarchy is not to prevail. It is necessary to distinguish between situations in which a State claims to act in self-defense; situations in which a State is posing a threat to others outside its borders; and situations in which the threat is primarily internal and the issue is the responsibility to protect a State's own people. In all cases, we believe that the Charter of the United Nations, properly understood and applied, is equal to the task: Article 51 needs neither extension nor restriction of its long-understood scope, and Chapter VII fully empowers the Security Council to deal with every kind of threat that States may confront. The task is not to find alternatives to the Security Council as a source of authority but to make it work better than it has.

That force *can* legally be used does not always mean that, as a matter of good conscience and good sense, it *should* be used. We identify a set of guidelines—five criteria of legitimacy—which we believe the Security Council (and anyone else involved in these decisions) should always address in considering whether to authorize or apply military force. The adoption of these guidelines (seriousness of threat, proper purpose, last resort, proportional means and balance of consequences) will not produce agreed conclusions with push-button predictability, but should significantly improve the chances of reaching international consensus on what have been in recent years deeply divisive issues.

We also address here the other major issues that arise during and after violent conflict, including the needed capacities for peace enforcement, peacekeeping and peacebuilding, and the protection of civilians. A central recurring theme is the necessity for all members of the international community, developed and developing States alike, to be much more forthcoming in

Secretary General of the United Nations, (December 2, 2004).

providing and supporting deployable military resources. Empty gestures are all too easy to make: an effective, efficient and equitable collective security system demands real commitment.

Using Force: Rules and Guidelines

The framers of the Charter of the United Nations recognized that force may be necessary for the "prevention and removal of threats to the peace, and for the suppression of acts of aggression or other breaches of the peace." Military force, legally and properly applied, is a vital component of any workable system of **collective** security, whether defined in the traditional narrow sense or more broadly as we would prefer. But few contemporary policy issues cause more difficulty, or involve higher stakes, than the principles concerning its use and application to individual cases.

The maintenance of world peace and security depends importantly on there being a common global understanding, and acceptance, of when the application of force is both legal and legitimate. One of these elements being satisfied without the other will always weaken the international legal order—and thereby put both State and human security at greater risk.

A. The Question of Legality

The Charter of the United Nations, in Article 2, expressly prohibits Member States from using or threatening force against each other, allowing only two exceptions: self-defense under Article 51, and military measures authorized by the Security Council under Chapter VII [Articles 39–51] (and by extension for regional organizations under Chapter VIII [Articles 52–54]) in response to "any threat to the peace, breach of the peace or act of aggression."

For the first 44 years of the United Nations, Member States often violated these rules and used military force literally hundreds of times, with a paralyzed Security Council passing very few Chapter VII resolutions and Article 51 only rarely providing credible cover. Since the end of the cold war, however, the yearning for an international system governed by the rule of law has grown. There is little evident international acceptance of the idea of security being best preserved by a balance of power, or by any single—even benignly motivated—superpower.

But in seeking to apply the express language of the Charter, three particularly difficult questions arise in practice: first, when a State claims the right to strike preventively, in self-defense, in response to a threat which is not imminent; secondly, when a State appears to be posing an external threat, actual or potential, to other States or people outside its borders, but there is disagreement in the Security Council as to what to do about it; and thirdly, where the threat is primarily internal, to a State's own people.

Article 51 of the Charter of the United Nations and self-defense   The language of this article is restrictive: "Nothing in the present Charter shall impair the inherent right of individual or collective self-defense if an armed attack occurs against a member of the United Nations, until the Security Council has taken measures to maintain international peace and security." However, a threatened State, according to long established international law, can take military action as long as the threatened attack is *imminent,* no other means would deflect it and the action is proportionate. The problem arises where the threat in question is not imminent but still claimed to be real: for example the acquisition, with allegedly hostile intent, of nuclear weapons-making capability.

Can a State, without going to the Security Council, claim in these circumstances the right to act, in anticipatory self-defense, not just preemptively (against an imminent or proximate threat) but preventively (against a non-imminent or non-proximate one)? Those who say "yes" argue that the potential harm from some threats (e.g., terrorists armed with a nuclear weapon) is so great that one simply cannot risk waiting until they become imminent, and that less harm may be done (e.g., avoiding a nuclear exchange or radioactive fallout from a reactor destruction) by acting earlier.

The short answer is that if there are good arguments for preventive military action, with good evidence to support them, they should be put to the Security Council, which can authorize such action if it chooses to. If it does not so choose, there will be, by definition, time to pursue other strategies, including persuasion, negotiation, deterrence and containment—and to visit again the military option.

For those impatient with such a response, the answer must be that, in a world full of perceived potential threats, the risk to the global order and the norm of non-intervention on which it continues to be based is simply too great for the legality of unilateral preventive action, as distinct from collectively endorsed action, to be accepted. Allowing one to so act is to allow all. We do not favour the rewriting or reinterpretation of Article 51.

Chapter VII of the Charter of the United Nations and external threats   In the case of a State posing a threat to other States, people outside its borders or to international order more generally, the language of Chapter VII is inherently broad enough, and has been interpreted broadly enough, to allow the Security Council to approve any coercive act ion at all, including military action, against a State when it deems this "necessary to maintain or restore international peace and security." That is the case whether the threat is occurring now, in the imminent future or more distant future; whether it involves the State's own actions or those of non-State actors it harbors or supports; or whether it takes the form of an act or omission, an actual or potential act of violence or simply a challenge to the Council's authority.

We emphasize that the concerns we expressed about the legality of the preventive use of military force in the case of self-defense under Article 51 are not applicable in the case of collective action authorized under Chapter VII. In the world of the twenty-first century, the international community does have to be concerned about nightmare scenarios combining terrorists, weapons of mass destruction and irresponsible States, and much more besides, which may conceivably justify the use of force, not just reactively but preventively and before a latent threat becomes imminent. The question is not whether such action can be taken: it can, by the Security Council as the international community's collective security voice, at any time it deems that there is a threat to international peace and security. The Council may well need to be prepared to be much more proactive on these issues, taking more decisive action earlier, than it has been in the past.

Questions of legality apart, there will be issues of prudence, or legitimacy, about whether such preventive action *should* be taken: crucial among them is whether there is credible evidence of the reality of the threat in question (taking into account both capability and specific intent) and whether the military response is the only reasonable one in the circumstances. We address these issues further below.

It may be that some States will always feel that they have the obligation to their own citizens, and the capacity, to do whatever they feel they need to do, unburdened by the constraints of collective Security Council process. But however understandable that approach may have been in the cold war years, when the United Nations was manifestly not operating as an effective collective security system, the world has now changed and expectations about legal compliance are very much higher. One of the reasons why States may want to bypass the Security Council is a lack of confidence in the quality and objectivity of its decision-making. The Council's decisions have often been less than consistent, less than persuasive and less than fully responsive to very real State and human security needs. But the solution is not to reduce the Council to impotence and irrelevance: it is to work from within to reform it, including in the ways we propose in the present report. The Security Council is fully empowered under Chapter VII of the Charter of the United Nations to address the full range of security threats with which States are concerned. The task is not to find alternatives to the Security Council as a source of authority but to make the Council work better than it has.

Chapter VII of the Charter of the United Nations, internal threats and the responsibility to protect The Charter of the United Nations is not as clear as it could be when it comes to saving lives within countries in situations of mass atrocity. It "reaffirm(s) faith in fundamental human rights" but does not do much to protect them, and Article 2 prohibits intervention "in matters which are essentially within the jurisdiction of any State." There has been, as a result, a long-standing argument in the international community between those who insist on a "right to intervene" in man-made catastrophes and those who argue that the Security Council, for all its powers under Chapter VII to "maintain or restore international security," is prohibited from authorizing any coercive action against sovereign States for whatever happens within their borders.

Under the Convention on the Prevention and Punishment of the Crime of Genocide (Genocide Convention), States have agreed that genocide, whether committed in time of peace or in time of war, is a crime under international law which they undertake to prevent and punish. Since then it has been understood that genocide anywhere is a threat to the security of all and should never be tolerated. The principle of non-intervention in internal affairs cannot be used to protect genocidal acts or other atrocities, such as large-scale violations of international humanitarian law or large-scale ethnic cleansing, which can properly be considered a threat to international security and as such provoke action by the Security Council.

The successive humanitarian disasters in Somalia, Bosnia and Herzegovina, Rwanda, Kosovo and now Darfur, Sudan, have concentrated attention not on the immunities of sovereign Governments but their responsibilities, both to their own people and to the wider international community. There is a growing recognition that the issue is not the "right to intervene" of any State, but the "responsibility to protect" of *every* State when it comes to people suffering from avoidable catastrophe—mass murder and rape, ethnic cleansing by forcible expulsion and terror, and deliberate starvation and exposure to disease. And there is a growing acceptance that while sovereign Governments have the primary responsibility to protect their own citizens from such catastrophes, when they are unable or unwilling to do so that responsibility should be taken up by the wider international community—with it spanning a continuum involving prevention, response to violence, if necessary, and rebuilding shattered societies. The primary focus should be on assisting the cessation of violence through mediation and other tools and the protection of people through such measures as the dispatch of humanitarian, human rights and police missions. Force, if it needs to be used, should be deployed as a last resort.

The Security Council so far has been neither very consistent nor very effective in dealing with these cases, very often acting too late, too hesitantly or not at all. But step by step, the Council and the wider international community have come to accept that, under Chapter VII and in pursuit of the emerging norm of a collective international responsibility to protect, it can always authorize military action to redress catastrophic internal wrongs if it is prepared to declare that the situation is a "threat to international peace and security," not especially difficult when breaches of international law are involved. We endorse the emerging norm that there is a collective international responsibility to protect, exercisable by the Security Council authorizing military intervention as a last resort, in the event of genocide and other large-scale killing, ethnic cleansing or serious violations of international humanitarian law which sovereign Governments have proved powerless or unwilling to prevent.

B. The Question of Legitimacy

The effectiveness of the global collective security system, as with any other legal order, depends ultimately not only on the legality of decisions but also on the common perception of their legitimacy—their being made on solid evidentiary grounds, and for the right reasons, morally as well as legally. If the Security Council is to win the respect it must have as the primary body in the collective security system, it is critical that its most important and influential decisions, those with large-scale life-and-death impact, be better made, better substantiated and better communicated. In particular, in deciding whether or not to authorize the use of force, the Council should adopt and systematically address a set of agreed guidelines, going directly not to whether force *can* legally be used but whether, as a matter of good conscience and good sense, it *should* be. The guidelines we propose will not produce agreed conclusions with push-button predictability. The point of adopting them is not to guarantee that the objectively best outcome will always prevail. It is rather to maximize the possibility of achieving Security Council consensus around when it is appropriate or not to use coercive action, including armed force; to maximize international support for whatever the Security Council decides; and to minimize the possibility of individual Member States bypassing the Security Council.

In considering whether to authorize or endorse the use of military force, the Security Council should always address—whatever other considerations it may take into account—at least the following five basic criteria of legitimacy:

a. *Seriousness of threat.* Is the threatened harm to State or human security of a kind, and sufficiently clear and serious, to justify prima facie the use of military force? In the case of internal threats, does it involve genocide and other large-scale killing, ethnic cleansing or serious violations of international humanitarian law, actual or imminently apprehended?

b. *Proper purpose.* Is it clear that the primary purpose of the proposed military action is to halt or avert the threat in question, whatever other purposes or motives may be involved?

c. *Last resort.* Has every non-military option for meeting the threat in question been explored, with reasonable grounds for believing that other measures will not succeed?

d. *Proportional means.* Are the scale, duration and intensity of the proposed military action the minimum necessary to meet the threat in question?

e. *Balance of consequences.* Is there a reasonable chance of the military action being successful in meeting the threat in question, with the consequences of action not likely to be worse than the consequences of inaction?

The above guidelines for authorizing the use of force should be embodied in declaratory resolutions of the Security Council and General Assembly. We also believe it would be valuable if individual Member States, whether or not they are members of the Security Council, subscribed to them.

Peace Enforcement and Peacekeeping Capability

When the Security Council makes a determination that force must be authorized, questions remain about the capacities at its disposal to implement that decision. In recent years, decisions to authorize military force for the purpose of enforcing the peace have primarily fallen to multinational forces. Blue helmet peacekeepers—in United Nations uniform and under direct United Nations command—have more frequently been deployed when forces are authorized with the consent of the parties to conflict, to help implement a peace agreement or monitor ceasefire lines after combat.

Discussion of the necessary capacities has been confused by the tendency to refer to peacekeeping missions as "Chapter VI operations" and peace enforcement missions as "Chapter VII operations"—meaning consent-based or coercion-based, respectively. This shorthand is also often used to distinguish missions that do not involve the use of deadly force for purposes other than self-defense, and those that do.

Both characterizations are to some extent misleading. There *is* a distinction between operations in which the robust use of force is integral to the mission from the outset (e.g., responses to cross-border invasions or an explosion of violence, in which the recent practice has been to mandate multinational forces) and operations in which there is a reasonable expectation that force may not be needed at all (e.g., traditional peacekeeping missions monitoring and verifying a ceasefire or those assisting in implementing peace agreements, where blue helmets are still the norm).

But both kinds of operation need the authorization of the Security Council (Article 51 self-defense cases apart), and in peacekeeping cases as much as in peace-enforcement cases it is now the usual practice for a Chapter VII mandate to be given (even if that is not always welcomed by troop contributors). This is on the basis that even the most benign environment can turn sour—when spoilers emerge to undermine a peace agreement and put civilians at risk—and that it is desirable for there to be complete certainty about the mission's capacity to respond with force, if necessary. On the other hand, the difference between Chapter VI and VII mandates can be exaggerated: there is little doubt that peacekeeping missions operating under Chapter VI (and thus operating without enforcement powers) have the right to use force in self-defense—and this right is widely understood to extend to "defense of the mission."

The real challenge, in any deployment of forces of any configuration with any role, is to ensure that they have (a) an appropriate, clear and well understood mandate, applicable to all the changing circumstances that might reasonably be envisaged, and (b) all the necessary resources to implement that mandate fully.

The demand for personnel for both full-scale peace-enforcement missions and peacekeeping missions remains higher than the ready supply. At the end of 2004, there are more than 60,000 peacekeepers deployed in 16 missions around the world. If international efforts stay on track to end several long-standing wars in Africa, the numbers of peacekeepers needed will soon substantially increase. In the absence of a commensurate increase in available personnel, United Nations peacekeeping risks repeating some of its worst failures of the 1990s. At present, the total global supply of personnel is constrained both by the fact that the armed forces of many countries remain configured for cold war duties, with less than 10 per cent of those in uniform available for active deployment at any given time, and by the fact that few nations have sufficient transport and logistic capabilities to move and supply those who are available. For peacekeeping, and in extreme cases peace enforcement, to continue to be an effective and accepted instrument of collective security, the availability of peacekeepers must grow. The developed States have particular responsibilities here, and should do more to transform their existing force capacities into suitable contingents for peace operations.

Prompt and effective response to today's challenges requires a dependable capacity for the rapid deployment of personnel and equipment for peacekeeping and law enforcement. States that have either global or regional air- or sea-lift capacities should make these available to the United Nations, either free of charge or on the basis of a negotiated fee-based structure for the reimbursement of the additional costs associated with United Nations use of these capacities. Member States should strongly support the efforts of the Department of Peacekeeping Operations of the United Nations Secretariat, building on the important work of the Panel on United Nations Peace Operations (see A/55/305–S/2000/809), to improve its use of strategic deployment stockpiles, standby arrangements, trust funds and other mechanisms to meet the tighter deadlines necessary for effective deployment.

However, it is unlikely that the demand for rapid action will be met through United Nations mechanisms alone. We welcome the European Union decision to establish standby high readiness, self-sufficient battalions that can reinforce United Nations missions. Others with advanced military capacities should be encouraged to develop similar capacities at up to brigade level and to place them at the disposal of the United Nations.

Steven L. Kenny  **NO**

The National Security Strategy Under the United Nations and International Law

We make war so that we may live in peace. (Aristotle)

In response to an international order of growing terrorism, trans-national crime, "rogue" and "failed" states potentially armed with WMD [weapons of mass destruction] and willing to use them, the [U.S. document] *National Security Strategy* has invoked an escalation of the right of self-defense as it prosecutes the Global War on Terrorism. Termed preemption, it is in fact a policy of preventive self-defense.

The *National Security Strategy* policy of preventive self-defense has been generally condemned throughout the international arena and also within the U.S. However, this condemnation is not universal. This study will show that a significant amount of validity can be conferred on the National Security Strategy due to: (1) the failure of the UN to enforce its charter, essentially abandoning the purposes of the UN (2) the continued use and threat of use of preventive self-defense by many states and previous U.S. administrations (3) state practice (4) customary international law (5) the slowly changing body of international law that is responding to and inferring more significance due to the rise of transnational terrorists and WMD proliferation over state sovereignty.

The National Security Strategy of the United States of America

In the *Overview of The National Security Strategy of the United States of America,* September 2002, President George W. Bush put forth a number of idealistic aspirations [regarding spreading democracy and securing peace throughout the world]. . . . While quite laudable, . . . these generated a muted level of interest and discussion. The overwhelming attention of both the United States and the international community focused almost singularly on another significant tenet espoused throughout the document. [This included:]

- Identifying and destroying the threat before it reaches our borders. . . . we will not hesitate to act alone if necessary, to exercise our right of self-defense by acting preemptively against such terrorists.

Strategy Research Project, U.S. Army War College, (March 19, 2004).

- The United States has long maintained the option of preemptive actions to counter a sufficient threat to our national security. The greater the threat, the greater is the risk of inaction—and the more compelling the case for taking anticipatory action to defend ourselves, even if uncertainty remains as to the time and place of the enemy's attack. To forestall or prevent such hostile acts by our adversaries, the United States will, if necessary, act preemptively.
- The United States will not use force in all cases to preempt emerging threats, nor should nations use preemption as a pretext for aggression. Yet in an age where the enemies of civilization openly and actively seek the world's most destructive technologies the United States cannot remain idle while dangers gather.

Anticipatory? Preemption? Preventive?

The words anticipatory, preemptive, and preventive when associated with the self-defense of a nation generated extensive debate before the United Nations was even a dream. However, there is no need for an exhaustive review and discussion of this history to discern an opinion or conclusion on what these terms have come to mean today within the international community and the United Nations. Current publications . . . provide definitions quite acceptable to the vast majority of international legal scholars and members of the United Nations.

From the Department of Defense, Dictionary of Military and Associated Terms:

> "Preemptive Attack—An attack initiated on the basis of incontro-vertible evidence that an enemy attack is imminent."
>
> "Preventive War—A war initiated in the belief that military con-flict, while not imminent, is inevitable, and that to delay would involve greater risk."

From the United States Army, Judge Advocate General's School, Operational Law Handbook, 2002:

> "Anticipatory self-defense finds its roots in the 1842 Caroline case and a pronouncement by then Secretary of State Daniel Webster that a state need not suffer an actual armed attack before taking defensive action, but may engage in anticipatory self-defense if the circumstances leading to the use of force are "instantaneous, overwhelming, and leaving no choice of means and no moment for deliberation."

From these definitions, one can discern an obvious hierarchy based on the level of imminence the threat presents. Anticipatory self-defense associated with an "instantaneous" or truly, imminent threat. Preemptive attack associ-ated with "incontrovertible evidence that an enemy attack is imminent." Pre-ventive war associated with an "inevitable" future threat, but not linked in any way with the concept of an imminent threat.

One can form an association between anticipatory self-defense and preemptive attack based on their respective references to a requirement for some level of an imminent threat. Based on this requirement of imminence, the distinction between anticipatory self-defense and preemptive attack has become blurred and these terms are often used interchangeably. However, the lack of any reference to an imminent threat in the definition of preventive war would clearly distinguish it from anticipatory self-defense and preemptive attack.

Interestingly, a review of the use of the words anticipatory and preemptive in the *National Security Strategy* reveals an obvious disconnect with the Department of Defense and United States Army, Judge Advocate General definitions. In most cases "preventive" can be substituted for anticipatory and preemption within the National Security Strategy and the document is transformed to agree with these definitions.

For the purposes of this paper, it will be stipulated that when the *National Security Strategy of the United States* uses the words anticipatory and preemption in the context of the nation's self-defense, it is in fact referring to concepts that are more commonly accepted as preventive self-defense.

While the legality of initiating the use of force in self-defense remains an area of much debate within the United Nations and international law, one can clearly delineate a significant difference in this arena when comparing the use of anticipatory/preemptive to preventive. In fact, it is quite evident that most of the world (including much of the United States) would support the argument that the use of preventive in the context of self-defense is not a matter of self-defense at all. The vast majority of legal debate, argument, and opinion declares that the concept of preventive self-defense is illegal under international law and the Charter of the United Nations.

One might easily dismiss the validity of the National Security Strategy based on the above conclusion. However, international law and the United Nations have been and remain a dynamic entity. Taking a stance in this arena is an open invitation for a debate. Perhaps there is a future for the National Security Strategy.

Use of Force in Self-Defense Under the Provisions of the Charter of the United Nations

A nation and its right of self-defense is a controversial and active part of the international legal debate, even more than 50 years since most of the world's nations became signatories of the charter of the United Nations. Why? Because the world has suffered many conflicts in the past 50 plus years and self-defense is claimed as a factor in most of them. Self-defense of a nation remains the most common legal justification under international law and the United Nations for the use of coercive force between states.

Under the charter of the United Nations, the generally accepted sections applicable to the use of force in self-defense are:

Chapter One, Article 2 (Principles), Paragraph 4

> "All members shall refrain in their international relations from the threat or use of force against the territorial integrity or political independence of any state, or in any other manner inconsistent with the Purposes of the United Nations."

Chapter 7 (actions with respect to threats to the peace, breaches of peace, and acts of aggression), Article Fifty-One

> "Nothing in the Charter shall impair the inherent right of individual or collective self-defense if an armed attack occurs against a Member of the United Nations, until the Security Council has taken measures necessary to maintain international peace and security. Measures taken by Members in the exercise of this right of self-defense shall be immediately reported to the Security Council and shall not in any way affect the authority and responsibility of the Security Council under the present Charter to take at any time such action as it deems necessary in order to maintain or restore international peace and security."

These two articles appear fairly straightforward. They could be boiled down to no use of force except in self-defense after an attack and then only until the Security Council takes necessary measures to "restore international peace and security." There exists a substantial amount of legal opinion in the arena of international law that supports this simple, somewhat literal, interpretation of these articles. Any use of force outside of this interpretation would be considered a violation of international law and the charter of the United Nations. Is it really this simple?

At least in practice, no. Columbia University international security policy expert Richard K. Betts wrote,

> I am aware of no case in which international law has blocked a decision to wage war—that is, a case in which a government decided that strategic necessity required war yet refrained because international law was deemed to forbid it. "He further notes that once the decision is made by a state to go to war," they find a lawyer to tell the world that international law allows it. . . .

United Nations Charter and the Use of Force—Framer's Intent

Professor Timothy Kearly, University of Wyoming School of Law, conducted an interesting analysis of the 1967 book, *Foreign Relations of the United States,* which contained the minutes of the United States delegation to United Nations Conference on International Organization (UNCIO), held in San Francisco, April 25–June 25, 1945. The UN Charter's final form was constructed at this conference. The minutes covered the U.S. delegation's internal meetings and meetings with the other "Great Powers" who would eventually become the five permanent members of the United Nations Security Council. His article, "Regulation of Preventive and Preemptive Force in the United Nations Charter: A Search for Original Intent," conducted an extensive review of these minutes, focusing on the discussions concerning the development of the provisions on the use of force in self-defense under the UN Charter. His purpose was to determine if one could ascertain the intent of the framers of the UN Charter from these minutes. The intent of the framers is important because it is often invoked in the international arena to support a position in the contentious arguments over the use of force in self-defense. . . .

The analysis reveals that there were significant differences among the Great Powers. They all brought their own concerns that didn't always coincide with the other's concerns. This is reflected in Kearly's conclusion that, "there were substantial, unresolved disagreements . . . about the circumstances under which states should be able to use force without Security Council approval . . . combined with time pressures . . . [this] resulted in Charter use of force provisions that are imprecise, somewhat inconsistent, and open to interpretation." He goes on to note "the drafters were not concerned with their lack of precision because they assumed the permanent members of the Security Council would negotiate judgments concerning uses of force case by case in good faith.

This conclusion confirms that considerable ambiguity is built into the charter. The ambiguity was acceptable to the framers because they wanted an agreement; without the ambiguity, it is likely there would be no agreement due to the differing concerns and motives of the Great Powers. The fact that the framers introduced ambiguity reveals exactly what the framers intended. . . .

This indicates that the framers intended the law applying organ, i.e. the Security Council to make decisions case by case in good faith as the need arose in ambiguous situations. Conversely, it does not appear the framers intended international jurists to interpret the charter and establish new legal principles. . . .

Preventive Self-Defense

Critics of the *National Security Strategy* typically renounce the U.S. as embarking on unilateral, hegemonic mission to overturn the guarantee of international peace secured in 1945 by the UN Charter. They cry that the concept of preventive self-defense was eliminated for good on that day. Noam Chomsky, a prominent MIT professor and political dissident recently wrote, "Preventive war is, very simply, the 'supreme crime' condemned at Nuremburg." A rather harsh condemnation considering that the concept of preventive self-defense is part of the UN Charter. Critics of the National Security Strategy such as Chomsky typically ignore or summarily dismiss the fact that in 1945, the UN Charter actually contained a provision authorizing the very crime they denounce so vehemently, preventive self-defense.

Chapter 17, Article 107

> Nothing in the present Charter shall invalidate or preclude action, in relation to any state which during the Second World War has been an enemy of any signatory to the present Charter, taken or authorized as a result of that war by the Governments having responsibility for such action.

Article 107 was created due to the desires of the Soviet Union, Great Britain and France. They had suffered greatly in the two World Wars at the hands of aggressive powers that did not respond to peaceful efforts to resolve matters. Kearly in his previously mentioned review concluded, "With respect to preventive force . . . the charter's drafters intended to prohibit such assertive action except as specifically authorized in the form of . . . Article 107 actions against former enemy states." They wanted "an explicit authorization under the charter to use force preventively against their most likely foes, but did not want other states to have that authorization."

There is some ambiguity in Article 107 and a restrictionist [one who argues the UN charter strictly limits when countries can use force] might propose to limit Article 107 to actions "taken or authorized as a result of that war." This was addressed in 1951 by Hans Kelsen in a legal analysis of fundamental problems with the UN Charter. He concluded that it would be impossible to limit the use of Article 107 precisely due to the very ambiguity of this phrase. An additional conclusion from Kearly's review, the framers "assumed the permanent members of the Security Council would negotiate judgments concerning uses of force case by case in good faith." The framers understood the concerns of the European allies and they supported this article based on good faith. Although Article 107 does not apply today, it has to be recognized that preventive self-defense is not a new concept to the UN and its members.

Preventive self-defense as expressed in the National Security Strategy could be fairly evaluated on a case-by-case basis within the Security Council to determine if it is in concert with the purposes of the UN. Just as it was when Article 107 was created. For the UN and international community to laconically declare that any use of preventive self-defense is a violation of the UN Charter simply ensures they won't be consulted and opens the door to the National Security Strategy option of unilateral action.

Interestingly, it would be a mistake to believe the U.S. is the sole keeper of the preventive self-defense flame. In September 2003, the French Ministry of Defense stated, "Outside our borders, within the framework of prevention and projection-action, we must be able to identify and prevent threats as soon as possible. Within this framework, possible preemptive action is not out of the question, where an explicit and confirmed threat has been recognized." Although the French Ministry calls for "preemptive action," the use of "explicit and confirmed threat" only indicates only a clear, unambiguous threat. There is no requirement expressed for the threat to be of an imminent nature. Thus, this statement appears to be indicating that France is prepared to take actions of a preventive nature in self-defense. More similarity to the National Security Strategy is found in the French 2003–2008 Military Program Bill of Law, "especially as transnational terrorist networks develop and organize outside our territory, in areas not governed by states, and even at times with the help of enemy states."

State Practice

In 1970 Thomas Franck, a [scholar] . . . in the field of international law . . . , quipped "the high-minded resolve of Article 2 (4) mocks us from its grave."

He pointed out that in the first 25 years of the UN, there were "one hundred separate outbreaks of hostility between states." In only one occasion was the UN "able to mount a collective enforcement action." The eternal failure of the UN to enforce its mandate results in an endemic use of force self-defense. There is no way to establish aggressor and aggrieved in the international system resulting in both parties claiming to have used force only in self-defense. Thirty years later, Franck's observation remains the status quo. In 1999 alone, there were 44 countries involved in conflict. Of the 44 countries, 20 suffered fatalities of at least 1000 and many suffered even higher numbers. . . .

Professor of Law and the Fletcher School of Law and Diplomacy, Michael Glennon, updated the record regarding hostility between states in 2002. "Between 1945 and 1999, two-thirds of the members of the United Nations— 126 States out of 189—fought 291 interstate conflicts in which over 22 million people were killed."

Glennon related congressional testimony by former Secretary of Defense, William Perry, who stated "we will attack the launch sites of any nation that threatens to attack the U.S. with nuclear or biological weapons." The reservation of the right of first use of nuclear weapons has always been the stated policy of the members of the Security Council. This would clearly violate Article 51 as an act of preventive self-defense. The very threat itself is a violation of Article 2 (4).

Glennon concluded that "international 'rules' concerning use of force are no longer regarded as obligatory by states," declaring that Article 2 (4) and Article 51 are invalidated by state practice.

Franck recognized that the UN Charter did not have the mechanisms required for the modern world. The framers of the UN Charter were building on their experience, "large military formations preceded by mobilization and massing of troops." This allowed time for preparation and negotiation and was the type of aggression the framers intended to address by Article 2 (4) and Article 51. Franck noted "Modern warfare, however, has inconveniently by-passed these Queensberry-like practices. One too small and the other too large to be encompassed effectively . . . first, wars of agitation, infiltration and subversion carried on by proxy through national liberation movements; and second, nuclear wars involving the instantaneous use, in a first strike, of weapons of near-paralyzing destructiveness."

The *National Security Strategy* is making the same argument today. However, the environment is even more dangerous as the real fear is the "One too small" (terrorists) could come to possess and use the "weapons of near-paralyzing destructiveness." Article 2 (4) and Article 51 simply aren't designed to address this threat and the Security Council has refused to consider it.

International Law

Customary international law is not necessarily what is written down, but what states actually practice. Accepting that preventive self-defense is illegal under the UN Charter, use of preventive self-defense as proposed under the *National*

Security Strategy would be considered illegal. However, if preventive self-defense reflects customary international law, it could be considered lawful.

Georgetown University professor, author and international law expert Anthony Clark Arend states, "International law is created through consent of states expressed through treaties and customs." If conflicts arise concerning treaties (such as the UN Charter) and customs, the "conflict is resolved by determining the rules to which states consent at the present time." Arend lists 19 incidents from 1948 to 1999 where force has been used against "the political independence and territorial integrity of states" without the authorization of the Security Council and where no reasonable claim of self-defense could be made. Arend notes incidents such as the Soviet invasion of Czechoslovakia in 1948, the Argentine invasion of the Falkland Islands in 1982, the U.S. invasion of Grenada in 1983, the Iraqi attack on Kuwait in 1990, the NATO/U.S. actions against Yugoslavia in the Kosovo situation in 1999 and states that there have been "numerous acts of intervention in domestic conflict, covert actions, and other uses of force" throughout this period. According to Arend, "Given this historical record of violations, it seems very difficult to conclude that the charter framework is truly controlling of state practice, and if it is not controlling, it cannot be considered to reflect existing international law."

Arend concludes that a customary prohibition on the use of force solely for annexation of territory such as Kuwait in 1990 remains under current customary law. However, current customary international law otherwise bears no resemblance to any prohibition contained in Article 2 (4) and that "For all practical purposes, the UN Charter framework is dead." He adds that since the Article 2 (4) is not reflected in state practice, "the Bush doctrine of preemption does not violate international law."

The Future of International Law

Michael N. Schmitt, Professor of International Law at the George C. Marshall European Center for International Affairs, conducted an extensive study on the response of international law to conflict over time. Law is not static; it is dynamic, responding and adjusting to the community on whose behalf it operates. It does not respond on a case-by-case basis, but moves in a general direction which can be predictive of its future. Professor Schmitt offers a compelling analysis that indicates the international community may already be moving in a direction that will accommodate the *National Security Strategy* under international law. . . .

[He] proposes a legal basis for the violation of the territorial integrity in the pursuit of terrorists, . . . [suggesting] a modification to the concept of imminency. First, he holds that imminency must accommodate the principle of self-defense. He submits that imminency should be defined as "the last viable window of opportunity, the point at which any further delay would render a viable defense ineffectual. . . . Any other interpretation would gut the right of self-defense."

On the subject of preemption, he states that the condemnation of such a policy is based on the fact that terrorist attacks are mischaracterized as isolated incidents. Considering al-Qa'ida for example, which has been involved in a terror campaign since 1993. "Once a terrorist campaign is launched, the issue of preemption becomes moot because an operation already underway cannot, by definition, be preempted." Nor would a response be considered preventive in nature.

Schmitt's conclusion, "There is little doubt that events of the last five years are signaling a sea of change in jus ad bellum [just cause of war]. Slowly but surely this body of law is becoming more permissive in response to the demise of nuclear armed bipolar competition and the rise of both transnational terrorists and WMD proliferation."

Conclusion

> It is revolting to have no better reason for a rule of law than that it was laid down in the time of Henry IV. It is still more revolting if the grounds upon which it was laid down have vanished long since, and the rule simply persists from blind imitation.
>
> Oliver Wendell Holmes

Since the formation of the UN, there have been nearly 300 interstate conflicts resulting in the deaths of 22 million people. The hope of the joint declaration of President [Franklin D.] Roosevelt and Prime Minister [Winston S.] Churchill "that all nations of the world must come to the abandonment of the use of force" has never materialized.

Success of the UN depended on a Security Council that makes decisions on a case-by-case basis in good faith and enforces them. The UN never matured into the enforcement organization the framers intended and that was required for its success. It is essentially a political organization and as Secretary of State Colin Powell warned, it is close to becoming "a feckless debating society."

In response to an international order of growing terrorism, transnational crime, "rogue" and "failed" states potentially armed with WMD and will to use them, the National Security Strategy has invoked an escalation of the right of self-defense. Termed preemption, it is in fact a policy of preventive self-defense.

The National Security Strategy policy of preventive self-defense has been condemned throughout the international arena and also within the U.S. However, this condemnation is not universal. It has been shown that a significant amount of validity can be conferred on the National Security Strategy due to: (1) the failure of the UN enforce its charter, essentially abandoning the purposes of the UN (2) the continued use and threat of use of preventive self-defense by many states and previous U.S. administrations (3) state practice (4) customary international law (5) the slowly changing body of international law that is responding to and inferring more significance on the rise of transnational terrorists and WMD proliferation over state sovereignty.

There is no doubt that this is a path fraught with peril. The Global War on Terrorism will go on for decades. Any use of preventive self-defense must retain the principles of jus ad bellum and jus in bello [just conduct of war]. It should be a tool of last resort utilized only after careful consideration combined with efforts exercising all elements of national power. However, it is a tool that will be required as the U.S engages and defeats its enemies in the Global war on Terrorism.

POSTSCRIPT

Is Preemptive War an Unacceptable Doctrine?

The report by the High Level Panel on Threats, Challenges, and Change to UN Secretary General Kofi Annan rejecting preemptive war reinforced his existing view. In September 2003, Annan had told the UN General Assembly that the argument behind preemptive war:

> . . . represents a fundamental challenge to the principles on which, however imperfectly, world peace and stability have rested for the last fifty-eight years. My concern is that, if it were to be adopted, it could set precedents that resulted in a proliferation of the unilateral and lawless use of force, with or without justification.

Perhaps the secretary general is correct, but there is a relatively small percentage of people around the world who would agree with him categorically. A survey conducted in 20 countries in 2003 found that only 32 percent of the respondents thought that preemptive was "never justified." But when the 22 percent who answered, "rarely justified" are added to this total, it is clear that most people are either opposed to or very wary of the principle enunciated in the Bush Doctrine. More at ease with it are the 14% who replied "often justified" and the 27% who said "sometimes justified," with the remaining 5% unsure. Among Americans, the replies were 22 percent often justified, 44 percent sometimes justified, 17 percent rarely justified, 13 percent never justified, and 3 percent unsure. More on preemptive war within the changing threat environment of the early twenty-first century can be found in Michael Walzer, *Arguing About War* (Yale University Press, 2004), Joel Rosenthal, "New Rules for War," *Naval War College Review* (Fall 2004), and the several articles included in "Symposium: War and Self-Defense," *Ethics & International Affairs* (Winter 2004).

At least part of the problem is that many people believe that the United Nations too seldom acts with decisiveness to meet threats, part of the evaluation of the world body addressed in Issue 16. Whatever the cause of the UN's inability or unwillingness to act, some argue that it creates a security gap that justifies national action even without UN authorization. A 2004 poll in nine countries found that in only three was there a majority of people willing to say their country should wait for UN approval to act militarily to deal with an international threat. In the other six, more respondents felt that their country could act because getting UN approval was too difficult. Among Americans, 48 percent rejected waiting for UN authorization to act, 41 percent favoring waiting, and 10 percent unsure.

As suggested in the report by the High Level Panel on Threats, Challenges, and Change, one answer to the new spectrum of threats may be to substantially improve both the decision-making process in the UN and the capabilities of the forces that it can utilize. The panels entire 95-page report is available at http://www.un.org/secureworld/. Secretary General Annan clearly recognized the need for change in his September 2003 address, commenting, "It is not enough to denounce [preemptive force] unless we also face up squarely to the concerns that make some states feel uniquely vulnerable, since it is those concerns that drive them to take unilateral action. We must show that those concerns can, and will, be addressed effectively through collective action." Keep this matter in mind when pondering the points in Issue 18.

ISSUE 13

Does the United States Have a Sound Strategy for the War on Terrorism?

YES: George W. Bush, from "President Discusses War on Global Terror," Speech to the Military Officers Association of America (September 5, 2006)

NO: Bruce Hoffman, from "Combating Al Qaeda and the Militant Islamic Threat," Testimony before the Armed Services Committee, Subcommittee on Terrorism, Unconventional Threats and Capabilities, U.S. House of Representatives (February 16, 2006)

ISSUE SUMMARY

YES: George W. Bush, president of the United States, warns that the road ahead in the war on terrorism is going to be difficult and will require more sacrifice, but also assures his listeners that the strategy to defeat terrorism means that they can have confidence in the outcome.

NO: Bruce Hoffman, corporate chair in Counterterrorism and Counterinsurgency of RAND, a think tank, and senior fellow at the Combating Terrorism Center, U.S. Military Academy, West Point, New York, argues that U.S. strategy needs to change from waging a global war on terrorism that overemphasizes military action to a broader global counterinsurgency approach that adds equally critical political, economic, diplomatic, and developmental efforts to the military campaign.

Although the use of terrorism extends far back into history, recent decades have seen a rise in the practice for numerous reasons. Some of these have more to do with modern technology than politics. One such factor is that more than in the past, governments are armed with aircraft and other high-tech weapons that are unavailable to opposition forces, making it nearly suicidal for dissidents to use conventional tactics. Second, terrorist targets are now more readily available than in the past because people are more concentrated in large buildings, in airliners, and other locations. Third, modern television and satellite communication makes it easy for terrorists to gain an audience. This is important because terrorism is not usually directed at its victims as such. Rather, it is intended to frighten others. Fourth, technology has led to the creation of increasingly lethal weapons that terrorists can use to kill and injure large numbers of people. These include biological, chemical, nuclear, and radiological weapons.

Other causes cited for the rise of terrorism are more political and more controversial. Most generally, there is the grinding poverty that billions of people, especially in less developed countries, experience. Reflecting this view, President Alejandro Toledo of Peru advised a UN conference, "To speak of development is to speak also of a strong and determined fight against terrorism." The rapid pace of change in the world, which is causing cultural dislocation and feeling of alienation in many people, is also cited as a cause of the type of personal alienation and anger felt by many terrorist groups. For example, a survey found that 78 percent of the Muslims in the Middle East and 46 percent of Muslims globally felt that their religion was under attack. Many analysts also believe that terrorism by Muslim groups is sparked by the overwhelming view among Muslims that Israel is oppressing the Palestinians and that the United States favors Israel. Also cited is the presence of U.S. forces in the Middle East, especially those in Saudi Arabia near the holiest sites of Islam in Mecca and Medina. Prominent in the view of the Bush administration is the argument that terrorists want to impose their religious or political ideas on others and therefore hate democracy.

Understanding the roots of terrorism is critical. In the short-term, it is of course wise to guard against the symptoms, which are the terrorists acts perpetrated on innocent victims. Everyone agrees this should be done. The split is on the long-term. One view favors measures meant to kill or capture terrorists and so destroy their organizations in the belief that they can be decimated to the point that they no longer present a threat. The other view is that the most effective long-term counterterrorism approach is to eliminate or ameliorate as many of the causes as possible. As you will see in the debates that follow, disagreement about the causes of terrorism is important because differing views lead to differing prescriptions for countering it.

Another conundrum is how to know whether or not one is winning. The easiest way is counting attacks and casualties. But even here there are problems. The mostly widely cited data source, the U.S. State Department, is controversial. In addition to technical problems, the line between military action and terrorism is not precise. Some people argue that the State Department tends to count the action of enemies more readily than allies. Additionally, actions conducted by uniformed military forces arguably sometimes fall into the category of terrorism, and these are also usually not reflected in the State Department's data. Most recently, the State Department data has shown a sharp increase in terrorist attacks by counting thousands of instances in Iraq that critics say would be better understand as guerilla warfare against the occupation forces or examples of civil warfare.

Not long ago, Americans were mostly unconcerned about terrorism. The September 11, 2001, terrorist attacks shattered this sense of security. In response President Bush declared war on terror, and that campaign is still prominent in Americans' sense of priorities. In the first reading, President Bush outlines his war on terrorism strategy and claims it is making progress. Disagreeing in the second reading, Bruce Hoffman contends that the campaign against terrorism has been bogged down and requires a new approach.

YES

George W. Bush

The President Discusses
Global War on Terror

We're engaged in a global war against an enemy that threatens all civilized nations. And today the civilized world stands together to defend our freedom; we stand together to defeat the terrorists; and were working to secure the peace for generations to come.

Next week, America will mark the fifth anniversary of September the 11th, 2001 terrorist attacks. As this day approaches, it brings with it a flood of painful memories. We remember the horror of watching planes fly into the World Trade Center, and seeing the towers collapse before our eyes. We remember the sight of the Pentagon, broken and in flames. We remember the rescue workers who rushed into burning buildings to save lives, knowing they might never emerge again. We remember the brave passengers who charged the cockpit of their hijacked plane, and stopped the terrorists from reaching their target and killing more innocent civilians. We remember the cold brutality of the enemy who inflicted this harm on our country—an enemy whose leader, Osama bin Laden, declared the massacre of nearly 3,000 people that day—I quote—"an unparalleled and magnificent feat of valor, unmatched by any in humankind before them."

In five years since our nation was attacked, al Qaeda and terrorists it has inspired have continued to attack across the world. They've killed the innocent in Europe and Africa and the Middle East, in Central Asia and the Far East, and beyond. Most recently, they attempted to strike again in the most ambitious plot since the attacks of September the 11th—a plan to blow up passenger planes headed for America over the Atlantic Ocean.

Five years after our nation was attacked, the terrorist danger remains. We're a nation at war—and America and her allies are fighting this war with relentless determination across the world. Together with our coalition partners, we've removed terrorist sanctuaries, disrupted their finances, killed and captured key operatives, broken up terrorist cells in America and other nations, and stopped new attacks before they're carried out. We're on the offense against the terrorists on every battlefront—and we'll accept nothing less than complete victory.

Address to the Military Officers Associations of America, George W. Bush, (September 5, 2006).

In the five years since our nation was attacked, we've also learned a great deal about the enemy we face in this war. We've learned about them through videos and audio recordings, and letters and statements they've posted on websites. We've learned about them from captured enemy documents that the terrorists have never meant for us to see. Together, these documents and statements have given us clear insight into the mind of our enemies—their ideology, their ambitions, and their strategy to defeat us.

We know what the terrorists intend to do because they've told us—and we need to take their words seriously. So today I'm going to describe—in the terrorists' own words, what they believe . . . what they hope to accomplish, and how they intend to accomplish it. I'll discuss how the enemy has adapted in the wake of our sustained offensive against them, and the threat posed by different strains of violent Islamic radicalism. I'll explain the strategy we're pursuing to protect America, by defeating the terrorists on the battlefield, and defeating their hateful ideology in the battle of ideas.

The terrorists who attacked us on September the 11th, 2001, are men without conscience—but they're not madmen. They kill in the name of a clear and focused ideology, a set of beliefs that are evil, but not insane. These al Qaeda terrorists and those who share their ideology are violent Sunni extremists. They're driven by a radical and perverted vision of Islam that rejects tolerance, crushes all dissent, and justifies the murder of innocent men, women and children in the pursuit of political power. They hope to establish a violent political utopia across the Middle East, which they call a "Caliphate"—where all would be ruled according to their hateful ideology. Osama bin Laden has called the 9/11 attacks—in his words—"a great step towards the unity of Muslims and establishing the Righteous . . . [Caliphate]."

This caliphate would be a totalitarian Islamic empire encompassing all current and former Muslim lands, stretching from Europe to North Africa, the Middle East, and Southeast Asia. We know this because al Qaeda has told us. About two months ago, the terrorist [Ayman al-] Zawahiri—he's al Qaeda's second in command—declared that al Qaeda intends to impose its rule in "every land that was a home for Islam, from [Spain] to Iraq. He went on to say, "The whole world is an open field for us."

We know what this radical empire would look like in practice, because we saw how the radicals imposed their ideology on the people of Afghanistan. Under the rule of the Taliban and al Qaeda, Afghanistan was a totalitarian nightmare—a land where women were imprisoned in their homes, men were beaten for missing prayer meetings, girls could not go to school, and children were forbidden the smallest pleasures like flying kites. Religious police roamed the streets, beating and detaining civilians for perceived offenses. Women were publicly whipped. Summary executions were held in Kabul's soccer stadium in front of cheering mobs. And Afghanistan was turned into a launching pad for horrific attacks against America and other parts of the civilized world—including many Muslim nations.

The goal of these Sunni extremists is to remake the entire Muslim world in their radical image. In pursuit of their imperial aims, these extremists say there can be no compromise or dialogue with those they call "infidels"—a category that includes America, the world's free nations, Jews, and all Muslims who reject their extreme vision of Islam. They reject the possibility of peaceful coexistence with the free world. Again, hear the words of Osama bin Laden earlier this year: "Death is better than living on this Earth with the unbelievers among us."

These radicals have declared their uncompromising hostility to freedom. It is foolish to think that you can negotiate with them. We see the uncompromising nature of the enemy in many captured terrorist documents. Here are just two examples: After the liberation of Afghanistan, coalition forces searching through a terrorist safe house in that country found a copy of the al Qaeda charter. This charter states that "there will be continuing enmity until everyone believes in Allah. We will not meet [the enemy] halfway. There will be no room for dialogue with them." Another document was found in 2000 by British police during an anti-terrorist raid in London—a grisly al Qaeda manual that includes chapters with titles such as "Guidelines for Beating and Killing Hostages." This manual declares that their vision of Islam "does not . . . make a truce with unbelief, but rather confronts it." The confrontation . . . calls for . . . the dialogue of bullets, the ideals of assassination, bombing, and destruction, and the diplomacy of the cannon and machine gun."

Still other captured documents show al Qaeda's strategy for infiltrating Muslim nations, establishing terrorist enclaves, overthrowing governments, and building their totalitarian empire. We see this strategy laid out in a captured al Qaeda document found during a recent raid in Iraq, which describes their plans to infiltrate and take over Iraq's western Anbar Province. The document lays out an elaborate al Qaeda governing structure for the region that includes an Education Department, a Social Services Department, a Justice Department, and an "Execution Unit" responsible for "Sorting out, Arrest, Murder, and Destruction."

According to their public statements, countries that . . . they have targeted . . . stretch from the Middle East to Africa, to Southeast Asia. Through this strategy, al Qaeda and its allies intend to create numerous, decentralized operating bases across the world, from which they can plan new attacks, and advance their vision of a unified, totalitarian Islamic state that can confront and eventually destroy the free world.

These violent extremists know that to realize this vision, they must first drive out the main obstacle that stands in their way—the United States of America. According to al Qaeda, their strategy to defeat America has two parts: First, they're waging a campaign of terror across the world. They're targeting our forces abroad, hoping that the American people will grow tired of casualties and give up the fight. And they're targeting America's financial centers and economic infrastructure at home, hoping to terrorize us and cause our economy to collapse.

Bin Laden calls this his "bleed-until-bankruptcy plan." And he cited the attacks of 9/11 as evidence that such a plan can succeed. With the 9/11 attacks, Osama bin Laden says, "al Qaeda spent $500,000 on the event, while America . . . lost—according to the lowest estimate—$500 billion . . . Meaning that every dollar of al Qaeda defeated a million dollars" of America. Bin Laden concludes from this experience that "America is definitely a great power, with . . . unbelievable military strength and a vibrant economy, but all of these have been built on a very weak and hollow foundation." He went on to say, "Therefore, it is very easy to target the flimsy base and concentrate on their weak points, and even if we're able to target one-tenth of these weak points, we will be able [to] crush and destroy them."

Secondly, along with this campaign of terror, the enemy has a propaganda strategy. Osama bin Laden laid out this strategy in a letter to the Taliban leader, Mullah Omar, that coalition forces uncovered in Afghanistan in 2002. In it, bin Laden says that al Qaeda intends to "[launch]," in his words, "a media campaign . . . to create a wedge between the American people and their government." This media campaign, bin Laden says, will send the American people a number of messages, including "that their government [will] bring them more losses, in finances and casualties." And he goes on to say that "they are being sacrificed . . . to serve . . . the big investors, especially the Jews." Bin Laden says that by delivering these messages, al Qaeda "aims at creating pressure from the American people on the American government to stop their campaign against Afghanistan."

Bin Laden and his allies are absolutely convinced they can succeed in forcing America to retreat and causing our economic collapse. They believe our nation is weak and decadent, and lacking in patience and resolve. And they're wrong. Osama bin Laden has written that the "defeat of. . . American forces in Beirut" in 1983 is proof America does not have the stomach to stay in the fight. He's declared that "in Somalia . . . the United States [pulled] out, trailing disappointment, defeat, and failure behind it." And last year, the terrorist Zawahiri declared that Americans "know better than others that there is no hope in victory. The Vietnam specter is closing every outlet."

These terrorists hope to drive America and our coalition out of Afghanistan, so they can restore the safe haven they lost when coalition forces drove them out five years ago. But they've made it clear that the most important front in their struggle against America is Iraq—the nation bin Laden has declared the "capital of the Caliphate." Hear the words of bin Laden: "I now address . . . the whole . . . Islamic nation: Listen and understand . . . The most . . . serious issue today for the whole world is this Third World War . . . [that] is raging in [Iraq]." He calls it "a war of destiny between infidelity and Islam." He says, "The whole world is watching this war," and that it will end in "victory and glory or misery and humiliation." For al Qaeda, Iraq is not a distraction from their war on America—it is the central battlefield where the outcome of this struggle will be decided.

Here is what al Qaeda says they will do if they succeed in driving us out of Iraq: The terrorist Zawahiri has said that al Qaeda will proceed with "several incremental goals. The first stage: Expel the Americans from Iraq. The second stage: Establish an Islamic authority or amirate, then develop it and support it until it achieves the level of Caliphate . . . The third stage: Extend the jihad wave to the secular countries neighboring Iraq. And the fourth stage: . . . the clash with Israel."

These evil men know that a fundamental threat to their aspirations is a democratic Iraq that can govern itself, sustain itself, and defend itself. They know that given a choice, the Iraqi people will never choose to live in the totalitarian state the extremists hope to establish. And that is why we must not, and we will not, give the enemy victory in Iraq by deserting the Iraqi people.

Last year, the terrorist Zarqawi declared in a message posted on the Internet that democracy "is the essence of infidelity and deviation from the right path." The Iraqi people disagree. Last December, nearly 12 million Iraqis from every ethnic and religious community turned out to vote in their country's third free election in less than a year. Iraq now has a unity government that represents Iraq's diverse population—and al Qaeda's top commander in Iraq breathed his last breath.

Despite these strategic setbacks, the enemy will continue to fight freedom's advance in Iraq, because they understand the stakes in this war. Again, hear the words of bin Laden, in a message to the American people earlier this year. He says: "The war is for you or for us to win. If we win it, it means your defeat and disgrace forever."

Now, I know some of our country hear the terrorists' words, and hope that they will not, or cannot, do what they say. History teaches that underestimating the words of evil and ambitious men is a terrible mistake. In the early 1900s, an exiled lawyer in Europe published a pamphlet called "What Is To Be Done?"—in which he laid out his plan to launch a communist revolution in Russia. The world did not heed Lenin's words, and paid a terrible price. The Soviet Empire he established killed tens of millions, and brought the world to the brink of thermonuclear war. In the 1920s, a failed Austrian painter published a book in which he explained his intention to build an Aryan super-state in Germany and take revenge on Europe and eradicate the Jews. The world ignored Hitler's words, and paid a terrible price. His Nazi regime killed millions in the gas chambers, and set the world aflame in war, before it was finally defeated at a terrible cost in lives.

Bin Laden and his terrorist allies have made their intentions as clear as Lenin and Hitler before them. The question is: Will we listen? Will we pay attention to what these evil men say? America and our coalition partners have made our choice. We're taking the words of the enemy seriously. We're on the offensive, and we will not rest, we will not retreat, and we will not withdraw from the fight, until this threat to civilization has been removed.

Five years into this struggle, it's important to take stock of what's been accomplished—and the difficult work that remains. Al Qaeda has been weakened by our sustained offensive against them, and today it is harder for al Qaeda's leaders to operate freely, to move money, or to communicate with their operatives and facilitators. Yet al Qaeda remains dangerous and determined. Bin Laden and Zawahiri remain in hiding in remote regions of this world. Al Qaeda continues to adapt in the face of our global campaign against them. Increasingly, al Qaeda is taking advantage of the Internet to disseminate propaganda, and to conduct "virtual recruitment" and "virtual training" of new terrorists. Al Qaeda's leaders no longer need to meet face-to-face with their operatives. They can find new suicide bombers, and facilitate new terrorist attacks, without ever laying eyes on those they're training, financing, or sending to strike us.

As al Qaeda changes, the broader terrorist movement is also changing, becoming more dispersed and self-directed. More and more, we're facing threats from locally established terrorist cells that are inspired by al Qaeda's ideology and goals, but do not necessarily have direct links to al Qaeda, such as training and funding. Some of these groups are made up of "homegrown" terrorists, militant extremists who were born and educated in Western nations, were indoctrinated by radical Islamists or attracted to their ideology, and joined the violent extremist cause. These locally established cells appear to be responsible for a number of attacks and plots, including those in Madrid, and Canada, and other countries across the world.

As we continue to fight al Qaeda and these Sunni extremists inspired by their radical ideology, we also face the threat posed by Shia extremists, who are learning from al Qaeda, increasing their assertiveness, and stepping up their threats. Like the vast majority of Sunnis, the vast majority of Shia across the world reject the vision of extremists—and in Iraq, millions of Shia have defied terrorist threats to vote in free elections, and have shown their desire to live in freedom. The Shia extremists want to deny them this right. This Shia strain of Islamic radicalism is just as dangerous, and just as hostile to America, and just as determined to establish its brand of hegemony across the broader Middle East. And the Shia extremists have achieved something that al Qaeda has so far failed to do: In 1979, they took control of a major power, the nation of Iran, subjugating its proud people to a regime of tyranny, and using that nation's resources to fund the spread of terror and pursue their radical agenda.

Like al Qaeda and the Sunni extremists, the Iranian regime has clear aims: They want to drive America out of the region, to destroy Israel, and to dominate the broader Middle East. To achieve these aims, they are funding and arming terrorist groups like Hezbollah, which allow them to attack Israel and America by proxy. Hezbollah, the source of the current instability in Lebanon, has killed more Americans than any terrorist organization except al Qaeda. Unlike al Qaeda, they've not yet attacked the American homeland. Yet they're directly responsible for the murder of hundreds of Americans abroad. It was Hezbollah that was behind the 1983 bombing of the U.S. Marine barracks in Beirut that killed 241 Americans. And Saudi Hezbollah was behind the 1996 bombing of Khobar Towers in Saudi Arabia that killed 19 Americans, an attack conducted by terrorists who we believe were working with Iranian officials.

Just as we must take the words of the Sunni extremists seriously, we must take the words of the Shia extremists seriously. Listen to the words of Hezbollah's leader, the terrorist [Hassan] Nasrallah, who has declared his hatred of America. He says, "Let the entire world hear me. Our hostility to the Great Satan [America] is absolute . . . Regardless of how the world has changed after 11 September, Death to America will remain our reverberating and powerful slogan: Death to America."

Iran's leaders, who back Hezbollah, have also declared their absolute hostility to America. Last October, Iran's President declared in a speech that some people ask—in his words—"whether a world without the United States and Zionism can be achieved . . . I say that this . . . goal is achievable." Less than three months ago, Iran's President declared to America and other Western powers: "open your eyes and see the fate of pharaoh . . . if you do not abandon the path of falsehood . . . your doomed destiny will be annihilation." Less than two months ago, he warned: "The anger of Muslims may reach an explosion point soon. If such a day comes . . . [America and the West] should know that the waves of the blast will not remain within the boundaries of our region." He also delivered this message to the American people: "If you would like to have good relations with the Iranian nation in the future . . . bow down before the greatness of the Iranian nation and surrender. If you don't accept [to do this], the Iranian nation will . . . force you to surrender and bow down."

America will not bow down to tyrants.

The Iranian regime and its terrorist proxies have demonstrated their willingness to kill Americans—and now the Iranian regime is pursuing nuclear weapons. The world is working together to prevent Iran's regime from acquiring the tools of mass murder. The international community has made a reasonable proposal to Iran's leaders, and given them the opportunity to set their nation on a better course. So far, Iran's leaders have rejected this offer. Their choice is increasingly isolating the great Iranian nation from the international community, and denying the Iranian people an opportunity for greater economic prosperity. It's time for Iran's leader to make a different choice. And we've made our choice. We'll continue to work closely with our allies to find a diplomatic solution. The world's free nations will not allow Iran to develop a nuclear weapon.

The Shia and Sunni extremists represent different faces of the same threat. They draw inspiration from different sources, but both seek to impose a dark vision of violent Islamic radicalism across the Middle East. They oppose the advance of freedom, and they want to gain control of weapons of mass destruction. If they succeed in undermining fragile democracies, like Iraq, and drive the forces of freedom out of the region, they will have an open field to pursue their dangerous goals. Each strain of violent Islamic radicalism would be emboldened in their efforts to topple moderate governments and establish terrorist safe havens.

Imagine a world in which they were able to control governments, a world awash with oil and they would use oil resources to punish industrialized nations. And they would use those resources to fuel their radical agenda, and pursue and purchase weapons of mass murder. And armed with nuclear weapons, they would blackmail the free world, and spread their ideologies of hate, and raise a mortal threat to the American people. If we allow them to do this, if we retreat from Iraq, if we don't uphold our duty to support those who are desirous to live in liberty, 50 years from now history will look back on our time with unforgiving clarity, and demand to know why we did not act.

I'm not going to allow this to happen—and no future American President can allow it either. America did not seek this global struggle, but we're answering history's call with confidence and a clear strategy. Today we're releasing a document called the "National Strategy for Combating Terrorism." This is an unclassified version of the strategy we've been pursuing since September the 11th, 2001. This strategy was first released in February 2003; it's been updated to take into account the changing nature of this enemy. This strategy document is posted on the White House website—whitehouse.gov. And I urge all Americans to read it.

Our strategy for combating terrorism has five basic elements:

First, we're determined to prevent terrorist attacks before they occur. So we're taking the fight to the enemy. The best way to protect America is to stay on the offense. Since 9/11, our coalition has captured or killed al Qaeda managers and operatives, and scores of other terrorists across the world. The enemy is living under constant pressure, and we intend to keep it that way—and this adds to our security. When terrorists spend their days working to avoid death or capture, it's harder for them to plan and execute new attacks.

We're also fighting the enemy here at home. We've given our law enforcement and intelligence professionals the tools they need to stop the terrorists in our midst. We passed the Patriot Act to break down the wall that prevented law enforcement and intelligence from sharing vital information. We created the Terrorist Surveillance Program to monitor the communications between al Qaeda commanders abroad and terrorist operatives within our borders. If al Qaeda is calling somebody in America, we need to know why, in order to stop attacks.

I want to thank [supportive members of Congress] for working with us to give our law enforcement and intelligence officers the tools necessary to do their jobs. And over the last five years, federal, state, and local law enforcement have used those tools to break up terrorist cells, and to prosecute terrorist operatives and supporters in New York, and Oregon, and Virginia, and Texas, and New Jersey, and Illinois, Ohio, and other states. By taking the battle to the terrorists and their supporters on our own soil and across the world, we've stopped a number of al Qaeda plots.

Second, we're determined to deny weapons of mass destruction to outlaw regimes and terrorists who would use them without hesitation. Working with Great Britain and Pakistan and other nations, the United States shut down the world's most dangerous nuclear trading cartel, the A. Q. Khan network. [Abdul Qadeer Kahn headed Pakistan nuclear weapons program and illegally sold nuclear weapons technology to Iran, Libya, and North Korea.] This network had supplied Iran and Libya and North Korea with equipment and know-how that advanced their efforts to obtain nuclear weapons. And we launched the Proliferation Security Initiative, a coalition of more than 70 nations that is working together to stop shipments related to weapons of mass destruction on land, at sea, and in the air. The greatest threat this world faces is the danger of extremists and terrorists armed with weapons of mass destruction—and this is a threat America cannot defeat on her own. We applaud the determined efforts of many nations around the world to stop the spread of these dangerous weapons. Together, we pledge we'll continue to work together to stop the world's most dangerous men from getting their hands on the world's most dangerous weapons.

Third, we're determined to deny terrorists the support of outlaw regimes. After September the 11th, I laid out a clear doctrine: America makes no distinction between those who commit acts of terror, and those that harbor and support them, because they're equally guilty of murder. Thanks to our efforts, there are now three fewer state sponsors of terror in the world than there were on September the 11th, 2001. Afghanistan and Iraq have been transformed from terrorist states into allies in the war on terror. And the nation of Libya has renounced terrorism, and given up its weapons of mass destruction programs, and its nuclear materials and equipment. Over the past five years, we've acted to disrupt the flow of weapons and support from terrorist states to terrorist networks. And we have made clear that any government that chooses to be an ally of terror has also chosen to be an enemy of civilization.

Fourth, we're determined to deny terrorist networks control of any nation, or territory within a nation. So, along with our coalition and the Iraqi government, we'll stop the terrorists from taking control of Iraq, and establishing a new safe haven from which to attack America and the free world. And we're working with friends and allies to deny the terrorists the enclaves they seek to establish in ungoverned areas across the world. By helping governments reclaim full sovereign control over their territory, we make ourselves more secure.

Fifth, we're working to deny terrorists new recruits, by defeating their hateful ideology and spreading the hope of freedom—by spreading the hope of freedom across the Middle East. For decades, American policy sought to achieve peace in the Middle East by pursuing stability at the expense of liberty. The lack of freedom in that region helped create conditions where anger and resentment grew, and radicalism thrived, and terrorists found willing recruits. And we saw the consequences on September the 11th, when the terrorists brought death and destruction to our country. The policy wasn't working.

The experience of September the 11th made clear, in the long run, the only way to secure our nation is to change the course of the Middle East. So America has committed its influence in the world to advancing freedom and liberty and democracy as the great alternatives to repression and radicalism. We're taking the side of democratic leaders and moderates and reformers across the Middle East. We strongly support the voices of tolerance and moderation in the Muslim world. We're standing with Afghanistan's elected government against al Qaeda and the Taliban remnants that are trying to restore tyranny in that country. We're standing with Lebanon's young democracy against the foreign forces that are seeking to undermine the country's sovereignty and independence. And we're standing with the leaders of Iraq's unity government as they work to defeat the enemies of freedom, and chart a more hopeful course for their people. This is why victory is so important in Iraq. By helping freedom succeed in Iraq, we will help America, and the Middle East, and the world become more secure.

During the last five years we've learned a lot about this enemy. We've learned that they're cunning and sophisticated. We've witnessed their ability to change their methods and their tactics with deadly speed—even as their murderous obsessions remain unchanging. We've seen that it's the terrorists who have declared war on Muslims, slaughtering huge numbers of innocent Muslim men and women around the world.

We know what the terrorists believe, we know what they have done, and we know what they intend to do. And now the world's free nations must summon the will to meet this great challenge. The road ahead is going to be difficult, and it will require more sacrifice. Yet we can have confidence in the outcome, because we've seen freedom conquer tyranny and terror before. In the 20th century, free nations confronted and defeated Nazi Germany. During the Cold War, we confronted Soviet communism, and today Europe is whole, free and at peace.

And now, freedom is once again contending with the forces of darkness and tyranny. This time, the battle is unfolding in a new region—the broader Middle East. This time, we're not waiting for our enemies to gather in strength. This time, we're confronting them before they gain the capacity to inflict unspeakable damage on the world, and we're confronting their hateful ideology before it fully takes root.

We see a day when people across the Middle East have governments that honor their dignity, and unleash their creativity, and count their votes. We see a day when across this region citizens are allowed to express themselves freely, women have full rights, and children are educated and given the tools necessary to succeed in life. And we see a day when all the nations of the Middle East are allies in the cause of peace.

We fight for this day, because the security of our own citizens depends on it. This is the great ideological struggle of the 21st century—and it is the calling of our generation. All civilized nations are bound together in this struggle between moderation and extremism. By coming together, we will roll back this grave threat to our way of life. We will help the people of the Middle East claim their freedom, and we will leave a safer and more hopeful world for our children and grandchildren.

Combating Al Qaeda and the Militant Islamic Threat

Four and a half years into the war on terrorism, the United States stands at a crossroads. The sustained successes of the war's early phases appear to have been stymied by the protracted insurgency in Iraq and our inability either to kill or capture Usama bin Laden and his chief lieutenant, Ayman al-Zawahiri. More consequential, but less apparent perhaps, has been our failure to effectively counter our enemies' effective use of propaganda and related information operations. Their portrayal of America and the West as an aggressive and predatory force waging war on Islam not only continues to resonate among large segments of the Muslim world but also continues to undermine our own efforts to break the cycle of recruitment and regeneration that sustains al Qaeda and the militant, global jihadi movement it champions.

Although many reasons are often cited for the current stasis in America's war on terrorism—from the diversion of attention from bin Laden and al-Zawahiri caused by Iraq to inchoate U.S. public diplomacy efforts—the real cause is at once as basic as it is prosaic: we still don't know, much less, understand our enemy.

"If you know the enemy and know yourself," Sun Tzu famously advised centuries ago, "you need not fear the results of a hundred battles." The war on terrorism has now lasted longer than America's involvement in World War II: yet, even today we cannot claim with any credibility, much less, acuity to have fulfilled Sun Tzu's timeless admonition. Indeed, what remains missing four and a half years since this war began is a thorough, systematic understanding of our enemy: encompassing motivation as well as mindset, decision-making processes as well as command and control relationships; and ideological constructs as well as organizational dynamics.

Forty years ago the United States understood the importance of building this foundation in order to effectively counter an enigmatic, unseen enemy motivated by a powerful ideology who also used terrorism and insurgency to advance his cause and rally popular support. Although America of course encountered many frustrations during the Vietnam conflict, a lack of understanding of our adversary was not among them. Indeed, as early as 1965, the Pentagon had begun a program to analyze Vietcong morale and motivation based on detailed interviews conducted among thousands of guerrilla detainees. These voluminously

Testimony before the Armed Services Committee, Subcommittee on Terrorism, Unconventional Threats and Capabilities, Bruce Hoffman, (February 16, 2006).

detailed studies provided a roadmap of the ideological and psychological mindset of that enemy: clearly illuminating the critical need to win what was then often termed the "other war"—the ideological struggle for the hearts and minds of the Vietnamese people. Even if the fundamental changes required in U.S. military strategy to overcome the Vietcong's appeal went ignored, tremendous effort and resources were devoted to understanding the enemy.

Today, Washington has no such program in the war on terrorism. America's counterterrorism strategy appears predominantly weighted towards a "kill or capture" approach targeting individual bad guys. This line of attack assumes that America's contemporary enemies—be they al Qaeda or the insurgents in Iraq—have a traditional center of gravity. It also assumes that these enemies simply need to be killed or imprisoned so that global terrorism or the Iraqi insurgency will both end. Accordingly, the attention of the U.S. military and intelligence community is directed almost uniformly towards hunting down militant leaders or protecting U.S. forces—not toward understanding the enemy we now face. This is a monumental failing not only because decapitation strategies have rarely worked in countering mass mobilization terrorist or insurgent campaigns, but also because al Qaeda's ability to continue this struggle is ineluctably predicated on its capacity to attract new recruits and replenish its resources.

The success of U.S. strategy will therefore ultimately depend on Washington's ability to counter al Qaeda's ideological appeal—and thus effectively address the three key elements of their strategy:

- the continued resonance of their message;
- their continued ability to attract recruits replenishing their ranks; and,
- their capacity for continual regeneration and renewal.

To do so, we first need to better understand the origins of the al Qaeda movement, the animosity and arguments that underpin it and indeed the region of the world from which its struggle emanated and upon which its hungry gaze still rests. Without knowing our enemy we cannot successfully penetrate their cells; we cannot knowledgeably sow discord and dissension in their ranks and thus weaken them from within; and, we cannot fulfill the most basic requirements of an effective counterterrorist strategy—pre-empting and preventing terrorist operations and deterring their attacks. Until we recognize the importance of this vital prerequisite, America will remain perennially on the defensive: inherently reactive rather than proactive—deprived of the capacity to recognize, much less anticipate, important changes in our enemy's modus operandi, recruitment and targeting.

Knowing the Enemy: The State of Al Qaeda in Early 2006

The Department of Defense's recently published Quadrennial Defense Review (QDR) accurately describes America's war on terrorism as the "long war." A critical, though unstated, dimension of this "long war" is the main reason for its longevity: an enemy that is at once as adaptive and resilient as it is malleable and implacable. Since 9/11 al Qaeda has clearly shown itself to be a nimble, flexible, and adaptive entity. Indeed, al Qaeda's greatest achievement has been the makeover it has given itself since 2001. The current al Qaeda thus exists more as an ideology than as an identifiable, unitary terrorist organization. It has become a vast enterprise—an international franchise with like-minded local representatives, loosely connected to a central ideological or motivational base, but advancing the remaining center's goals at once simultaneously and independently of each other. Hence, unlike the hierarchical, pyramidal structure that typified terrorist groups of the past, the current al Qaeda movement in the main is flatter, more linear and organizationally networked.

The result is that today there are many al Qaedas rather than the single al Qaeda of the past. It is now a more loosely organized and connected movement that mixes and matches organizational and operational styles whether dictated by particular missions or imposed by circumstances. Nonetheless, it would be mistaken to believe that al Qaeda does not still retain some important characteristics or aspects of a more organized entity with a central command and control structure, however weakened and reduced. Al Qaeda today, accordingly, can perhaps be usefully conceptualized as comprising four distinct, but not mutually exclusive, dimensions. In descending order of sophistication, they are:

1. **Al Qaeda Central.** This category comprises the remnants of the pre-9/11 al Qaeda organization. Although its core leadership includes some of the familiar, established commanders of the past, there are a number of new players who have advanced through the ranks as a result of the death or capture of key al Qaeda senior-level managers such as KSM [Khalid Sheikh Mohammed, alleged head of al Qaeda's internnational terrorism network], Abu Atef, Abu Zubayda, and Hambali [*nom de guerre* of Indonesian jihadist Riduan Isamuddin], and most recently, Abu Faraj al-Libi and Abu Hamza al-Masri. It is believed that this hardcore remains centered in or around Pakistan and continues to exert some coordination, if not actual command capability, in terms of commissioning attacks, directing surveillance and collating reconnaissance, planning operations, and approving their execution.

   This category comes closest to the al Qaeda operational template or model evident in the 1998 East Africa embassy bombings and 9/11 attacks. Such high value, "spectacular" attacks are entrusted only to al Qaeda's professional cadre: the most dedicated, committed and absolutely reliable element of the movement. Previous patterns suggest that these "professional" terrorists are deployed in predetermined and carefully selected teams. They will also have been provided with very specific targeting instructions. In some cases, such as the East Africa bombings, they may establish contact with, and enlist the assistance of, local sympathizers and supporters. This will be solely for logistical and other attack-support purposes or to enlist these locals to actually execute the attack(s). The operation, however, will be planned and directed by the "professional" element with the locals clearly subordinate and playing strictly a supporting role (albeit a critical one, though).

2. **Al Qaeda Affiliates and Associates.** This category embraces formally established insurgent or terrorist groups who over the years have benefited from bin Laden's largesse and/or spiritual guidance and/or have received training, arms, money and other assistance from al Qaeda. Among the recipients of this assistance have been terrorist groups and insurgent forces in Uzbekistan and Indonesia, Chechnya and the Philippines, Bosnia and Kashmir, among other places. By supporting these groups, bin Laden's intentions were three-fold. First, he sought to co-opt these movements' mostly local agendas and channel their efforts towards the cause of global jihad. Second, he hoped to create a jihadi "critical mass" from these geographically scattered, disparate movements that would one day coalesce into a single, unstoppable force. And, third, he wanted to foster a dependency relationship whereby as a quid pro quo for prior al Qaeda support, these movements would either undertake attacks at al Qaeda's behest or provide essential local, logistical and other support to facilitate strikes by the al Qaeda "professional" cadre noted above.

This category includes groups such as: al-Ittihad al-Islami (AIAI), Abu Musab Zarqawi's al Qaeda in Mesopotamia (formerly *Jamaat al Tawhid wa'l Jihad*), Asbat al-Ansar, Ansar al Islam, Islamic Army of Aden, Islamic Movement of Uzbekistan (IMU), Jemaah Islamiya (JI), Libyan Islamic Fighting Group (LIFG), Moro Islamic Liberation Front (MILF), Salafist Group for Call and Combat (GSPC), and the various Kashmiri Islamic groups based in Pakistan—e.g., Harakat ul Mujahidin (HuM), Jaish-e-Mohammed (JeM), Laskar-e-Tayyiba (LeT), and Laskar I Jhangvi (LiJ).

3. **Al Qaeda Locals.** These are amorphous groups of al Qaeda adherents who are likely to have had some prior terrorism experience, will have been bloodied in battle as part of some previous jihadi campaign in Algeria, the Balkans, Chechnya, and perhaps more recently in Iraq, and may have trained in some al Qaeda facility before 9/11. They will therefore have had some direct connection with al Qaeda—however tenuous or evanescent. Their current relationship, and even communication, with a central al Qaeda command and control apparatus may be equally tenuous, if not actually dormant. The distinguishing characteristic of this category, however, is that there is some previous connection of some kind with al Qaeda.

Specific examples of this adversary include Ahmed Ressam, who was arrested in December 1999 at Port Angeles, Washington State, shortly after he had entered the U.S. from Canada. Ressam, for instance, had a prior background in terrorism having belonged to Algeria's Armed Islamic Group (GIA). After being recruited to al Qaeda, he was provided with a modicum of basic terrorist training in Afghanistan. In contrast to the professional cadre detailed above, however, Ressam was given very non-specific, virtually open-ended targeting instructions before being dispatched to North America. Also, unlike the well-funded professional cadre, Ressam was given only $12,000 in 'seed money' and instructed to raise the rest of his

operational funds from petty thievery. He was also told to recruit
members for his terrorist cell from among the expatriate Muslim
communities in Canada and the U.S.

4. **Al Qaeda Network.** These are home-grown Islamic radicals—from
North Africa, the Middle East, and South and South East Asia—as
well as local converts to Islam mostly living in Europe, Africa and
perhaps Latin America and North America as well, who have no
direct connection with al Qaeda (or any other identifiable terrorist
group), but nonetheless are prepared to carry out attacks in solidarity with or support of al Qaeda's radical jihadi agenda. They are
motivated by a shared sense of enmity and grievance felt towards the
United States and West in general and their host-nations in particular. In this case, the relationship with al Qaeda is more inspirational
than actual; abetted by profound rage over the U.S. invasion and
occupation of Iraq and the oppression of Muslims in Palestine,
Kashmir, Chechnya, and elsewhere. Critically, these people are neither part of a known, organized group nor even a very cohesive
entity unto themselves.

Examples of this category, which comprises small cells of like-
minded locals who gravitate towards one to plan and mount terrorist
attacks completely independent of any direction provided by al
Qaeda, include the group of mostly Moroccan Islamic radicals based
in Spain who carried out the March 2004 Madrid bombings and
their counterparts in the Netherlands responsible for the November
2004 murder of Theo Van Gogh, among others.

The most salient threat posed by the above categories, however, continues to come from al Qaeda Central and then from its affiliates and associates.
However, an additional and equally challenging threat is now posed by less
discernible and more unpredictable entities drawn from the vast Muslim
Diaspora in Europe. As far back as 2001, the Netherlands' intelligence and
security service had detected increased terrorist recruitment efforts among
Muslim youth living in the Netherlands whom it was previously assumed had
been completely assimilated into Dutch society and culture. Thus, representatives of Muslim extremist organizations had already succeeded in embedding
themselves in, and drawing new sources of support from, receptive elements
within established Diaspora communities. In this way, new recruits could be
drawn into the movement who likely had not previously come under the scrutiny of local or national law enforcement agencies.

This new category of terrorist adversary, moreover, also has proven more
difficult for the authorities in these countries to track, predict and anticipate.
They comprise often previously unknown cells whom it is otherwise difficult,
if not impossible, to effectively profile. Although the members may be marginalized individuals working in menial jobs from the lower socio-economic
strata of society, some of whom with long criminal records or histories of
juvenile delinquency; others may well come from solidly middle and upper-
middle class backgrounds with university and perhaps even graduate degrees
and prior passions for cars, sports, rock music and other completely secular,
more ethereal interests. What they will have in common is a combination of a

deep commitment to their faith—often recently re-discovered; admiration of bin Laden for the cathartic blow struck against America on 9/11; hatred of the U.S. and the West; and, a profoundly shared sense of alienation from their host countries. These new recruits are the anonymous cogs in the worldwide al Qaeda enterprise and include both long-standing residents and new immigrants found across Europe, but specifically in countries with large expatriate Muslim populations such as Britain, Spain, France, Germany, Italy, the Netherlands, and Belgium.

The al Qaeda Movement's Ideological Resiliency and Continued Resonance

Despite the damage and destruction and losses of key leaders and personnel that al Qaeda has suffered over the past four-plus years, it stubbornly adheres to its fundamental raison d'etre: continuing to inspire and motivate the broader radical jihadi community. The principle of jihad is the ideological bond that unites this amorphous movement: surmounting its loose structure, diverse membership and geographical separation. The requirement to engage in jihad is relentlessly expounded in both video- and audio-tapes of bin Laden and al-Zawahiri and other senior al Qaeda personalities, on myriad jihadi web-sites, and by radical clerical/lay-preachers speaking in mosques or addressing informal circles of adherents in more private settings.

The struggle is cast in narrow defensive terms: extolling the duty of the faithful to defend Islam by the sword. Imitation by example is encouraged through the depiction of the sacrifices of past martyrs (suicide terrorists and others who perished in battle against the infidel) coupled with messages about the importance of continuous battle against Islam's enemies. "It is no secret that warding off the American enemy is the top duty after faith and that nothing should take priority over it," bin Laden wrote in his seminal 1996 declaration of war.

Such exhortations continue to resonate today when many Muslims harbor a deep sense of humiliation and resentment over the invasions of Afghanistan and Iraq, the continued bloodletting of their co-religionists in Palestine, Chechnya, and Kashmir among other places, the ill-treatment of detainees at Abu Ghraib and Guantanamo alongside the myriad other reasons jihadis have for hating the United States. Indeed, the expostulated theological requirement to avenge the shedding of innocent Muslim blood—and particularly that of Muslim children who have been killed in Iraq and Palestine—has repeatedly been invoked by bin Laden. These calls for revenge coupled with the terrorists' own abiding faith in the potential regenerative power of even a single, new dramatic terrorist attack to breathe new life into the jihadi movement, ensure that the war on terrorism will be won neither easily nor soon.

Terrorist morale is also sustained by propaganda portraying the 9/11 attacks as a great victory and America's involvement in Iraq as a quagmire that will ultimately bring about the U.S.'s downfall. The connection between the destruction of the World Trade Center and the blow struck against the U.S.

economy by the 9/11 attacks has been a persistent jihadi theme. It was repeated by bin Laden himself in the videotape broadcast on 29 October 2004, when he explained, "So we are continuing this policy in bleeding America to the point of bankruptcy. Allah willing, and nothing is too great for Allah."

Parallels are also drawn with the mujahideen's defeat of the Red Army in Afghanistan, the alleged chain reaction it set in motion that led to the demise of the Soviet Union and collapse of communism with the current travails the U.S. faces in Iraq and the inevitability of our defeat there at the hands of contemporary jihadis. Indeed, al Qaeda propaganda has long described the U.S. as a "paper tiger," on the verge of financial ruin and total collapse much as the USSR once was, with the power of Islam poised similarly to push America over the precipice. Bin Laden emphasized this very point in his last publicly known address to his fighters in December 2001, when he declared that, "America is in retreat by the grace of God Almighty and economic attrition is continuing up to today. But it needs further blows. The young men need to seek out the nodes of the American economy and strike the enemy's nodes." And, he repeated it again in the aforementioned videotape released just days before the 2004 American presidential elections. "This is in addition to our having experience in using guerrilla warfare and the war of attrition to fight tyrannical superpowers, as we, alongside the Mujahideen, bled Russia for ten years, until it went bankrupt and was forced to withdraw in defeat. All Praise is due to Allah." This strategy thus continues to guide jihadi target selection and tactics today.

The al Qaeda movement's ability to continue to prosecute this struggle is also a direct reflection of its capacity to attract new recruits and replenish expended resources. Its survival may also be dependent upon the preservation of some core leadership cadre to champion and lead this campaign. In this respect, al Qaeda appears to retain at least some depth in managerial personnel as evidenced by its ability to produce successor echelons for the mid-level operational commanders who have been killed or captured. But the main challenge for al Qaeda and the wider jihadi movement is to promote and ensure its durability as an ideology and concept. It can only achieve this by staying in the news: elbowing itself into the limelight through dramatic and bloody attack, thereby promoting its continued relevance as the defenders and avengers of Muslims everywhere. Violence will thus continue to be key to ensuring its continued presence as an international political force. Hence, al Qaeda and the wider movement's resiliency—if not, longevity—will thereby be predicated on its continued ability to recruit new cadre, mobilize the Muslim masses, and marshal support—both spiritual and practical—for jihad.

Amazingly, al Qaeda also claims that it is stronger and more capable now than it was on 9/11. Al Qaeda propagandists on web sites and other forums, for instance, repeatedly point to a newfound vitality that has facilitated an operational capacity able to carry out at least two major attacks per year since 9/11 compared to the one attack every two years that it could implement before 9/11. "We are still chasing the Americans and their allies everywhere," al-Zawahiri crowed in December 2003, "even in their homeland." Irrespective of whether our definition of a major attack and al Qaeda's are the same, propaganda doesn't have to be true to be believed: all that matters is that it is communicated effectively and persuasively—precisely the two essential components of information operations that al Qaeda has mastered.

What bin Laden also doubtless understands is that in the post-9/11 world, terrorism's power to coerce, and intimidate; to force changes in our daily lives; and to influence our policies and affect how and on what we spend money, have all increased enormously. In this respect, the stakes have not only grown, but public fears and expectations have as well. More and more, the metric of success in the war on terrorism is defined as the ability of intelligence agencies and law enforcement organizations to prevent, pre-empt and deter attacks. Conversely, the metric of success for the terrorists has become simply the ability to act. Although there is a world of difference between bombing a bar on a Saturday night in Bali and laying the World Trade Towers to waste and severely damaging the Pentagon, the impact is no longer completely dissimilar.

The tragic loss of innocent life in any attack linked to al Qaeda is calculated by its masterminds to rekindle worldwide the same profound fears and anxieties that the attacks on 9/11 ignited. Al Qaeda's stature and receptiveness in parts of the world today is still a product of the extraordinary success achieved and attention generated by the attacks that day. In these circumstances, we have to be careful to avoid impatience and the temptation to declare victory in the war on terrorism—and not least precipitous optimism. Countering terrorism is akin to taking a time series of photographs. The image captured on film today is not the same as yesterday nor will it be the same tomorrow. Terrorism, accordingly, is constantly changing, evolving: no more so, and indeed, far more rapidly and consequentially, in the period of time since 9/11.

The Iraqi Insurgency As A Harbinger of the Future

The escalating insurgency in Iraq has emerged as a critical front in al Qaeda's struggle. Iraq had already emerged as an important rallying cry for al Qaeda and the radical jihadi movement even before the actual invasion began. The call to arms that al Qaeda issued, however, was not in support of Saddam Hussein or his regime, but in resistance to what was—and is still—perceived as continued U.S. and Western aggression against Muslims and neo-colonialist encroachment on Muslim lands. In fact, the idea that al Qaeda wanted to make Iraq the central battlefield of jihad was first suggested by al Qaeda itself. In February 2003, a month before the U.S.-led coalition even invaded Iraq, the movement's information department released the fifth and sixth installments of a series of on-line articles entitled *In the Shadow of the Lances* that had begun to appear shortly after the 9/11 attacks. Although the previous installments had been written by al Qaeda's chief spokesman, Sulaiman Abu Ghaith, who had been trained as a theologian and

Muslim cleric, these two, new issues were authored by Saif al-Adel, the movement's chief of military operations, one of its most senior commanders and a warrior by training who had been an officer in the Egyptian Army's Special Forces and a military trainer at al Qaeda's al-Farook camp in Afghanistan. In these two issues, al-Adel imparted practical advice to Iraqis and foreign jihadis on how guerrilla warfare tactics could be used against the American and British troops. "Turn the mujahedin military force into small units with good administrative capabilities," he suggested, since this "will spare us big losses. Large military units pose management problems," al-Adl further explained. "They occupy large areas which are difficult to conceal from air reconnaissance and air attack." His exhortations echoed previous statements made by bin Laden since at least 1996 about the asymmetric virtues of guerrilla warfare.

Indeed, the al Qaeda leader has often cited the victory he claims was achieved with this tactic against American forces in Mogadishu, Somalia during October 1993—when 18 U.S. Army Rangers and Delta Force commandos were killed in fighting with Somali militiamen and, according to bin Laden, al Qaeda fighters too. "[I]t must be obvious to you," bin Laden had stated in his 1996 declaration of war, "that, due to the imbalance of power between our armed forces and the enemy forces, a suitable means of fighting must be adopted, i.e. using fast moving light forces that work under complete secrecy. In other words to initiate a guerrilla warfare, were [sic] the sons of the nation, and not the military forces, take part in it." For bin Laden, the withdrawal of American military forces that followed is proof that terrorism and guerrilla warfare can defeat more powerful opponents.

Al Qaeda's entreaties to jihadis to descend on Iraq and confront the U.S. and coalition military forces only intensified after the fall of Baghdad. For example, a statement posted on the movement's al neda.com website on 9 April 2003—which was clearly written after American forces had entered the Iraqi capital, lauded the virtues of guerrilla warfare against conventional military opponents. Under the heading 'Guerrilla Warfare Is the Most Powerful Weapon Muslims Have, and It Is The Best Method to Continue the Conflict with the Crusader Enemy,'" these lessons of history were cited to rally jihadis for renewed battle. "With guerilla warfare," it explained, the Americans were defeated in Vietnam and the Soviets were defeated in Afghanistan. This is the method that expelled the direct Crusader colonialism from most of the Muslim lands, with Algeria the most well known. We still see how this method stopped Jewish immigration to Palestine, and caused reverse immigration of Jews from Palestine. The successful attempts of dealing defeat to invaders using guerilla warfare were many, and we will not expound on them. However, these attempts have proven that the most effective method for the materially weak against the strong is guerrilla warfare.

The clearest explication of al Qaeda's strategy in Iraq was provided by Zawahiri himself on the occasion of the second anniversary of the 9/11 attacks. "We thank God," he declared, "for appeasing us with the dilemmas in Iraq and Afghanistan. The Americans are facing a delicate situation in both countries. If they withdraw they will lose everything and if they stay, they will continue to bleed to death." On the attacks' third anniversary, he issued a slightly different version of the same statement, now proclaiming that U.S. defeat in Iraq and Afghanistan "has become just a question of time. . . . The Americans in both countries are between two fires," Zawahiri explained. "[I]f they continue, they will bleed until death, and if they withdraw, they will lose everything."

Indeed, what U.S. military commanders optimistically described in late 2003 as the jihadi "magnet" or terrorist "flytrap" orchestrated by the U.S. invasion of Iraq is thus viewed very differently by al Qaeda. "Two years after Tora Bora," Zawahiri observed in December 2003, "the American bloodshed [has] started to increase in Iraq and the Americans are unable to defend themselves." For al Qaeda, accordingly, Iraq has likely been a very useful side-show: an effective means to preoccupy American military forces and distract U.S. attention while al Qaeda and its confederates make new inroads and strike elsewhere. On a personal level, it may have also provided bin Laden and al-Zawahiri with the breathing space that they desperately needed to further obfuscate their trail. But most importantly, Iraq has figured pro-minently in al Qaeda and jihadi plans and propaganda as a means to rein-vigorate the jihadi cause and sustain its momentum as well as engage U.S. forces in battle and thus perpetuate the image of Islam cast perpetually on the defensive with no alternative but to take up arms against American and Western aggressors. In addition, the ongoing violence in Iraq coupled with the inability of U.S. and coalition and Iraqi security forces to maintain order and the Abu Ghraib revelations along with other disadvantageous dev-elopments, have all doubtless contributed to America's poor standing in the Muslim world.

Finally, whatever the outcome of the current conflict in Iraq, its conse-quences will likely be felt for years to come. Much like Afghanistan after the struggle against the Soviet occupation ended in that country, the surviving foreign jihadis who fought in Iraq will eventually return to their home coun-tries or the émigré communities that they came from. Having been bloodied in battle in Iraq, they will possess the experience, cachet and credibility useful for both jihadi recruitment and operational purposes elsewhere. Moreover, in contrast to the mujahideen who returned home from Afghanistan a decade and a half ago who were mostly trained in rural guerrilla warfare, this new generation of jihadis will have acquired in Iraq invaluable first-hand experi-ence in urban warfare—including the construction of vehicular and roadside IEDs [improvised explosive devices], the use of stand-off weaponry like mor-tars and similar remote-control fired devices, assassination and kidnapping techniques, and sniper and ambush tactics. The application of these newly learned capabilities to urban centers in Europe, North Africa, the Middle East, South Asia and elsewhere could result in a precipitous escalation of bloodshed and destruction, reaching into countries and regions that hitherto have expe-rienced little, if any, organized jihadi violence. While the threat to Europe is perhaps the most serious, the danger may be greatest in Saudi Arabia: the country from which the overwhelming majority jihadis (61 percent) fighting in Iraq hail.

Conclusion

The "Long War" posited by the recent Quadrennial Defense Review argues that the U.S. is likely to still be fighting the war on terrorism, countering insurgency, and involved in nation-building efforts for at least the next decade or more. To a significant degree, our ability to carry out such missions effectively will depend on the ability of American strategy to adjust and adapt to changes we see in the nature and character of our adversaries. At the foundation of such a dynamic and adaptive policy must be the ineluctable axiom that successfully countering terrorism as well as insurgency is not exclusively a military endeavor but also involves fundamental parallel political, social, economic, and ideological activities. As this testimony has previously argued, the predominantly tactical "kill or capture" approach and metric that currently guides our counterterrorist and counterinsurgent efforts is too narrow and does not sufficiently address the complexities of these unique operational environments. The adversaries and the threats we face today, however, are much more elusive and complicated to be vanquished by mere decapitation.

Moreover, what worked for the U.S. during the initial operations of the war on terrorism in 2001 and 2002—when we faced a differently configured and structured al Qaeda, for instance, and before the intensification of the insurgency in Iraq—will likely not prove as effective given the recent changes and evolution we have witnessed in both. In so fluid an environment, our strategy must accordingly change and adapt as well. What will be required today and in the future to ensure continued success, therefore, is a more integrated, systems approach to a complex problem that is at once operationally durable, evolutionary and elusive in character. In sum, we will need to adjust and adapt our strategy, resources, and tactics to formidable opponents that, as we have seen, are widely dispersed and decentralized and whose many destructive parts are autonomous, mobile, and themselves highly adaptive.

That the above description conforms as much as to the current insurgency in Iraq as to the new form that al Qaeda and the radical jihadi threat has assumed, says volumes about the challenge this operational environment poses to U.S. national security. An effective response will thus ineluctably be predicated upon a strategy that effectively combines the tactical elements of systematically destroying and weakening enemy capabilities (the "kill or capture" approach) alongside the equally critical, broader strategic imperative of breaking the cycle of terrorist and insurgent recruitment and replenishment that have respectively sustained both al Qaeda's continued campaign and the ongoing conflict in Iraq.

Accordingly, rather than viewing the fundamental organizing principle of American national defense strategy in this unconventional realm as a global war on terrorism (GWOT) as it has been to date, it may be more useful to re-conceptualize it in terms of a global counterinsurgency (GCOIN). Such an approach would a priori knit together the equally critical political, economic, diplomatic, and developmental sides inherent to the successful prosecution of counterinsurgency to the existing dominant military side of the equation.

Greater attention to this integration of American capabilities would provide incontrovertible recognition of the importance of endowing a GCOIN with an overriding and comprehensive, multidimensional, policy. Ideally, this policy would embrace several elements: including a clear strategy, a defined structure for implementing it, and a vision of inter-government agency cooperation, and the unified effort to guide it. It would have particular benefit with respect to the gathering and exploitation of "actionable intelligence." By updating and streamlining interagency coun-terterrorism and counterinsurgency systems and procedures both strategi-cally as well as operationally between DoD [Department of Defense], the Department of State, and the intelligence community, actionable intel-ligence could likely be acquired, analyzed and disseminated faster and operations mounted more quickly. A more focused and strengthened inter-agency process would also facilitate the coordination of key themes and messages and the development and execution of long-term "hearts and minds" programs.

In any event, success in the campaign against global terrorism and radi-cal jihadism will ultimately depend on how effectively the U.S. can build bridges and untangle lines of authority, de-conflict overlapping responsibili-ties and improve the ability to prioritize and synchronize interagency opera-tions in a timely and efficient manner. Organizations will therefore have to do—or be compelled to do—what they have been reluctant to do in the past: reaching across bureaucratic territorial divides and sharing resources in order to defeat terrorists, insurgencies, and other emerging threats. Clarifying these expectations and processes is a critical step in efficiently addressing contem-porary threats to U.S. security as is creating incentives to more effectively blend diplomacy, justice, development, finance, intelligence, law enforcement, and military capabilities and coherently generating and applying resources to defeat terrorist and insurgent threats.

Even the best strategy will be proven inadequate if military and civilian agency leaders are not prepared to engage successfully within ambiguous environments and reorient their organizational culture to deal with irregular threats. A successful GCOIN transcends the need for better tactical intel-ligence or new organizations. It is fundamentally about transforming the attitudes and mindsets of leaders so that they have the capacity to take deci-sive, yet thoughtful action against terrorists and/or insurgents in uncertain or unclear situations based on a common vision, policy, and strategy. In addition to traditional "hard" military skills of "kill or capture" and destruction and attrition; "soft" skills such as negotiations, psychology, social and cultural anthropology, foreign area studies, complexity theory, and systems manage-ment will become increasingly important in the ambiguous and dynamic environment in which irregular adversaries circulate. Arguably, by combating irregular adversaries in a more collaborative and integrative manner with key relevant civilian agencies, those charged with countering terrorism and insur-gency can better share critical information, track the various moving parts in terrorist/insurgency networks, and develop a comprehensive picture of this enemy—including their supporters, nodes of support, organizational and operational systems, processes, and plans. With this information in hand, the U.S. would then be better prepared to systematically disrupt or defeat all of the critical nodes that support the entire terrorist/insurgent network, thus rendering them ineffective.

Achieving this desideratum, however, will necessitate the coordination, de-conflicting, and synchronization of the variety of programs upon which the execution of American counterterrorist and/or counterinsurgency planning are dependent. An equally critical dimension of this process will be aligning the training of host nation counterparts with U.S. counterterrorism and counterinsurgency operations: building synergy; avoiding duplication of effort; ensuring that training leads to operational effectiveness; and ensuring that the U.S. interagency team and approach is in complete harmony. In other words, aligning these training programs with operations to build indigenous capabilities in counterterrorism and counterinsurgency will be absolutely fundamental to the success of such a strategy. In sum, new times, new threats, and new challenges ineluctably make a new strategy, approach and new organizational and institutional behaviors necessary. The threat posed by elusive and deadly irregular adversaries emphasizes the need to anchor changes that will more effectively close the gap between detecting irregular adversarial activity and rapidly defeating it. The effectiveness of U.S. strategy will be based on our capacity to think like a networked enemy, in anticipation of how they may act in a variety of situations, aided by different resources.

This goal requires that the American national security structure in turn organize itself for maximum efficiency, information sharing, and the ability to function quickly and effectively under new operational definitions. With this thorough understanding in mind, we need to craft an approach that specifically takes into account the following key factors to effectively wage a GCOIN:

1. Separating the enemy from the populace that provides support and sustenance. This, in turn, entails three basic missions:
   a. Denial of enemy sanctuary
   b. Elimination of enemy freedom of movement
   c. Denial of enemy resources and support;
2. Identification and neutralization of the enemy;
3. Creation of a secure environment—progressing from local to regional to global;
4. Ongoing and effective neutralization of enemy propaganda through the planning and execution of a comprehensive and integrated information operations and holistic civil affairs campaign in harmony with the first four tasks;
5. Interagency efforts to build effective and responsible civil governance mechanisms that eliminate the fundamental causes of terrorism and insurgency.

The key to success will be in harnessing the overwhelming kinetic force of the U.S. military as part of a comprehensive vision to transform capabilities in order to deal with irregular and unconventional threats. A successful strategy will therefore also be one that thinks and plans ahead with a view towards addressing the threats likely to be posed by the terrorist and insurgent generation beyond the current one.

POSTSCRIPT

Does the United States Have a Sound Strategy for the War on Terrorism?

As the preceding readings indicate, the debate on whether or not the war of terrorism is succeeding can be divided into two basic parts. One is measurement. At least from an American perspective, it is possible to argue that as of this writing in October 2006, success can be demonstrated by the fact that there have been no successful attacks on Americans within the United States since 9/11. Moreover, if the bomb attacks on U.S. forces in Iraq using car bombs and other convert methods are not counted, there have been no major terrorist attacks on U.S. forces akin in severity to the boat bomb attack in October 2000 that wreaked havoc on the USS *Cole* and killed 17 sailors while the ship was in Port Aden, Yemen, taking on fuel.

From a less optimistic perspective, it is myopic to claim progress if the most notorious terrorist leader, Osama bin Laden, remains at large and active, occasionally creating tapes aired on Muslim and other news broadcasts in December 2004. One called for the overthrow of the Saudi monarchy, the other declared a holy war against U.S. forces in Iraq and on cooperating Iraqis and called for a boycott of the planned elections. Moreover, terrorist attacks in Saudi Arabia and elsewhere were widely attributed to either al-Qaeda directly or to bin Laden's influence. Moreover, a national intelligence report to President Bush in September 2006 that represents a consensus of all the various U.S. intelligence agencies concluded that the U.S. and allied occupation of Iraq was promoting the growth of terrorism by fuelling Muslim anger.

Many other aspects of the effort to thwart terrorism are even less certain. Little or no public information exists to gauge the degree to which the flow of finances to and among terrorists has been hindered. Knowing whether any progress is being made in the struggle for "the hearts and minds" of Muslims and others is also very difficult. Among those who believe that the war on terrorism is going well is Edwin J. Feulner, "Winning the War," Heritage Foundation Commentary (June 18, 2004) at http://www.heritage.org/Press/Commentary/. Taking the opposite view is Charles V. Peña, *Winning the Un-War: A New Strategy for the War on Terrorism* (Potomac Books, 2006).

The second and related aspect of the debate relates to counterterrorism tactics. A prime source for the U.S. approach is the president's "National Strategy for Combating Terrorism" (September 2006), available at http://www.whitehouse.gov/nsc/nsct/2006/. The annual reports on terrorism by the State Department and other information about the U.S. anti-terrorist efforts are available from the Office for the Coordinator for Counterterrorism at http://www.state.gov/s/ct/. For commentary on the State Department's reporting on terrorist activity, see the report by the Congressional Research Service, "Trends on Terrorism: 2006" (July 21, 2006) at http://www.fas.org/sgp/crs/terror/RL33555.pdf. For views that differ with the administration and urge a different course of action, see Stephen Van Evera, "Assessing U.S. Strategy in the War on Terror," *Annals of the American Academy of Political and Social Science* (September 2006) and Anthony H. Cordesman, "Winning the 'War on Terrorism': A Fundamentally Different Strategy," *Middle East Policy* (September 2006). For an alarming view that failure to win the war on terror and in general defusing the issues that make the Middle East so volatile could lead to World War II, read Niall Ferguson, "The Next War of the World," *Foreign Affairs* (September/October 2006).

ISSUE 14

Is Patient Diplomacy the Best Approach to Iran's Nuclear Program?

YES: Frank G. Wisner, from "Iran, the United States and the International Community: The Time Is Right to Engage," Testimony during Hearings on "Iran's Political/Nuclear Ambitions and U.S. Policy Options," before the Committee on Foreign Relations, U.S. Senate (May 18, 2006)

NO: James Phillips, from "U.S. Policy and Iran's Nuclear Challenge," Testimony during Hearings on "Iran's Political/Nuclear Ambitions and U.S. Policy Options," before the Committee on Foreign Relations, U.S. Senate (May 18, 2006)

ISSUE SUMMARY

YES: Frank G. Wisner, vice chairman for External Affairs of the American International Group, in New York City, says it is not clear that Iran is determined to build nuclear weapons and urges a policy signaling that the United States not only seeks agreement that will contain the nuclear crisis but is prepared to consider normalizing relations with and giving security guarantees to Iran.

NO: James Phillips, research fellow for Middle Eastern Affairs in the Douglas and Sarah Allison Center for Foreign Policy Studies at the Heritage Foundation in Washington, D.C., tells Congress that the United States should mobilize an international coalition to pressure Iran to cease its nuclear weapons development program and, if that fails, should consider military options to set back Iran's nuclear weapons program.

The global effort to control the spread of nuclear weapons centers on the Nuclear Non-Proliferation Treaty (NPT) of 1968. Under it, 85 percent of the world's countries that adhere to the NPT pledge not to transfer nuclear weapons or assist a nonnuclear state to make or otherwise acquire nuclear weapons. Nonnuclear countries also agree not to build or accept nuclear weapons and to allow the UN's International Atomic Energy Agency (IAEA) to monitor their nuclear facilities to ensure their exclusive use for peaceful purposes.

The NPT has not been a complete success. India and Pakistan both tested nuclear weapons in 1998. Israel's possession of nuclear weapons is an open secret. None of them agreed to the treaty. Currently, there are tensions over two countries that have agreed to the NPT. One of those countries is North Korea, which adhered to the NPT in 1970, then violated the treaty in the early 1990s by moving toward building nuclear weapons. Diplomacy failed to halt the development program, and North Korea tested a nuclear weapon in 2006.

Iran, like North Korea, agreed to the NPT in 1970. At that time, Iran was ruled by a pro-Western monarch, Shah Mohammad Reza Pahlavi, who was overthrown in 1979. After the Shah fled, the Ayatollah Ruhollah Khomeini returned from exile and founded a theocratic political system that condemned Western values and influence.

During the 1980s Iran fought a horrendous eight-year war with Iraq, one in which Iraq used chemical weapons. Partly because of that war and the assumption that Iraq had nuclear weapons ambitions, Iran moved to produce enriched uranium and to take other steps necessary to produce nuclear fuel for energy, but also nuclear weapons. This program also reflected a combination of Iran's desire to become a regional power and its fear of the United States. Among other concerns, President George W. Bush had said Iran was one of the "axis of evil" countries promoting terrorism and had ordered the U.S. invasion of two neighboring Muslim countries, Afghanistan in 2001 and Iraq in 2003. The United States by 2003 was urging international pressure to make Iran give up its program. Three European Union countries—France, Germany, and Great Britain (the EU-3)—took the lead trying to persuade Iran to end its dual-use efforts. Iran negotiated, but also claimed that its intentions were peaceful and that it had the sovereign right to develop nuclear power. With no progress being made, the council of the IAEA voted overwhelmingly in February 2006 to refer the matter to the UN Security Council. There the matter stood at the time Frank Wisner recommended in the first reading that patient diplomacy was the best approach to Iran. James Phillips disagreed. He conceded that peaceful diplomacy should be the initial approach, but predicted that it was likely to fail and therefore had to be followed by a willingness to soon impose sanctions on Iran and perhaps even take military action against it.

YES

Frank G. Wisner

Iran, the United States and the International Community: The Time Is Right to Engage

The United States, the international community and Iran are in crisis. The crisis broke out last year in the wake of Iran's decision to proceed with its nuclear enrichment program and limit its cooperation with the International Atomic Energy Agency [IAEA]. But the crisis runs deeper. It is rooted in broad international concern over Iran's clandestine efforts to develop an enrichment program, which have put into question the spirit of Iran's compliance with the Non-Proliferation Treaty.

In fact, the origins of the crisis are long standing. For over a quarter of a century and as a result of the overthrow of the Shah's regime, Iran's clerically dominated government has been at odds with the United States and frequently with its neighbors. The regime's aggressive assertion of its religious identity has frightened Sunni Muslim nations in the Gulf, the Middle East and elsewhere in the region. Iran's espousal of Hezbollah and Hamas has put the country on the front lines of the war against terror. The Iranian leadership's unwillingness to accept the existence of the State of Israel has further undermined the ability of the United States to find common ground with it.

In response to the Iranian Government's policies and the principles it espouses, the United States, during the Bush administration, has identified Iran as an opponent of the United States and a candidate for "regime change." The Congress' involvement in legislation to fund activities which would undermine clerical rule in Iran has sent the strong signal of aggressive American intent. To a nation historically under siege and more recently at odds with the United States, these threats have hit hard and have stirred broad Iranian insecurities.

I come to this meeting over the future of American policy toward Iran, having read Iran's history closely and having followed attentively its recent actions and our relationship. I bring to this session my thirty-seven years of experience in our nation's diplomatic service as well as a four year association with "track two" [unofficial] discussions with knowledgeable Iranians. These discussions have been organized under the auspices of the United Nations'

Testimony before the Foreign Relations Committee, U.S. Senate, by Frank G. Wisner (May 18, 2006).

Association of the United States (UNA-USA). The results have been regularly shared with officials of the United States government.

In addition, I represented the United States Government in 1997 in discussions with Russia's authorities over the transfer of missile technology from the Russian Federation to Iran. This said, I have no access to official intelligence on Iran, its nuclear program nor the workings of Iranian domestic politics.

I intend, in the course of my testimony, to answer four questions— 1) Will Iran develop a nuclear weapon; 2) Is that outcome imminent; 3) Is Iran's leadership united behind the development of a nuclear weapon and 4) What is the way ahead for the United States.

Will Iran Develop a Nuclear Weapon?

The answer to that question is not obvious. It is clear Iran believes it has the right to enrich uranium and fuel a nuclear power system. Iran further argues that this right is part of its commitment to the NPT. It is also true that Iran has pursued a nuclear ambition since the days of the Shah. Finally, it is obvious that Iran has developed its fuel enrichment system clandestinely and in violation of its international obligations.

It is my view that Iran has not made a nuclear weapons decision and that its house is divided on the subject. There are Iranians who believe Iran would be better off with a nuclear weapon; there are others who argue that a weapon will increase the dangers which Iran faces. Virtually all Iranians, including those who live outside the country, share the opinion that their country needs nuclear power and that an enrichment program is a legitimate assertion of the nation's right. Moreover, the nuclear program has become in Iranian eyes a question of national honor and prestige.

It is possible that Iran will proceed down the path of enrichment, stopping just short of a nuclear weapon, leaving open the option to acquire such a capacity. Given Iran's dangerous record on other fronts and the lack of confidence in its government's behavior, that outcome is unacceptable to the United States and our friends in Europe. In a word, we must deal with the nuclear issue and seek to contain it.

Is a Weapon Imminent?

Again, I advise caution in concluding that the United States faces an immediate, threat. Estimates of the time it would take Iran to assemble adequate amounts of fissionable material vary sharply. Like you, I have seen figures that range from three to ten years, depending on the urgency with which Iran pursues the goal, the technology and resources available to it and the international environment. The design and weaponization of a nuclear device is another matter but not one for "tomorrow morning." I argue, therefore, that we have time to consider carefully our strategy for dealing with the very real threat which Iran's enrichment program poses. There need be no rush to judgment; and we have time to explore and exercise the option of diplomacy.

Let me make this point in a different way.

Is Iran's Leadership United Behind the Development of a Nuclear Weapon?
Once again my experience leads me to be careful about concluding Iran's leadership and political class are united. Those, who state with confidence that they know Iran's intentions, have been consistently wrong. Our insights into the politics of the clerical regime are limited; our estrangement from Iran has impeded serious analysis of political trends and developments. This state of affairs is regrettable and I suggest it is in the interests of the United States to increase the attention we pay to Iran, its politics, economics, and social trends—within government and in academic and research communities.

It is my view that Iran's leadership, broadly defined, is not united on a wide range of issues of national importance, including nuclear weaponization. Power is divided. The Supreme Leader retains control over Iran's Revolutionary Guards, its intelligence services and the nuclear program. Mahmoud Ahmadinejad, the President and author of deeply offensive and inflammatory statements about Israel, the region, Iran's nuclear intentions and the United States, does not directly control these institutions and programs. But he won the election to the Presidency with a solid majority and with clerical sympathy. Today he is playing Iranian politics with consummate skill. Ahmadinejad will be a significant factor in Iranian politics for years to come. He has developed a strong base among young Iranians and he appeals effectively to the street's instincts. Moreover he enjoys substantial standing with the Supreme Leader and the Guardians. In the election campaign and his brief time in office Ahmadinejad has eclipsed the reformers; his leverage in Iranian politics is rising. This said, so are his opponents who are questioning the President's assertions about national security policy and his profligate interventions in the economy.

Finally, it has been my experience that the exercise of power has the potential of educating its holders in the realities of international and domestic life. This has been Iran's recent experience. The country's original revolutionary fervor has run thin. We are in Ahmadinejad's early days. There is more to come, but the present situation of crisis strengthens the Iranian President's hand. There is reason therefore to lessen, if we can, the intensity of the present crisis.

What are the United States Choices?

I suggest that the nuclear stand-off with Iran will play out over a period of time—months if not years. There are no quick fixes and we need the time to examine, select and pursue our options. The United Nations' Security Council is divided. Our European friends, deeply opposed to Iran's nuclear program, seek a diplomatic resolution.

Is there a military solution to enrichment? There is no obvious way to deal with Iran's intention to proceed with nuclear enrichment. It is my view that military action can only disrupt Iranian facilities. Worse yet, the consequences of an American attack on Iranian intentions will be severe. If Iran's leaders have not crossed the nuclear threshold, they would in the wake of American military action. We would have to anticipate direct Iranian retaliation against our forces in Iraq and other American targets in the Gulf and the Middle East—if not beyond. I have not seen any evidence that our intelligence is adequate to pinpoint Iran's nuclear enrichment system and make it vulnerable to a decisive military strike.

The political consequences of an American attack would be even more devastating. I can assure you that there will be an eruption of protest across the Muslim world; public opinion in allied nations would be hostile and our standing in international fora would be undermined. We must also calculate the economic consequences. I have no way to predict where the price of oil will go in the wake of military action against Iran or counter moves which impeded the Straits of Hormuz [between the Persian Gulf and the Indian Ocean].

Military action should always be the last choice—and never excluded. But I do not believe that we have reached the end of the road and can therefore justify or appropriately use military force to stop Iran's enrichment program.

Will Economic Sanctions Deter Iran?

The United States has committed the majority of its sanctions arsenal against Iran in the past and has few decisive instruments left. While the possibility of greater allied cooperation in the face of a nuclear threat is somewhat better, our allies have been hard to bring along in the past. Ordinary trade sanctions will be very difficult to enforce, given Iran's long borders and proximity to trading entrepôts, [commercial centers] like Dubai. Financial sanctions come at the cost of disruption of our complicated, international financial system. Sanctions against the movement of Iranian officials are hardly significant. Sanctions generally work when they are targeted, short term and multilateral. It is hard to imagine the Iranian nuclear crisis being either of short duration or subject to resolution only through the imposition of sanctions.

The Case for Engagement

The first choice in conflict resolution should be diplomacy. There are diplomatic options available to the United States.

Does this mean that military means or sanctions have no place in addressing the crisis we face with Iran? Of course not. They are and must remain arrows in our quiver. Diplomacy, without strength and the ability to deliver pressure, is rarely successful. For the moment, military force and additional sanctions are more effective as threats which its leaders must contemplate.

Our leverage lies elsewhere. Iran is an isolated nation. Apart from a few states, like Syria, whose association with Iran is based on tactical considerations, Iran has few friends and no allies. If the international community, notably Russia and China, are divided from us about how to deal with Iran, there are no divisions over the issue of Iran's nuclear pretensions nor her historic sponsorship of violence in her region. Cut off from acceptance within the international community, Iran is also isolated in the mainstream of world economics. She sells oil but she receives virtually no investment. Existing sanctions, especially those put in place by the United States, limit foreign capital flows. And these sanctions can be deepened. Iran receives little to no technology and will not as long as she continues to stand outside the norms of acceptable international behavior.

Iran's isolation, born of her policies of confrontation, aggravates her perception of threat and preoccupies her leaders and intelligentsia. At heart, they know that Iran cannot force her way into respectability, partnership and security. Sooner or later, Iran must meet all of us "half way" or she will remain threatened and denied the capital flows, investment partnerships and technology her lagging economy and highly dissatisfied and deprived population requires. In a word, Iran's understanding of her isolation and our capacity to sustain and intensify it are powerful weapons in addressing the nuclear crisis we face and the other threats Iran poses to our interests. Equally, our willingness to offer a path away from isolation is a powerful tool.

Then How Do We Deal with Iran?
Our ability to respond militarily is "on the table" and it should remain there. Sanctions are in place and selectively, for example a multilateral agreement aimed at the denial of official credits, can be added over time. We have drawn our "lines in the sand" and the time is right to move on and engage Iran politically.

The time is right, moreover, to signal that the United States not only seeks agreement which will contain the nuclear crisis but that we are prepared to consider normalizing relations, provided, of course, that Iran is similarly disposed and acts accordingly. Engagement, through diplomatic dialogue, means addressing the broad array of issues that divide Iran from us and the international community—the issues that leave her marginalized and insecure—in other words, the issues that undergird distrust of Iran.

The questions, which we and Iran must address, are obvious and they deal with subjects of vital importance to the United States—Iran's nuclear pretensions; the future of Iraq and Afghanistan; the security of the Gulf; the prevalence of terror in the Middle East; political instability in the Arab East; and peace between Israel and Palestine. The US plays a very special role in Iran's thinking. The questions she wishes to address with us are her isolation; the sanctions' regimes she faces; her search for acceptance in the international community and her insecurity in a deeply troubled region. In particular, Iran needs access to the international economy if she is to provide employment for her young.

Our record of engagement with Islamic Iran is a poor one. Past attempts, born of initiatives to address a single issue, have failed. They will fail again if we and Iran do not address the totality of our relationship and if we and Iran are not prepared to set as an ultimate objective, the normalization of our relationship. And that means, simply stated, a reciprocal readiness to live in peace and mutual respect, no matter how sharply divided we are over our view of each others' political systems.

History is replete with examples of the United States finding a working basis for our relationships with those from whom we were sharply divided over ideology, national ambition, and questions of vital national security concern. I have in mind our ability to find common ground, through detente, with the erstwhile Soviet Union and through the Shanghai Communiqué, with the People's Republic of China.

Engagement begins with a commitment at the top of our political system. On our side, it starts with an undertaking by the President to a normalized relationship. It means a willingness to set aside the rhetoric of "axis of evil" and measures legislatively mandated to undermine Iran's regime. Our concerns are legitimately with Iran's external ambitions and absent any confidence in those ambitions, its nuclear intentions. Its domestic orientation is another question. Iranians have changed their regimes in the past and they will do so again. In a situation of greater peace and security, that day may even come sooner. Our objective must be the stability of the region and our interests there—not Iran's domestic order. We have our principles; the clerics have theirs. Let's see on whose side history sits.

I believe there is an opportunity today to pursue engagement with Iran. Based on my assessment of Iran's policies, I conclude that Iran's clerical leaders are more comfortable with the country's elected government and are willing to give it the freedom to maneuver internationally, including with us. This was not the case in Khatami's time. In addition Iran's leaders are less intimidated by our ability to deliver on the threats they feel we have articulated. They know we are bogged down in Iraq. Therefore they feel they can approach us on a more equal footing. Our European allies want us to enter the dialogue; Russia and China clearly share that view. I suspect they would welcome a signal the United States is ready to seek normalized relations with Iran and to live in peace.

Ahmadinejad's recent letter, as bizarre and objectionable as its content are, is based on a sense of self confidence. It deserves an answer—not rejection. We are under no obligation to reply to the terms which the letter offers. We are free to state our case and spell out our objectives for a dialogue.

I do not have a neat formula to resolve the nuclear crisis. I doubt Iran will renounce enrichment but will it enter into cooperative, internationally based arrangements for the production and supervision of enriched fuel? Is it possible to find common ground over Iraq and Afghanistan where Iranian interests have been served by the elimination of Saddam and the Taliban? I believe so, especially if we make it clear the United States does not intend to be a permanent fixture in Iraq or Afghanistan and that we will not use our position in either country to threaten Iran. Can the concerns of Sunni Arabs be addressed? I contend there is room for a regional conference to elaborate security guarantees. Can Iran address the dangers posed by Hezbollah and Hamas and can Iran be brought to be a more responsible player in the Israeli-Palestinian equation? Perhaps, but it will be difficult. But it is reasonable to conclude Iran sees in Hamas' victory in the Palestinian elections a vindication and because Hamas is now in power, a two state solution can be pursued.

This said, I return to my core contention: the starting point in negotiations with Iran is our willingness to seek normalization. The United States must deal with the nuclear crisis. We have time, leverage and the authority to do so. But to repeat, our approach should be a broad one; aimed at a full exploration of the several issues of concern to us and with the objective of a normalized relationship. . . .

James Phillips  **NO**

U.S. Policy and Iran's Nuclear Challenge

The efforts of the United States and its allies to dissuade Iran from pursuing its long-sought goal of attaining a nuclear weapons capability have so far failed to yield satisfactory results. Iran made temporary tactical concessions in October 2003 under strong international pressure to temporarily freeze its uranium enrichment operations and submit to increased inspections of its nuclear facilities by the International Atomic Energy Agency (IAEA). Tehran feared that referral to the Security Council could result in diplomatic isolation, economic sanctions, or possible military attack. It undoubtedly also was motivated by the examples set by the rapid overthrow of the Taliban regime in Afghanistan in 2001 and Saddam Hussein's regime in Iraq in early 2003 by U.S.-led coalitions.

Tehran made enough tactical concessions to stave off international sanctions and engage the European Union in diplomatic negotiations led by Britain, France, and Germany (the EU-3) to temporarily defuse the crisis. But Tehran later dropped the charade of negotiations after it apparently concluded that the international situation had shifted in its favor. It now apparently believes that it is in a much stronger position due to the continued need for U.S. military forces in Iraq and Afghanistan; the rise in oil prices which has given it greater bargaining leverage with oil importers; and its diplomatic cultivation of China and Russia, which can dilute or veto resolutions brought before the U.N. Security Council.

The installation of a new hard-line government led by President Mahmoud Ahmadinejad in August 2005 also was a major factor that led Tehran to renege on its agreement with the EU-3. Iran's new president is firmly committed to Iran's nuclear program and vehemently criticized Iran's previous government for making too many concessions in past negotiations with the EU-3. Shortly thereafter Iran resumed operations at the Isfahan uranium conversion facility, converting yellowcake into uranium hexafluoride, a preliminary step before enrichment. In January 2006 Iran announced its intention to resume uranium enrichment activities and removed IAEA seals at its Natanz facility. Iran remains determined to develop a complete nuclear fuel cycle, which would eventually give it the fissile material for a nuclear

Testimony during Hearings on "Iran's Political/Nuclear Ambitions and U.S. Policy Options" before the Committee on Foreign Relations, U.S. Senate, James Phillips (May 18, 2006).

weapons capability. Thus far, Iran has escaped paying any significant price for its apparent violations of its commitments under the NPT and failure to fully cooperate with the IAEA.

The U.S. should mobilize an international coalition to raise the diplomatic, economic, domestic political, and potential military costs to Tehran of continuing to flout its obligations under its nuclear safeguards agreements. This "coalition of the willing" should seek to isolate the Ahmadinejad regime, weaken it through targeted economic sanctions, explain to the Iranian people why their government's nuclear policies will impose economic costs and military risks on them, contain Iran's military power, and encourage democratic change. If Tehran persists in its drive for nuclear weapons despite these escalating pressures, then the United States should consider military options to set back the Iranian nuclear weapons program.

The Growing Threat of Ahmadinejad's Iran

Mahmoud Ahmadinejad rose up through the ranks of the Islamic Revolutionary Guard Corps (IRGC), the praetorian guard dedicated to advancing and exporting the revolution that Ayatollah Ruhollah Khomeini inspired in Iran in 1978–1979. Ahmadinejad is a true believer in Khomeini's radical vision of Iran's role as the vanguard of a global Islamic revolution. He has lambasted the U.S. as "a failing power" and a threat to the Muslim world.

In sharp contrast to his predecessor, former President Mohammad Khatami, who advocated a conciliatory "dialogue of civilizations" but was blocked by the strong opposition of the ideological hardliners, Ahmadinijad has returned to the fiery rhetoric of the Khomeini era. In September he delivered a truculent speech at the United Nations, warning foreign governments against meddling in Iranian affairs. On October 26, he made a venomous speech attacking Israel in which he quoted Khomeini: "As the Imam said, Israel must be wiped off the map."

Ahmadinejad's vehement return to Khomeini's radical line has been accompanied by a purge of pragmatists and reformers within the regime. Forty of Iran's senior ambassadors have been recalled from overseas posts, including diplomats who were involved in the EU-3 negotiations in Britain, France, Germany, and at the United Nations in Geneva. Ahmadinejad has appointed many of his IRGC cronies to key positions throughout the government.

Iran also has been increasingly aggressive in stirring up trouble inside Iraq. In October, the British government charged that the Iranians had supplied sophisticated bombs with shaped charges capable of penetrating armor to clients in Iraq who used them in a series of attacks on British forces in southern Iraq. Iran also has given discreet support to insurgents such as Moqtada al-Sadr, who twice has led Shiite uprisings against coalition forces and the Iraqi government.

Iranian hardliners undoubtedly fear that a stable democratic Iraq would present a dangerous alternative model of government that could undermine their own authority. They know that Iraq's pre-eminent Shiite religious leader,

Grand Ayatollah Ali al-Sistani, whose religious authority is greater than that of any member of Iran's ruling clerical regime, rejects Khomeini's radical ideology and advocates traditional Shiite religious doctrines. Although Iran continues to enjoy considerable influence with many Iraqi Shiites, particularly with Iraq's Supreme Council for the Islamic Revolution in Iraq and the Dawa Party, the moderate influence of Sistani dilutes their own revolutionary influence. Therefore, Tehran plays a double game in Iraq, using the young firebrand al-Sadr to undermine Sistani and keep pressure on the U.S. military to withdraw, while still maintaining good relations with Shiite political parties who revere Sistani and need continued American support.

In addition to its destabilizing role in Iraq, Iran continues to be the world's leading sponsor of terrorism. Secretary of State Condoleezza Rice recently called Iran "the central banker" of international terrorism. It has close ties to the Lebanon-based Hezballah terrorist group, which it organized and continues to finance, arm, and train. Tehran also has supported a wide variety of Palestinian terrorist groups, including Fatah, Hamas, and Palestinian Islamic Jihad, as well as Afghan extremists such as Gulbuddin Hekmatyar. Iran was involved in the 1996 Khobar Towers bombing, which killed 19 American military personnel deployed in Saudi Arabia. Moreover, Iran reportedly continues to give sanctuary to elements of al-Qaeda, including at least one of Osama bin Laden's sons, Saad bin Laden, and Saif al-Adil, a top operations coordinator.

This long and deep involvement in terrorism, continued hostility to the United States, and repeated threats to destroy Israel, provide a strong warning against the dangers of allowing such a radical regime to develop nuclear weapons.

Leading an International Response to Iran's Nuclear Challenge

Diplomatic efforts centered on the United Nations to pressure Iran to abandon its clandestine nuclear efforts are unlikely to solve the problem, in part due to the institutional weaknesses of the U.N. Security Council, where a lack of consensus often leads to paralysis or lowest common denominator policies that are not effective. Nevertheless, the Bush Administration must resolutely press the diplomatic case at the Security Council to set the stage and improve the U.S. position in the push for possible diplomatic and economic sanctions targeted at Iran's recalcitrant regime, or, as a last resort, possible future military action.

Another goal should be to make sure that the end result of the Security Council's interactions with Iran clearly lays the responsibility of any failure on Tehran, not Washington. Washington should seek to focus the Security Council debate on the critical issue—the threat posed by Iran's nuclear program—not the broader question of whether to seek a multilateral "grand bargain" with an untrustworthy revolutionary power that exploited and sabotaged past American efforts to stage a rapprochement under the Carter and Reagan Administrations and failed to respond to the tentative détente offered by the Clinton Administration. Getting drawn into a multilateral dialogue with Iran through the auspices of the United Nations would allow Iran to divert attention from its safeguard violations and history of terrorism, while subjecting the United States to growing international pressure to bribe Iran with diplomatic carrots to comply with international legal commitments that it already has violated and could renege on again in the future. Iran already has provided ample evidence that it has no intention to fully cooperate with the IAEA or end the uranium enrichment activities that eventually will give it a nuclear weapons capability. If it merely seeks a nuclear power capability for economic reasons, as it insists, then it would not have rejected the Russian offer to enrich uranium at facilities in Russia, which would have saved it considerable costs in building and operating uranium enrichment facilities. Moreover, Iran also would have received additional economic benefits from the EU-3 if it had not broken off those negotiations. Under these circumstances, the EU-3's recent undertaking to put together a new package of incentives for Iran is the triumph of wishful thinking over experience. Beginning a new round of negotiations while Iran continues to work to perfect its uranium enrichment technology will enable Tehran to buy time for its nuclear weapons program, forestall sanctions, and weaken the perceived costs of violating the nuclear non-proliferation regime in the eyes of other countries who may consider following Iran's path. To change Iran's course, the EU-3 should be considering larger disincentives, not just larger incentives.

Forge a Coalition to Impose the Strongest Possible Sanctions on the Iranian Regime

Although it has greatly benefited from the recent spike in world oil and natural gas prices, Iran's economic future is not a promising one. The mullahs have sabotaged economic growth through the expansion of state control of the economy, economic mismanagement and corruption. Annual per capita income is only about two thirds of what it was at the time of the 1979 revolution. The situation is likely to get worse as President Ahmadinejad follows through on his populist promises to increase subsidies and give Iran's poor a greater share of Iran's oil wealth.

Iranians are sending large amounts of their capital out of the country due to fears over the potentially disastrous policies of the new government. Shortly after Ahmadinejad gave his October 26 speech threatening Israel, Iran's stock market plunged to its lowest level in two years. Many Iranian businessmen understand, even if Ahmadinejad does not, that Iran's economic future depends on access to world markets, foreign investment, and trade.

The US should push for the strongest possible sanctions at the U.N. Security Council. But experience has demonstrated that Washington cannot rely on the U.N. to halt the Iranian nuclear program. Russia and China, who have extensive economic, military, and energy ties to Iran, may veto or dilute any effective resolution. The U.S. therefore should make contingency plans to work with Britain, France, Germany, the EU, and Japan to impose sanctions outside the U.N. framework if necessary.

An international ban on the import of Iranian oil is a non-starter. It is unrealistic to expect oil importers to stop importing Iranian oil in a tight, high-priced oil market. Instead, the focus should be on denying Iran loans, foreign investment, and favorable trade deals. Washington should cooperate with other countries to deny Iran loans from international financial institutions such as the World Bank and to deny Iran loans for a proposed natural gas pipeline to India via Pakistan.

Although Iran is one of the world's leading oil exporters, it is also an importer of gasoline due to mismanagement and inadequate investment in its refinery infrastructure. An international ban on gasoline exports to Iran would deprive Tehran of approximately 40 percent of its daily gasoline consumption. This would significantly drive up the price of Iranian gasoline and underscore to the Iranian people the shortsighted policies of Iran's ruling regime.

In addition to economic sanctions, the U.S. should press its allies and other countries to ban nuclear assistance, arms sales, and the export of dual use technology to Iran. Symbolic sanctions, such as a travel ban on Iranian officials or ban on Iranian participation in international sports events, would drive home to the Iranian people that international opposition to Iran's nuclear program is widespread and not an artificial issue created by the United States, as their government claims.

Support Iran's Democratic Opposition

The Bush Administration has correctly aligned the U.S. with the Iranian people in their efforts to build a true democracy, but it has held back from a policy of regime change, partly in deference to the EU-3 negotiations with Iran about its nuclear program. However, now that it is clear that Iran has reneged on its promises to the EU-3, Washington should discreetly aid all Iranian groups that support democracy and reject terrorism, either through direct grants or indirectly through nongovernmental organizations. The Iran Freedom and Support Act of 2005 (H.R. 282 and S. 333), currently under consideration by Congress would authorize such aid and tighten U.S. economic sanctions on Iran.

Iran has a well-educated group of young reformers who seek to replace Iran's current mullahcracy with a genuine democracy that is accountable to the Iranian people. They have been demoralized by the failure of former President Khatami to live up to his promises of reform and his lack of support for the student uprisings of 1999, but are likely to be re-energized by a brewing popular disenchantment with the policies of Ahmadinejad's hard-liners.

The U.S. and its allies should discreetly support all Iranian opposition groups that reject terrorism and advocate democracy by publicizing their activities internationally and within Iran, giving them organizational training indirectly through western NGOs, and inviting them to attend international conferences and workshops outside Iran, preferably in European or other countries where Iranians could travel relatively freely with minimal fear of being penalized upon their return to Iran.

Educational exchanges with western students would be an important avenue for bolstering and opening up communication with Iran's restive students, who historically have played a leading role in Iran's reform movements. Women's groups also could play a key role in strengthening support for political reforms among young Iranian women, a key element opposing the restoration of harsh social restrictions by Iran's resurgent Islamic ideologues.

The United States also should covertly subsidize opposition publications and organizing efforts, as it did to aid the anti-communist opposition during the Cold War in Europe and Asia. But such programs should be strictly segregated from the public outreach efforts of the U.S. and its allies, to avoid putting Iranian participants in international forums at risk of arrest or persecution when they return home.

The United States should not try to play favorites among the various Iranian opposition groups, but should encourage them to cooperate under the umbrella of the broadest possible coalition. But Washington should rule out support for the People's Mujahideen Organization (PMO), which is also known as the Mujahideen Khalq, or its front group, the National Council of Resistance. The PMO is a non-democratic Marxist terrorist group that was part of the broad revolutionary coalition that overthrew the Shah, but was purged in 1981 and aligned itself with Saddam Hussein's dictatorship.

While this cult-like group is one of the best-organized exile organizations, it has little support inside Iran because of its alliance with arch-enemy Iraq during the Iran-Iraq war. Moreover, the PMO resorted to terrorism against the Shah's regime and was responsible for the assassinations of at least four American military officers in Iran during the 1970s. It demonstrated in support of the Soviet invasion of Afghanistan in 1979 and against the release of the American hostages in 1981. The U.S. cannot afford to support an organization with such a long history of terrorism, if it expects Tehran to halt its own terrorism.

Launch a Public Diplomacy Campaign to Explain to the Iranian People How the Regime's Nuclear Weapons Program and Hard-line Policies Hurt Their Economic and National Interests

Iran's clerical regime has tightened its grip on the media in recent years, shutting down more than 100 independent newspapers, jailing journalists, closing down websites, and arresting bloggers. The U.S. and its allies should work to defeat the regime's suppression of independent media by increasing Farsi broadcasts by government sponsored media such as the Voice of America, Radio Free Europe (Radio Farda), and other information sources. The free flow of information is an important prerequisite for the free flow of political ideas. The Iranian people need access to information about the activities of Iranian opposition groups, both within and outside Iran, and the plight of dissidents.

The internet is a growing source of unfiltered information for many Iranians, particularly Iranian students. Farsi is reportedly the fourth most popular language used online and there has been a proliferation of political blogs devoted to Iranian issues. The U.S. should consider ways of assisting

Iranians outside the country to establish politically-oriented websites that could be accessed by activists and other interested people inside Iran.

Mobilize Allies to Contain and Deter Iran

The bellicose resurgence of Iran's hardliners, Iran's continued support for terrorism, and the prospective emergence of a nuclear Iran pose threats to many countries. President Ahmadinejad's belligerence gives Washington greater opportunity to mobilize other states, particularly those living in growing shadow of Iranian power. The United States should maintain a strong naval and air presence in the Persian Gulf to deter Iran and strengthen military cooperation with the Gulf States.

The US and its European allies should strengthen military, intelligence, and security cooperation with threatened states, such as Iraq, Turkey, Israel and the members of the Gulf Cooperation Council (Bahrain, Kuwait, Oman, Qatar, Saudi Arabia, and the United Arab Emirates), which was founded in 1981 to provide collective security for Arab states threatened by Iran. Such a coalition could help contain the expansion of Iranian power and possibly would cooperate in facilitating military action, if necessary against Iran.

Washington could also offer to deploy or transfer anti-ballistic missile defense systems to threatened states, enhance joint military planning, and step up joint military and naval exercises. In particular, the U.S. and its allies should stage multilateral naval exercises to demonstrate the will and capability to defeat Tehran's threats to block the Strait of Hormuz, through which flow about one fifth of the world's oil exports.

Prepare for the Use of Military Force as a Last Resort

A strong U.S. military posture is essential to dissuading and deterring Iran from fielding nuclear weapons and supporting terrorism, and when necessary responding decisively and effectively to Iranian threats. To deal with a nuclear or terrorist threat from Iran several military capabilities are particularly important. They include (1) expanding and strengthening the proliferation security initiative; (2) theater missile defense; (3) robust special operations forces and human intelligence (HUMINT) assets; (4) assured access to bases and staging areas in the theater for both special operations and conventional ground, air, and sea forces, and; (5) Energy security preparations.

Proliferation security initiative (PSI) PSI is a multi-national effort to track down and breakup networks that proliferate chemical, biological, and nuclear weapons technologies and materials. The administration should field more modern capabilities that can provide the right intelligence, reconnaissance, surveillance, and interdiction assets for the U.S. military. In particular, modernization of Coast Guard and Naval forces that can help prevent seaborne trafficking of weapons material is vital.

Theater missile defense (TMD) TMD is also essential. Missile defenses provide the means to intercept a ballistic missile in flight and destroy it before the missile can deliver a nuclear warhead to its target. The United States should work with its friends and allies to provide theater missile defense to countries in the region. The United States should continue to pursue a mix of air, land, and sea-based missile defense systems.

Special operations forces and HUMINT   These military and intelligence assets provide the capacity for focused operations against specific targets. Today, these forces are overstretched, performing many missions in the global war on terrorism. The Pentagon must end the use of special operations for training foreign militaries and other tasks that can be done by conventional military units. In addition, the administration must bolster the ranks of the special forces and HUMINT assets that might be required to operate in Iran, ensuring they have the right language skills, area knowledge, and detailed, actionable intelligence.

Theater access   The United States must ensure it retains the means to deploy and sustain forces in the theater. The Pentagon should work to secure a variety of basing options for staging military operations. In addition, the military must have robust means to ensure its ability to operate in the Gulf and defeat "anti-access" weapons that Iran might employ such as cruise missiles, sea-based mines, terrorist attacks, and biological or chemical weapons.

Energy security preparations   In the event of a military clash with the United States, Iran undoubtedly will try to follow through on its threats to close the Strait of Hormuz to oil tankers and disrupt oil exports from other Persian Gulf oil exporters. Washington should take immediate steps to limit the future impact of such oil supply disruptions by working with the Arab gulf states to help them reduce the vulnerability of their oil infrastructure to Iranian military and terrorist attacks; pressing U.S. allies and other oil importers to expand their strategic oil stockpiles; encouraging Saudi Arabia to expand its excess oil production capacity; and asking Saudi Arabia to upgrade the Trans Saudi Arabian pipeline to increase its capacity and make preparations to bring the Iraq-Saudi pipeline back online to reroute oil exports away from the Persian Gulf to the Red Sea oil export terminals.

The Nightmare Scenario of a Nuclear Iran

There is no guaranteed policy that can halt the Iranian nuclear program short of war, and even a military campaign may only delay Iran's acquisition of a nuclear weapons capability. But U.S. policymaking regarding the Iranian nuclear issue inevitably boils down to a search for the least-bad option. And as potentially costly and risky as a preventive war against Iran would be, allowing Iran to acquire nuclear weapons would result in far heavier potential costs and risks.

The U.S. probably would be able to deter Iran from a direct nuclear attack on American or Israeli targets by threatening massive retaliation and the assured destruction of the Iranian regime. But there is a lingering doubt that a leader such as President Ahmadinejad, who reportedly harbors apocalyptic religious beliefs regarding the return of the Mahdi, would have the same cost-benefit calculus about a nuclear war as other leaders. The bellicose leader, who boldly called for Israel to be "wiped off the map" before he acquired a nuclear weapon, might be sorely tempted to follow through on his threat after he acquired one. Moreover, his regime might risk passing nuclear weapons off to terrorist surrogates in hopes of escaping retaliation for a nuclear surprise attack launched by an unknown attacker.

Even if Iran could be deterred from considering such attacks, an Iranian nuclear breakout would undermine the NPT and trigger a nuclear arms race in the Middle East that could lead Saudi Arabia, Egypt, Turkey, Iraq, and Algeria to build or acquire their own nuclear weapons. Each new nuclear power would multiply the risks and uncertainties in an already volatile region.

Iran also may be emboldened to step up its support of terrorism and subversion, calculating that its nuclear capability would deter a military response. An Iranian miscalculation could easily lead to a future military clash with the United States or an American ally that would impose exponentially higher costs than a war with a non-nuclear Iran. Even if it could not threaten a nuclear missile attack on U.S. territory for many years, Tehran could credibly threaten to target the Saudi oil fields with a nuclear weapon, thereby gaining a potent blackmail threat over the world economy. I believe that Senator John McCain was correct when he concisely stated: "There is only one thing worse than the U.S. exercising a military option, and that is a nuclear-armed Iran."

POSTSCRIPT

Is Patient Diplomacy the Best Approach to Iran's Nuclear Program?

The debate over Iran's nuclear program raises a host of important, long-term issues that extend far beyond the immediate concern. One is that fashioning an appropriate response to another country's action is often difficult because you are not sure what is motivating the other country. It is possible that Iran is sincere that it has no intention of building nuclear weapons. It is also possible, and more likely, that Iran's desire to build nuclear weapons is defensive. Recall from the introduction that Iraq had nuclear weapons ambitions and had attacked Iran with chemical weapons in the 1980s. Iran also faces a nuclear-armed Russia to its north and an often hostile and nuclear armed United States, which has troops on Iran's western and eastern flanks. Further, Muslims were and are angry over condemnations of their attempts to build nuclear weapons by countries that simultaneously ignore Israel's possession of a substantial number of nuclear weapons. It may also be that Iran's intentions are aggressive, that it wants nuclear weapons to support its effort to dominate the Persian Gulf region and to enhance its dreams of returning to the glory of the ancient Persian Empire. Alarm was heightened by President Ahmadinejad's statement that Israel is a "disgraceful stain on the Islamic world" that should be "wiped away." Moreover, if Iran is allowed to acquire weapons, that can also lead other countries to similarly stake a claim to a right to develop weapons of mass destruction.

Further complicating matters is the view of Iranians and many others that the United States is at least partly motivated by maintaining as much of its nuclear predominance as possible and forestalling Iranian nuclear weapons that would make a future U.S. action against Iran much more difficult. It strikes a sympathetic chord with some when President Ahmadinejad argues that the United States is hypocritical about nuclear weapons and should promote peace by giving up its own nuclear weapons. There is also a matter of sovereignty, and the belief in Iran and many other smaller countries that outside interventions by U.S.-led, largely Western forces are a form of neoimperialism.

A third set of difficulties arise from the possible implications of any course of action. Peaceful diplomacy could fail, allowing Iran to complete a nuclear weapons system. A deal with Iran would also include substantial concessions, and there are those who reject the idea of rewarding countries, such as Iran and North Korea, for ceasing to violate treaty obligations. But there would also almost surely be negative consequences to attacking Iran, even if the action destroyed its nuclear program. Iran might increase its support of terrorism; seek to disrupt the flow of oil, thus skyrocketing energy prices; and take other actions. The task of occupying Iran would be at least as challenging as doing so has been in Iraq. So beware anyone who argues that it is "clear" that one option is better than others. Each constitutes a roll of the dice betting on a not fully foreseeable future.

For an additional argument for taking a hard stand on Iran, see Efraim Inbar, "The Need to Block a Nuclear Iran," *Middle East Review of International Affairs* (March 2006). Taking the opposite view based on the argument that the United States wants a weak Iran, read Robert Dreyfuss, "Next We Take Tehran," *Mother Jones* (July/August 2006). Also opposed to war with Iran, but from the view that it will be very difficult and perhaps ultimately counter-productive is Richard K. Betts, "The Osirak Fallacy," *The National Interest* 83 (Spring 2006).

ISSUE 15

Is North Korea an
Aggressive Rogue State?

YES: Nicholas Eberstadt, from Testimony during Hearings on "North Korea's WMD Program: Purposes and Implications," before the Committee on International Relations, U.S. House of Representatives, Subcommittee on Asia and the Pacific (February 17, 2005)

NO: Leon V. Sigal, from "A Rogue by Any Other Name," *Foreign Service Journal* (October 2005)

ISSUE SUMMARY

YES: Nicholas Eberstadt, Henry Wendt Scholar in Political Economy at the American Enterprise Institute, Washington, D.C., asserts that North Korea's acquisition of nuclear weapons is designed to facilitate the reunification of the now-divided Korean peninsula under the rule of the Pyongyang regime.

NO: Leon V. Sigal, director of the Northeast Cooperative Security Project at the Social Science Research Council, New York City, contends that since 1988, North Korea has been trying to end its historic enmity against the United States but has been frustrated by U.S. policy.

$\mathbf{A}$s the discussion in Issue 14 of Iran's alleged nuclear weapons indicates, North Korea is one of the vast majority of countries that agreed to the Nuclear Non-Proliferation Treaty (NPT) of 1968. This treaty pledged the North Koreans not to build nuclear weapons or acquire them from another country and to allow the UN's International Atomic Energy Agency (IAEA) to monitor their nuclear facilities to ensure they are being used exclusively for peaceful purposes.

The immediate background of the debate in this issue dates to early 1993 when North Korea announced its withdrawal from the NPT. Alarm about a possible North Korean nuclear weapons program was heightened by media reports that North Korea might already have one or two nuclear weapons. The image of a nuclear-armed North Korea created grave concerns for three reasons. One is the possibility that it might use them in a war on the ever-tense Korean peninsula. A second worry is that the possession of nuclear weapons by North Korea might push both South Korea and Japan to develop their own nuclear arsenals. Third, analysts worried that desperately poor North Korea might be tempted to sell nuclear weapons or components and technology to others.

North Korea's announcement created a confrontation with Washington, which was determined to persuade or force Pyongyang to abide by the NPT. Tensions neared military confrontation in 1994, but then eased when North Korea agreed to remain a party to the NPT, to gradually dismantle its nuclear energy program, and to allow the IAEA inspections. The United States and its allies pledged that they—principally Japan and South Korea—would spend approximately $4 billion to build two nuclear reactors in North Korea that were not capable of producing plutonium for bomb building. The allies also agreed to help meet North Korea's energy needs by annually supplying it with millions of gallons of petroleum until the new reactors were ready.

Tensions soared again beginning in late 2002 when North Korea once again renounced the NPT, expelled IAEA inspectors, and moved to restart its Yongbyon nuclear power plants capable of producing weapons-grade plutonium and uranium. Moreover, the CIA estimated that North Korea had the material to build a half-dozen nuclear weapons within several months and the capacity to create two or more nuclear weapons a year after that. The CIA also warned that Americans faced a "near term" threat from North Korea's extensive missile program.

Washington and Pyongyang accused one another of violating the 1994 agreements, and dark threats volleyed back and forth across the Pacific. Soon, however, the United States eased its stance, recognizing that, first, it was on the edge of war with Iraq, and, second, that war, even a conventional war with North Korea, might unleash massive damage on South Korea, which has population centers (including its capital, Seoul) within artillery range of the border. Third, almost all the other concerned countries, including South Korea and Japan, favored patient diplomacy. That took the form of the Six-Party Talks that began in 2003 among China, Japan, North Korea, Russia, South Korea, and the United States. These negotiations were underway in late 2005 when Nicholas Eberstadt told Congress in the first reading that North Korea is a dangerous dictatorship under Kim Jong-il determined to acquire nuclear weapons and use them to support its drive to dominate the Korean Peninsula. Leon V. Sigal, in the second essay, disagrees that North Korea is a rogue state and argues that much of the problem for the recurring crisis rests with the United States.

YES

Nicholas Eberstadt

North Korea's WMD Program: Purposes and Implications

Last week's declaration by the Democratic People's Republic of Korea (DPRK, aka North Korea) that Pyongyang possessed nuclear weapons, and would hold on to its nuclear arsenal "under any circumstances", was greeted with shock and astonishment around the world. The most surprising part of last week's momentous development, however, was that North Korea's bold move was so widely regarded as genuinely unexpected, both in Washington and abroad.

The North Korean government did not opt to join the world's nuclear weapons club suddenly, on a bizarre and inexplicable whim. To the contrary: last week's announcement represents the entirely predictable culmination of decades of steady, deliberate effort and careful, methodical progress on a multifaceted program of weapons of mass destruction (WMD)—a program that includes work not only on nuclear weapons, but also on chemical weapons, biological weapons, and ballistic missiles.

This WMD program is propelled not by irrational impulses, but rather by a carefully considered strategy—a strategy so deeply wedded to purposes of state that can be described as integrally fused into the very logic of the North Korean system. [1] That strategy, and the logic that undergirds it, may be intuitively unfamiliar to those of us with modern, "globalization era" sensibilities. But unless and until we appreciate the thinking that animates North Korea's WMD quest, we will face the prospect of ever more unpleasant and expensive surprises from Pyongyang.

In a very real sense, the DPRK is a state unlike any other on the face of the earth today. It is a political construct specially and particularly built for three entwined purposes: to conduct a war, to settle a historical grievance, and to fulfill a grand ideological vision.

That *vision* is the reunification of the now-divided Korean peninsula under the unfettered "independent, socialist" rule of the Pyongyang regime— in other words, unconditional annexation of present-day South Korea and liquidation of the government of the Republic of Korea (ROK) so that Kim Jong II & Co. might exercise total command over the entire Korean race (*minjok* in Korean).

U.S. House of Representatives, Subcommittee on Asia and the Pacific, Nicholas Eberstadt (February 17, 2005).

If that vision sounds preposterous and utterly impracticable to us, please understand that it looks very different from Pyongyang. North Korean state-craft has been predicated on that very vision for over half a century. To this day, "Sunshine Policy" and all the rest notwithstanding, Pyongyang grants diplomatic status to only one "government mission" from Seoul: this being the legation of the so-called "South Korean National Democratic Front (SKNDF)", an invented resistance group supposedly based in the South, which regularly uses North Korean airwaves to denounce the Republic of Korea as an illegitimate colonial police state.

The *grievance* is the failure of the famous June 1950 surprise attack against South Korea—an assault that might well have unified all Korea on Pyongyang's terms but for America's unexpected military intervention in defense of the ROK. In Pyongyang's telling, it is only America's continuing and malign imperialistic support that has permitted an otherwise rotten, unstable and utterly irredeemable ROK government to survive since 1950.

The total-mobilization war state that Pyongyang has painfully erected over the decades (at among other costs, the North Korean famine of the 1990s) is a response to this grievance, and an instrument for fulfilling this vision. And the *war* that North Korea has prepared for is not some future theoretical contingency. Quite the contrary: in the view of North Korean leaders, their country is at war today, here and now.

Although we ourselves are sometimes inattentive to it, the fact of the matter is that the Korean War's battles were only halted through a cease-fire agreement (the Armistice of 1953)—there has never been a peace treaty bring-ing the hostilities to a formal and conclusive end. The Korean War is, from the DPRK's standpoint, an *ongoing* war—and North Korea's leadership is commit-ted to an eventual, unconditional victory in that war, however long that may take, however much that may cost.

Against all odds, North Korean leadership still attempts to support a vast conventional military force—long rehearsed for an anticipated reprise of June 1950—on a dysfunctional and failing Soviet-type economy. Despite the ingenu-ity and bravery of North Korean People's Army officers and soldiers, this force cannot hope to prevail over the combined ROK-U.S. alliance that awaits them on the other side of the DMZ. Thus the neutralization, and effective removal, of the United States and the U.S. alliance system from the Korean equation is utterly essential from Pyongyang's perspective.

That objective, however, cannot be achieved by the DPRK's conventional capabilities—today or in any foreseeable future. To deter, coerce, and punish the United States, the DPRK must possess nuclear weaponry and the ballistic missiles capable of delivering these into the heart of the American enemy. This central strategic fact explains why North Korea has been assiduously pursuing its nuclear development and missile development programs for over thirty years—at terrible expense to its people's livelihood, and despite all adverse repercussions on its international relations.

Although Pyongyang rails against "globalization" in other contexts, North Korea's own conception of the uses of WMD are fully "globalized." Thanks largely (though not exclusively) to its short-range "SCUD"-style missiles and bio-chemical weapons, primarily targeted on South Korea, Pyongyang can always remind counterparts in the Blue House that the enormous metropolis of Seoul is a hostage to fate, to be destroyed at a moment on Kim Jong Il's say-so. Intermediate "No Dong" type missiles capable of striking Japan (and American bases in Japan) with nuclear warheads put Japanese political leaders on permanent warning of the possible costs of incurring North Korea's anger, and the potential dangers of siding with the United States in any time of Peninsular crisis. Finally, long-range missiles of the improved "Taepo Dong" variety may be capable of striking the United States mainland, now or in the relatively near future. [2]

Several important implications flow from the DPRK's conception of, and strategy for, its WMD program.

First, continuing and escalating international tensions are not the accidental and unwelcome side-effects of the program: they are instead its central purpose. Simply stated, the DPRK's growing WMD arsenal, and the threats it permits the North Korean regime to pose to other governments, are the key to the political and economic prizes Pyongyang intends to extract from an otherwise hostile and unwilling world.

Second, WMD threats—and especially nuclear and missile threats—have *already* been used by North Korea with great success: as an instrument for extracting *de facto* international extortion payments from the United States and its allies, and as a lever of forcing the United States to "engage" Pyongyang diplomatically, and on Pyongyang's own terms. [3]

The greatest potential dividends for North Korean nuclear and ballistic diplomacy, however, still lie in store—and this bring us to a third point. For half a century and more U.S. security policy has been charged with imposing "deterrence" upon Pyongyang. Shouldn't we expect that Pyongyang has also been thinking about how to "deter" the U.S. over those same long decades?

Nuclear weapons (especially long-range nuclear missiles) might well answer the "deterrence question" for the North Korean state, as former Secretary of Defense William J. Perry incisively recognized in his 1999 "Perry Process" report: faced with the risk of nuclear attack on the U.S. mainland, he warned, Washington might hesitate at a time of crisis in the Korean peninsula. But if Washington's security commitment to the ROK were not credible in a crisis, the military alliance would be hollow: and vulnerable to collapse under the weight of its own internal contradictions. North Korea's WMD program, in short, may be the regime's best hope for achieving its long-cherished objectives of breaking the U.S.-ROK military alliance, and forcing American troops out of the Korean peninsula.

Fourth, those who hope for a "win-win" solution to the North Korean nuclear impasse must recognize the plain fact that Pyongyang does not now engage in "win-win" bargaining, and never has. The historical record is completely clear: Pyongyang believes in "zero-sum" solutions, preferring outcomes that entail not only DPRK victories, but also face-losing setbacks for its opponents. From the DPRK's perspective, "win-win" solutions are not only impractical—they leave adversaries unnecessarily strong—but actually immoral.

Finally, those who believe that a peaceful and voluntary de-nuclearization of the DPRK is still possible through yet further rounds of international "conference diplomacy", or through some future "negotiating breakthrough," must be ready to consider what such an outcome would look from North Korea today—that is to say, from the standpoint of the real existing North Korean state, not some imaginary DPRK we'd rather be talking to.

No matter how large the pay-off package, no matter how broad and comprehensive the attendant international formula for recognition and security, the Western desideratum of "complete verifiable irreversible denuclearization" (CVID) would irrevocably consign North Korea to a world in which it is the metrics of peaceful international competition that matter—and thus irrevocably to a role in international affairs for the DPRK more in consonance with the size of its GNP. No North Korean leader is likely to mistake such a proposal for a bargain.

Even worse from Pyongyang's standpoint: a genuine agreement to denuclearize might well threaten to undermine the authority and legitimacy of the North Korean state. Since its founding in 1948, the DPRK has demanded terrible and continuing sacrifices from its population—but it has always justified these in the name of its historic vision for reunifying the Korean race. Today, however, forswearing its WMD options would be tantamount to forswearing the claim to unify the Korean peninsula on Pyongyang's own terms. Shorn of its legitimating vision, what then, exactly, would be the rationale for absolutist North Korean rule?

The unsettling thrust of this analysis is not just that North Korean leadership today may positively prefer a strategy that augments the government's WMD capabilities: it may also positively fear a strategy that does anything less.

To conclude: the task now before us is to make the world safe *from the DPRK*. Kim Jong Il, by contrast, is doing his best to make the world safe *for the DPRK*. Making the world safe *from* North Korea promises to be a difficult, expensive, and dangerous undertaking. For America and her allies, however, the costs and dangers of making the world safe *for* North Korea stand to be incalculably higher.

Notes

1. Parts of this testimony draw upon the author's contributions to a recent study by the National Institute for Public Policy (NIPP) on the North Korean challenge to U.S. missile defense. Thanks go to NIPP's Dr. Keith A. Payne and Amb. David J. Smith for supporting and encouraging my research in that effort.
2. There is no indication, incidentally, that North Korean decision-makers view WMD as "special weapons," to be held in reserve—on the contrary, missiles and nuclear devices seem to figure integrally in North Korean official thinking and are *already* being used on a regular basis in North Korean statecraft, as the government's ongoing foray's in "blackmail diplomacy" attest. And despite Pyongyang's emphasis of race doctrine, there is no indication

whatsoever that North Korean leadership would hesitate to use such weapons on *minjok*—race brothers—in South Korea. Pyongyang did not blink at starving perhaps one million of its *own* people for reasons of state in the 1990s. It regards the South Korean state as a cancerous monstrosity, and those who support it as corrupt and worthless national traitors.

3. Despite the North Korean regime's seemingly freakish face to the world, North Korean leadership's capabilities for making subtle and skillful calculations is underscored by the bottom line in its negotiations with the United States government over the past decade. Between 1995 and 2004, by calculations of the Congressional Research Service, Pyongyang secured more than $1 billion in foreign aid from the U.S.—a state the DPRK regards as its prime international enemy.

Leon V. Sigal    **NO**

A Rogue by Any Other Name

What's in a name? Plenty, if that name is "rogue state" or "pariah state." Rogue states, or pariahs with aggressive intent, are said to be the main proliferation menace in the world. Yet the United States does not brand Pakistan with either of those labels, even though it may have done more than any other country to enable other states to obtain nuclear arms.

North Korea has not been as fortunate as Pakistan. To many Americans, the Democratic People's Republic of Korea is the archetypal rogue state: implacable and inimical, with a master plan to deceive the world and acquire nuclear weapons. Its one-man rule, its internal regimentation and its dogmatism would alienate any freedom-loving American. Pyongyang's harsh diatribes against Washington, its penchant for brinkmanship and its nasty habit of floating concessions on a sea of threats all continue to antagonize even the most level-headed observers. So did its past acts of terrorism, like the 1983 bombing in Rangoon that barely missed South Korea's President Chun Doohwan and killed 17 members of his entourage.

Yes, in many respects, North Korea makes a perfect foe. Yet ever since 1988, it has been trying to end its historic enmity against the United States. Beginning in that year, it stopped sponsoring terrorist acts against other states, and even softened its anti-American rhetoric. Nevertheless, the image of a rogue state ruled by a latter-day Genghis Khan has been difficult to shake, leaving the North an easy target for demonization.

Name-calling does more than foster a domestic political climate of hostility. It also infects official thinking. Epithets like "rogue" or "pariah" become a pernicious premise of U.S. policy and intelligence estimates, blinding officials to the motives of states for acquiring nuclear weapons. They predispose American policymakers to take a coercive approach to stopping the spread of nuclear arms, threatening isolation, economic sanctions and military force. And they impede diplomatic give-and-take, which is the best way to probe the intentions of such states and try to induce them to change course.

After all, a rogue is a criminal, and the only way to handle criminals is to punish them.

Yet, again and again, the crime-and-punishment approach has failed to dissuade states from seeking their own nuclear arsenals. By contrast, American reassurances and inducements have a long record of accomplishment. They helped convince South Korea, Taiwan, Sweden, Brazil, Argentina, South Africa,

From *Foreign Service Journal*, October 2005, pp. 37–38, 40–44. Copyright © 2005 by American Foreign Service Association. Reprinted by permission.

Ukraine, Belarus and Kazakhstan to abandon their nuclear ambitions. Only with Iraq and Pakistan did such efforts fail.

The Good Cop Approach

Branding potential proliferators as rogue states actually gets in the way of disarming them. Washington would be better off referring to them by a more appropriate name—perhaps "insecure states"—and treating them accordingly. That means offering encouragement and incentives instead of threats to get such governments to stop arming, and moving to contain and deter them only if that approach fails.

Hard-liners dismiss such talk as sympathy for the aggressor. They take it on faith, for example, that Pyongyang is motivated by paranoid hostility to America and will not stop its campaign to become a full-fledged nuclear power. So what if it is reaching out to its neighbors and the world and establishing diplomatic ties with them? That's just a tactic. So what if it agreed to freeze its plutonium program in 1994—the only nuclear weapons program it then had? That was just a ruse to dupe the credulous while it began acquiring the means to enrich uranium.

So what if the DPRK is now offering to freeze and dismantle its nuclear weapons programs—if only the United States will normalize political and economic relations and provide assurances that it won't attack, interfere in its internal affairs, or impede its economic development by maintaining sanctions and discouraging aid and investment from its neighbors? Even to discuss such proposals, say the hard-liners, would amount to coddling criminals, or in their favorite turn of phrase, rewarding bad behavior.

But the trouble is that by not upholding the 1994 Agreed Framework, the United States failed to reward North Korea's good behavior, even though the accord gave Washington what it most wanted up front: a freeze of Pyongyang's plutonium production, a program that by now could have generated enough nuclear material for at least 50 bombs. But when the Republicans won control of Congress just days after the October 1994 accord was signed, they quickly denounced the deal as appeasement. Shying away from taking them on, the Clinton administration backpedaled on implementing the agreement. As a result, Washington did little easing of sanctions until 2000. Having pledged to provide two nuclear power plants "by a target date of 2003," it did not even pour concrete for the first foundation until August 2002. It did deliver heavy fuel oil as promised, but seldom on schedule. Above all, it did not live up to its commitment in Article II of the accord to "move toward full normalization of political and economic relations"—to end enmity and lift sanctions.

When Washington was slow to fulfill the terms of the accord, Pyongyang threatened to break out of it in 1997. Its acquisition of gas centrifuges to enrich uranium from Pakistan began soon thereafter. Yet that was a pilot program, not the operational capability U.S. intelligence says it moved to acquire in 2001 after the Bush administration refused talks and instead disclosed that the North was a target for nuclear attack. However, U.S. hard-liners took it as conclusive evidence (as if they needed any) that North Korea was hellbent on arming. After confronting Pyongyang over enrichment in October 2002, Washington retaliated by halting shipment of heavy fuel oil promised under the Agreed Framework.

The Road to Pyongyang

Hard-liners were convinced that Iraq's fate would chasten North Korea. On the day Saddam Hussein's statue was toppled from its pedestal in Baghdad, Under Secretary of State John Bolton declared, "We are hopeful that a number of regimes will draw the appropriate lesson from Iraq."

Yet, far from becoming more pliable, North Korea became more determined to arm itself—and will remain so until the United States changes course. In 2003, as U.S. troops were deploying to the Persian Gulf, Pyongyang challenged Washington by lighting two nuclear fuses. It resumed reprocessing to extract plutonium from nuclear fuel rods that it had removed from its reactor in 1994 but had stored since then at Yongbyon under international inspectors' scrutiny. And it resumed making plutonium-laden spent fuel by refueling and restarting its nuclear reactor.

In an official statement on the start of the war in March 2003, North Korea noted that the United States had first demanded that Iraq submit to inspections, and it had. The United States next demanded that Baghdad disarm, and it began to do so. The United States then attacked it anyway. "This suggests that even the signing of a non-aggression treaty with the U.S. would not help avert war," a DPRK Foreign Ministry spokesman said on April 6, 2003. "Only military deterrent force, supported by ultra-modern weapons, can avert a war and protect the security of the nation. This is the lesson drawn from the Iraqi war."

Pyongyang's rhetoric and tactics convinced many in Washington that it was determined to arm and should therefore be punished for breaking its commitments. Other policy-makers interpreted its actions as extortion, intended to secure economic aid without giving up anything in return. In fact, it was doing neither, but simply playing tit for tat—cooperating whenever Washington cooperated and retaliating when Washington reneged. It still is.

Hard-liners call this approach blackmail. But that's a misnomer. It's blackmail when a man menaces you with a baseball bat and demands that you hand over your wallet—and you do. It's not blackmail when he hands you his bat and says, let's play ball, and you don't. That's what North Korea did after October 1994 and says it is willing to do again now.

Skeptics may ask why we should believe Pyongyang would be willing to re-engage in the face of implacable hostility from Washington. One answer lies in President Kim Jong Il's October 2001 decision to reform his country's moribund economy, a policy he formally promulgated in July 2002. As a result of that policy shift, the North Korean economy has begun to revive—but reform cannot succeed without a political accommodation with the United States, Japan and South Korea that facilitates reallocation of resources from military use and attracts aid and investment from the outside.

Misreading the Situation

In the belief that North Korea was on the verge of collapse, however, Bush administration hard-liners kept pushing for an economic embargo and naval blockade to strangle it to death. Yet all the North's neighbors think that regime change can best be achieved through prolonged engagement. They know that attempts to isolate and starve Pyongyang will provoke it to arm even faster, which is why they won't try. Instead, they have pursued talks of their own with North Korea, which persuaded them that it seems willing to deal.

So why, in contrast, have U.S. policy-makers been so unwilling to countenance negotiating with North Korea before reaching for their guns? For many, it is a blank screen on which to project their own predispositions and prejudices. Given the endemic uncertainty about the DPRK's nuclear capabilities and intentions, the years of hostility and the deep mistrust on both sides, the image of North Korea as a rogue state filled the vacuum of knowledge.

A prudent response to uncertainty would have been to treat estimates of North Korean nuclear capabilities and intentions as rough guesses rather than facts, and to probe Pyongyang's intentions through diplomatic give-and-take without running a high risk of war. The hard-liners' response, instead, has been to leak worst-case assessments and pursue rash policies—threats of political isolation and economic coercion, even armed force.

By impeding a cooperative solution, the unilateralists have put Washington on a collision course not just with Pyongyang but, more importantly, with America's allies in Asia. This approach threatens to erode political support for the alliance in South Korea and Japan and jeopardize the U.S. troop presence in the region. In fact, the hard-liners would apparently rather pick a fight with China than negotiate with North Korea.

Their intransigence has been the catalyst for unprecedented cooperation in Northeast Asia aimed at reining in the United States. The January 2003 Japan-Russia summit meeting and the Japan-DPRK summit meetings of 2002 and 2004 should be seen in this light, as should South Korea's warming relations with China. Given the history of antagonism in the region, such cooperation would have seemed unthinkable just a few short years ago.

"Action for Action"

The best way for the United States to avoid further erosion in its position in the region is to negotiate in earnest with North Korea and test whether it makes a deal and lives up to it.

An agreement in principle stating what each side wants at the end is a useful starting point. North Korea needs to agree to rid itself of its nuclear weapons programs and abandon plans to build longer-range missiles. The United States, in turn, should join other nations in providing written security assurances and move to normalize relations as the North eliminates its weapons and the means of making them.

The most urgent need for the United States is to restore inspectors' control over the plutonium that North Korea removed from its reactor at

Yongbyon in 1994, and again earlier this year, and to shut down that reactor to keep it from generating more plutonium in its spent fuel. Shutting down and resealing the DPRK's reprocessing plant is another priority.

Satellites and other technical means can monitor a freeze of activity at the Yongbyon reactor and reprocessing plant, though not enrichment sites at unknown locations. Inspections of these sites, as desirable as they are, will take time to arrange. But they can wait: U.S. intelligence estimates the North cannot produce much highly enriched uranium until later in this decade. Conversely, delaying a freeze to negotiate a detailed verifiable agreement on enrichment will simply allow time for Pyongyang to generate more plutonium, fabricate bombs and increase its negotiating leverage.

The key to verification is what the International Atomic Energy Agency calls an "initial declaration," listing all the North's nuclear facilities, equipment and fissile material, in whatever form they may now be. Once that declaration is cross-checked against what U.S. intelligence has already ascertained, elimination can begin. The time for challenge inspections will come, but it is not yet here. Why waste time and bargaining chips negotiating to verify that the North has what it says it has when the aim is to get rid of its weapons programs altogether?

Pyongyang's missile program can be dealt with in parallel. The first priority is what the North offered in Beijing—a ban on missile test launches and exports of missile technology. Next is to negotiate the dismantling of missiles and production sites.

Washington will have to reciprocate for each of these steps, of course. It will not get something for nothing. Words alone will not placate Pyongyang. Given the deep mistrust on both sides, and the belief on each side that the other reneged on the Agreed Framework, this cautious approach makes sense. Each side needs concrete results from the other to enable it to build trust and move forward.

The good news is that Pyongyang seems ready to deal. It says it wants to exchange "words for words" and "action for action." By "words for words" it means an agreement in principle that if Washington "gives up its hostile policy," it will "transparently renounce all nuclear-weapons related programs." By "action for action," it means phased, reciprocal steps. To start, it is offering a freeze on "all the facilities related to nuclear weapons," shutting down its nuclear reactor and reprocessing plant at Yongbyon. Whether Pyongyang has "facilities" to enrich uranium or is in the process of building them it has yet to clarify. That discussion could begin if Washington engages in direct dialogue with its foe.

Most important, the proposed freeze covers "even products achieved through reprocessing," which meant putting the plutonium acquired in 1994—five to six bombs' worth—back under inspection. In return, Pyongyang wants Washington to "participate" in providing heavy fuel oil promised under the Agreed Framework, take it off the list of "state sponsors of terrorism" and lift related sanctions. North Korea's negotiating stance is intended to drive home the point that if the United States remains its foe, it feels threatened and will seek nuclear arms to counter that threat. Conversely, if the United States takes steps to end its enmity, it will reciprocate.

North Korea insists on dealing directly with the United States, whether or not China, South Korea, Japan and Russia are also at the negotiating table, because none of them can provide such assurances on behalf of the United States. Direct dialogue is also the least a state can do to end enmity. To refuse to talk face-to-face is to deny the DPRK's legitimacy as a state.

Testing the Waters

For the past four years the United States has watched North Korea arm without trying what South Korea and Japan think just might get it to stop: negotiating in earnest. Instead, the Bush administration prefers to demonize North Korea as a rogue state and stick with a crime-and-punishment approach to disarming it. This is not surprising, given that most hard-liners are unilateralists who could not care less what allies think. (*As the* Journal *went to press, news came of a tentative agreement at the six-party talks.*)

The Bush administration insists that the six-party talks are succeeding in isolating North Korea and that additional pressure by China and others will bring it to heel. And if not, well, the prospect of a nuclear-armed Pyongyang will at least drive Seoul and Tokyo further into Washington's arms.

But many Asians see a negotiated resolution as both desirable and possible. Indeed, the Washington hard-liners' uncompromising stance has led some in Seoul and Tokyo to wonder whether they can rely on the U.S. for their security. That suspicion is threatening to unravel U.S. alliances in Northeast Asia and enhance China's influence there. Indeed, far from isolating the North, Washington is itself becoming odd man out in the region, dissipating political support for pressuring Pyongyang and enhancing China's influence.

The great divide in American foreign policy thinking is between those who believe that to get its way in the world the United States has to push other countries around, and those who think that cooperation can sometimes reduce threats to security.

Does Pyongyang mean what it says? The surest way to find out is sustained diplomatic give-and-take. That will require the United States to make a strategic decision to spell out the steps it is prepared to take to end enmity if North Korea eliminates its nuclear weapons programs—and this time carry them out.

POSTSCRIPT

Is North Korea an Aggressive Rogue State?

As of this writing, the situation related to North Korea has deteriorated seriously. North Korea broke off the Six-Party Talks in late 2005 after Washington pressured a bank in Macau, China, to freeze North Korean funds it held. The U.S. Treasury department charged that the funds were part of a money-laundering scheme connected with Pyongyang's involvement in counterfeiting U.S. currency and selling narcotics. Pyongyang rejected the accusations. Tensions grew further in July 2006 when North Korea launched seven missiles probably capable of carrying nuclear warheads. Six were medium-range missiles and splashed down in the Sea of Japan. They carried a clear warning to Japan. The seventh missile, a longer-range Taepodong-2 that some analysts believe could reach the U.S. West Coast, failed 40 seconds into its flight. Washington let it be known that a retest of a Taepodong-2 might lead to a U.S. effort to intercept and destroy it using the still unproven U.S. ballistic-missile defense system. Then bringing the crisis to perhaps its worse point in its 12-year history, North Korea tested a nuclear weapon in early October 2006. Strong condemnation poured in from every side, even from China, one of the few countries generally supportive of Pyongyang. Japan and the United States were among the harshest critics. President Bush labeled the test a "provocative act" and a "threat to international peace and security," and the United States asked for an emergency meeting of the UN Security Council to impose sanctions including international inspections of all cargo moving into and out of North Korea to look for weapons-related material. That precaution highlighted the concern that the North Koreans would try to earn desperately needed outside funds by selling nuclear technology and perhaps even weapons to other countries and even to terrorists. Bush warned that doing so "would be considered a grave threat to the United States," which "would hold North Korea fully accountable of the consequences of such action."

How subsequent events unfolded is part of the ongoing saga that you should catch up on. A good source for the U.S. perspective is the U.S. State department's Bureau of East Asian and Pacific Affairs http://www.state.gov/p/eap/. North Korea's home page is at http://www.korea-dpr.com/, but a better source for the government's view is the Korean Central New Agency at http://www.kcna.co.jp/. Taking the view that tensions with North Korea and Iran are the result of countries seeking nuclear weapons to deter U.S. aggression and post-9/11 United States heightened its determination not to be threatened by weapons of mass destruction is Derek D. Smith, *Deterring America: Rogue States and the Proliferation of Weapons of Mass Destruction* (Cambridge University

Press, 2006). The most important question, of course, is how to address the issue. One discussion of various strategies can be found in Victor D. Cha (Author), David C. Kang, *Nuclear North Korea: A Debate on Engagement Strategies* (Columbia University Press, 2005). Also read an article on an overall peace strategy for the Korean Peninsula by then South Korean foreign minister and, beginning on January 1, 2007, United Nations Secretary General Ban Ki-moon, "For Permanent Peace," *Harvard International Review* (Summer 2006).

Internet References . . .

The United Nations Department of Peacekeeping Operations

This UN site is the gateway to not only all the functions of the United Nations, but also to many associated agencies.

http://www.un.org/

The International Law Association

The International Law Association, which is currently headquartered in London, was founded in Brussels in 1873. Its objectives, under its constitution, include the "study, elucidation and advancement of international law, public and private, the study of comparative law, the making of proposals for the solution of conflicts of law and for the unification of law, and the furthering of international understanding and goodwill."

http://www.ila-hq.org

United Nations Treaty Collection

The United Nations Treaty Collection is a collection of 30,000 treaties, addenda, and other items related to treaties and international agreements that have been filed with the UN Secretariat since 1946. The collection includes the texts of treaties in their original language(s) and English and French translations.

http://untreaty.un.org

Jurist: Terrorism Law and Policy

This site maintained by the University of Pittsburgh is a good source for the many complex legal issues involved in defining and combating terrorism.

http://jurist.law.pitt.edu/terrorism/htm

International Law and Organization Issues

*P*art *of the process of globalization is the increase in scope and importance of both international law and international organizations. The issues in this section represent some of the controversies involved with the expansion of international law and organizations into the realm of military security. Issues here relate to increasing international organizations' responsibility for security, the effectiveness of international financial organizations, and the proposal to authorize international courts to judge those who are accused of war crimes.*

- Does the United Nations Deserve Support?

- Is U.S. Refusal to Join the International Criminal Court Wise?

- Should Accused Terrorists Have Legal Rights Similar to Prisoners of War?

ISSUE 16

Does the United Nations Deserve Support?

YES: Betty McCollum, from Address to the Board of Directors, United Nations Association of the United States of America (UNA-USA) (June 8, 2006)

NO: Clifford D. May, from "The United Nations: Realities and Responses," Commentary on the Web site of the Foundation for the Defense of Democracy (January 23, 2005)

ISSUE SUMMARY

YES: Betty McCollum, member of the United States House of Representatives (D-MN), admits that the United Nations has flaws and needs reforms, but argues that the world is far better off than it would be if the UN did not exist.

NO: Clifford D. May, president of the Foundation for the Defense of Democracy, argues that the UN has largely been a failure, that the prospects to reform it are dim, and that the United States and other democracies should create a new international organization to promote global peace, prosperity, and democracy.

T he United Nations was established in 1945 as a reaction to the failure of its predecessor, the League of Nations, to prevent World War II with its horrendous destruction of life and property. From this perspective, founding the UN in 1945 represented something akin to a sinner resolving to reform. In this case, a world that had just barely survived a ghastly experience pledged to organize itself to preserve the peace and improve humanity.

More than six decades later, international violence continues, global justice and respect for international law remain goals rather than reality, and grievous economic and social ills still afflict the world. Further, people have come to recognize the environmental threats the world faces, but many of these continue to worsen rather than be arrested or reversed through international cooperation. Does the United Nations continue to merit or support?

Despite the many high-flown phrases in its Charter, the UN has been and remains principally a political organization in which the countries of the world maneuver to advance their political agendas. For example, the United States, which was the prime mover behind the creation of the UN, worked to make the Security Council the focus of UN collective security decision making involving military action, economic sanctions, and other coercive measures. Then to ensure its central role, the United States (along with its wartime allies the British, Chinese, French, and Russians/Soviets) secured a permanent seat on the 15-country council and also established the ability of these permanent members to cast a veto and with their one vote halt UN action, block the selection of the UN secretary general, and otherwise bring many UN functions to a halt.

For a quarter century most UN members were U.S. allies. This allowed Washington to usually dominate the UN, although the Soviets had become enemies and often used their veto to block action. However, the UN's membership began to change increasingly during the 1960s and 1970s when dozens of former colonies in Africa, Asia, and elsewhere gained independence and joined the UN as sovereign countries. These newer member-countries often saw things differently than the United States, and by the 1980s the U.S. ability to almost muster a majority in the UN General Assembly had waned. American influence in the Security Council also ebbed. China's seat in the UN and on the council was shifted from the government on Taiwan to the communist government in Beijing in 1972, and France became increasingly independent-minded and critical of U.S. policy.

Official U.S. frustration with the UN intensified prior to the U.S. invasion of Iraq in March 2003 due to President George W. Bush's inability to win Security Council support for military action. "I think unless the United Nations shows some backbone and courage, it could render the Security Council irrelevant," an irritated Bush warned. There have also been widespread charges that the UN's bureaucracy is excessive and inefficient. Partly in reaction to that, Congress in 2002 mandated a 12-percent reduction in the percentage of the basic UN budget funded by the United States and has rarely appropriated enough money to even meet the new, lower figure. Even more recently, several scandals have rocked the UN. From 1996 to 2003, it ran an "oil-for-food" program that permitted Iraq to sell oil and use the receipts to buy food, medicine, and other humanitarian supplies under UN supervision. Persistent rumors about corruption in the $67 billion program led to an investigation in 2004 that found substantial corruption, including the program administrator taking bribes to ignore Iraq diverting huge sums to the purchase of munitions and other banned uses. The UN's image was further sullied in 2004 when evidence came to light of UN peacekeeping troops and personnel trading food and other necessities of life to obtain sex from those they were supposedly protecting.

What should be done? In the first reading, Betty McCollum argues that the UN is a worthwhile organization, and that it can and should be reformed to make it even better. Clifford May disagrees in the second reading. He rejects not only the UN itself as flawed, but the very premise on which it was founded as wanting. He recommends abandoning the UN in favor of a league of democracies.

YES

Betty McCollum

Address to the United Nations Association of the United States of America

I am an advocate for the UN and strong supporter of active U.S. engagement and leadership at the UN—including paying our dues—in full and on time. I believe in the mission and I support the tremendous work of the UN as it impacts people in every corner of the world.

I have seen the work and I admire the men and women who dedicate their lives to working for peace, security, development and human rights. These are people to be admired for their courage, their dedication and their willingness to work in the most dangerous and desperate situations confronting mankind.

Your work [as members of the United Nations Association of the United States of America]—[serving] as advocates, educators and opinion leaders—on behalf of important global issues and the work of the UN is vitally important. . . . It is not easy to carry out this mission here on the Hill in what are too often hostile political conditions, but you must not be deterred. The American people need to be educated, informed and then reminded again and again about the tremendous value and benefit the UN provides our nation and our citizens.

As you know, I am from Minnesota. . . . I am very proud to represent St. Paul, Minnesota here in Congress. We are a progressive, diverse and outward looking community that welcomes immigrants and refugees as well as a constant in migration from rural Minnesota of retiring Norwegian bachelor farmers searching for a new life in the big city.

At the same time, we have a unique connection to the United Nations— we could call it a "bi-polar" connection. St. Paul is the home of a wonderful institution of higher learning, Macalester College, which claims [UN Secretary General] Kofi Annan as a distinguished alumnus. Many of us are very proud to have this special connection to the Secretary General.

Minnesota is clearly the heartland of America—and maybe this does put us at the heart of the battle regarding the domestic political debate surrounding the UN. Which brings me to the "speech"—which some detractors will likely call the 6-6-6 speech since it was delivered on the sixth day of the six month of this century's sixth year.

United Nations Association of the United States of America, by Betty McCollum (June 8, 2006).

Of course, I am referring to the speech made earlier this week by [UN] Deputy Secretary General Mark Malloch Brown that has stirred controversy and has been harshly criticized by [U.S.] Ambassador [to the United Nations John R.] Bolton in the news today. I've read the Deputy Secretary General's speech and I would call it a brave speech, an accurate speech and a speech that reflects the sentiments of the millions of Americans who believe the United States should be a responsible super-"partner"—as well as superpower and leader of the free world.

I am sure it was shocking to Ambassador Bolton when the organization that has been his personal punching bag for so long punched back.

Mr. Malloch Brown described the information disseminated to the American public regarding the work of the UN this way, "much of the public discourse that reaches the U.S. heartland has been largely abandoned to its loudest detractors such as Rush Limbaugh and Fox News," and may I add a certain Minnesota senator to that list.

Mr. Malloch Brown is right and those of us who care about the UN and its vital role in the world need to speak up and reach out to the American people—as your organization does.

In my opinion, Mr. Malloch Brown's speech was an honest and legitimate assessment.

The world's greatest multilateral organization is constantly being attacked and undermined by politicians in Washington for short-term political gain. I say this because there are voices in Congress who wish to dissolve the UN. There are others who wish to render it impotent. Still others wish to make the UN an extension of American power—a multilateral institution run by Washington. Others, legitimately, wish to see the UN succeed but have used excessively punitive and heavy-handed approaches to achieve their policy objectives.

After sixty years, of course the United Nations needs reforming. We all agree on that.

And, no one understands that better than Secretary General Annan and Mr. Malloch Brown who have made constructive recommendations and are working to make positive changes. They have dedicated their professional lives to the UN and they—along with all of us—want to see the organization strong, effective, transparent and relevant to the tremendous challenges facing our world.

It disturbs and disappoints me greatly to hear the empty rhetoric about the UN coming from voices here in Congress. An honest and forthright policy critique is absolutely necessary—regarding the UN as well as U.S. foreign policy—here in Congress. This critique needs to be done in a constructive fashion both in Washington among policy makers and in New York among member states. Dialogue, not destruction, is the answer.

Unfortunately, raw power, confrontation and a disregard for dialogue have become the norm in Washington. Why would Congress or the administration treat the UN any differently than we treat each other? Clearly, confrontation was the intended message when the president sent our permanent representative to New York to represent the United States without the consent of the U.S.

Senate. As a nation we can do better, which I believe means leading the world towards consensus based solutions, without unilateral threats or tantrums.

My tone and cynicism is harsh and for this I apologize, but I came to Washington in January 2001—three weeks before President Bush was sworn in. I came to Washington believing we are the United Nations. By this I mean the UN is only as effective and meaningful as the members who comprise the body—especially the United States.

The U.S. is a member state. We have a permanent seat on the Security Council. We have the veto. But this superpower doesn't get to win all the time. When we are confronting the challenges of today's world—Darfur, avian influenza, Iran's nuclear program, the South Asia tsunami, Middle East peace—it should never be about winning. It should be about saving lives, preventing conflict, promoting peace, building trust, and restoring hope. We need the world. The world needs us. And, the world and the U.S. need the UN.

Politicians in Washington can bash and berate the UN, but let's face it, it is coming off pretty empty to the rest of the world and the hypocrisy is now far too transparent.

At one time I believe some nine congressional committees were investigating the oil-for-food scandal. Yet, the U.S. government cannot account for $8.8 billion in Iraq that was under the control of the Coalition Provisional Authority.

Ambassador Bolton can condemn the composition of the new UN Human Rights Council on legitimate grounds. But how does he reconcile Guantanamo Bay [the U.S. naval base where many terrorist suspects are imprisoned], Abu Ghraib [the prison in Iraq where U.S. service personnel abused Iraqi prisoners], and the vile practice of extraordinary rendition with the values stated in the Universal Declaration of Human Rights? He can't, because torture and the mistreatment of prisoners are indefensible.

I admit I have been a harsh critic of the unilateral approach to foreign policy over and over again advanced by this White House. I have called the decision and deception that led our nation to war in Iraq the greatest foreign policy disaster in American history. And, as we all know, it's not even close to being over yet.

But I commend Secretary [of State Condoleezza] Rice for her recent leadership with the Quartet [an informal consultative group consisting of the United States, the United Nations, the European Union, and Russia seeking diplomatic solutions to tensions in the Middle East]. Finally, after so much destructive unilateral decision making, Secretary Rice is effectively working multilaterally to confront Hamas and avoid a crisis in the Middle East. Her efforts and the efforts of the Quartet are to be commended and supported.

Yet only two weeks ago in the House of Representatives we again demonstrated a shameful disdain for the UN. The House passed a punitive sanctions bill that risks fomenting a humanitarian crisis among the Palestinian people and contains language requiring mandatory withholding of U.S. contributions to the United Nations unless reforms to UN programs operating in the Palestinian Authority are certified by our president. Here again, Congress is targeting our partner in the Quartet, and sending the message that the UN, along with Hamas, is the enemy. Sadly, only 47 of us did not support this bill.

The critics, the skeptics, and the unilateralists will never be comfortable with multilateral cooperation. It is hard work that requires listening, dialogue, diplomacy, consensus building and, often times, compromise. Tragically, in this Congress the concept of compromise and working to find shared success reflects weakness rather than necessary reality. The inability to compromise is obvious and reflected in the poor quality of the legislation coming out of Congress.

Today, we have the Security Council's permanent members along with Germany engaging Iran. This isn't weakness, this is the strength of multilateral diplomacy at work and for the sake of the entire world I pray that it does work.

Let me shift focus for a moment and say that the bluster and bashing and threats of funding cuts to the UN by this Congress and the White House comes at a cost—a real human cost.

Do you think for one second that the 1.3 billion people around the world who live on a dollar a day—living in misery and fear and hopelessness care about the speech given by the Deputy Secretary General or Ambassador Bolton's outrage [at the speech]?

What about the 30,000 parents around the world who today watched their child die from a preventable or treatable disease?

Or, the thousands of children who today became orphans because their parent died of AIDS?

For tens of millions of people—maybe even a billion—every day is about survival.

In the past year, I have traveled to Darfur, Democratic Republic of the Congo, and Malawi. In each place I have met UN workers, and in each place I met people struggling to survive who have a better chance of surviving because the UN was there.

Politics can save lives, there is no doubt about it. Politics—the politics of cynicism and hypocrisy and scoring cheap political points can also cost lives. Are we in Congress willing to offer our voices and our votes to invest our nation's resources in saving lives, promoting peace and building a better future for our planet's most vulnerable people?

Many are of my colleagues are, and I know this because ninety-nine of my House colleagues have co-sponsored H. Con. Res. 172, a resolution I introduced that commits the U.S. to be actively leading to help achieve the United Nation's Millennium Development Goals (MGDs). [Note: In 2000 at the Millennium Summit at the UN, the assembled world leaders agree that their countries would cooperate to strive by 2015 to meet 8 millennium developmental goals: (1) halve extreme poverty and hunger, (2) achieve universal primary education, (3) empower women and promote equality between women and men, (4) reduce under-five mortality by two-thirds, (5) reduce maternal mortality by three-quarters, (6) reverse the spread of diseases, especially HIV/AIDS and malaria, (7) ensure environmental sustainability, and (8) create a global partnership for development with targets for foreign aid, trade, and debt relief.]

Everything we do here in Congress is about setting priorities, making choices and investing in the future—this is why I so strongly support the MDGs. The United States—our president, this Congress and the American people—have the power to lead the fight to help to eliminate extreme poverty, to save the lives of millions of newborns, to overcome the devastating human suffering caused by AIDS. We have the power to invest in solutions that will end food insecurity, keep girls in school and promote healthy families around the world.

Right now, the U.S. is remarkable in its leadership in responding to emergencies around the globe such as the South Asia tsunami, earthquakes in Pakistan and Indonesia, and the crisis in Darfur. But, we cannot ignore the fact that more than a billion people around the world live on $1 a day. Their daily misery is not to be discounted—they deserve the help of the world community.

The U.S., in partnership with the world community, must address emergencies as they arise, but we also need to invest much more than we are in long-term development solutions that builds human capacity and enhances human dignity among our brothers and sisters who have the least.

I am working for a world that is more secure, hopeful and peaceful. But it shouldn't be considered an act of political courage to vote to increase [foreign aid] funding to support girls' education, keep mothers and newborns healthy or provide safe drinking water. Why are massive investments in saving lives and enhancing human dignity more controversial for Congress than spending $7 billion every month for a war in Iraq?

It is time for Congress to look out and see the world as it really is inter-connected, interdependent, and filled with a common human desire for hope, opportunity and respect—especially among those who have the least. I am committed to working to add my voice to the millions of Americans who care deeply about achieving the MDGs—because to do so reflects both our values and our national interests as Americans.

I am hopeful we are on the right track, not because of any action by Congress, but because earlier this year in March I attended a Model UN in St. Paul which focused on the MDGs. Those hundreds of children were smart, serious and not to be stopped. Their faces reflected the faces of the world and their spirit reflected the best of America. They participated because they not only were learning about the UN—but because they want to believe in the UN. They want the UN to be successful because it will make the world they are about to inherit more successful.

Thank you for inviting me here. Thank you, all of you, for empowering a new generation of Americans to understand and believe in the value of the United Nations.

Clifford D. May    **NO**

The United Nations:
Realities and Responses

I want to offer a broad view of the United Nations, what it's become, what we can—and cannot—expect from it. Finally, I will offer a modest proposal.

As I'm sure you all are aware, the United Nations was born just after World War II. Its pre-war predecessor, the League of Nations, died after it failed to stand up to the threats posed by German Nazism, Italian Fascism and Japanese Militarism. The UN was supposed to do better.

Unfortunately, that hasn't happened. The UN never lived up to the hope and expectations of its more idealistic founders. According to the UN Charter, among its central purposes was to "maintain international peace and security, and to that end: to take effective collective measures for the prevention and removal of threats to the peace."

According to the UN Universal Declaration of Human Rights "Everyone has the right to life, liberty and security of person" and "no one shall be subjected to torture or to cruel, inhuman or degrading treatment or punishment." The UN was supposed to take sides with victims against aggressors. It has rarely done so.

Consider China: When [Communist Party Chairman Mao Zedong] Mao's Cultural Revolution [1966–1969] killed millions, the UN did nothing. After Beijing used ruthless violence for political objectives in Tiananmen Square [1989] the UN was silent again.

This pattern was repeated over the years and around the world. When the Khmer Rouge [the communist guerilla group and then government] was slaughtering the population of Cambodia [1975–1979], the UN failed to act. When genocide against the Tutsis was carried out in Rwanda, the UN sat on its hands. Actually, it was worse than that: A small UN force that was in the country was pulled back—lest anyone wearing a blue helmet be killed along with the intended victims.

When mass murder was waged against the people of Bosnia and Kosovo, the UN made the situation worse. Srebrenica was the site of the worst case of genocide in Europe since World War II. In July 1995, the Bosnian Serb army invaded a UN safe area—and with no opposition from UN peacekeepers—separated Muslim families and murdered over 7,000 men and boys.

Yet when President Clinton intervened militarily Bosnia and Kosovo [in 1994 and 1998, respectively], it had to be without UN authorization.

The UN turned a blind eye when Afghanistan was hijacked by al Qaeda terrorists. It allowed Somalia to collapse into anarchy.

The UN was feckless in its efforts to stop the slaughter of black Christians in southern Sudan, and the slaughter of black Muslims in western Sudan [in Darfur, ongoing].

The UN did not respond to Saddam Hussein's genocidal attacks on the Kurds in the late 1980s and his slaughters of the Shia in the early 1990s.

UN officials ignored and may have helped facilitate the theft of billions of dollars by Saddam from the Iraqi people under the UN's Oil for Food Program—the biggest financial swindle in world history.

UN peacekeepers working in the Congo sexually abused girls as young as 13.

In the Indian Ocean areas hit by the tsunami last month [December 2004], UN officials have rushed to take charge and take credit—with little evidence of useful expertise or resources. As one American diplomat recently wrote: "To avoid running into the UN, we must go out to where the quake and tsunami actually hit. As we come up on two weeks since the disaster struck, the U.N. is still not to be seen where it counts—except when holding well-staged press events."

Have there been any exceptions, any successes? Well, in 1967, when Egypt, Syria, Jordan and other Arab countries were mobilizing for a war to wipe Israel off the face of the Earth, the UN did do something: It removed its "peacekeepers" so they would not get in the way.

The UN never became a maker of international law or a source of moral authority—though through a combination of wishful thinking and clever public relations many people have been misled to believe otherwise.

Instead, the UN has been a cozy retreat for transnational bureaucrats. Leave aside such lofty goals as peace-making, peace-keeping and the spread of human rights. The UN also has been a failure at contributing to economic development. Name one country—just one—more prosperous now than a generation ago due to UN economic expertise and assistance. It certainly was not thanks to UN "development experts" that Taiwan has become an economic powerhouse.

Nor has the UN even been an efficient provider of relief, which is what you must administer when development fails and disasters strike. As a *New York Times* correspondent in Africa in the 1980s, I saw first-hand how much superior were the relief efforts of such faith-based organizations as World Vision and Catholic Relief Services.

The United Nations, of course, are not really united. There is no "international community." The word "community" implies common traditions and values. What traditions and values unite the people of the United States with the dictators of North Korea and Syria, or with the mullahs of Iran?

But, yes, with Britain, Australia and Canada, we Americans do share traditions. The newly freed nations of Eastern Europe understand in their bones why Americans refuse to appease tyrants. Israel, Turkey and India are free and democratic, too.

And Americans share values with the people of Taiwan. More Americans need to understand that the people of Taiwan have created a democratic society, a vibrant society that embraces freedom and human rights and opportunity just as we do.

The UN is a mixture of democracies and dictatorship. Institutionally, the UN does not prefer the one over the other—though it has long been the dictatorships that have held sway.

Joshua Muravchik, a scholar at the American Enterprise Institute in Washington, who is now completing a study of the UN [*The Future of the UN*: AEI Press, 2005], recently added that it is not entirely true that the UN, as sometimes argued, "is no more than the sum of its members states."

He notes that "collective or derivative bodies take on lives of their own." The Secretary General, for example, commands a budget of $3 billion and a staff of 15,000.

Between attackers and defenders—the UN is generally neutral. The UN Human Rights Commission is a wonderful organization for human rights violators to join—because by so doing they make themselves virtually immune to sanctions or even serious criticisms.

As Muravchik has pointed out, "year after year, fully half of the governments that Freedom House cites as 'the worst of the worst' human-rights violators secure seat on the body overseeing human rights abuses. They include China, Cuba, Sudan, Syria, Saudi Arabia, and Libya, which recently held the chair. . . . [N]either China nor Saudi Arabia has ever suffered a word of censure."

Does any UN official think this is an outrage? If so, he's kept his opinion to himself.

The challenge posed by terrorism, by radical, fascist Islamist groups that seek the destruction of democratic societies is not something the UN is willing to tackle or, indeed, even assist with.

On the contrary, a 1970 resolution of the General Assembly essentially says that those who claim to represent "national liberation movements" have a license to commit murder. The resolution essentially validates suicide bombing as an exercise of human rights.

What does the UN care about? Shashi Tharoor, Secretary-General Kofi Annan's deputy says that it is "the exercise of American power" that "may well be the central issue in world politics today."

Despite all this, there are those who would like to see the UN elevated into some sort of world government. Such ambitions must be discouraged. The UN does not have the moral authority for such a role. Its resume does not qualify it for such a job.

As for Taiwan's membership in the United Nations, there is no question that all the reasonable arguments are on Taiwan's side. But reasonable arguments, as I hope I've demonstrated, carry little weight at the UN as it is presently constituted.

The UN's so-called "principle of universality," provided for in Paragraph 1 of Article 4 of the UN Charter, says that membership in the United Nations is open to "peace-loving states."

In reality, of course, many states that obviously do not love peace have been welcomed into the UN. And, since this article applies only to "states," Beijing can and will argue that Taiwan does not qualify, that Taiwan is not an independent state. Again, logic and morality are on the side of Taiwan—which has not been ruled from Beijing since 1895.

But, again, logic and morality seldom count for much in the halls of the United Nations.

Let me add this caution: Any move toward independence carries with it significant risks for the Taiwanese people—you know that much better than I do.

Within the democratic institutions that the Taiwanese have so courageously built, there will continue to be a meaningful debate regarding those risks, regarding the consequences of insisting on rights to which the Taiwanese are entitled, but which Beijing—obsessed with preserving the legitimacy of the Chinese Communist Party and willing to use the Taiwan issue to stoke mainland nationalism—does not recognize.

I have confidence in the wisdom of the Taiwanese people, confidence that they will proceed thoughtfully and carefully, understanding the risks, and recognizing that their decisions will have real-word consequences.

Today, halfway through the first decade of the 21st century, the world looks very different from the way it appeared in 1945. But there are similarities too.

The democratic societies—indeed the democratic experiment—are threatened by a witch's brew of rogue dictators, terrorists and weapons of mass destruction.

To cope with these dangers will require fresh and creative thinking, and hard choices.

I don't believe the UN is going to be abolished. I also don't believe it will be successfully reformed.

With that in mind, I would argue that it's time to explore alternative institutions and structures, time to explore new models in which democratic societies could work together against common enemies and for common goals.

And I think it's clear that the Taiwanese people—who have built the first democracy in 4,000 years of Chinese history—should be given the right to choose whether they would want to be a charter member of such an organization.

That won't happen if, as has been suggested, a caucus of democracies is established within the current structure of the UN. A better idea, I believe, is that proposed by Dore Gold, the Israeli author of *Tower of Babble* [Crown Forum, 2004], a sharp criticism of the UN. Dr. Gold advocates the creation of a Community of Democracies outside the UN as a sort of substitute or alternative.

Membership in such a community needn't be limited to entities universally recognized as "states." It could gather and organize a variety of democratic societies.

In such a forum, Taiwan's achievements and values would be better appreciated than they ever would be at the UN as it is currently structured.

In the 20th century, the democratic experiment was endangered by totalitarianism, which took such forms as Nazism, Fascism, Japanese Militarism and Communism.

Today, in the 21st century, the democratic experiment is again endangered. Those who want to ensure the survival of democracy have a right and an obligation to work together more diligently and more creatively than ever before.

POSTSCRIPT

Does the United Nations Deserve Support?

Evaluating the value of the UN has a great deal to do with what standard of evaluation you adopt. One standard is akin to asking whether a glass is half full or half empty. Undoubtedly, the UN has not come anywhere near achieving the lofty goals set out in its Charter. Thus, the evaluative glass is at least half empty. However, it is also true that the UN has accomplished a great deal. Dozens of UN peacekeeping operations have been fielded, and some of them have made an important contribution. For all the human abuse and poverty that remain, there is greater justice and better living conditions in the world now than existed a few decades ago. Again, the UN can legitimately claim some of the credit. So from this perspective, the glass is at least fuller than it once was.

It is also important to decide whether to evaluate the UN from a global or a national perspective. President Bush argued that the UN was veering toward irrelevance because it did not agree with his desire to wage war on Iraq. From the perspective of U.S. national interests or at least Washington's preferences then (see Issues 7 and 12), the UN failed. But most of the other countries of the world opposed taking action at that point. And if their collective view constitutes the world's evaluation of its interest, then arguably the UN succeeded by resisting the superpower's pressure. Indeed, one could contend that if the UN failed, it was in that it could not prevent the United States and the so-called coalition of the willing from taking unilateral action. Yet another standard of measurement has to do with the old adage about being careful when throwing stones in glass houses. The UN has sometimes wasted money, its workers have not always performed admirably, and even Secretary General Kofi Annan (1997–2006) conceded that to some degree the UN's administration had "become fragmented, duplicative, and rigid." Yet every government, including the U.S. government, is subject to the same accusation. Annan was able to implement many changes, and his successor beginning in 2006, Secretary General Ban Ki-moon has said continued reform will be a top priority. It is also the case that a small number of UN troops and personnel behaved immorally, but the equally if not more abominable performance of a few American soldiers at Abu Ghraib Prison and elsewhere show how the actions of the reprehensive few can besmirch the reputations of the honorable many.

The ultimate question is if not the UN, then what? Calls to "fix" the UN are many and varied, and debating what should be done and what is possible are worthwhile. Perhaps creating a successor organization would be a good idea. Then there is Clifford May's suggestion of essentially abandoning the

UN and having democratic countries to create a new international organization. Ask yourself whether that would open the way to a safer, more prosperous, more just world or even further your country's national interests. Arguing that the UN is beyond repair and should be replaced by a more minimalist organization is Joshua Muravchik in *The Future of the United Nations: Understanding the Past to Chart a Way Forward* (AEI Press, 2005). Disagreeing on both counts is Paul Kennedy in *The Parliament of Man: The Past, Present, and Future of the United Nations* (Random House, 2006). For a commentary on some of the particular problems facing the new secretary general and some advice on tackling them read Anne-Marie Slaughter, "A New U. N. for a New Century," *Fordham Law Review* (May 2006), and Brian Urquhart, "The Next Secretary-General: How to Fill a Job with No Description," *Foreign Affairs* (September/October 2006).

ISSUE 17

Is U.S. Refusal to Join the International Criminal Court Wise?

YES: John R. Bolton, from "The United States and the International Criminal Court," Remarks to the Federalist Society (November 14, 2002)

NO: Briony MacPhee, from "The International Criminal Court: A Case for Conservatives," *The American Non-Governmental Organizations Coalition for the International Criminal Court* (August 30, 2005)

ISSUE SUMMARY

YES: John R. Bolton, at the time U.S. Under Secretary State for Arms Control and International Security and beginning in 2005, U.S. Ambassador to the United Nations, explains why President George W. Bush had decided to reject membership in the International Criminal Court.

NO: Briony MacPhee, a professional volunteer associate with the American Non-Governmental Organizations Coalition for the International Criminal Court, a program of the United Nations Association of the United States of America, argues that conservatives should join many liberals in supporting the United States to become a party to the International Criminal Court.

Historically, international law has focused primarily on countries. More recently, individuals have increasingly become subject to international law. The first major step in this direction was the convening of the Nuremberg and Tokyo war crimes trials after World War II to try German and Japanese military and civilian leaders charged with various war crimes. There were no subsequent war crimes tribunals until the 1990s when the United Nations established two of them. One sits in The Hague, the Netherlands, and deals with the horrific events in Bosnia. The other tribunal is in Arusha, Tanzania, and provides justice for the genocidal massacres in Rwanda. These tribunals have indicted numerous people for war crimes and have convicted and imprisoned many of them. Nevertheless, there was a widespread feeling that such ad hoc tribunals needed to be replaced by a permanent international criminal tribunal.

In 1996 the UN convened a conference in Rome to do just that. At first the United States was supportive, but it favored a very limited court that could only prosecute and hear cases referred to it by the UN Security Council (where the United States had a veto) and, even then, could only try individuals with the permission of the defendant's home government. Most countries disagreed, however, and in 1998 the Rome conference voted to overwhelmingly create a relatively strong court. The Rome Statute of the International Criminal Court (ICC) gives the ICC jurisdiction over wars of aggression, genocide, and other crimes, but only if the home country of an alleged perpetrator fails to act.

Although the ICC treaty was open for signature in July 1998, President Bill Clinton showed either ambivalence or a desire not to have it injected as an issue into the 2000 presidential election by waiting until December 31, 2000 to have a U.S. official sign the treaty. If Clinton had his doubts, his successor, George W. Bush, did not. He was adamantly opposed to the treaty. As directed by the White House, State Department official John R. Bolton, the author of the first reading, sent a letter dated May 6, 2002 to UN Secretary General Kofi Annan informing him that "in connection with the Rome Statute of the International Criminal Court . . . , the United States does not intend to become a party to the treaty . . . [and] has no legal obligations arising from its signature on December 31, 2000." The Bush administraton also launched an effort to persuade other countries to sign "Article 98" agreements by which countries agree not to surrender U.S. citizens to the International Criminal Court.

This letter formally notifying the United Nations that the United States does not intend to become a party to the Rome statute also ended any U.S. participation in the workings of the court. In the first reading, John Bolton explains just a few months after his letter to the UN why the Bush administration had decided to reject the ICC treaty. The U.S. position did not, however, prevent the ICC from coming into being. That occurred soon after Bolton's letter when upon ratification by the sixtieth country, the treaty went into effect on July 1, 2002. Since then, the ICC has begun to function, and in the second reading Briony MacPhee tries to answer the arguments put forth by Bolton and other conservatives against the ICC.

YES

John R. Bolton

The United States and the International Criminal Court

I've been asked to [make] remarks about the pressures of national security on American government. With this in mind, I'd like to address the topic of the International Criminal Court [ICC] and detail our [the Bush administration's] reasons for opposing it. As I will explain, the problems inherent in the ICC are more than abstract legal issues—they are matters that touch directly on our national security and our national interests.

For a number of reasons, the United States decided that the ICC had unacceptable consequences for our national sovereignty. Specifically, the ICC is an organization whose precepts go against fundamental American notions of sovereignty, checks and balances, and national independence. It is an agreement that is harmful to the national interests of the United States, and harmful to our presence abroad.

U.S. military forces and civilian personnel and private citizens are currently active in peacekeeping and humanitarian missions in almost 100 countries at any given time. It is essential that we remain steadfast in preserving the independence and flexibility that America needs to defend our national interests around the world. As President Bush said,

> The United States cooperates with many other nations to keep the peace, but we will not submit American troops to prosecutors and judges whose jurisdiction we do not accept. . . . Every person who serves under the American flag will answer to his or her own superiors and to military law, not to the rulings of an unaccountable International Criminal Court.

So in order to protect our citizens, we are in the process of negotiating bilateral agreements with the largest possible number of states, including non-Parties [to the ICC Treaty: countries that have not ratified it]. These Article 98 agreements, as they are called, provide American citizens with essential protection against the Court's purported jurisdiction claims, and allow us to remain engaged internationally with our friends and allies. To date, 14 countries have signed Article 98 agreements with us. It is a misconception that the United States wants to use these Article 98 agreements to undermine the ICC. To the contrary, we are determined to work with States Parties, utilizing a

American Enterprise Institute, John R. Bolton, (November 14, 2002).

mechanism prescribed within the Rome Statute itself, to find an acceptable solution to one of the main problems posed by the ICC.

In the eyes of its supporters, the ICC is simply an overdue addition to the family of international organizations, an evolutionary step ahead of the Nuremberg tribunal, and the next logical institutional development over the ad hoc war crimes courts for the Former Yugoslavia and Rwanda. The Statute of Rome establishes both substantive principles of international law and creates new institutions and procedures to adjudicate these principles. The Statute confers jurisdiction on the ICC over four crimes: genocide, crimes against humanity, war crimes, and the crime of aggression. The Court's jurisdiction is "automatic," applicable to covered individuals accused of crimes under the Statute regardless of whether their governments have ratified it or consent to such jurisdiction. Particularly important is the independent Prosecutor, who is responsible for conducting investigations and prosecutions before the Court. The Prosecutor may initiate investigations based on referrals by States Parties, or on the basis of information that he or she otherwise obtains.

So described, one might assume that the ICC is simply a further step in the orderly march toward the peaceful settlement of international disputes, sought since time immemorial. But in several respects, the court is poised to assert authority over nation states, and to promote its prosecution over alternative methods for dealing with the worst criminal offenses.

The Court's flaws are basically two-fold, substantive, and structural. As to the former, the ICC's authority is vague and excessively elastic, and the Court's discretion ranges far beyond normal or acceptable judicial responsibilities, giving it broad and unacceptable powers of interpretation that are essentially political and legislative in nature. This is most emphatically *not* a Court of limited jurisdiction. Crimes can be added subsequently that go beyond those included in the Rome Statute. Parties to the Statute are subject to these subsequently-added crimes only if they affirmatively accept them, but the Statute purports automatically to bind non-parties, such as the United States, to any such new crimes. It is neither reasonable nor fair that these crimes would apply to a greater extent to states that have not agreed to the terms of the Rome Statute than to those that have.

Numerous prospective "crimes" were suggested at Rome and commanded wide support from participating nations, such as the crime of "aggression," which was included in the Statute, but not defined. Although frequently easy to identify, "aggression" can at times be something in the eye of the beholder. For example, Israel justifiably feared in Rome that certain actions, such as its initial use of force in the Six Day War, would be perceived as illegitimate preemptive strikes that almost certainly would have provoked proceedings against top Israeli officials. Moreover, there seems little doubt that Israel will be the target of a complaint in the ICC concerning conditions and practices by the Israeli military in the West Bank and Gaza. Israel recently decided to declare its intention not to become a party to the ICC or to be bound by the Statute's obligations.

A fair reading of the treaty leaves one unable to answer with confidence whether the United States would now be accused of war crimes for legitimate but controversial uses of force to protect world peace. No U.S. Presidents or their advisors could be assured that they would be unequivocally safe from politicized charges of criminal liability.

As troubling as the ICC's substantive and jurisdictional problems are, the problems raised by the Statute's main structures—the Court and the Prosecutor— are still worse. The ICC does not, and cannot, fit into a coherent, international structural "constitutional" design that delineates clearly how laws are made, adjudicated or enforced, subject to popular accountability and structured to protect liberty. There is no such design, nor should there be. Instead, the Court and the Prosecutor are simply "out there" in the international system. Requiring the United States to be bound by this treaty, with its unaccountable Prosecutor and its unchecked judicial power, is clearly inconsistent with American standards of constitutionalism. This is a macro-constitutional issue for us, not simply a narrow, technical point of law.

We are considering, in the Prosecutor, a powerful and necessary element of executive power, the power of law-enforcement. Never before has the United States been asked to place any of that power outside the complete control of our national government without our consent. Our concern goes beyond the possibility that the Prosecutor will target for indictment the isolated U.S. soldier who violates our own laws and values by allegedly committing a war crime. Our principal concern is for our country's top civilian and military leaders, those responsible for our defense and foreign policy. They are the ones potentially at risk at the hands of the ICC's politically unaccountable Prosecutor, as part of an agenda to restrain American discretion, even when our actions are legitimated by the operation of our own constitutional system.

Unfortunately, the United States has had considerable experience in the past two decades with domestic "independent counsels," and that history argues overwhelmingly against international repetition. Simply launching massive criminal investigations has an enormous political impact. Although subsequent indictments and convictions are unquestionably more serious, a zealous independent Prosecutor can make dramatic news just by calling witnesses and gathering documents, without ever bringing formal charges.

Indeed, the supposed "independence" of the Prosecutor and the Court from "political" pressures (such as the Security Council) is more a source of concern than an element of protection. "Independent" bodies in the UN system have often proven themselves more highly politicized than some of the explicitly political organs. True political accountability, by contrast, is almost totally absent from the ICC.

The American concept of separation of powers, imperfect though it is, reflects our settled belief that liberty is best protected when the various authorities legitimately exercised by government are, to the maximum extent possible, placed in separate branches. So structuring the national government, the Framers believed, would prevent the excessive accumulation of power in a limited number of hands, thus providing the greatest protection for individual liberty. Continental European constitutional structures do not, by and large, reflect a similar set of beliefs. They do not so thoroughly separate judicial from executive powers, just as their parliamentary systems do not so thoroughly separate executive from legislative powers. That, of course, is entirely

Europe's prerogative, and may help to explain why Europeans appear to be more comfortable with the ICC's structure, which closely melds prosecutorial and judicial functions in the European fashion.

In addition, our Constitution provides that the discharge of executive authority will be rendered accountable to the citizenry in two ways. First, the law-enforcement power is exercised through an elected President. The President is constitutionally charged with the responsibility to "take Care that the Laws be faithfully executed," and the constitutional authority of the actual law-enforcers stems directly from the only elected executive official. Second, Congress, all of whose members are popularly elected, through its statute-making authority, its confirmation authority and through the appropriations process, exercises significant influence and oversight. When necessary, the congressional impeachment power serves as the ultimate safeguard.

In the ICC's central structures, the Court and Prosecutor, these sorts of political checks are either greatly attenuated or entirely absent. They are effectively accountable to no one. The Prosecutor will answer to no superior executive power, elected or unelected. Nor is there any legislature anywhere in sight, elected or unelected, in the Statute of Rome. The Prosecutor is answerable only to the Court, and then only partially, although the Prosecutor may be removed by the Assembly of States Parties. The Europeans may be comfortable with such a system, but Americans are not.

By long-standing American principles, the ICC's structure utterly fails to provide sufficient accountability to warrant vesting the Prosecutor with the Statute's enormous power of law enforcement. Political accountability is utterly different from "politicization," which we can all agree should form no part of the decisions of either Prosecutor or Court. Today, however, precisely contrary to the proper alignment, the ICC has almost no political accountability, *and* carries an enormous risk of politicization. Even at this early stage in the Court's existence, there are concerns that its judicial nomination process is being influenced by quota systems and back-room deals.

Under the UN Charter, the Security Council has primary responsibility for the maintenance of international peace and security. The ICC's efforts could easily conflict with the Council's work. Indeed, the Statute of Rome substantially minimized the Security Council's role in ICC affairs. While the Security Council may refer matters to the ICC, or order it to refrain from commencing or proceeding with an investigation or prosecution, the Council is precluded from a meaningful role in the ICC's work. In requiring an affirmative Council vote to *stop* a case, the Statute shifts the balance of authority from the Council to the ICC. Moreover, a veto by a Permanent Member of such a restraining Council resolution leaves the ICC completely unsupervised. This attempted marginalization of the Security Council is a fundamental *new* problem created by the ICC that will have a tangible and highly detrimental impact on the conduct of U.S. foreign policy. The Council now risks having the ICC interfering in its ongoing work, with all of the attendant confusion between the appropriate roles of law, politics, and power in settling international disputes. The Council already has had to take action to dilute the disincentive the ICC poses to nations considering troop contributions to UN-related peacekeeping operations.

Paradoxically, the danger of the ICC may lie in its potential weakness rather than its potential strength. The most basic error is the belief that the ICC will have a substantial deterrent effect against the perpetration of crimes against humanity. Behind their optimistic rhetoric, ICC proponents have not a shred of evidence supporting their deterrence theories. In fact, they fundamentally confuse the appropriate roles of political and economic power, diplomatic efforts, military force, and legal procedures. Recent history is filled with cases where even strong military force or the threat of force failed to deter aggression or gross abuses of human rights. ICC proponents concede as much when they cite cases where the "world community" has failed to pay adequate attention, or failed to intervene in time to prevent genocide or other crimes against humanity. The new Court and Prosecutor, it is said, will now guarantee against similar failures.

But deterrence ultimately depends on perceived effectiveness, and the ICC fails badly on that point. The ICC's authority is far too attenuated to make the slightest bit of difference either to the war criminals or to the outside world. In cases where the West in particular has been unwilling to intervene militarily to prevent crimes against humanity as they were happening, why will a potential perpetrator feel deterred by the mere possibility of future legal action? A weak and distant Court will have no deterrent effect on the hard men like Pol Pot most likely to commit crimes against humanity. Why should anyone imagine that bewigged judges in The Hague will succeed where cold steel has failed? Holding out the prospect of ICC deterrence to the weak and vulnerable amounts to a cruel joke.

Beyond the issue of deterrence, it is by no means clear that "justice" as defined by the Court and Prosecutor is always consistent with the attainable political resolution of serious political and military disputes. It may be, or it may not be. Human conflict teaches that, much to the dismay of moralists and legal theoreticians, mortal policy makers often must make tradeoffs among inconsistent objectives. This can be a painful and unpleasant realization, confronting us as it does with the irritating facts of human complexity, contradiction, and imperfection.

Accumulated experience strongly favors a case-by-case approach, politically and legally, rather than the inevitable resort to adjudication. Circumstances differ, and circumstances matter. Atrocities, whether in international wars or in domestic contexts, are by definition uniquely horrible in their own times and places.

For precisely that reason, so too are their resolutions unique. When the time arrives to consider the crimes, that time usually coincides with events of enormous social and political significance: negotiation of a peace treaty, restoration of a "legitimate" political regime, or a similar milestone. At such momentous times, the crucial issues typically transcend those of administering justice to those who committed heinous crimes during the preceding turbulence. The pivotal questions are clearly political, not legal: How shall the formerly warring parties live with each other in the future? What efforts shall be taken to expunge the causes of the previous inhumanity? Can the truth of what actually happened be established so that succeeding generations do not make the same mistakes?

One alternative to the ICC is the kind of Truth and Reconciliation Commission created in South Africa. In the aftermath of apartheid, the new government faced the difficult task of establishing and legitimizing truly democratic governmental institutions while dealing simultaneously with earlier crimes. One option was widespread prosecutions against the perpetrators of human rights abuses, but the new government chose a different model. Under the Commission's charter, alleged offenders came before it and confessed past misdeeds. Assuming they confessed truthfully, the Commission in effect pardoned them from prosecution.

This approach was intended to make public more of the truth of the apartheid regime in the most credible fashion, to elicit admissions of guilt, and then to permit society to move ahead without the prolonged opening of old wounds that trials, appeals, and endless recriminations might bring.

I do not argue that the South African approach should be followed everywhere, or even necessarily that it was correct for South Africa. But it is certainly fair to conclude that that approach is radically different from the ICC, which operates through vindication, punishment, and retribution.

It may be that, in some disputes, neither retribution nor complete truth-telling is the desired outcome. In many former Communist countries, citizens are still wrestling with the handling of secret police activities of the now-defunct regimes. So extensive was the informing, spying, and compromising in some societies that a tacit decision was made that the complete opening of secret police and Communist Party files will either not occur, or will happen with exquisite slowness over a very long period. In effect, these societies have chosen "amnesia" because it is simply too difficult for them to sort out relative degrees of past wrongs, and because of their desire to move ahead.

One need not agree with these decisions to respect the complexity of the moral and political problems they address. Only those completely certain of their own moral standing, and utterly confident in their ability to judge the conduct of others in excruciating circumstances can reject the amnesia alternative out of hand. Invariably insisting on international adjudication is not necessarily preferable to a course that the parties to a dispute might themselves agree upon. Indeed, with a permanent ICC, one can predict that one or more disputants might well invoke its jurisdiction at a selfishly opportune moment, and thus, ironically, make an ultimate settlement of their dispute more complicated or less likely.

Another alternative, of course, is for the parties themselves to try their own alleged war criminals. Indeed, there are substantial arguments that the fullest cathartic impact of the prosecutorial approach to war crimes occurs when the responsible population itself comes to grips with its past and administers appropriate justice. The Rome Statute pays lip service to the doctrine of "complementarity," or deference to national judicial systems, but this is simply an assertion, unproven and untested. It is *within* national judicial systems where the international effort should be to encourage the warring parties to resolve questions of criminality as part of a comprehensive solution to their disagreements. Removing key elements of the dispute to a distant forum, especially the emotional and contentious issues of war crimes and crimes against humanity, undercuts the very progress that these peoples, victims and per-petrators alike, must make if they are ever to live peacefully together.

In the absence of the means or political will to address grave violations, the United States has supported the establishment and operation of ad hoc tribunals such as those in Yugoslavia and Rwanda. Unlike the ICC, these are created and overseen by the UN Security Council, under a UN Charter to which virtually all nations have agreed.

As the ICC comes into being, we will address our concerns about the ICC's jurisdictional claims using the remedy laid out for us by the Rome Statute itself and the UN Security Council in the case of the peacekeeping force in the former Yugoslavia. Using Article 98 of the Rome Statute as a basis, we are negotiating bilateral, legally-binding agreements with individual States Parties to protect our citizens from being handed over to the Court. Since the European Union's decision in September to permit its member states to conclude Article 98 agreements with the United States, our negotiators have been engaged in bilateral discussions with several EU countries. In the near future we will also be holding discussions on the issue with several countries in the Middle East and South Asia. Our ultimate goal is to conclude Article 98 agreements with every country in the world, regardless of whether they have signed or ratified the ICC, regardless of whether they intend to in the future. These agreements will allow us the necessary protections in a manner that is legally permissible and consistent with the letter and spirit of the Rome Statute.

In order to promote justice worldwide, the United States has many for-eign policy instruments to utilize that are fully consistent with our values and interests. We will continue to play a worldwide leadership role in strengthening domestic judicial systems and promoting freedom, transparency and the rule of law. As Secretary Powell has said:

We are the leader in the world with respect to bringing people to justice. We have supported a tribunal for Yugoslavia, the tribunal for Rwanda, trying to get the tribunal for Sierra Leone set up. We have the highest standards of accountability of any nation on the face of the earth.

It is important to note that we are not seeking immunity for our citizens, but a simple, non-surrender agreement as contemplated in the Rome Statute. We fully commit ourselves to, where appropriate, investigate and prosecute serious, credible allegations of war crimes, crimes against humanity and geno-cide that have been made against any of our people.

We respect the decision of States Parties to join the ICC, but they in turn must respect our decision not to be bound by jurisdictional claims to which we have not consented. As President Bush stated in his National Security Strategy,

We will take the actions necessary to ensure that our efforts to meet our global security commitments and protect Americans are not impaired by the poten-tial for investigations, inquiry, or prosecution by the International Criminal Court, whose jurisdiction does not extend to Americans and which we do not accept.

Signatories of the Statute of Rome have created an ICC to their liking, and they should live with it. The United States did not agree to be bound, and must not be held to its terms.

Briony MacPhee  **NO**

The International Criminal Court: A Case for Conservatives

Since negotiations began on the first permanent International Criminal Court (ICC or Court) in 1995, conservatives in the United States have been concerned about its creation and its implications for American sovereignty and international actions. This range of concerns has led many conservatives to conclude that the Court does not merit U.S. support and involvement. This paper examines the important concerns that conservative Americans have expressed regarding the ICC, and responds to them. Close examination of the Court indicates that the values that are important to conservatives are implemented and carried out by the ICC.

The ICC in Operation

On July 1, 2002, the ICC came into existence following the necessary 60th ratification of its Rome Statute, with jurisdiction over crimes committed after this date. The ICC advances global peace through internationally administered justice. It is unprecedented as a permanent tribunal to try individuals, regardless of nationality, for the most serious crimes, including genocide, crimes against humanity, war crimes, and when defined, the crime of aggression. The states which support the ICC are democratic and free, thus the judges elected will be from democratic countries, as evidenced in those that have been elected so far. Moreover, the staff of the ICC is drawn from countries all over the world, both members and non-members of the Court.

For example, an American is a senior prosecutor, responsible for managing the Uganda case. The ICC is up and running, with the support of nearly 100 countries that have ratified the Rome Statute. The governments of the Democratic Republic of the Congo (DRC), Uganda and the Central African Republic (CAR) are among the first to refer situations to the ICC. In addition, the United Nations Security Council has referred the situation in Darfur (Sudan) to the ICC, and the Ivory Coast has consented to the Court's jurisdiction. Investigations have already begun in the DRC, Uganda and Darfur, and arrest warrants are expected soon.

Conservative support was among the factors encouraging the Bush administration to abstain on the Darfur referral, which allowed the referral to take

The American Non-Governmental Organizations Coalition for the International Criminal Court, Briony MacPhee (August 30, 2005).

place. Conservatives thus spearheaded an important international action against the atrocities. Americans overwhelmingly supported the referral. Public opinion polls indicate that 91% of Americans feel that the U.S. should cooperate with the ICC to help bring to justice those responsible for the atrocities in Darfur. In light of the recent actions concerning the Court, namely the Darfur referral, some conservatives have begun to reexamine their concerns about the Court.

History   The sheer scale of horror committed during the Holocaust made the international community brutally aware of the power of ethnic hate, and the evil of leaders who are not called to account for planning and creating atrocities. American troops led the effort to liberate Nazi concentration camps, playing a noble role to end the atrocities. The United States also led the effort to establish the subsequent Nuremberg and Tokyo tribunals, holding the perpetrators to account, and helping to establish the principle of individual accountability for war crimes.

Although "never again" was the battle cry after World War II, the success of the Nuremberg and Tokyo tribunals did not lead to the establishment of a permanent court to try such crimes. The Cold War made it impossible politically to create a court. The consequences of this failure are apparent in the recent atrocities committed in Sierra Leone, Rwanda, East Timor, and the former Yugoslavia, along with other cases. The ad hoc tribunals were the pilot project, but their experiences made it evident that a permanent court was needed and that the UN Security Council could not create it.

Motives That Led to the Creation of the Court

The motives of other countries and their historical experiences were among the factors that led to the creation of the ICC. Many countries who drafted the Rome Statute recently emerged from dictatorships to democracy. It was their unstable and violent past, coupled with the desire to have a permanent court to deal with atrocities that continue to happen around the world, which led them to create the Court.

The experience of the ad hoc tribunals also motivated the creation of the ICC. Although there have been difficulties with their operation, the tribunals have worked. Currently more than 50 individuals have been prosecuted and are serving sentences for the crimes they committed in the former Yugoslavia and Rwanda. This demonstrates that tribunals such as these can be successful, but their cost, their temporariness, and their inability to deter continuing crimes because they act only after the atrocities are over, makes the need for a permanent court obvious.

Concerns

The ICC implements most American values about trials and justice, and has thus far demonstrated its impartiality, independence and international acceptance. However, in the United States there is still fear and deep doubt about the reach, mandate and operation of the Court. The concerns of conservatives include: that the Court will be able to try and prosecute Americans, that U.S. participation may be unconstitutional, that there will be a loss of American sovereignty, that there is an absence of safeguards, especially when the U.S. is not a party to the Court, that the Court will have the defects of the ad hoc tribunals and finally, that the Court will limit America's ability to act in its national interest.

Concern 1: The Ability of the Court to Prosecute Americans

It is highly unlikely that the Court will ever prosecute Americans. This is partly, but not only, because of the calculated and widespread manner in which the crimes must be committed, and the limited kinds of crimes that the ICC can prosecute. Countries such as America reject and abhor the kind of atrocities that the Court has been created to adjudicate. It is only the tyrannical leaders of countries that repeatedly violate the most fundamental and basic human rights that will be brought before the Court and held to account. The Rome Statute also limits the Court's jurisdiction to individuals who are citizens of a country party to the ICC or who have committed crimes in the territory of such a country. Only if the Security Council refers a case, or a country accepts the Court's jurisdiction, can the ICC act when the states involved are not party to the Court.

In order for an American servicemember to be tried before the ICC, an American would have to commit crimes of the horrible nature described in the Statute, the U.S. would not investigate the crime or a trial by one of the most respected legal systems in the world would be deemed biased by the ICC, neither the U.S. nor its allies could convince the ICC prosecutor not to investigate, and/or the Pre-Trial Chamber of the Court, composed of elected judges, would approve the Prosecutor's decision to investigate. Finally, despite U.S. influence, the Security Council would also have to refuse to defer the investigation, which is under its mandate. Even if such an unlikely scenario should occur, the accused American would come before a court whose due process requirements are virtually identical to those provided in U.S. courts.

These provisions of the Rome Statute are identical to those in the U.S. Bill of Rights. The Statute includes rights such as the right to a speedy trial, the right to remain silent and the right to be questioned with counsel present. The only difference between the rights provided for Americans in U.S. courts and the ICC is that there is no trial by jury. However, a jury trial for Pol Pot [of Cambodia], Idi Amin [of Uganda], Saddam Hussein or Adolf Hitler would be an impractical mockery of the whole meaning and purpose of juries. Who exactly would be the peers of such men? The ICC provides instead for trial by judges schooled in the highest legal principles of the Court, thus ensuring that their rulings will be rooted in them. It is clear that the ICC is not a biased, but is rather a court that is founded on the basic rights and privileges awarded to all Americans, ensuring that Americans would receive a proper and fair trial before the ICC.

Concern 2: U.S. Participation Is Unconstitutional

Some Americans declare that U.S. participation in the ICC will be unconstitutional. They argue that the Court circumvents the powers of Congress to establish the federal judicial system and that an American who has committed a crime in the U.S. cannot be tried in a court located outside of the country, one which Congress neither created nor drafted its rules.

This would not be the first time that the United States would subject its nationals to be tried in a judicial system other than an American one. The U.S. has entered into previous treaties that allow its nationals to be brought before foreign courts. Examples of such extraterritorial judicial reach are the extradition treaties that the U.S. has established and continuously honors with many countries. For example, if an American commits a crime in another country, and the United States has an extradition treaty with that country, the U.S. is obliged to send that person to that country. A state has absolute and exclusive jurisdiction over those who commit crimes within its territory. This has been an accepted concept that has been a part of American law as far back as 1812. Furthermore, Supreme Court cases have made apparent that it is not unconstitutional to try Americans in foreign courts. It is abundantly clear from these cases that Americans can be extradited, and have been extradited, to countries whose judicial systems are very dissimilar to American courts—for example, courts that do not have trial by jury.

The ICC is not the kind of American court in which the Congress is authorized to establish under Article III of the U.S. Constitution. Instead, it is a court outside the U.S. and in that respect is similar to the courts of foreign countries. Therefore, the U.S. is not escaping the Court's jurisdiction if it does not sign onto the ICC. As long as America is not party to the Statute and does not wish to make its nationals available to the Court, the ICC will only be able to prosecute Americans who are physically in foreign nations, which would have primary jurisdiction over them even without the ICC. In fact, given this reach of foreign courts even without American endorsement of the ICC, U.S. membership in the Court may actually serve to increase its influence and clout in such cases.

Concern 3: Loss of American Sovereignty

The creation of this Court is not an attempt to check American power, nor a step toward world government. Moral considerations prompted the ICC's formation. The Court was a reaction to a brutal history and a refusal to accept perpetual atrocities. The fact that the ICC was created by a group of nations indicates that it is not an outside institution which simply materialized by its own accord to impose its will on the United States. Rather than violate the principle of sovereignty, the ICC is its expression. It is an act of sovereignty for countries to join treaties and organizations. The countries that drafted the Rome Statute, and subsequently signed and ratified it, are exercising their right to create an international organization. These countries still have the right to legislate and enforce the law within their own borders, and they are encouraged to do so.

The Court's restricted jurisdiction is deliberate. The Court's Statute begins by stating that the jurisdiction of the Court "shall be complementary to national criminal jurisdiction." A case may not be brought before the Court if it is being investigated by a concerned state. This principle of complementarity ensures that sovereignty is not lost, but rather upheld and "complemented" when a nation becomes a party to the ICC. It is only when ICC judges determine that a country cannot or will not try someone that the Court may refuse to defer to a national legal system.

In addition, Americans are concerned that it is an invasion of our sovereignty for ICC judges to have the power to determine whether a criminal proceeding was conducted in good faith. If the ICC ever had to make such a decision, it would apply only to the particular case involved and would not be an overall judgment of the U.S. legal system. Such a judgment would only be an examination of what the U.S. did or did not do in a particular situation. It is of fundamental importance, if the Court is to function effectively, that its judges be able to independently determine the quality of a trial. Although there is a technical possibility that judges could conclude that a U.S. trial was not conducted in good faith, this is very unlikely since the international community is very aware that the U.S. judicial system has functioned with judicial rigor and independence over the last 200 years.

Concern 4: No Safeguards or a System of Checks and Balances

Conservatives are worried that the Court does not have the necessary safeguards to prevent politically motivated investigations and prosecutions, especially against Americans. However, the Court only has jurisdiction over "the most serious crimes of concern to the international community as a whole," which necessitates that criminal acts must have occurred on a large scale and be the result of deliberate plans or policies by a nation or organization.

If U.S. enemies do seek to use the ICC to achieve anti-American political objectives, there are numerous safeguards against this. The negotiators of the Rome Statute anticipated attempts to politically pervert the Court and quite wisely took careful precautions to prevent the abuse of the Court for political gain. If used in conjunction, such protections may provide nearly total exemption for any country with a well-functioning legal system. Perhaps the most significant limitation and check on the Court is that it is a court of last resort.

As discussed above, the Court is obliged to defer to national proceedings unless it can be shown that the state with jurisdiction over a case is unable or unwilling to act. Such a state must be notified if the Court is beginning an investigation and therefore has the ability to invoke complementarity to demonstrate that it can try the resulting cases.

Moreover, the ICC has four independent organs that serve as a check for one another. The Assembly of States Parties (ASP), the governing body of the

Court, is comprised of the states that have ratified the Court's statute. The ASP has ultimate oversight authority over the Court. It is the Assembly, not the Court that is responsible for managing the administration of the Court, deciding what measures to take when a member fails to cooperate, and controlling the budget. In addition, if a judge, the Prosecutor, or the Registrar does not act independently or is biased, the Assembly can remove him or her. The ASP demonstrates that the ICC is controlled by states, not faceless bureaucrats. Many of these states are our allies, whose national interests are close to our own. Thus, if America ratifies the Rome Statute, we will have the power to work with our allies to shape the work of the ICC and hold it accountable.

There are also provisions that limit the powers of the Prosecutor. For instance, the Prosecutor's office has no authority to decide on its own to pursue a case. He or she cannot begin a formal field investigation without the approval of the Pre-Trial Chamber of judges. Furthermore, the judges and Prosecutor are responsible for overseeing each other's impartiality whenever it might reasonably be doubted on any ground. Additionally, the Security Council can defer an investigation for 12 months and renew deferrals indefinitely. The ICC judges not only should have very high credentials to be nominated, but must also be elected by a two-thirds majority of the ASP. In addition, no two judges may be nationals of the same state. Similarly, the Prosecutor and Deputy Prosecutor must be elected by an absolute majority of the ASP and must be of different nationalities. The election of the first 18 judges demonstrates a precedent of required excellence. American participation would be a very powerful way to ensure that this continues to happen.

Concern 5: The Court will be Like the Ad Hoc Tribunals

Although previous ad hoc tribunals have helped a great deal in bringing to justice those responsible for the atrocities committed in the former Yugoslavia and Rwanda, they have failed to deter atrocities because they are established only after the crimes they address have been committed. The early corruption of the International Criminal Tribunal for Rwanda, the chaotic start of the International Criminal Tribunal for the former Yugoslavia, and the occasional failure of the tribunals to follow the rules and safeguards in their statutes, are all pointed to as failures of the process. The setbacks of the tribunals came from their improvised nature, lack of a permanent mandate, and inadequate oversight by the Security Council. As each was established, it had to start from scratch in operations, investigations, prosecutions, personnel recruitment and financing.

The permanence of the Court greatly reduces these problems. For example, the Court has its own set of rules and standards for procedure and evidence, personnel recruitment and the election of judges, all of which are carefully discussed and reviewed before approval by the ASP. The ability of the ICC to organize itself permanently before its first indictments gives the institution a huge advantage over the ad hoc tribunals. In fact, many of the tribunals' staff were closely involved in ICC negotiations, and some have even been elected to serve as judges or members of the Registry. These individuals can take their past experiences and transform them into positive reinforcement for the Court.

Concern 6: The Court will Limit America's Ability to Act in the National Interest

A final concern is that the ICC will inhibit policymakers to act or make choices in the interest of the country. One fear, especially felt by many military officials, is that military operations may constitute crimes against humanity, or, once defined, the crime of aggression. Such concerns are unnecessary because the ICC was not designed to prosecute citizens of democratic countries which normally do not plan and commit atrocities. In fact, it is unthinkable that Americans would ever commit such crimes since they are calculated and strategic, not the collateral damage of warfare.

The crimes under the Court's jurisdiction must be extremely serious and executed as a matter of official policy, within a repeated pattern of abuse. This ensures that only a very particular type of criminal will come before the ICC. The war crimes the Statute describes can be found in the military manuals of the U.S. army and the definitions of their elements were shaped, supported and finally approved by the U.S. and Department of Defense in negotiations on the ICC. The crime of genocide requires the intent to destroy a national, ethnic, racial or religious group. Crimes against humanity and war crimes have to be committed as part of a broad and consistent policy, not an inadvertent act. Therefore the U.S. need not fear prosecution from an error or combat miscalculation. It is unthinkable that a U.S. official would ever commit such crimes. Since the end of World War II, it is arguable that no actions taken by Americans would qualify for the ICC's jurisdiction.

In addition, conservatives should not fear that the worldwide deployment of Americans to serve our country will expose them to the political abuses of the ICC. Article 98 of the Statute provides for protection of U.S. citizens serving in the military or as officials abroad. It requires the ICC to defer to Status of Forces Agreements (SOFAs), which protect U.S. soldiers, sailors, air force personnel and marines abroad, and to Status of Mission Agreements (SOMAs) for U.S. officials.

Therefore, it may even be argued that the Court will aid in the protection of Americans, especially servicepersons, because of its many protective provisions. Concern over possible prosecution for the crime of aggression is understandable. However, there will be jurisdiction over the crime of aggression only when a provision is adopted defining the crime and the conditions for such jurisdiction. If the U.S. ratifies the Statute before such a definition is adopted, it will be able to participate in negotiations surrounding its adoption. As a State Party [a country that has ratified the Treaty of Rome], the U.S. will also have the right to reject the definition and thus not be bound by the ICC's jurisdiction for this crime. Thus, for the U.S., the jurisdiction of the court can easily remain only war crimes, genocide, and crimes against humanity.

Conclusion

Freedom, democracy and equality—these are all profoundly American values upon which the United States was founded. The U.S. should use its strength and influence in the world to support those values on an international scale and thus put its power to good use. Personal accountability and respect for the rule of law is a fundamental value on which America was built, protection of which is also fundamental at the international level.

Many conservatives often support humanitarian efforts to help those in need. They frequently mount substantial efforts to aid individuals victimized by violent conflict, genocide, and political upheaval. Conservatives respect and make sacrifices for the principle that ignoring a mutilated man, a raped woman or a starving child, no matter how far overseas, is a moral outrage. Although the American people overwhelmingly support humanitarian efforts, their resolve is often tested by the substantial costs in American lives and tax dollars. In addition, humanitarian relief efforts rarely lead to a permanent solution. If the ICC does indeed have a deterrent effect, much of the humanitarian work sponsored by the U.S. abroad may no longer be necessary, allowing Americans to continue to advance their humanitarian ideals while potentially avoiding the deaths of American soldiers and rerouting the millions spent on humanitarian aid.

While such efforts are crucial and greatly aid victims, the goal should be to prevent these atrocities when they occur, and to punish the perpetrators. This is the mandate of the ICC. It holds to account individuals that commit horrible acts. Americans fight to end horrible crimes such as human trafficking, slavery, religious persecution and mutilation. Such crimes are included in the jurisdiction of the Court. The Court's aims and objectives demonstrate that the ICC shares similar values and moral history that America was founded upon, and that common ground exists both for the Court and U.S. acceptance of it.

POSTSCRIPT

Is U.S. Refusal to Join the International Criminal Court Wise?

With the ICC treaty in effect, the countries that were a party to it met in 2003 and elected the court's 18 judges and its chief prosecutor. By 2004 the ICC was ready to begin operations at its seat in The Hague, the Netherlands. Soon thereafter, several African countries soon filed complaints of atrocities by various government and rebel forces in the long and gruesome fighting in and near Uganda in central Africa. In response, the ICC prosecutor launched three investigations. A fourth investigation began in 2005 after the Security Council asked the ICC to probe charges of criminal activity in civil war in the Darfur region of Sudan. The ICC prosecutor has issued five arrest warrants related to these cases, and in March 2006, the ICC took charge of its first prisoner, Thomas Lubanga, after the Democratic Republic of the Congo extradited him. Lubanga is a former rebel leader alleged to have committed the war crime, as defined by the ICC treaty, of conscripting children under the age of 15 into an armed force. His trial is expected to begin in early 2006. The Web site of the ICC at http://www.icc-cpi.int/ is an excellent source of information about its organization, personnel, and activities.

As of October 2006, 102 countries had formally agreed to the Statue of Rome and joined the Assembly of State Parties that constitutes the ICC's governing board. The United States remained among the absent, and it is unlikely this status will change before a new U.S. president takes office in 2009. Meanwhile, the Bush administration continues to press other governments to sign Article 98 agreements. About 100 countries have done so, but most have been small countries subject to U.S. pressure. Among the countries that have not signed Article 98 agreements with the United States are all the countries of Europe, all the other permanent members of the UN Security Council, Japan, Canada, Mexico, and all South American countries except Colombia. For an analysis of U.S. policy, read the Congressional Research Service report, "U.S. Policy Regarding the International Criminal Court" (June 14, 2006) on the Web at http://fpc.state.gov/documents/organization/68799.pdf. A recent article critical of U.S. policy is Robert C. Johansen, "The Impact of U.S. Policy Toward the International Criminal Court on the Prevention of Genocide, War Crimes, And Crimes Against Humanity," *Human Rights Quarterly* (May 2006). Taking a more skeptical view of international courts is Helena Cobban, "International Courts," *Foreign Policy* (April 2006).

Even when a new president takes office, American sensitivity to U.S. sovereignty and to the image of an American being tried by an international court will make adherence to the ICC treaty very controversial. When asked a general question about an international criminal court to try war criminals if their home country would not do so, 71 percent of Americans thought the United States should participate. However, a poll that asked Americans, "Should the International Criminal Court be allowed to try United States soldiers accused of war crimes if the United States government refuses to try them?" found 50 percent of the respondents replying no, compared to 37 percent saying yes, and 12 percent unsure. More on the future of the ICC can be found in Joanna Harrington, ed., *Bringing Power to Justice?: The Prospects of the International Criminal Court* (McGill-Queen's University Press, 2006)

ISSUE 18

Should Accused Terrorists Have Legal Rights Similar to Prisoners of War?

YES: Katherine Newell Bierman, from Testimony on "Military Commissions in Light of the Supreme Court Decision in *Hamdan v. Rumsfeld*," before the Committee on Armed Services, U.S. Senate (July 19, 2006)

NO: Steven G. Bradbury, from Testimony on "*Hamdan v. Rumsfeld*: Establishing a Constitutional Process," before the Committee on the Judiciary, U.S. Senate (July 11, 2006)

ISSUE SUMMARY

YES: Katherine Newell Bierman, Counterterrorism Counsel, U.S. Program of Human Rights Watch, urges Congress to ensure that terrorist suspects captured on the battlefield are prosecuted according to the standards of the Uniform Code of Military Justice.

NO: Steven G. Bradbury, Acting Assistant Attorney General, U.S. Department of Justice, contends that it is neither necessary nor wise to require that military commissions follow all of the procedures of a court-martial when dealing with terrorists for their war crimes.

$\mathbf{A}$n important advance of international law during modern history has been near universal adoption of several treaties governing the treatment of military prisoners of war. These treaties also govern the treatment of captured members of irregular forces, such as guerillas. The most important of these treaties are the four Geneva Conventions (1864, 1929, 1949, and 1949) supplemented by amendments (called protocols: two in 1977, 2005).

The question here is whether and to what degree the Geneva Conventions should apply to terrorists both those taken in battle and those seized abroad and charged with supporting terrorist operations. While this issue is not wholly new, it came into sharp focus in relation to prisoners captured by the United States in Afghanistan and held largely at the U.S. naval base at

Guantánamo Bay, Cuba. Eventually, the Bush administration eventually classified Taliban prisoners as soldiers subject to the Geneva Conventions' protections. By contrast, al Qaeda members were labeled "enemy combatants," on the grounds that they were not members of an organized military. Therefore, the administration held that al Qaeda prisoners do not have the protection of the Geneva Conventions or of many of the rights accorded to prisoners of war tried in military courts.

Some of the differences relate to procedures such as whether a detainee has to be charged and brought to a speedy trial, the use of evidence, and the right to counsel. Beyond matters of legal process, there is also the question of what, if any, extraordinary measures can be used to persuade/coerce prisoners to reveal information that U.S. interrogators want to learn. Critics of such measures refer to them all as torture, but defenders of threatening sleep deprivation, and other tactics claim that they are permissible and necessary when dealing with lawless terrorists. The issue came to a head when Salim Ahmed Hamdan, an alleged al Qaeda fighter captured in Afghanistan in 2001, filed suit in U.S. court challenging the legality of the plan of U.S. Secretary of Defense Donald Rumsfeld to try him before a military commission established by the president rather than before a court-martial operating under the Uniform Code of Military Justice. The Supreme Court ruled in *Hamden v. Rumsfeld* (2006) that the president had no authority under any existing statute or under the president's constitutional authority to create special military courts and that without such authority, the legal process for prisoners like Hamdan had to conform to existing U.S. law and to the Geneva Conventions. The court's decision did, however, leave the way open for Congress to enact law that would set up special procedures for the treatment of Hamdan-like prisoners.

That is where this debate takes up. Congress began to consider proposals about the treatment and trial of such prisoners. In the first reading, Katherine Newell Bierman contends that they should be afforded all the protections extended to anyone tried under the Uniform Code of Military Justice (UCMJ). Steven G. Bradbury disagrees, arguing that it is neither legally necessary or feasible to do so. In particular, Bierman and Bradbury differ over the applicability of "Common Article 3," language common to all the Geneva Conventions that, as Article 3 in Section 1 requires that prisoners no longer taking an "active part in the hostilities . . . shall in all circumstances be treated humanely," and:

To this end, the following acts are and shall remain prohibited:

(a) violence to life and person, in particular murder of all kinds, mutilation, cruel treatment and torture;
(b) taking of hostages;
(c) outrages upon personal dignity, in particular humiliating and degrading treatment;
(d) the passing of sentences and the carrying out of executions without previous judgment pronounced by a regularly constituted court affording all the judicial guarantees which are recognized as indispensable by civilized peoples.

YES

Katherine Newell Bierman

Military Commissions in Light of the Supreme Court Decision in *Hamdan v. Rumsfeld*

The Supreme Court's decision in *Hamdan* presents the Congress and the administration with an opportunity—to start bringing accused terrorists to justice in a way that will both protect America's security and uphold its values. I hope that Congress seizes this opportunity, by reaffirming the United States' longstanding commitment to Common Article 3 of the Geneva Conventions, and ensuring that trials of terrorist suspects captured on the battlefield go forward in accordance with the standards of the Uniform Code of Military Justice, which have served this country so well for so long. If the Congress and the administration choose that course, it will help to rebuild America's moral authority in the world, reaffirm America's commitment to the rule of law, and reclaim America's greatest tool in the war on terror: our integrity.

If, on the other hand, the Congress and the administration try to find a way around *Hamdan*, by shirking the Geneva Conventions or creating substandard tribunals, the tribunal system will remain on trial, instead of the terrorists. That would be a profoundly unfortunate result, whether the goal is an effective fight against terrorism or upholding the rule of law.

Common Article 3 of the Geneva Conventions Applied to al-Qaeda

In *Hamdan*, the Supreme Court determined that Common Article 3 of the Geneva Conventions ("Common Article 3") applied to Mr. Hamdan as a member of al-Qaeda captured on the battlefield. The Court determined the military commissions established by the President to try Mr. Hamdan and other "enemy combatants" violated the requirements of Common Article 3.

In 2002, the Administration had decided that no part of the Geneva Conventions, including Common Article 3, would apply in a legally binding way to the armed conflict with al-Qaeda. Since the *Hamdan* decision was announced, some have suggested that this ruling somehow imposes a new or alien requirement on the U.S. military, and that it is inappropriate to apply Common Article

Committee on Armed Services, U.S. Senate, Katherine Newell Bierman (July 19, 2006).

3 to al-Qaeda because it is not a signatory to the Geneva Conventions and because its members defy the laws of war and any fundamental regard for human rights.

This argument misrepresents the purpose and requirements of Common Article 3. It is true that al-Qaeda is an irregular force that does not abide by the rules of war and is not a signatory to the Geneva Conventions. As such, its members are not entitled to prisoner of war status, or covered by many of the other provisions of the Third Geneva Convention concerning prisoners of war.

But the framers of the Geneva Conventions intended to establish a minimal standard that would cover *everyone* involved in an armed conflict, regardless of the nature of the conflict or an individual's status or behavior. Common Article 3 is that standard. It is specifically designed to apply to conflicts between a state that is party to the Conventions (like the US) and a non-state force, like al Qaeda, that, by definition, could not be a signatory. It is a narrow rule with the broadest application, and establishes the barest minimum safeguards for humane treatment and fair justice. It ensures that no one caught up in an armed conflict is completely beyond the reach of law.

Common Article 3 of the Geneva Conventions and Humane Treatment

The Administration also argues that the terms of Common Article 3 are too vague. In particular, proponents point to the prohibition on "outrages against personal dignity," and say that the U.S. military would be unable to apply Common Article 3 in practice. But the Pentagon has been clear about the meaning of Common Article 3 and its obligations for decades, as the standards it embodies are already part of U.S. military doctrine, policy, and training. The U.S. military has long treated Common Article 3 and, in fact, the much higher standard for the treatment of POWs, as standard operating procedure. This Committee heard testimony last week to this effect from Judge Advocates Generals. [Note: The judge advocate general for each of the U.S. military services is its top legal officer.] Following the *Hamdan* decision, U.S. Deputy Secretary of Defense Gordon England issued a memorandum to all Department of Defense units stating unequivocally that existing Department of Defense orders, policies, directives, execute orders, and doctrine already comply with the standards of Common Article 3. I sincerely doubt that the Deputy Secretary of Defense would make such a statement if the Pentagon was unclear about the meaning of the terms of Common Article 3.

The U.S. has been steadfast in applying the full protections of the Geneva Conventions (i.e., far more than just Common Article 3) to enemy fighters, even when not required to do so. U.S. adherence to the highest standards has improved treatment of captured American service members, even when capturing governments claimed American servicemen were unprotected by Geneva.

The U.S. even applied the full protections of the Geneva Conventions to soldiers of governments who insisted the Conventions did not bind them, and when the Conventions technically did not apply. Examples include the conflict against the Viet-Cong in Vietnam, covert operations against the Soviet Union in Afghanistan, and against forces loyal to Somali warlords targeting international peacekeepers. The current conflict is not the last Americans will ever fight—it is only a matter of time before governments who might otherwise avoid the appearance of illegality will exploit America's efforts to carve out exceptions to the Geneva Conventions to justify poor treatment of captured Americans.

Were Congress to repudiate in some way the application of Common Article 3 to this or any conflict, it would be reversing decades of U.S. law and policy and sending a message to U.S. troops that is diametrically opposed to their training.

Congress has also set standards. The humane treatment standard required by Common Article 3 is essentially the same standard that Congress already mandated when it passed the McCain Amendment last year, which stated as law, "No individual in the custody or under the physical control of the United States Government, regardless of nationality or physical location, shall be subject to cruel, inhuman, or degrading treatment or punishment."

For decades, the United States has accepted the substance of Common Article 3 as both an obligation under treaty and customary international law. If Congress were to step back from that obligation, it would in effect be establishing a reservation to the Geneva Conventions. No country in the world has ever before formally renounced these obligations under Common Article 3. Such a step would send a message that America's enemies would all-too willingly amplify: the United States *affirmatively* seeks to treat people inhumanely . . ., *intends* to try and execute people without fair trials, and *willingly* defies its own allies and history to do so.

Common Article 3 is not just a matter of human rights. Like many laws of war, it is good war-fighting. . . . Insurgent captives are not guaranteed full protection under the articles of the Geneva Conventions relative to the handling of EPWs [enemy prisoners of war]. However, Article 3 of the Conventions requires that insurgent captives be humanely treated and forbids violence to life and person—in particular murder, mutilation, cruel treatment, and torture. It further forbids commitment of outrages upon personal dignity, taking of hostages, passing of sentences, and execution without prior judgment by a regularly constituted court.

Humane treatment of insurgent captives should extend far beyond compliance with Article 3, if for no other reason than to render them more susceptible to interrogation. The insurgent is trained to expect brutal treatment upon capture. If, contrary to what he has been led to believe, this mistreatment is not forthcoming, he is apt to become psychologically softened for interrogation. Furthermore, brutality by either capturing troops or friendly interrogators will reduce defections and serve as grist for the insurgent's propaganda mill.

Common Article 3 of the Geneva Conventions and War Crimes

In the War Crimes Act of 1997, Congress made it a felony for any U.S. military personnel or U.S. national to engage in conduct that violates Common Article 3. Reports indicate that the Administration encouraged interrogators to adopt techniques that violated Common Article 3 by telling them they would be immune from prosecution.

In the wake of the *Hamdan* decision, some have expressed concern that applying Common Article 3 to al Qaeda would leave American troops vulnerable to frivolous prosecution.

To accept such a proposition, one would have to believe that the likelihood of war crimes prosecutions by the United States has no relation to the reality of current or historical practice. No soldier can be prosecuted for violations of the War Crimes Act unless military prosecutors decide to bring charges against him. The military justice system is highly unlikely to take action against soldiers for trivial or ambiguous offenses under this Act, especially since it has never done so even to prosecute even extremely serious crimes. To date, no U.S. service member has ever been prosecuted for any violation of the War Crimes Act, even in situations such as the war in Iraq, where everyone agrees the Geneva Conventions fully apply—much less for violations of Common Article 3 occurring under less clear circumstances.

The fact is, American military prosecutors, and not anyone else, will make the decision to prosecute. It is hard to understand why we would suddenly not trust the Executive to judge whether a U.S. service member's suspected crime was sufficiently grave and substantiated to merit prosecution.

The Administration also argues that, because Common Article 3 is an international standard interpreted by foreign courts, these courts will somehow create frivolous standards that U.S. courts will use to prosecute Americans. This proposition disregards the fact that foreign judicial opinions are not binding on U.S. courts, and it is extremely unlikely that a U.S. prosecutor would pursue a case or a U.S. court would hold someone criminally responsible under a strained interpretation of this standard. The provision of Common Article 3 concerning "outrages upon personal dignity" has always been interpreted as prohibiting very serious abuses. According to the official commentary on the Geneva Conventions, it was meant to prohibit acts "which world opinion finds particularly revolting—acts which were committed frequently during World War II."

Judicial opinions from international criminal tribunal opinions reflect that level of severity. "Outrages upon personal dignity" as a criminal act are usually a form of violence, determined in part by severity and duration, and the intensity and duration of the resulting physical or mental suffering. Typically a crime of an "outrage against human dignity" is prosecuted alongside other egregious or violent acts to cover behavior outrageous precisely because it offends all sense of decency.

For example, international criminal tribunal cases often prosecute outrages against human dignity alongside charges such as murder, rape, and torture— men who forced women to dance naked on tables before they raped them, murderers who forced women to strip naked in public before they were killed, or interrogators who rubbed a knife on a woman's thigh and threatened to put it in her during torture. Justice demanded those prosecutions address such humiliating treatment as separate outrages in their own right. While "outrages" do not have to take place only in the context of rape or murder, they have generally been prosecuted in the context of the most extreme situations of abuse. I would add that the U.S. Constitution gives us a lot of words that are hard to define: for example, due process, free speech, cruel and unusual punishment, unreasonable searches. Americans believe in the principles embodied in these terms, even though their precise legal meaning is not self-evident. We don't say, "I can't define due process in ten words or less, so let's not have any." Americans have worked out the meaning of these terms over 200 years. The precise meaning of the terms of the Geneva Conventions have also become broadly understood in the 50 years since the Conventions were drafted, and are well understood by the U.S. military. It was the administration's decision to ignore the Conventions that confused our troops, not the Supreme Court's decision to respect Geneva. If the Congress wants clarity, the best thing it can do is to reaffirm that Common Article 3 applies.

Common Article 3 is actually much easier than you might think, because it isn't the gold standard, like granting prisoner-of-war rights. It's the barest minimum. The list of prohibited conduct is short precisely because the drafters of the Geneva Conventions agreed to apply it broadly.

Finally, we should remember that the War Crimes Act not only permits prosecution of American troops who commit such crimes against others, but prosecution of foreign nationals who commit such crimes against Americans. If we were to deny the application of Common Article 3 to this conflict, we would deny ourselves one avenue to try terrorists who perpetrate these offenses against Americans. *If we want an act that was committed* against *an American to be a crime, it also has to be a crime when it is committed* by *an American.* I think it is hard to disagree with that bottom line.

Common Article 3 and Fair Trials

People captured on the battlefield and suspected of having committed war crimes or other serious offenses should be brought to justice. Military commissions that prosecute these persons must meet international fair trial standards. The rules and procedures for the military commissions should be based upon those provided for general courts-martial. Any departures from these standards must be exceptional, narrowly tailored to meet the interests of justice, and uniformly established before any proceedings begin. In particular, some principles must not be compromised.

Military Commissions and Coerced Evidence

Through the adoption of the McCain Amendment to the Detainee Treatment Act, Congress established a prohibition on cruel, inhuman, or degrading treatment or punishment expressly to address abusive interrogation techniques. International and U.S. law have long recognized that one way to curb official abuses in gathering information is to prohibit the use of any evidence obtained through such actions in judicial proceedings. Otherwise, the goal of obtaining a conviction becomes an incentive to coerce confessions from suspects. This is the fundamental logic behind international rules against prosecuting people with evidence obtained through torture, and behind rules in U.S. courts against the use of involuntary confessions or evidence obtained through other unlawful means.

The bottom line: *Congress cannot effectively prohibit abusive interrogation techniques if rules for military commissions do not explicitly and effectively keep evidence obtained through those techniques out of subsequent legal proceedings.* Evidence obtained through interrogations that violate the Detainee Treatment Act shouldn't be used in military commission hearings. Anything less than this will cut the heart out of the McCain amendment. Upholding this rule provides the McCain amendment with an enforcement mechanism.

Furthermore, any rules and procedures must make such a prohibition meaningful. For this reason, rather than starting from scratch, Congress should ensure that military commissions use the rules and procedures in the Manual for Courts-Martial and accompanying case law necessary to prohibit the use of coerced evidence. In the U.S. military justice system, an involuntary statement obtained through the use of coercion generally may not be received in evidence against an accused who made the statement. The accused must move to suppress, or object to the evidence. If the military judge thinks there is sufficient doubt about the statement, the prosecution—the party with the best access to the story behind the statement—then has the burden of establishing the admissibility of the evidence. The military judge must find by a preponderance of the evidence that a statement by the accused was made voluntarily before it may be received into evidence. Statements of witnesses not present before the court are presumptively inadmissible. The proponent must show the statement meets limited exceptions to this rule designed to weed out questionable evidence.

The failed military commission rules demonstrate a stark contrast. On March 24, 2006, the General Counsel of the Department of Defense adopted a change to the military commission rules to prohibit the use of evidence obtained through torture. However, the rule provided few safeguards to make the prohibition meaningful. It failed to indicate whether the commission on its own would make inquiries into the possible use of torture and whether the U.S. government must provide the information the commission requests to determine whether a statement was extracted through torture. It also failed to provide guidance on whether the prosecution must make its own independent determination of whether interrogation methods constituted torture, or whether it must accept determinations made by others, e.g., those conducting the interrogations, or senior Pentagon or Department of Justice officials.

The Use of Hearsay Evidence in Military Commissions

Opponents of the use of the U.S. military justice system's rules concerning hearsay evidence say that such rules will stymie prosecutions by limiting evidence essential to the prosecution of accused terrorists. They suggest that rules regarding hearsay—which admit "second hand" statements only in exceptional circumstances—will require military commanders to be called in from war-fighting duties to testify at proceedings thousands of miles away; that key witnesses in Afghanistan and elsewhere will refuse to travel to testify; and that valuable and reliable evidence will be lost to logistics.

In fact, the U.S. courts-martial system has rules and procedures to address these concerns, and allows in more hearsay evidence that these arguments suggest. Hearsay exceptions in U.S. courts-martial are generally the same kinds used in U.S. federal courts. Summaries of statements made by witnesses in an excited state, at a time of high stress, or just after perceiving an event are all admissible—and the actual witnesses who made the statements need not be present. In all of these cases, soldiers or arresting officers can simply describe what witnesses on the scene told them; the person making the battlefield utterance who wouldn't have to. In this sense, there is some modest burden on the military, but it's worth it given the alternative, which allows easy cover-up of coercive interrogation. In addition, there are many other ways to adhere to the existing rules against hearsay without imposing excessive travel burdens on witnesses who are located far away. Witnesses can testify by closed circuit television, or their depositions by both sides can be taped and played in court. Moreover, the Military Rules of Evidence allow a declarant to be determined "unavailable" by reason of military necessity, opening the door to a number of hearsay exceptions.

The bottom line concerning hearsay evidence should be this: *Any rules or procedures that allow hearsay should not allow the government to convict people on the basis of secret interrogations without producing the witness, either in person, by closed-circuit television, or by deposition.* Our concern is that such interrogations are likely to be described by only the interrogator, or possibly only the interrogator's supervisor or colleague, or a government official who spoke to an interrogator from a foreign country. This is fundamentally unfair for two reasons.

First, if you are listening to a report from an interrogator about a confession or admission, how do you test whether the statement was coerced or even tortured out of the declarant? You are deciding whether the interrogation used torture by asking the interrogator himself. If the declarant also testifies, at least then the fact-finder can decide based on two sides to that story—the declarant and any interrogator who might refute claims of mistreatment.

The second reason does not relate to statements by interrogators, but statements made by one detainee implicating another. When the statement is second-hand, you can't directly test its credibility. According to the Administration, al-Qaeda members are trained to lie during interrogation. No one should be convicted on the basis of the testimony of such allegedly unsavory characters without the opportunity to question the witness directly. An interrogator's hearsay account of what one detainee said about another deprives the suspect of this essential confrontation right.

Some advocates adopt the evidentiary rules and procedures of international criminal tribunals to accommodate hearsay evidence. However, to be effective and fair, such a step would need to do more than simply adopt an evidentiary standard. International criminal tribunals use a panoply of evidentiary and other rules to ensure fairness. Generally, their rules allow the factfinder to admit any relevant evidence that he or she deems to have probative value. But, there are other rules that work with this standard.

For example, the tribunal is made up of legally trained judges who have experience making fine distinctions on the reliability and value of different forms of evidence that a jury or even a panel of non-lawyer officers simply won't have. There is a clear prohibition on any evidence that is obtained by a violation of internationally recognized human rights norms if "the violation casts substantial doubt on the reliability of the evidence; or the admission of the evidence would be antithetical to and would seriously damage the integrity of the proceedings." The judges can decide this issue on their own; a party doesn't have to raise the matter. The judges are instructed to look at "indicia of [a statement's] reliability" such as its truthfulness and trustworthiness along with whether or not the statement was voluntarily given. The judges can decide to disregard testimony after it has been given rather than keeping it out in the first place. In ruling on admissibility, including the relevance or probative value of hearsay evidence, the court must give reasons that are placed in the record of the proceedings.

Hearsay admissibility is one of the most misunderstood rules in the U.S. system, with many careful and complex rules interwoven over time, but the U.S. military judge advocate corps knows them well. If the Administration has a good reason to proceed differently, let the Administration make the case. But concerns about "getting in the evidence" should not obscure the bottom line: *Any rules or procedures that allow hearsay should not allow the government to convict people on the basis of secret interrogations without producing the witness.* The invitation to abuse is simply too great.

"*Miranda* Warnings" and Military Commissions

The administration witnesses before the Judiciary Committee say that using the U.S. military justice system's requirements for rights warnings and exclusion of evidence would compromise military operations—that U.S. troops in the field would face a choice between reciting *Miranda* warnings as they conducted urban warfare, and thereby potentially discouraging valuable intelligence information, or forgoing prosecution of suspected terrorists.

But the rules and procedures for courts-martial have already dealt with this issue. The rights warning is not required when someone is interrogated for the purpose of gathering intelligence. Moreover, the failure to give a rights warning does not keep evidence obtained through an intelligence interrogation out of court. Only if an interrogation is begun for the purposes of law enforcement or disciplinary proceedings is a rights warning required for the resulting statements to be admissible. Whether the interrogation is disciplinary or law enforcement is determined by assessing all the facts and circumstances at the time of the interview to determine whether the questioner was acting or could reasonably be considered to be acting in an official law enforcement or disciplinary capacity.

Evidence obtained through intelligence interrogations is generally admissible. The other side can challenge that evidence for a number of reasons, the most relevant here being that it was coerced (or that the interrogations were really for law enforcement). If the judge decides evidence from intelligence interrogations cannot be admitted, the next question is whether the evidence from the law enforcement interrogation was tainted by a coerced intelligence interrogation. Evidence from intelligence interrogations can in principle be given to law enforcement interrogators, but if the evidence from an intelligence interrogation was coerced, that may keep out evidence from both interrogations.

This issue typically comes up when US service members are questioned for intelligence-gathering purposes, which is not unusual. For example, when troops return to base after combat, they are often debriefed by intelligence personnel—a form of intelligence interrogation. Should the debriefer determine that a US serviceman may have been involved in a crime, the purpose of the questioning might shift, with the purpose determining the admissibility of unwarned statements that the serviceman might make. The classic legal opinion on this rule is *U.S. v. Lonetree* [Court of Military Appeals, 1992], which dealt with a Marine Corps embassy guard stationed in Moscow who was charged, among other things, with committing espionage by passing confidential information to Soviet agents. He was debriefed for intelligence purposes and only later interrogated for prosecution. The court knew the difference, and unwarned statements made during the course of the intelligence debriefing came in.

That's the rule now. Again, if the Administration has a good reason for changing the rules, let it make the case. The bottom line regarding Miranda warnings is this: *no one should be forced to testify against themselves or to confess guilt.* This is another reason why statements which have been made as the result of torture may not be used as evidence in any proceedings. The protections in a general court-martial that prevent forced self-incrimination require that people be warned of their right to remain silent and their right to an attorney fairly early in a law enforcement or disciplinary process. As with rules and procedures that give effect to the ban on abusive interrogations, Congress should look to the rules already in place, already tested, already used in training, and use the U.S. military justice system to its best advantage.

In closing I want to see terrorists brought to justice. I was in the room when accused al-Qaeda propaganda minister Ali Hamza al Bahlul called the proceedings illegitimate. Of course he said that, but that's not what's important. What killed me was the knowledge that any objective observer would have to agree with him. Please do what's necessary to set the bottom line where it should be, and let's make it happen.

Steven G. Bradbury  **NO**

Concerning the Supreme Court's Decision in *Hamdan v. Rumsfeld*

T he Supreme Court's decision in *Hamdan v. Rumsfeld* . . . is a decision without historical analogue. Since the Revolutionary War, the United States has used military commissions in time of armed conflict to bring to justice unlawful combatants for violations of the laws of war. Indeed, *Hamdan* recognized that the Supreme Court itself has sanctioned the use of military commissions on multiple occasions in the past. Yet the Court in *Hamdan* held that the military commissions that the President established were inconsistent with the Uniform Code of Military Justice and the Geneva Conventions.

The Court's reasoning in *Hamdan* may be surprising and disappointing to many of us, but it is not my intent to reargue the case this morning. The Administration will, of course, as the President [George W. Bush] has said, abide by the decision of the Court.

It is important to point out that the Court did not call into question the authority of the United States to detain enemy combatants in the War on Terror, and that the Court's decision does not require us to close the detention facilities at Guantanamo Bay or release any terrorist held by the United States. Moreover, the Court implicitly recognized several fundamental government positions: The Court confirmed our view that the atrocities committed by al Qaeda on September 11 have triggered our right to use military force in self-defense and that we are involved in an armed conflict with al Qaeda to which the laws of war apply.

And the Supreme Court made clear that its decision rested only on an interpretation of current statutory and treaty-based law. The Court did not address the President's constitutional authority and did not reach any constitutional question. Indeed, the Court did not accept the petitioner's arguments that the Constitution precludes the use of military commissions.

Therefore, the *Hamdan* decision now gives Congress and the Administration a clear opportunity to work together to address the matters raised by the case, including the appropriate procedures governing military commissions. As Justice [Stephen G.] Breyer stated in his separate opinion, "Nothing prevents the President from returning to Congress to seek the authority he believes necessary."

Committee on the Judiciary, U.S. Senate, by Steven G. Bradbury (July 11, 2006).

In its decision, the Court also addressed the application of the Geneva Conventions to al Qaeda fighters in our War on Terror. On this point, it is important to emphasize that the Court did not decide that the Geneva Conventions as a whole apply to our conflict with al Qaeda or that members of al Qaeda are entitled to the privileges of prisoner of war status. The Court did hold, rather, that the basic standards contained in common Article 3 of the Geneva Conventions apply to the conflict with al Qaeda.

Of course, the terrorists who fight for al Qaeda have nothing but contempt for the laws of war. They have killed thousands of innocent civilians in New York, Washington, and Pennsylvania—and thousands more in London, Madrid, Kenya, Tanzania, Yemen, Jordan, Indonesia, Iraq, and Afghanistan. They advocate unrestrained violence and chaos. As a matter of course, they kidnap relief aid workers, behead contractors, journalists, and U.S. military personnel, and bomb shrines, wedding parties, restaurants, and night clubs. They openly mock the rule of law, the Geneva Conventions, and the standards of civilized people everywhere, and they will attack us again if given the chance.

The Supreme Court's conclusion that common Article 3 applies to members of al Qaeda is a significant development that must be considered as we continue the healthy discussion between the political Branches about the standards and procedures that ought to govern the treatment of terrorist detainees.

Courts-Martial and Military Commissions

In moving forward after *Hamdan*, the basic question we must answer together is how best to pursue the prosecution of al Qaeda and other terrorists engaged in armed conflict with the United States.

The *Hamdan* majority held that Congress had greatly restricted the President's authority to establish procedures for military commissions. The Court read the Uniform Code of Military Justice, or "UCMJ," to require presumptively that captured enemy combatants, including unlawful combatants such as al Qaeda terrorists, are entitled to the very same military court-martial procedures that are provided for the members of our Armed Forces.

In trying al Qaeda terrorists for their war crimes, we firmly believe that it is neither appropriate as a matter of national policy, practical as a matter of military reality, nor feasible in protecting sensitive intelligence sources and methods, to require that military commissions follow all of the procedures of a court-martial.

For example, when members of the U.S. Armed Forces are suspected of crimes, the UCMJ, in Article 31(b), provides that they must be informed of their Miranda rights, including the right to counsel, prior to any questioning. The right of access to a lawyer in the military justice system is even more protective than in civilian courts, since it applies as soon as the service member is suspected of an offense. Granting terrorists prophylactic Miranda warnings and extraordinary access to lawyers is inconsistent with security needs and with the need to question detainees for intelligence purposes. The very notion of our military personnel regularly reading captured enemy combatants Miranda warnings on the battlefield is nonsensical.

The rules that apply to courts-martial under the UCMJ also impose strict requirements on the admission of evidence in court-martial proceedings that are wholly unworkable for military commission trials of unlawful combatants in the War on Terror. Court-martial rules require that the chain of custody for evidence be preserved, and that all documents admitted be painstakingly authenticated. But it is extremely difficult during an armed conflict to gather evidence in a way that meets strict criminal procedure requirements, whether collected on the battlefield, during military intelligence operations, or during interrogations of detainees.

Furthermore, court-martial rules prohibit the use of hearsay in ways very similar to the civilian rules of evidence. Yet reliable hearsay statements from the battlefield and from fellow terrorists are often the only probative evidence readily available. In these situations, use of court-martial procedures may mean that the most relevant and probative evidence will be inadmissible. Securing properly sworn and authenticated evidence would also require members of the Armed Forces to leave the front lines to attend legal proceedings, in effect, requiring them to fight al Qaeda members twice, once on the battlefield and then again through legal proceedings.

Article 46 of the UCMJ, and the procedures prescribed under it, require that prosecutors share classified information with the accused if the information will be introduced as evidence at trial. We cannot put at risk our Nation's most sensitive secrets in the War on Terror by exposing them to terrorist detainees. The disclosure of classified information about intelligence sources and methods would compromise national security and could endanger the lives of Americans at home and around the world. That is a risk that can be avoided, while still ensuring that military commission trials are fundamentally fair.

The insistence upon the protections of the UCMJ may not always be easy in the military justice system, but it is often impossible on the battlefields of the present conflict. Our forces are dedicated to fighting this armed conflict; unsurprisingly, they cannot be expected to focus on the law enforcement tasks of gathering evidence and conducting criminal investigations. Such duties would, at best, distract from the military's central mission—fighting and winning the war. Congress has never embraced the notion that dangerous foreign terrorists are entitled to the same procedural protections as American citizens who risk their lives for the Nation.

All of the issues with military commissions identified by the Supreme Court can be addressed and resolved through legislation. The Administration stands ready to work with Congress to do just that. We would like to see Congress act quickly to establish a solid statutory basis for the military commission process, so that trials of captured al Qaeda terrorists can move forward again.

The United States may continue to detain the terrorists we have captured. But as of right now, we cannot effectively punish those who have committed war crimes. That is unacceptable.

The Court's Jurisdiction Under the DTA

In addition to developing appropriate procedures for military commissions, we will need to consider carefully how any new legislation should clarify the scope of judicial review. In this connection, I want to comment briefly on the Court's threshold conclusion in *Hamdan* that it was proper for the Court to exercise jurisdiction over the case.

The role of the Supreme Court in the separation of powers depends crucially upon the principle that the jurisdiction of federal courts extends only to cases that properly arise under the laws enacted by Congress. Last December, in the Detainee Treatment Act of 2005, Congress expressly established procedures for the review of military commission decisions. The DTA provided that judicial review of military commission proceedings would be strictly limited to post-trial review of the final judgments of military commissions; the DTA expressly deprived the federal courts of jurisdiction to hear pre-trial habeas petitions, such as *Hamdan*'s.

It has long been a canon of interpretation, firmly established by what the dissenting Justices called "[a]n ancient and unbroken line of authority," that statutes removing jurisdiction from the courts have immediate effect in all pending cases. Congress was entitled to legislate against the background of that traditional canon when it enacted the DTA. *Hamdan* makes clear, however, that if Congress seeks to limit the Court's jurisdiction in future cases, it may be well advised to enact statutory provisions that are ironclad and leave absolutely no wiggle room with respect to Congress's intent.

Common Article 3 of the Geneva Conventions

Finally, we will need to address the Court's ruling that common Article 3 of the Geneva Conventions applies to our armed conflict with al Qaeda.

The United States has never before applied common Article 3 in the context of an armed conflict with international terrorists. When the Geneva Conventions were concluded in 1949, of course, the drafters of the Conventions certainly did not anticipate, and did not agree to cover, armed conflicts with international terrorist organizations such as al Qaeda.

In directing that our Armed Forces would treat all detainees humanely regardless of their legal status, the President specifically determined in February 2002 that common Article 3 does not apply to the conflict with al Qaeda on the ground that the War on Terror is decidedly an "international" conflict. It involves the projection of U.S. force to different states to combat a transnational terrorist movement with global reach and a proven record of targeting the United States in multiple countries. The President's conclusion on this point was plainly reasonable. Indeed, it reflects what is a fundamental truth about the Geneva Conventions—that they were not designed as a framework for addressing the kind of conflict we are in with al Qaeda.

We are now faced with the task of implementing the Court's decision on common Article 3. Last year, Congress engaged in a significant public debate on the standard that should govern the treatment of captured al Qaeda terrorists.

Congress codified that standard in the McCain Amendment, part of the Detainee Treatment Act, which prohibits "cruel, inhuman, or degrading treatment or punishment," as defined by reference to the established meaning of our Constitution, for all detainees held by the United States, regardless of nationality or geographic location. Congress rightly assumed that the enactment of the DTA settled questions about the baseline standard that would govern the treatment of detainees by the United States in the War on Terror.

That assumption may no longer be true. By its interpretation of common Article 3 in *Hamdan*, the Supreme Court has imposed another baseline standard—common Article 3—that we must now interpret and implement.

On the one hand, when reasonably read and properly applied, common Article 3 will prohibit the most serious and grave offenses. Most of the provisions of common Article 3 prohibit actions that are universally condemned, such as "violence to life," "murder," "mutilation," "torture," and the "taking of hostages." These are a catalog of the most fundamental violations of international humanitarian law. In fact, they neatly sum up the standard tactics and methods of warfare utilized by our enemy, al Qaeda and its allies, who regularly perpetrate gruesome beheadings, torture, and indiscriminate slaughter through suicide bombings. Consistent with that view, some in the international community, including the International Committee of the Red Cross, have stated that the actions prohibited by common Article 3 involve conduct of a serious nature.

On the other hand, although common Article 3 should be understood to apply only to serious misconduct, it is undeniable that some of the terms in common Article 3 are inherently vague. Common Article 3 prohibits "[o]utrages upon personal dignity, in particular, humiliating and degrading treatment," a phrase that is susceptible of uncertain and unpredictable application. It is also unclear what precisely is meant by "judicial guarantees which are recognized as indispensable by civilized peoples."

Furthermore, the Supreme Court has said that in interpreting a treaty provision such as common Article 3, the meaning given to the treaty language by international tribunals must be accorded "respectful consideration," and the interpretations adopted by other state parties to the treaty are due "considerable weight." Accordingly, the meaning of common Article 3—the baseline standard that now applies to the conduct of U.S. personnel in the War on Terror—would be informed by the evolving interpretations of tribunals and governments outside the United States. Many of these interpretations to date have been consistent with the reading that we would give to common Article 3. Nevertheless, the application of common Article 3 will create a degree of uncertainty for those who fight to defend us from terrorist attack.

We believe that the standards governing the treatment of detainees by the United States in the War on Terror should be certain, and that those standards should be defined by U.S. law, in a manner that will fully satisfy our international obligations.

The meaning and application of the vague terms in common Article 3 are not merely academic questions. The War Crimes Act, 18 U.S.C. § 2441, makes any violation of common Article 3 a felony offense.

The difficult issues raised by the Court's pronouncement on common Article 3 are ones that the political Branches need to consider carefully as they chart a way forward after *Hamdan*. We think this, too, is an area that Congress should address.

Notwithstanding the problematic aspects of the Court's opinion I have described, the decision in *Hamdan* gives the political branches an opportunity to work as one to reestablish the legitimate authority of the United States to rely on military commissions to bring the terrorists to justice. It is also an opportunity to come together to reaffirm our values as a Nation and our faith in the rule of law.

We in the Administration look forward to working with Congress to protect the American people and to ensure that unlawful terrorist combatants can be brought to justice, consistent with the Supreme Court's guidance.

POSTSCRIPT

Should Accused Terrorists Have Legal Rights Similar to Prisoners of War?

After a protracted political struggle within Congress and between legislators and the president, Congress and the White House eventually agreed on a new law governing the treatment and prosecution of terrorist combatants. The Military Commission Act of 2006 can be accessed at http://thomas.loc.gov/cgi-bin/query/D?c109:2:./temp/~c109imPE7n::.

President Bush and those who agreed with him got a great deal of what they wanted. The September 2006 law allows the president to set up special military commissions to try terrorists, to allow the use of hearsay evidence, and, to some degree, even self-incrimination obtained by coercion falling short of "cruel, inhuman, or degrading treatment." The commissions can also bar the accused and their attorney from seeing evidence obtained from sensitive intelligence sources. The law also expansively defines an "unlawful enemy combatant" as anyone who has "purposefully and materially supported hostilities against the United States," gives the president the authority to interpret the meaning of the Geneva Conventions (such as what constitutes "outrages upon personal dignity"), and bars legal challenges to these interpretations based on the Geneva Conventions. Challenges can be mounted, however, based on the Detainee Treatment Act of 2005. The statute does bar "grave breaches" of the Geneva Conventions, but is not clear where the dividing line is. Overall, the detainees are probably better protected than they were before the law was passed, but are much less protected than prisoners of war, much less U.S. citizens charged with crimes in civilian or military courts. It is all but certain that various legal challenges to the law will be filed, claiming that various provisions such as barring the intervention of U.S. courts in some of the procedures are unconstitutional.

Probably the most contentious part of the bill involves what interrogation tactics are still available under the law. Certainly some would ring an alarm bell if used against Americans by U.S. officials in a regular criminal case. As for American attitudes on the subject, most people reject unlimited torture, but few oppose it altogether. For instance, a 2006 poll found that only 32 percent of them believed that torture was "never justified." Another 19 percent thought it was "rarely justified," while 28 percent thought torture was "sometimes justified," and 18 percent believed it as "often justified." Three percent were unsure. An essay supporting the limited use of torture is Andrew C. McCarthy, "Torture: Thinking About the Unthinkable,"

Commentary, July–August 2004. Opposing that stand is Michael Ignatieff, "Evil Under Interrogation: Is Torture Ever Permissible?" *The Financial Times*, May 15, 2004, at http://www.ksg.harvard.edu/news/opeds/. There are no organizations that, as such, support torture, but there are many that oppose it, including Human Right Watch at http://www.hrw.org/. More on the Geneva Conventions is available at http://www.genevaconventions.org/.

Internet References . . .

EarthTrends

An environmental information portal of the World Resources Institute sponsored by such diverse organizations as the Dutch government, the UN Development Programme, and the World Bank

http://earthtrends.wri.org/

Worldwatch Institute

The environmental-activist Worldwatch Institute offers a range of information and commentary on environmental, social, and economic trends. The institute's work revolves around the transition to an environmentally sustainable and socially just society—and how to achieve it.

http://www.worldwatch.org

The Common-Sense Environmentalist's Suite

The organizations listed on this links page offer research and commentary on environmental topics that take a skeptical view of many projections on looming environmental disaster.

http://www.heartland.org/archives/
suites/environment/links.htm

The Environment

*W*hen all is said and done, policy is, or at least ought to be, about values. That is, how do we want our world to be? There are choices to make about what to do (and what not to do). It would be easy if these choices were clearly good versus evil. But things are not usually that simple, and the issue in this part shows the disparity of opinions regarding the current state of the environment.

- Can Destructive Impacts from Global Warming Be Confidently Predicted?

ISSUE 19

Can Destructive Impacts from Global Warming Be Confidently Predicted?

YES: Ralph J. Cicerone, from Testimony on "Questions Surrounding the 'Hockey Stick' Temperature Studies: Implications for Climate Change Assessments," before the Committee on Energy and Commerce, Subcommittee on Oversight and Investigations, U.S. House of Representatives (July 27, 2006)

NO: John R. Christy, from Testimony on "Questions Surrounding the 'Hockey Stick' Temperature Studies: Implications for Climate Change Assessments," before the Committee on Energy and Commerce, Subcommittee on Oversight and Investigations, U.S. House of Representatives (July 27, 2006)

ISSUE SUMMARY

YES: Ralph J. Cicerone, president, National Academy of Sciences, tells Congress that while future climate change and its impacts cannot be precisely forecast, a broad-brush picture of how global warming may affect the Earth is emerging and it contains a range of worrisome impact.

NO: John R. Christy, professor of atmospheric science and director of the Earth System Science Center at the University of Alabama in Huntsville, argues that projections of drastic climate changes in the future from global warming have not been adequately proved, and it is important not to make radical changes in energy policy based on such projections.

We live in an era of almost incomprehensible technological boom. In a very short time—less than a long lifetime in many cases—technology has brought some amazing things. But these advances have had negative by-products. A great deal of prosperity has come through industrialization, electrification, the burgeoning of private and commercial vehicles, and a host of other inventions and improvements that, in order to work, consume massive amounts of fossil fuel (mostly coal, petroleum, and natural gas). The burning of fossil fuels gives off carbon dioxide (CO_2) into the atmosphere. The discharge of CO_2 from burning wood, animals exhaling, and some other sources is nearly as old as Earth itself, but the last century's advances have rapidly increased the level of discharge. Since 1950 alone, global CO_2 emissions have more than tripled to about 26 billion tons of CO_2 now being discharged annually. Much of this is retained in the atmosphere because the ability of nature to cleanse the atmosphere of the CO_2 through plant photosynthesis has been overwhelmed by the vast increases in fossil fuel burning and the simultaneous cutting of vast areas of the world's forests for habitation and agriculture.

Many analysts believe that as a result of this buildup of CO_2, we are experiencing global warming. The reason, they contend, is the greenhouse effect. As CO_2 accumulates in the upper atmosphere, it creates a blanket effect, trapping heat and preventing the nightly cooling of the Earth. Other gases, such as methane, also contribute to creating the thermal blanket. It is estimated that over the last century the Earth's average temperature has risen about 1.1 degree Fahrenheit. The 1990s was the warmest decade since temperature records were first kept in 1856, and the first decade of the 2000s is on track to be even warmer. The pattern of global warming over the last millennium or so is sometimes compared to a "hockey stick." Between A.D. 1000 and 1900, the average world temperature pattern was basically flat, resembling the long shaft of a hockey stick. Since 1900, however, the temperature has risen relatively rapidly upward, with the spike compared to the shorter blade of a hockey stick.

This warming of the atmosphere worries many, who believe that rainfall, wind currents, and other climatic patterns are and could be dramatically, and sometimes dangerously, altered. Among other impacts, the polar ice caps will melt more quickly, and sea levels will rise, displacing perhaps over a 100 million people on the continents' coasts during the coming century. Some weather experts also project an increase in the number and intensity of hurricanes and other catastrophic weather events. Ralph J. Cicerone lays out this argument in the first reading. Those who agree with Cicerone often call for significant changes in the levels of energy use and other changes in human activity that arguably will have a major impact on lifestyle.

Not everyone believes that global warming caused by a CO_2 buildup is occurring or worries about it. Some scientists do not believe that future temperature increases will be significant, either because they will not occur or because offsetting factors, such as increased cloudiness, will ease the effect. Others believe that whatever temperature increase is occurring is from natural trends in the Earth's warming and cooling process. They point out that the time since 1856 is a mere blip in climatological time and further note that in the last 1,300 years, two marked temperature changes, the Medieval Warm Period (800 to 1400) and the Little Ice Age (1600 to 1850) have occurred. Another criticism, and one represented by John R. Christy in the second reading, is that there is only mixed scientific evidence of a level of global warming that will have seriously negative effects. From this perspective, calls for significantly curtailing energy use and other dramatic measures to slow down or reverse global warming are overdrawn and should be approached carefully.

YES

Ralph J. Cicerone

Climate Change: Evidence and Future Projections

[In my remarks,] I will summarize the state of scientific understanding on climate change, based on the findings and recommendations in National Academy of Sciences [NAS] and National Research Council [NRC] reports and in recent refereed scientific publications. Although not part of the government, the National Academy of Sciences was chartered in 1863 to advise the government on matters of science and technology. Our reports, often written with the National Academy of Engineering and the Institute of Medicine, are the products of a study process that brings together leading scientists, engineers, public health officials, and other experts to provide consensus, peer-reviewed advice to the nation on scientific and technical questions.

The greenhouse effect is a natural phenomenon. Without greenhouse gases, the surface of the Earth would be about 60°F (33°C) colder than it is today. Now, humans are amplifying the greenhouse effect by increasing the concentrations of many greenhouse gases (carbon dioxide, methane, nitrous oxide, synthetic chlorofluorocarbons and other fluorocarbons, and tropospheric ozone) in the atmosphere. The extra energy trapped near Earth's surface by the human-amplified greenhouse effect is presently about 2.5 Watts per square meter, which is about 100 times larger than all human energy usage.

There is no doubt that the Earth is warming. Weather-station records and ship-based observations show that global average surface air temperature has increased by about 1.2°F (0.7°C) since the beginning of the 20th century, more than half of it since 1975. Scientists have also measured upward temperature trends in the lower atmosphere and in the upper oceans, and this continuing warming has been accompanied by worldwide changes in many other indicators, such as shifts in ecosystems and decreases in Arctic sea ice thickness and extent.

Last week [this committee] heard testimony from Dr. Gerald North, chair of the National Research Council committee that examined surface temperature reconstructions for the last 2,000 years derived from tree rings, boreholes, ice cores, glacier length records, and other types of proxy evidence. The committee concluded that the Earth was warmer during the last few decades of the 20th century than at any other time during at least the last 400 years, and potentially the last several thousand years. These temperature

Committee on Energy and Commerce, Subcommittee on Oversight and Investigations, U.S. House of Representatives, Ralph J. Cicerone (July 27, 2006).

reconstructions provide a useful context for evaluating late 20th century warming. However, they are not the primary evidence for the widely accepted view that global warming is occurring, that human beings are responsible, at least in part, for this warming, and that the Earth's climate will continue to change during the next century.

Many additional lines of evidence demonstrate that climate is changing:

- Measurements show large increases in carbon dioxide and other greenhouse gases (methane and nitrous oxide, for example) beginning in the middle of the 19th century. These increases in greenhouse gases are due to human activities such as burning fossil fuel for energy, industrial processes, and transportation. The concentration of carbon dioxide in the atmosphere is now at its highest level in 650,000 years and continues to rise.
- We understand how carbon dioxide and other greenhouse gases affect global temperature. Rigorous radiative transfer calculations of the temperature changes associated with increasing greenhouse gas concentrations, together with reasonable assumptions about climate feedbacks, provide a physically based theoretical explanation for the observed warming.
- State-of-the-art mathematical climate models are able to reproduce the warming of the past century only if human-caused greenhouse gases are included.
- Analysis of high-quality, precise measurements of the Sun's total brightness over the past 25 years shows that there has been little if any change in the long-term average of solar output over this time period. Thus, changes in the Sun can not explain the warming observed over the past 25 years.
- The oceans have warmed in recent decades and the stratosphere has cooled. Extratropical [outside the tropics] land masses in the Northern Hemisphere [such as the United States and Canada] have warmed even more than the oceans. These large-scale changes are consistent with the predicted spatial and temporal pattern of greenhouse surface warming.
- Ice covered regions of the Earth have experienced significant melting. For example, the annual average sea-ice extent in the Artic has decreased by about 8%, or nearly one million square kilometers, over the past 30 years. Measurements from Earth-orbiting satellites (from synthetic aperture radars and from Earth's gravity sensors) over the last few years have shown that both the Greenland and West Antarctic Ice Sheets are losing ice. [Note: 1 million square kilometers equals about 386,102 square miles, an area about equal to that of Texas and New Mexico combined].
- Several publications in 2005 and 2006 show that hurricane intensities have increased in some parts of the world, in lock step with oceanic warming.

While we are quite certain that the Earth's surface has warmed rapidly during the last 30 years and that it is warmer now than at any other time during at least the last 400 years, projecting what will happen to important climate variables in the future is more difficult. As stated in the 2001 NRC report, "climate change simulations . . . yield a globally averaged surface temperature increase by the end of the century of 2.5 to 10.4°F (1.4 to 5.8°C) relative to 1990." Since 2001, we have continued to make advances in our knowledge of the climate system and in our ability to model it mathematically. Yet, pinpointing the magnitude of future climate changes is hindered both by remaining gaps in our ability to simulate scientific phenomena, and by the fact that it is difficult to predict society's future actions, particularly in the areas of population growth, energy consumption, and energy technologies. In general, temperature is easier to predict than changes such as rainfall, storm patterns, and ecosystems.

While future climate change and its impacts are inherently uncertain, they are far from unknown. A broad-brush picture of how global warming may affect certain regions of the world is starting to emerge from climate modeling efforts. Models generally project more warming in continental regions than over the oceans and in polar regions than near the equator. Precipitation is expected to increase in the tropics, decrease in the subtropics, and increase in the midlatitudes. Rainfall is also expected to increase in the monsoon regimes in South Asia, West Africa, and South America; these changes may create the potential for stronger El Niño events. Some models indicate that midlatitude continents will likely be drier during the summer in a warmer climate, leading to an increased chance for summer drought conditions.

Even if no further increases in the atmospheric concentrations of greenhouse gases occur, we are very likely to experience additional warming of 0.7°F (0.4°C). In colder climates, such warming could bring less severe winters and longer growing seasons (if soil moisture is adequate). Several studies have projected that summertime ice in the Arctic could disappear by A.D. 2100. The combined effects of ice melting and sea water expansion from ocean warming will likely cause the global average sea level to rise by between 0.1 and 0.9 meters between 1990 and 2100. Those in coastal communities, many in developing nations, will experience increased flooding due to sea level rise and are likely to experience more severe storms and surges. Increasing acidification of the surface ocean (due to added carbon dioxide from the atmosphere) will harm marine organisms such as corals and some plankton species.

In summary, there are multiple lines of evidence supporting the reality of and human roles in global climate change. The task of mitigating and preparing for the impacts of climate change will require worldwide collaborative inputs from a wide range of experts, including natural scientists, engineers, social scientists, medical scientists, those in government at all levels, business leaders and economists. For example, researchers and resource managers have only begun to address how climate change will impact future demands for electricity and water. Society faces increasing pressure to decide how best to respond to climate change and associated global changes, and applied research in direct support of decision making is needed.

John R. Christy

 **NO**

Testimony on Global Warming Studies

This testimony covers a wide range of topics. I will discuss the idea of "consensus" in climate reports and how scientific results may be convoluted by that process. I will examine the issue of sharing computer code and data, and the way it led in our experience to a more reliable dataset. The issue of relative temperatures of the past 1,000 years as stated in the IPCC 2001 [Intergovernmental Panel on Climate Change report, *Climate Change 2001: Third Assessment*] will be addressed from my perspective as of one of the lead authors of that report explaining that we chose words signifying a relatively low level of confidence. I also will note my disappointment with the exclusion of information that pointed to a more complex picture of temperature variability over the last millennium. I touch on the imperceptible climate impacts of energy policy options being considered nowadays and close with some comments about the unfortunate demonization of energy, the resource that has produced uncountable benefits in human health, longevity and freedom from deprivation.

Consensus Reports and Science

In describing the process of generating scientific reports by consensus I was quoted in the *New York Times* as saying it was the worst way to gather scientific information except for all the others.

Consensus at its heart is a political notion. It is a process of selecting words that don't offend the combined sensibilities of a particular set of the authors and reviewers, and is often done grudgingly. It is almost certain that a different set of authors and reviewers would select a different set of words and interpretation even if given the same scientific material.

One example from the first report of the Climate Change Assessment Program's (CCSP) on surface and atmospheric temperature trends comes to mind. This may provide a window into the "science-by-consensus" process. The report's main task was to reach conclusions about temperature trends measured at the surface and those measured in the lower atmosphere. Projections from theoretical climate models indicated atmospheric trends should be warming faster than the surface, especially in the tropics. However,

Testimony before the Committee on Energy and Commerce Subcommittee on Oversight and Investigations, U.S. Senate, John R. Christy (July 27, 2006).

several observational datasets did not support the models, suggesting flaws in the way greenhouse theory was being expressed in those models. Was this discrepancy real?

The original headline was made public in the near-final drafts as, "There is no longer evidence of this discrepancy." This was constructed in a rather busy Chicago meeting in which various authors were working on finalizing their own chapters as well as dealing with this punchline. After sitting with this characterization for a few days I could not agree with its dogmatic tone of finality. The problem was that there was evidence for discrepancies within the report itself.

In terms of strict scientific defensibility the statement should have said, "The magnitude of the global discrepancies in trends is not significant." I made known my view and our lead Editor, Dr. Tom Karl, instigated a special, last minute conference call with the authors to let me make my case. I was basically unsuccessful at persuading the others. At one point I offered to have a footnote inserted that stated something like, "One author, John Christy, recommends the following version . . ." I didn't mind being singled out in print as having a different view. That idea was not accepted because, I presume, it violated the notion of consensus. Rather, the punchline statement was massaged a bit to give a little less dogmatism in its meaning to, "This significant discrepancy no longer exists."

The problem still for me is that discrepancies do indeed exist as clearly indicated in the raw numbers provided in the body of the report. However, error margins of the datasets included the *possibility* (not the *proof*) that there were no discrepancies. The difference in meaning of these two statements was apparent to me; rather than promoting a certainty of knowledge as does the first, my proposal acknowledged the uncertainty in our observations, and thus in model evaluation.

This example doesn't cast doubt on the credibility of the body of the report and the considerable information it provides. The many tables and figures display the real currency of science: numbers. The interpretation of those numbers, especially in the high profile Executive Summary, represents the political art of consensus, with the underlying knowledge that from this the headlines burst forth.

I often wonder what conclusions a completely different group of authors would have reached in the Executive Summary given the same scientific information. That would be a very interesting experiment to perform! My basic point is that one should recognize that scientific material *and* interpretation of that material are contained in these reports. The interpretation is difficult to test for accidental or even subtle bias. Specific statements may arise from the dogged advocacy of a small group and the fatigue of the remaining writers, but in the end is blanketed by the notion of "consensus." This leaves a murky path of accountability where "all" authors are accountable but at the same time "none" are.

I am risking something here. What future committee would ask me to serve if I might be tempted to later expose some deliberation to the public after all was said and done? I have been careful here to limit this example to one that involved only me, and that was made fully public in the process of final review. But, would the idea of public exposure and potential accountability constrain the typically free-wheeling discussions we as scientists enjoy in trying to reach conclusions? In any case, I hope this example will not threaten future opportunities for me while giving the committee a sense of the limitations of scientific consensus.

Consensus reports are not inerrant, nor infallible. And, as time goes on, new discoveries will demonstrate how science evolves and understanding improves. In the science of climate change we will never have the "Final Answer." I wish every one of these reports began with the line my high school physics teacher drilled into us, "At our present level of ignorance we think we know . . ." The National Academy of Sciences (NAS) recently released a report about surface temperature reconstructions of the past 2000 years. Regarding the NAS statement which evaluated MBH99 and how it was expressed in the IPCC 2001, I specifically recused myself from discussing that one paragraph since I was an author of the original IPCC statement. I did not want to be seen as having a conflict of interest and of opening the NAS to such a claim. [Note: Two studies published by scientists Michael Mann, Ray Bradley, and Malcolm Hughes and published in 1998 in *Nature* and in 1999 in *Geophysical Research Letters* that first showed a graph of temperature change resembling a hockey stick are referred to as MGH98 and MBH99 or collectively as MBH.]

As one of the lead authors of the Observations chapter in IPCC 2001, I helped craft the now infamous statement regarding the relative warmth of the temperature of the decade of the 1990s and the single year 1998 in the past millennium. We selected the qualifying term "likely" warmest rather than "very likely" or "virtually certain." In other words we chose the term which represented a relatively low level of confidence, being two thirds chance of being correct. "Very likely" meant 90% confidence while "virtually certain" demanded 99% confidence.

Through consensus, and I've indicated the dangers of applying consensus, we settled on "likely," meaning the evidence indicated to several of us that there still remained considerable uncertainty surrounding proxy temperature reconstructions and their errors.

Some IPCC authors were concerned that MBH99 was new and had not had time to be exposed to independent analysis to confirm or revise the result. We also learned at that time that a key anchor for the early part of the record was a western tree ring series that explained only 5% of the overall temperature variability. I was specifically concerned that the unavoidable constraints on the length and certainty of the calibration and validation periods prevented confident assignment of the relative warmth of century-scale temperatures. We eventually chose "likely" based on such concerns. I also remember that we casually discussed the possibility that this figure would become a prominent result of our chapter, but had no idea that it would receive the level of notoriety it eventually did. I think the wide but improper use of the figure promoted an idea that nothing happened for 900 years, then all of the sudden everything happened, giving a false impression of how climate varies over time.

A more disappointing aspect of IPCC 2001 regarding temperatures of the last 2000 years was that some important work was not included. Specifically, the work of Dahl-Jensen 2000, which I recommended to be included on a number of occasions, was completely missing in this section. [Note: The study is Dorthe Dahl-Jensen, "The Greenland Ice Sheet Reacts," *Science*, July 2000.] At that time, this particular analysis of borehole temperature records from Greenland was probably the most confident assessment of relative regional temperature values over the last millennium. Thus, in at least one location of the northern hemisphere we had high confidence that 1000 years ago there was a relatively long period of warmer temperatures than observed in the most recent decade. And, though Greenland's temperature may not be tightly connected to that of the entire northern hemisphere, Greenland in and of itself is important in dealing with claims of melting ice and sea level rise.

If Greenland were indeed warmer in the relatively recent past, as several proxy records indicated, what was its condition then? Was it melting around the edges in those earlier, warmer centuries as it appears to be melting now in our present cooler temperatures? I believe the IPCC 2001 missed an opportunity to show a more complex picture of climate variability on the planet by excluding this information in 2001.

Sharing data and computer code, Dr. Roy Spencer [University of Alabama in Huntsville] and I created the first satellite-based temperature dataset for climate studies in 1990. At present we are working on improvements for the 8th adjustment to the dataset brought about by the divergence of the most recent two satellites. Of the 7 previous changes in methodology, two were discovered by other scientists, while the other 5 were discovered by us. Satellite instruments and data are complicated and affected by processes which no one really understands completely. Since we cannot go back in time with better instruments, we have to study the ones that were in orbit then and do the best we can to understand how confounding influences affect the measurements. The computer code we employ consists of 6 complicated programs which at times run sequentially on 3 different machines. The raw data files are enormous. When asked, we have shared with others parts of the computer code that were important to understanding how our methodology worked as well as intermediate products which served as a test to check that methodology was doing what it was intended to do.

When asked, we provided Remote Sensing Systems (RSS) a section of our code which calculated part of the adjustment for the satellites' east-west drift as well as files with the actual values of the adjustment to be sure that our intention in the code and the output matched. They believed our accounting of this particular adjustment was incorrect. Frankly, this was a difficult process from a personal standpoint. By sharing this information, we opened ourselves up to exposure of a possible problem in the code which we had somehow missed. Or worse, a simple disagreement which would lead to arguments about obscure technical aspects of the problem might arise for which there was no simple answer. However, and more importantly, if there was a problem, we certainly wanted to know about it and fix it.

Not knowing the outcome of their work, I received a request from RSS for permission to publish one of the files that we had sent to them. In my formal scientific response I wrote, "Oh what the heck" . . . "I think it would be fine to use and critique . . . that's sort of what science is all about."

And so it was that in August 2005 RSS published a clear example of an artifact in our adjustment procedure which created erroneous values in our tropical temperature trend. In *Science* magazine the following November we published information about our now-corrected temperatures and expressed our gratitude to RSS for discovering our error. The UAH [University of Alabama at Huntsville] dataset is better as a result. RSS has also generated a set of satellite temperature products which still differ from ours in some aspects and explanations of those differences are being explored and documented in soon-to-be published material. The NAS report on temperature reconstructions made the point that when datasets and methods are fully exposed to independent eyes the results will carry more confidence within the scientific community. As best I can tell, this practice was not followed in the MBH99 situation, leading to the conflicts of the past few years. This brings me back to the CCSP and the evaluation of climate model projections. It was a requirement in the CCSP that all observational datasets used in the report be publicly available in easy-to-access format. Some of us thought the same requirement should be applied to the time series of the global and tropical averages from the climate model simulations, especially since those results had already been published the year before.

In a curious email debate, those who did not want public access given to the climate model averages prevailed. I've encountered this asymmetry before in the field of climate science in which it has typically been very difficult to obtain climate model output in a useful format if at all. Progress has been made with the archiving of the "Climate of the 20th Century" model output at the Dept. of Energy's Lawrence Livermore Laboratory, but the effort required to retrieve commonly used climate variables is still almost Herculean. Most investigators do not have the infrastructure and personnel to spend time acquiring the huge raw data files and then climb a very steep learning curve to process those files into something useful.

Further, it appears to me that climate model evaluation to this point has been performed mostly by the modelers themselves. It is my view and recommendation that policymakers would learn much from independent, hard-nosed assessments of these model simulations by those who are not directly vested in the outcome. Some of this is going on, but the level of support is minimal.

Science Panel Members—Vested or Non-Vested?

This leads me to another point regarding the CCSP and the NAS reports. In the case of the CCSP report, we as authors were ourselves the builders of the datasets or those who directly performed climate model simulations and evaluations. The process of selecting words to describe the conclusions sprang from those who arguably had strong vested interests. On the other hand, the

NAS report of surface temperature reconstructions was written by experts in climate, but who, as we say in Alabama, did not "have a dog in that fight."

After experiencing both situations in the past year, I prefer the approach of the National Academy of Sciences where, in theory, a better chance of producing unbiased and more critical statements is likely.

Global Warming

That greenhouse gases are increasing in concentration is clearly true and therefore the radiation budget of the atmosphere will be altered. In response, the surface temperature should rise due to this additional forcing. In our observational work however, we have not been able to show clear support for the manner or magnitude of this response as has been depicted by the present set of climate models.

For policy makers this is an important point. We cannot reliably project the trajectory of the climate for large regions within the U.S., for example. It would be a far more difficult task to reliably predict the effects of a policy that altered by a tiny amount the emissions which act to enhance the greenhouse effect. Simply put, we cannot say with any confidence to you or to the American tax payer that by adopting policy X we will cause an impact Y on the weather of the climate system. The basic problem is that if policy X is similar to those being proposed today, the impact on emissions will be essentially imperceptible and thus the attempt to measure or predict its consequence on the climate will be essentially impossible.

To understand the scale of what we are dealing with the following serves as a rough example. We know that we on Earth benefit from 10 terawatts of energy production today. To achieve a reduction of the CO_2 [carbon dioxide] representing 10% (1 terawatt) of that production we would need 1,000 nuclear power plants now (1 gigawatt each). Massive implementation of wind and solar does not achieve this result and would not provide the baseload power needed by economies today in any case. (They of course are worthy of investment if costs are reasonable.) Thus, to have a 10% impact on emissions from energy (that is growing at the same time) will require a tremendous and difficult and expensive restructuring of energy supplies.

I believe we will slowly decarbonize energy production and eventually this issue will fade away. But that path of decarbonization should be done with care, being aware of where we are in human economic development as described below. (However, there are other reasons, such as energy security, which may drive the nation to a different mix of energy sources for which economic outcomes may be more confidently predicted.)

Energy Policy

What I find disturbing in the policy sphere is the demonization of energy and its most common by-product, carbon dioxide. It is difficult for me to call CO_2 a pollutant when as an atmospheric gas it is the source of life on the planet.

The long history of CO_2 decline over the last millions of years is thought to have been leading to a slow starvation of the biosphere because CO_2 is, simply put, plant food.

But, as importantly, the extra CO_2 we have put in the atmosphere represents tremendous improvements in health, longevity and quality of human life. I suspect half of us in this Hearing room would not be here but for the benefits wrought by affordable and accessible energy. Energy has delivered to us longer and better lives. Energy use is not evil.

I feel I have some expertise not common to the average scientist that I believe is important in this whole discussion of energy and climate change. In the 1970's I taught science and math in Africa as a missionary teacher. I saw the energy system there. The "energy source" was wood chopped from the forest. The "energy transmission" system was the backs of women and girls, hauling the wood a U.N.-estimated average of 3 miles each day. The "energy use" system was burning the wood in an open fire indoors for heat and light. The consequence of that energy system was deforestation and habitat loss while for people it was poor respiratory and eye health. The U.N. estimates 1.6 million women and children die each year from the effects of this indoor smoke. Energy demand will grow, as it should, to allow these people to experience the advances in health and quality of life that we in the U.S. enjoy. They are far more vulnerable to the impacts of poverty, water and air pollution, and political strife than whatever the climate does. I simply close with a plea, please remember the needs and aspirations of the poorest among us when energy policy is made.

POSTSCRIPT

Can Destructive Impacts from Global Warming Be Confidently Predicted?

The debate over the causes, extent, and future impact of global warming is momentous. One ramification relates to the impact of the phenomenon as such. If those who issue alarmed warnings about global warming are correct, the impact could involve coastal settlements threatened and sometimes inundated by rising seas, increasingly frequent and violent hurricanes and other storms, wildfires in newly arid regions, and a host of other negative consequences. The second major consideration is what, if anything, to do about global warming. Most of the countries of the world, including the United States, negotiated a treaty called the Kyoto Protocol in 1997 that requires the industrialized countries to significantly cut their CO_2 emissions. Most countries have ratified the treaty, but the United States and a few others have not. The Bush administration takes the position that the alarm over global warming is not sufficiently proven to warrant the kind of harmful economic changes that the administration claims would have to take place to cut CO_2 emissions. For example, cars might have to be much smaller, gasoline prices higher, and electricity production and consumption curtailed. Also, many analysts project enormous costs. One study has concluded that a program to cut CO_2 emissions by 70 percent over a 40-year period would cost the U.S. economy $2.7 trillion. But the economic calculations cut both ways. For instance, there are projections of a $5 trillion savings in fuel costs. Other studies have pointed to the economic stimulus that would be provided by creating alternative energy technologies. Losses from storm damages will also drop, saving, perhaps, the cost of rebuilding many "New Orleans" shattered by storm-driven flooding.

If the decision is to take major steps to curb global warming, then the tough issue will be what to do. Polls in 2006 show that most Americans (67 percent) think global warming is a serious problem and (58 percent) that President Bush is doing too little to address the issue. A strong majority of Americans agree to offering companies tax breaks to become more energy efficient, but these tax breaks would either increase the already huge U.S. federal budget deficit or would have to be offset by tax increases. This latter idea leaves Americans cold, with 68 percent opposing increasing gasoline taxes and 81 percent opposing increasing electricity taxes to promote using less.

The U.S. Environmental Protection Agency has a good site on global warming at http://yosemite.epa.gov/oar/globalwarming.nsf/. An Internet site that takes a skeptical view of the alarm over global warming can be found at http://www.globalwarming.org/. Taking the opposite view is the Union of

Concerned Scientists at http://www.ucsusa.org/. A warnng about global warming and a plea to address the issue is given by former Vice President Al Gore in the documentary, *An Inconvenient Truth* (2006). The film is criticized in, "The *Real* 'Inconvenient Truth'," at http://www.junkscience.com/Greenhouse/.

Contributors to This Volume

EDITOR

JOHN T. ROURKE, Ph.D., is a professor of political science at the University of Connecticut. He has written numerous articles, book chapters, and papers, and is also the author of *Congress, the Executive, and U.S. Foreign Policymaking* (Westview Press, 1985); *International Relations on the World Stage*, 11th edition (McGraw-Hill, 1987–2006); *Making Foreign Policy: United States, Soviet Union, China* (Brooks/Cole, 1990); and *Presidential War and American Democracy: Rally Round the Chief* (Paragon House, 1993). Professor Rourke is the co-author of *Direct Democracy and International Politics: Deciding International Issues Through Referendums,* with Richard Hiskes and Cyrus E. Zirakzadeh (Lynne Rienner Publisher, 1992); *Making American Foreign Policy*, with Ralph Carter and Mark Boyer, 2nd edition (Brown & Benchmark, 1994, 1996); and *International Politics on the World Stage: Brief Edition* with Mark Boyer, 7th edition (McGraw-Hill, 1996–2007). In addition to this 13th edition of *Taking Sides: Clashing Views in World Politics* (McGraw Hill, 1987–2007), he is the editor of *Taking Sides: Clashing Views on Controversial Issues in American Foreign Policy,* 2nd edition (Dushkin Publishing Group, 2000, 2002) and *You Decide: Current Debates in American Politics,* 4th edition (Longman, 2004–2007). A long career in both the academic and applied sides of politics has convinced the author that politics impacts everyone and that those who become knowledgeable and get active to promote what they believe in, whether that is based on self-interest or altruism, are the single most important driving force in the ultimate contest: politics.

STAFF

Larry Loeppke	Managing Editor
Jill Peter	Senior Developmental Editor
Susan Brusch	Senior Developmental Editor
Beth Kundert	Production Manager
Jane Mohr	Project Manager
Tara McDermott	Design Coordinator
Nancy Meissner	Editorial Assistant
Julie Keck	Senior Marketing Manager
Mary Klein	Marketing Communications Specialist
Alice Link	Marketing Coordinator
Tracie Kammerude	Senior Marketing Assistant
Lori Church	Pemissions Coordinator

AUTHORS

PETER F. ALLGEIER is Deputy U.S. Trade Representative. He has also served as U.S. ambassador to the World Trade Organization (WTO) in Geneva, Switzerland. He has a Ph.D. in international economics from the University of North Carolina at Chapel Hill.

ROBERT BAUGH is executive director of the Industrial Union Council of the American Federation of Labor and Congress of Industrial Organizations (AFL-CIO).

PATRICIA BERLYN writes on Israelite history and culture and is a former associate editor for the *Jewish Bible Quarterly* in Jerusalem. She has also worked for the Council on Foreign Relations, as well as its journal, *Foreign Affairs*.

KATHERINE NEWELL BIERMAN is Counterterrorism Counsel for the U.S. Program of Human Rights Watch. She also served as a captain in the U.S. Air Force.

JOHN R. BOLTON is U.S. ambassador to the United Nations. Prior to that he served as Under Secretary of State for Arms Control and International Security, Assistant Secretary of State for International Organization Affairs, assistant attorney general in the U.S. Department of Justice, and as assistant administrator for Program and Policy Coordination and as general counsel in U.S. Agency for International Development. He has also been senior vice president of the American Enterprise Institute (AEI). He hold a J.D. from Yale Law School.

STEVEN G. BRADBURY is Assistant Attorney General in the Office of Legal Counsel at the U.S. Department of Justice. He served as a clerk to Associate Justice Clarence Thomas of the U.S. Supreme Court and holds a J.D. from the University of Michigan Law School.

GEORGE W. BUSH is president of the United States. He has also served as governor of Texas. Before that he was the owner of an oil and gas business and part owner of the Texas Rangers baseball team.

HUGO CHAVEZ has been president of Venezuela since 1998. A former career military officer, he was imprisoned for two years in the early 1990s for his part in a failed attempt to overthrow Venezuela's then-president Carlos Andres Perez.

RICHARD B. CHENEY is vice president of the United States. He has also served as White House Chief of Staff, Secretary of Defense, and a member of the U.S. House of Representatives from Wyoming. In Congress, colleagues elected him Chairman of the House Republican Conference and then House Minority Whip.

BARRY R. CHISWICK is UIC Distinguished Professor in and Head of the Department of Economics, University of Illinois at Chicago and director of the UIC Center for Economic Education. He holds a Ph.D. in economics from Columbia University.

JOHN R. CHRISTY is a professor and director of the Earth System Science Center, NSSTC University of Alabama in Huntsville. He holds a Ph.D. in atmospheric science from the University of Illinois.

RALPH J. CICERONE is president of the National Academy of Sciences. He is a former chancellor of the University of California, Irvine, where he was also a professor and chair of the Department of Earth System Science and Dean of Physical Science. He served as a senior scientist and director of the Atmospheric Chemistry Division at the National Center for Atmospheric Research in Boulder, Colorado. He holds a Ph.D. in electrical engineering from the University of Illinois.

COMMISSION FOR ASSISTANCE TO A FREE CUBA was established in October 2003 by President George W. Bush to develop a comprehensive U.S. policy toward Cuba. Its chair was Secretary of State Colin Powell, and its membership included representatives of most Cabinet departments and several leading independent agencies. Assistant Secretary of State for Western Hemisphere Affairs Roger Noriega oversaw the commission's day-to-day operations.

NICHOLAS EBERSTADT is the Henry Wendt Scholar in Political Economy at the American Enterprise Institute. He is also a member of the President's Council on Bioethics, the United States Commission on Helping to Enhance the Livelihood of People, and the Board of Scientific Counselors, National Center for Health Statistics, U.S. Department of Health and Human Services. He holds a Ph.D., in political economy and government from Harvard University

JOHN FRISBIE is president of the U.S.–China Business Council, an organization of U.S. companies engaged in business with the People's Republic of China.

JULIA GALEOTA was a high school senior at Holton Arms School in McLean, Virginia, at the time she wrote her essay. The essay won first place in the thirteen-to-seventeen-year-old age category of the 2004 *Humanist* Essay Contest for Young Women and Men of North America and was published in the *Humanist*. She has gone on to undergraduate studies at Yale University in New Haven, Connecticut.

TUCKER HERBERT is an undergraduate student at Stanford University and foreign affairs editor of the *Stanford Review*.

HIGH-LEVEL PANEL ON THREATS, CHALLENGES, AND CHANGE was established in November 2003 by Secretary-General Kofi Annan to examine the major threats and challenges the world faces in the broad field of peace and security. The panel was chaired by Anand Panyarachun, former prime minister of Thailand. Other panel members include, Robert Badinter (France, member of the French Senate and former Minister of Justice), João Clemente Baena Soares (Brazil, former secretary-general of the Organization of American States), Gro Harlem Brundtland (Norway, former Prime Minister of Norway and former girector-general of the World Health Organization), Mary Chinery-Hesse (Ghana, vice-chairman,

National Development Planning Commission of Ghana and former deputy director-general, International Labour Organization), Gareth Evans (Australia, president of the International Crisis Group and former minister for Foreign Affairs of Australia), David Hannay (United Kingdom, former ambassador of the United Kingdom to the United Nations), Enrique Iglesias (Uruguay, president of the Inter-American Development Bank), Amre Moussa (Egypt, secretary-general of the League of Arab States), Satish Nambiar (India, former Lt. General in the Indian Army and Force Commander of UN peacekeeping in Croatia), Sadako Ogata (Japan, former United Nations High Commissioner for Refugees), Yevgeny Primakov (Russia, former Prime Minister of the Russia), Qian Qichen (China, former vice prime minister and minister for Foreign Affairs of China), Nafis Sadik (Pakistan, former executive director of the United Nations Population Fund), Salim Ahmed Salim (Tanzania, former secretary-general of the Organization of African Unity), and Brent Scowcroft (United States, former Lt. General in the U.S. Air Force and National Security Adviser to President George H. W. Bush).

BRUCE HOFFMAN is corporate chair in Counterterrorism and Counterinsurgency at RAND and director of its Washington office. He is also a senior fellow at the Combating Terrorism Center at the U.S. Military Academy, West Point, and an adjunct professor in the security studies program at Georgetown University. He was the founding director of the Centre for the Study of Terrorism and Political Violence at the University of St. Andrews in Scotland. He hold a D. Phil in International relations from the University of Oxford, United Kingdom.

LOUIS JANOWSKI is a former U.S. diplomat with service in Vietnam, France, Ethiopia, Saudi Arabia, and Kenya.

STEVEN L. KENNY is a colonel in the U.S. Army.

ANN O. KRUEGER served as first deputy managing director of the International Monetary Fund from September 1, 2001 to August 31, 2006. Before coming to the fund, Ms. Krueger was the Herald L. and Caroline L. Ritch Professor in humanities and sciences in the department of economics at Stanford University and a senior fellow at the Hoover Institution. She hold a Ph.D. in economics from the University of Wisconsin.

PHILIPPE LEGRAIN is chief economist of Britain in Europe. He was previously special adviser to the director-general of the World Trade Organization and the trade and economics correspondent for *The Economist*. He has also written for *The Financial Times, The Wall Street Journal Europe, The Times, The Guardian, The Independent, New Statesman, Prospect* and *The Ecologist*, as well as *The New Republic, Foreign Policy*, and *The Chronicle Review*. He has a master's degree in economics from the London School of Economics.

BETTY MCCOLLUM is a member of the U.S. House of Representatives from Minnesota. Among other assignments, she is a member of the Committee on International Relations. Prior to that she served in the Minnesota

House of Representatives, in which she was assistant leader of the Democratic-Farmer-Labor Party, and she also served on the North St. Paul City Council.

ROBERT T. MCLEAN is a research associate at the Center for Security Policy in Washington, D.C.

MICHAEL MANDELBAUM is the Christian A. Herter Professor at and director of the American Foreign Policy Program at the Paul H. Nitze School of Advanced International Studies of The Johns Hopkins University. He has also taught at Harvard University, Columbia University, and the U.S. Naval Academy. He holds a Ph.D. in political science from Harvard University.

ALICE LYMAN MILLER is a research fellow at the Hoover Institution and visiting associate professor in the department of political science at Stanford. She is also a senior lecturer in the Department of National Security Affairs at the U.S. Naval Postgraduate School in Monterey, California. She has also taught at the School of Advanced International Studies (SAIS) at Johns Hopkins University. She also worked for the Central Intelligence Agency as a senior analyst in Chinese foreign policy and domestic politics. She holds a Ph.D. in history from George Washington University. Formerly H. Lyman Miller, she gender transitioned in 2006.

WILLIAM E. ODOM, is a senior fellow with Hudson Institute and an adjunct professor at Yale University. He is a retired Lieutenant General, U.S. Army. He also served as director of the National Security Agency and as the Army's assistant chief of staff for Intelligence. Additionally he has been military assistant to the president's assistant for National Security Affairs, and a staff member of the National Security Council, He hold a Ph.D. from Columbia University.

JAMES PHILLIPS is a research fellow in Middle Eastern Studies in the Douglas and Sarah Allison Center for Foreign Policy Studies, a division of the Kathryn and Shelby Cullom Davis Institute for International Studies, at the Heritage Foundation. He is a former research fellow at the Congressional Research Service.

WILLIAM RATLIFF is a research fellow and curator of the Americas Collection at the Hoover Institution. Before that he was a columnist and chief editorial writer for *Peninsula Times Tribune* in California. He has taught at Stanford University, San Francisco State University, the University of San Francisco, and Tunghai University in Taiwan. He hold a Ph.D. in Latin American and Chinese history from the University of Washington in Seattle.

DIANE RAUBE is an undergraduate student at Stanford University and a staff writer for the *Stanford Review.*

EUGENE RUMER is a senior fellow in the Institute for National Strategic Studies, at the National Defense University. Prior to that, he was a visiting scholar at the Washington Institute for Near East Policy, a member of the Secretary's Policy Planning Staff at the U.S. Department of State, and director for Russian, Ukrainian and Eurasian affairs at the National

Security Council. He hold a Ph.D. in Russian Studies from Georgetown University.

ROSEMANY SHINKO is coordinator of academic services at the Stamford Campus of the University of Connecticut. She hold a Ph.D. in political science from the University of Connecticut.

DAN SICILIANO is executive director of the program in law, economics, and business at Stanford Law School, where he teaches corporate law and practice. He has also headed a private law firm and a management consulting firm and practiced immigration law. He holds a J.D. from Stamford University.

LEON V. SIGAL is director of the Northeast Asia Cooperative Security Project at the Social Science Research Council. He has been a member of the editorial board of *The New York Times* and served in the Bureau of Politico-Military Affairs at the U.S. Department of State. He has been a member of the faculty at Wesleyan University. He holds a Ph.D. in government from Harvard University.

MARK STEYN is a Canadian journalist and columnist for the *Chicago Sun-Times*. He has also written for *Macleans, The Daily Telegram, Jerusalem Post, The National Review,* and *The Irish Times.*

LORI WALLACH is director of Public Citizen's Global Trade Watch, a division of Public Citizen. She is a graduate of Harvard Law School.

FRANK G. WISNER is vice chairman, American International Group. Prior to that he served in such government positions as U.S. ambassador to India, to the Philippines, to Egypt, and to Zambia, Under Secretary of Defense for Policy, Under Secretary of State for International Security Affairs, and Senior Deputy Assistant Secretary for African Affairs.

Index